SCRAMBLE FOR AFRICA

The Great Trek to the Boer War

Paul Kruger

Scramble for Africa

The Great Trek to the Boer War

ANTHONY NUTTING

E. P. DUTTON & CO., INC.

New York   1971

First Published in the U.S.A. 1971 by E. P. Dutton & Co., Inc.

FIRST EDITION

Library of Congress Catalog Card Number: 76-156265

SBN 0-525-19815-6

Contents

Illustrations

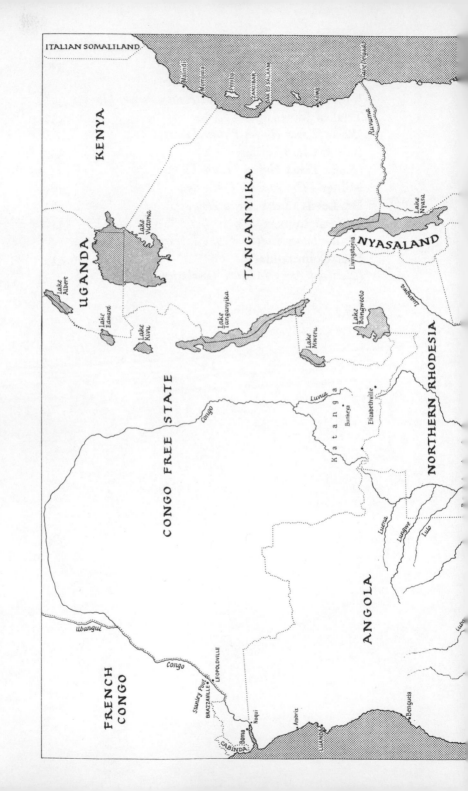

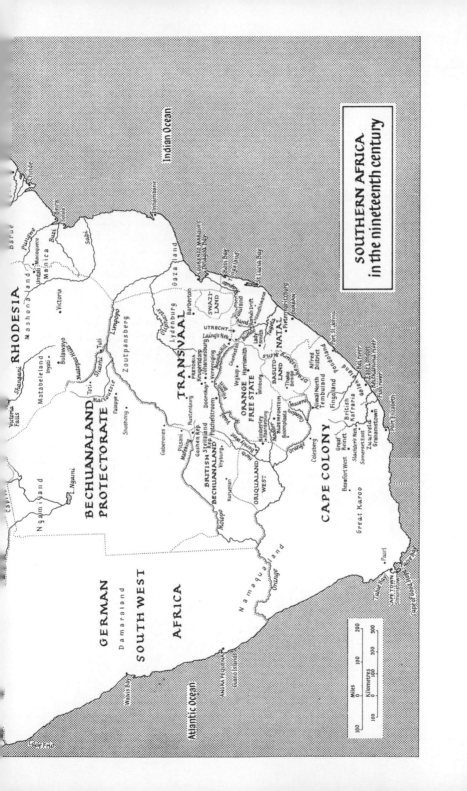

SOUTHERN AFRICA
in the nineteenth century

Acknowledgements

The Author wishes to acknowledge with grateful thanks the help given him by Miss Joan Davies and the Staff of the Government Archives Department in Cape Town and by Mr. T. Baxter and other members of the Archives Department in Salisbury, Rhodesia. He also wishes to express his gratitude to the Hon. Spencer Loch for the loan of the Personal Papers of Sir Henry Loch, 1890–1895.

Table of Principal Events in South Africa

1488 Bartolomew Diaz discovered and named the Cape of Good Hope.

1497 Vasco da Gama discovered Natal.

1510 D'Almeida, Portuguese Viceroy in India, killed by Hottentots at Table Bay.

1580 Sir Francis Drake sighted the Cape.

1602 Netherlands East India Company formed.

1652 Van Riebeeck landed at the Cape and formed the first settlement.

1688 Arrival of the first Huguenot settlers.

1713 First smallpox epidemic.

1760 Trek-Boers crossed Orange River.

1774 First mission station in South Africa established by Moravian Mission Society.

1778 Fish River made the eastern boundary of the Cape.

1780–83 War between Holland and England. Decline of the Netherlands East India Company.

1781 French troops landed at the Cape.

1784 French troops withdrawn.

1794 Netherlands East India Company declared bankrupt.

1795 First British occupation of the Cape.

1803 Cape returned to Batavian Republic of the Netherlands under Treaty of Amiens.

1806   Second British occupation of the Cape.

1814   The Cape formally ceded to Britain by Holland.

1819   Cape boundary extended to Keiskamma River.

1820   Arrival of 5,000 British settlers.

1828   Death of Zulu chief, Chaka.

1833   Slavery abolished in the Cape.

1836   Great Trek started.

1837   Voortrekker leader, Retief, entered Natal. Msilikazi's Matabeles crossed the Limpopo River.

1838   Dingaan's Zulus massacred Retief. Andries Pretorius avenged Retief's murder at Blood River. Dingaan overthrown.

1839   Vootrekker Republic proclaimed in Natal.

1842   British occupation of Natal. Republic of Potchefstroom founded.

1845   Natal proclaimed a British Colony.

1848   British sovereignty proclaimed between Orange and Vaal Rivers.

1852   Britain recognised independence of Transvaal Republics in Sand River Convention.

1854   Britain recognised independence of Orange Free State. First Parliament in Cape Colony.

1856   Self-destruction of Xosa tribes.

1858   War between Orange Free State and Basutos.

1862–63   Civil War among Transvaal Republics.

1864   M. W. Pretorius elected President of united Transvaal Republic.

1868   Basutoland annexed to Cape Colony.

1869   Diamonds discovered in Griqualand West.

1870   Griqualand West annexed by Britain.

1872   Responsible Government granted to Cape Colony.

1873   Gold discovered in Lydenburg district of Transvaal.

1877   Transvaal annexed by Britain.

1878 Walvis Bay proclaimed British territory.

1879 Zulu War. Cetewayo routed British army at Isandhl-wana. Cetewayo defeated and made prisoner at Ulundi. Formation of Afrikaner Bond by Jan Hofmeyr.

1880 First Anglo-Boer War. British troops defeated at Majuba Hill.

1881 Pretoria Convention. Transvaal regained independence under British sovereignty.

1883 Paul Kruger elected President of the Transvaal. Republics of Stellaland and Goshen founded in Bechuana territory.

1884 German Protectorate proclaimed over South-West Africa. London Convention granted Transvaal full independence except for rights to make treaties with foreign states and with Bantu tribes east and west of the Republic.

1885 Abolition of Republics of Stellaland and Goshen. Bechuanaland proclaimed a British Protectorate. Cape Town–Kimberley Railway opened. St. Lucia Bay annexed by Britain.

1886 Opening of Witwatersrand goldfields. Johannesburg founded.

1887 Zululand proclaimed British territory.

1888 British South Africa Company established. Matabeleland and Mashonaland declared British spheres of influence.

1889 Alliance between Orange Free State and Transvaal.

1890 Cecil Rhodes became Prime Minister of the Cape. B.S.A. Company occupied Mashonaland. Anglo-German treaty defining boundaries in south and east Africa. Swaziland Convention signed giving Transvaal access to Tongaland coast.

1891 Anglo-Portuguese Treaty defining boundaries in Zambezia.

1892 Cape Town–Johannesburg railway completed.

1893 B.S.A. Company invaded and seized Matabeleland.

1894 Pondoland annexed to Cape Colony. Delagoa Bay railway completed.

1895 Tongaland annexed by Britain. British Bechuanaland joined to Cape Colony. Chamberlain became Colonial Secretary. Invasion of Transvaal by B.S.A. Company troops under Dr. Jameson.

1896 Rhodes resigned as Cape Prime Minister. Matabele Rebellion in Rhodesia.

1897 House of Commons Select Committee enquiry into Jameson Raid.

1898 Kruger elected for fourth time as President of the Transvaal.

1899 Bloemfontein Conference between Kruger and Sir A. Milner, British High Commissioner. Second Anglo-Boer War began.

1902 Treaty of Vereeniging. Transvaal and Orange Free State became British Colonies. Death of Cecil Rhodes.

1 Prelude to the Scramble

AFRICA is in area larger than Asia without Russia and equal to the U.S.A., Australia, India and China put together. Yet only a hundred years ago at the start of the final quarter of the nineteenth century, the majority of this vast expanse was unknown to civilised man. And although for nearly all of the previous four hundred years the Portuguese, Dutch, English, Danes and French had sent merchants and missionaries, settlers and soldiers to lay claim to its shores, the extent of European colonisation was largely limited to a few scattered trading-posts situated at the mouths of Africa's greater rivers. Only in two areas had European colonisation penetrated to any depth—in the south where Dutch and English settlers had spread themselves in scattered communities across parts of what we know now as the Republic of South Africa, and in the north where the French were beginning to establish an overseas settlement for the Alsatian and Lorainian victims of the Franco-Prussian war. For the rest the secrets of the Dark Continent remained as unknown to man as the surface of the moon, inviolate to all but a handful of explorers.

Then suddenly, in the 1880s, the scramble for Africa got under way. And within the next two hectic decades, the map was marked off and divided by the European Powers into colonies and spheres of influence, which was to leave less than 4 per cent of this vast area—the states of Ethiopia and Liberia—as independent territories. France ended up with $4\frac{1}{4}$ million

15

square miles of empire, Britain with 3½ millions, while Germany, Portugal, Belgium and Italy shared most of the remainder in roughly equal portions of 900,000 square miles each.

It has become a commonplace among historians to contend that this phenomenally rapid and extensive effort in empire-building owed itself largely to a series of negative impulses, a chain reaction of dog-in-the-manger attitudes on the part of the powers concerned and most especially of Great Britain. There was, we are told, no conscious, active or positive desire in Britain or France or Germany to get involved in a colonial empire in Africa. The British only went into Africa to baulk the French and the Germans; the French were only trying to thwart the British; and as for the Germans, had not Bismarck pronounced that the quest for empire was not worth the bones of one Pomeranian grenadier?

Like many other generalisations, this one is too sweeping to be true. Admittedly, Britain's reasons for becoming involved in Egypt, first as overseer of the Khedive's finances and from 1882 onwards as the occupying power, had more to do with safeguarding her communications with her Indian empire than with any desire to lord it over the Nile valley. Likewise her subsequent moves into the Sudan and Kenya were more concerned to control the sources of the Nile in Uganda, and hence to protect her position in Egypt, than to add yet more square mileage to Her Majesty's already world-wide imperial dominions. And even the relatively rich pickings which men of enterprise, such as Sir George Goldie of the Royal Niger Company, had begun to develop in West Africa were regarded in London—at least until Mr. Joseph Chamberlain took charge of Britain's imperial affairs—as disposable assets, if it should prove necessary to barter them in order to strengthen Britain's hand in Egypt.

But what may have been true for North, West and East Africa was certainly not true for that part of the continent which lies south of the Zambezi river. For while the former case was largely governed by strategic requirements having little to do with Africa itself, in the latter British policy was driven by a deliberate and determined desire to establish a British dominion in South Africa. Unlike the foetid, steaming, malarial interiors of

Nigeria and Sierra Leone, or the unremitting desert wastes of Egypt and the Sudan, here in South Africa was a perfect temperate climate, in a fertile land relatively empty of human inhabitants, where white men could survive and prosper and into which the rapidly expanding British population could overflow in search of a new and better life.

Here the scramble for Africa had started between Briton and Boer almost as soon as England took over from the Dutch at the Cape of Good Hope during the Napoleonic Wars. Here the British were never content to establish a few coastal stations, where traders sat at the receipt of custom, packaging and shipping the pickings of the interior passed to them by the middlemen from up-river. Nor did they seek to preserve such curious fictions as later obtained in Egypt, where British officers and officials ran the army and the government under the guise of 'advisers' to a Turkish viceroy, for the sole purpose of maintaining a strategic base. Britain wanted the Cape to protect her communications with the Orient; but she also wanted South Africa for its own intrinsic merits, as an outright addition to her Empire, as a dominion to be settled as well as ruled by Britishers.

In South Africa, from the outset, from the advent of the 1820 settlers, the British were interested in colonisation, in creating a home from home for British migrants; and the British Government were even prepared to spend money to this end, to send troops to beat back native resistance, whether Boer or Bantu. The independence of the Boer Republics in the Transvaal and Orange Free State had to be suppressed and the military power of the Zulus, Basutos and Matabeles had to be broken to pave the way for British supremacy and a British dominion over all South Africa from the Zambezi river to the Cape of Good Hope.

To begin with, British colonial ambitions were limited to Cape Colony and a small coastal area of Natal. But as the Dutch settlers inspanned their oxen and trekked northwards to escape the interferences of the Cape Government with their traditional way of life, so the long arm of British administration was extended to catch up with them. And although the Boers were permitted to enjoy their coveted independence beyond the Orange and Vaal rivers for some twenty-five years while the

British were consolidating their settlements in Cape Colony and Natal, it was only a matter of time before the Imperial Government would resume their pressure and seek—as they did in the late seventies—to impose their rule as far north as the Transvaal. Whether it was the Confederation policy of Lord Carnarvon or the later concept of a South African union embraced by such Colonial Secretaries as Lord Knutsford and Joseph Chamberlain, the aim was the same—a British-ruled South Africa.

Then, towards the end of the nineteenth century, the country began to reveal that the wealth lying beneath its soil far exceeded that growing above it, which discovery attracted a new type of British settler—the miner, prospector and speculator—first to the diamond fields of Kimberley and later to the gold seams of the Rand. Henceforth the Imperial Government and the autonomous colonists of the Cape and Natal looked on South Africa with an even keener and more covetous eye. Kimberley's diamond diggings were promptly annexed to the Empire over the protests of the Boer Republics. But the riches of the Rand proved to be beyond Britain's grasp. And the attempts of successive Colonial Secretaries to bring them into the British fold by seeking to lure President Kruger into a union with the British Colonies were as unavailing as the effort of Cecil Rhodes to seize them by staging an armed invasion of the Transvaal. Worse still, thousands of Britishers from the Cape and Natal, as well as from the mother country, were drawn to the new Eldorado beyond the Vaal. Indeed, in the space of ten years, the wealth and influence of Kruger's independent Republic began to eclipse those of all the British territories combined. And so great became the fear that, unless they were forcibly subdued, the Boers would shortly usurp British supremacy in South Africa that, in the last months of the century, Britain and the British race were plunged into a war of conquest which was as disastrous in its execution as it was discreditable in its conception.

Inevitably, in all the European colonies in Africa, the initial momentum to penetrate and to possess sprang far more from the pioneers, the men-on-the-spot, than from the governments, still less the parliaments, of the homelands. G. M. Young's characterisation of British public opinion in the Victorian age as demonstrating 'a humane and frugal distrust of Empire . . .' could have been applied with equal truth to the people of France, Germany and the other European states with interests and possessions in Africa and elsewhere.

But in all things political, public opinion is and remains an inert force until moved by some vision or cataclysm which touches the people themselves. For the most part of the nineteenth century British opinion, unlike French or German, was not infected by any brooding desire to avenge defeat, nor by the intoxication of any sensational victory. Nationalism, of the kind which gripped the continent of Europe, was an unknown quantity in England. Yet there were other pressures, other visions, which led Britons to leave their homes and seek a new life under the British flag overseas. The depression following Waterloo and the desperate insecurity and poverty, which existed in a land where the average expectation of life among the working class in a big city was only fifteen years, overcame the innate insularity of the British race and made emigration the only escape. And although life was at first hard and even dangerous for many British migrants, their successful resettlement so caught and filled the imagination of their kinsmen at home that, in the thirty years after 1850, some 6½ millions out of a total population of only 26 millions left Britain's shores to settle in Canada, South Africa, Australia and New Zealand.

On a smaller scale and for different reasons similar movements of migrants came from other European countries, most notably from France. Young French army officers like General Faidherbe and Joseph-Simon Gallieni, on being posted to Senegal, dreamed of creating a second French empire in West and North Africa to replace the lost dominions of Richelieu and Colbert across the Atlantic. And as the nineteenth century advanced, the momentum of migration was accelerated by the cession of Alsace and Lorraine to Germany following the Franco-Prussian War and by the fligh of French wine-growers from the ravages of the phylloxera, which successive upheavals made it necessary for France to resettle large numbers of her dispossessed peasants in French Africa, and especially in Algeria. Likewise in Germany, once Bismarck had left the scene, influential groups sprang up, dedicated to winning for the newly united German nation a place among the colonial powers commensurate with the military supremacy which it had lately proven against Austria–Hungary and France. And to this end, German settlers began to emigrate to Germany's recently established colonies in Africa.

In their turn, these settlers—from Britain, France and elsewhere—were to force the pace of colonial development and expansion and, by creating a vision of imperial greatness, to excite and to goad politicians, newspaper editors, writers and poets at home into adopting and upholding the new imperialist creed. For the settlers had an influence over home opinion which no mere trader could ever emulate. As an established community of pioneers, a microcosm of the mother country overseas, who had staked life and limb to claim vast spaces in the name of the homeland, the settlers could command support from their governments, whereas the traders were regarded, and often treated, as expendable. Thus in Africa, the British Parliament could be brought to do things for the settlers in the south which they would not dream of doing for the traders on the west coast.

This is not to say that the British Treasury lavished huge sums on the South African colonies. On the contrary, Government and Parliament were at one in wanting an empire on the cheap; and so much the better if the taxpayers' money could be saved by entrusting the empire-building processes to Chartered Companies or by getting the local merchants and inhabitants to pay for the administration, even if this meant granting them self-government. The difference in treatment between South and West Africa lay in the fact that the self-governing colonials of the south knew that, if they got into difficulties, they could depend on military as well as moral support from Britain, while the traders of West Africa knew that they would have to rely largely, if not entirely, on their own resources. And when the colonists failed to gain their objective—as happened after Rhodes' abortive attempt to invade the Transvaal—or when Cape Colony or the British South Africa Company claimed more than was good for Britain's relations with Germany or Portugal, did the home government weigh in and take over the conduct of policy. Then the 'Imperial Factor' would intervene to coerce the Boers, to pacify the Basutos, or to prevent the Colonies from overreaching themselves and causing needless frictions with their European rivals.

But whether the deeds were done and the decisions made by self-governing colonists in the Cape and Natal, by Rhodes' enterprises acting under Royal Charter, or by agents, administrators and soldiers of the Imperial Government acting on orders from London, the policy in South Africa was ever to expand British dominion and to swallow up all who stood in the way of that expansion, whether white or black, Boer or Bantu. Occasionally the progression was halted, as when Gladstone's Liberal government conceded a qualified independence to the Transvaal following the defeat of British arms by the Boer commandos at Majuba. But such concessions were in effect little more than wayside pauses in a continuous, if often plodding, British march of conquest in southern Africa, just as such reverses as Majuba signified a failure of the Imperial Government not so much to underwrite policies of expansion, as to estimate correctly the odds against their fulfilment.

Thus South Africa was to the imperial, as well as the colonial, arm of British government a case apart from the rest of the Dark Continent. And because, right up to the last decade of the nineteenth century, London was content to leave the execution of policy largely to the autonomous Cape Colony, there was little, if any, coordination of British actions in the south with developments in other parts of Africa. Until Chamberlain took charge of Britain's imperial affairs, the plans and decisions that were made in South Africa bore little relation to British policy in the Nile or Niger valleys. The 'Cape to Cairo' concept was more a pipe-dream than a policy. South Africa and Egypt might have been on different planets, so totally divorced were the actions and reactions of their respective British rulers.

Not that the scramble for South Africa took place in a vacuum. On the contrary, British policy had to take account of more than the Boers of the Transvaal and Orange Free State and the natives of Bechuanaland whose territories gave access to the north. There were also the Germans in South-West Africa and

Tanganyika to be reckoned with, or more accurately to be used as a bogey to justify the continued advancement of Britain's frontiers. And there were the Portuguese, who were established, albeit in a somewhat ramshackle way, in Angola and Mozambique which they had held for nearly four centuries. The Portuguese too had their dreams and claims to empire, by virtue of prior exploration and discovery, and in southern Africa these took the form of a belt of territory stretching from east to west, linking the Indian and Atlantic Oceans and joining Mozambique with Angola from the Zambezi to the Congo river.

The importance of the Portuguese lay not only in the fact that their claims conflicted with Britain's plans to expand into the Zambezi valley. To begin with, it was also an essential ingredient of Britain's policy to enlist the aid of her oldest ally in coercing the irritatingly independent Boers. To this end, it was hoped to induce Portugal to cede the Delagoa Bay area of Mozambique—the nearest ocean outlet for the Transvaal—and, by thus imposing a British barrier between the Boers and the sea, to force the Republics into a British-ruled union of South Africa. But these tactics were frustrated when Britain failed to gain Delagoa Bay in an international arbitration and Portugal subsequently refused every offer of purchase. Thereafter all forbearance was abandoned and Portuguese claims in the Zambezi basin were brusquely overridden to pave the way for Rhodes' Chartered Company to expand his empire to the borders of Tanganyika and the Congo Free State. Portugal had to pay the inevitable price of failing to occupy the trans-African belt to which she had asserted her title and which threatened the extension of Britain's South African possessions.

But long before the British, or even the Dutch, came to settle and to expand in South Africa, the Portuguese had been established as the first European colonists. And the story of the scramble for southern Africa, therefore, naturally begins with those early pioneers and their descendants who, fired by the adventurous crusading vision of Prince Henry the Navigator, went forth from Portugal to claim a place on alien soil, thousands of miles away, from which even in this current age of decolonisation almost five hundred years later they have still to be evicted.

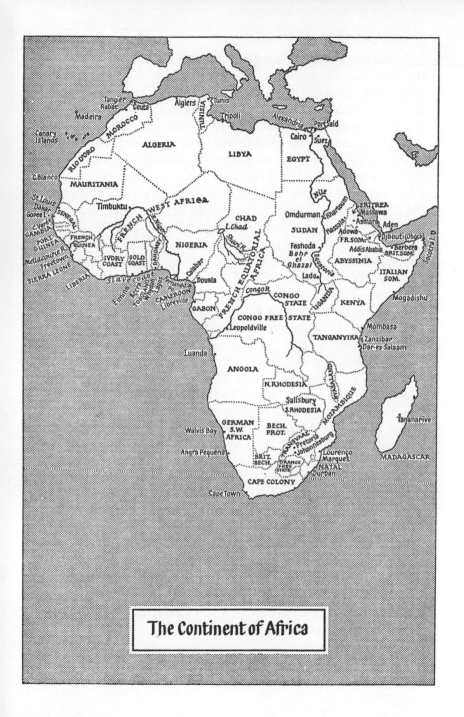

The Continent of Africa

At the beginning of the fifteenth century the momentum of the Christian reconquest of the Iberian peninsula had led the Portuguese to take the citadel of Ceuta and so to become the first Europeans to occupy a place in the African sun. This conquest was quickly followed by the colonisation of Madeira and the Azores and by the establishment of trade with Rio d'Oro, whence the first ten African slaves were brought back to Lisbon to revive in Europe the mediaeval custom of domestic slavery. But these were small advances compared with the ambitions of the patron-prince of early Portuguese imperialism, Henry the Navigator. For it was his dream that Portugal should, in the interests of Christianity and commerce, overthrow the Ottoman Sultan by sending her fleets round the continent of Africa and, in league with Prester John of Abyssinia, attack the Turks in their rear. Thus he would open up Europe's trade routes to the East which the Ottoman Empire had blocked, and from this he would go on to conquer the Indies 'for the glory of God and the profit of Portugal'.

To further his ambitions, Prince Henry was granted a monopoly of all African trade by his own Sovereign; and the reigning Pope, allegedly after His Holiness had received some of the first fruits of the new slave-trade, added his own inducements by granting remission of sins to all who took part in the Prince's crusade and by conferring on Portugal sole sovereignty over Africa's coasts and sole rights to convert its people to Christianity. But, in 1460, the 'Navigator' died with his dream unrealised. For at this point in time, Portugal's merchants and explorers had not penetrated beyond Guinea and the Gold and Slave Coasts. A fort had been built south of Cape Blanco in Morocco, Cape Verde and Senegal had been discovered and a Portuguese company had been formed to carry on trade with the Guinea coast in slaves and gold. But it was not until a quarter of a century after Prince Henry's death that Portuguese explorers discovered the estuary of the Congo and sailed up the river as far as Boma.

Thereafter the pace of exploration quickened and in 1488 Bartholomew Diaz rounded the southernmost point of Africa which he christened the Cape of Good Hope, from the encouragement which it gave him to press on to the discovery of the mysterious Indies. But his hopes were soon disappointed when, faced with a mutinous crew, he had to turn back. With Prince Henry dead and his venturesome spirit replaced by less daring counsellors who preferred to consolidate Portugal's conquests in Morocco and her trade with West Africa to pursuing the Indian odyssey, matters might have rested there had it not been for Columbus' voyage of discovery in 1492. Whether the Genoese explorer might be right or wrong in claiming to have found "the Indies", the Portuguese were now alerted to the fact of Spanish competition and to the need to lose no time in extending their own conquests and explorations as the only sure way of maintaining their monopoly rights.

Vasco da Gama was despatched five years later to take over where Diaz had left off. Sailing by the Cape Verde Islands and St. Helena, he rounded the Cape of Good Hope and, passing along the eastern coast of Africa, gave Natal its name from having discovered it at Christmastide. Still hugging the shore, he sailed on past Arab Mozambique as far as Malindi, on the coast of modern Kenya, and from there, guided by an Indian pilot and blown before the monsoon, he set out across the ocean to make his landfall at Calicut on the Indian coast, about halfway between the island of Ceylon and where the city of Bombay stands today. The pride and enthusiasm of the Portuguese which greeted da Gama's return in 1499 was almost boundless. Portugal had won the race to the Indies and, to mark the event, her King somewhat over-ambitiously styled himself 'Lord of the Conquest, Navigation and Commerce of Ethiopia, Arabia, Persia and China.'

For almost the next hundred years the Indian Ocean became a Portuguese sea. Triumphing with their cannon over the Arabs, Portugal's fleets commanded the entrances to the Persian Gulf and the Red Sea and established forts and harbours down the East African coast from Socotra, opposite Aden, to Mozambique. Jesuit priests were despatched to win the African natives to Christianity and to make converts from among the Moslems in the Arab zones of influence in East Africa. Settlements were established at Delagoa Bay and Mozambique, at Sofala—the old Arab sultanate and port whence for 1,500 years the gold of Manica had been shipped to the Red Sea and the Persian Gulf— at Kilwa and Zanzibar, Pemba, Mombasa, Malindi and Mogadishu on the east coast, at Quelimane, Sena and Tete on the Zambezi river, at St. Helena, and at Luanda and Kabinda in Angola and Congo.

In fact, neither the missionary effort nor the settlements were a success. The King of Congo embraced the Christian faith, taking the name of John after the Portuguese King, and sent an ambassador to reside in Lisbon and some twenty of his grandchildren to be educated in Portugal. Likewise the legendary Monomatopa, the black 'Emperor' of the Lower Zambezi valley, was baptised. But the missionaries spent more time caring for the souls of the half-caste products of the settlers' marriages with native women than they did in converting the tribes of the interior. And the fact that many of them kept slaves and some even engaged in slave-trading scarcely enhanced their influence with the natives. As for the settlers, stuck on a fever-ridden coast, they lacked both the energy and the resources to colonise or to trade other than in slaves and limited quantities of gold, brought to them from an interior to which access was barred by hostile tribes.

Beyond Africa, however, it was a more successful story. The copious wealth of the East and the rich cargoes of spices which da Gama's successors brought back from subsequent voyages helped the Portuguese to build a prosperous empire in India and the East Indies, while in the western hemisphere Brazil was annexed in the name of 'His Most Faithful Majesty'. By 1515, Goa was seized and Malacca too, which gave Portugal control over trade with the Far East. Portuguese ships even penetrated to Japan, while Macao, opposite Hongkong, was occupied together with the spice-trading Moluccas. In all, around the middle of the sixteenth century, Portugal held some 15,000 miles of coastline in Africa and the East, comprising some fifty-two trading stations and bases. So complete was their monopoly in these areas that the total of their overseas garrisons numbered no more than 20,000 soldiers, a paucity of strength which mattered little, so long as the native rulers remained friendly and no other power sought to dispute their occupation, but which in later years was to cost Portugal grave losses in territory and influence when her supremacy was challenged by native insurrections and European competition.

Such a challenge was not long in materialising. In 1580 the Portuguese House of Avis came to an end, after the young King Sebastian had fallen in battle attempting the conquest of Morocco. Philip II of Spain promptly laid claim to the vacant throne and Portugal was annexed for the next sixty years. Simultaneously, the Portuguese settlements at Mombasa, Kilwa and Tete were overrun and destroyed by one of those periodical waves of Bantu migration and invasion which mark the history of Black Africa. And although at the start of the sixteenth century the Congo Kings had welcomed the Portuguese as educators, addressed Portugal's sovereign as 'beloved brothers' and modelled their court on that of Lisbon from their style of dress down to the dinner service, these attitudes were destined to change before many years had elapsed. Due to the abuses of the Portuguese slave-traders and the attempts of Portuguese representatives to interfere in such delicate internal affairs as the succession to the throne, the early 'beloved brotherly' relationship was brought to an end. The sturdy sense of Congolese independence—a heritage of the mighty hunters armed with iron spears, or kongos, who founded this native state—duly asserted itself. After a bloody massacre in 1561, the Portuguese were driven from the Congo Basin and henceforth were obliged to confine their empire-building in West Africa to the coast of Angola, away to the south of the Congo estuary.

Added to all this, corruption became rife in the civil service of Portugal, as in the army and navy. Commands in Portuguese India were put up for auction, the spoils system was general and hordes of venal officials administered the royal monopoly in trade. With no Portuguese women in the new colonies, mixed marriages became the general rule. And before long, discipline collapsed as the Portuguese garrisons came increasingly to be manned by half-caste officers and soldiers with understandably little sense of loyalty to a fatherland which they had never seen.

27

Thus, within a hundred years of its creation, the Portuguese Empire in Africa and India had begun to decay. Only the profits of the slave-trade from West Africa kept it going with the aid of a nostalgic imperialism nurtured by the monarchy and by an evangelical Church. But it was a poor creature, which fell pitifully short of the ambitions which fired Prince Henry the Navigator, a classic example of a people who had overreached themselves in seeking to realise a dream far beyond their capabilities. And by way of tolling the bell for Portugal's imperial monopoly, that notable English mariner, Sir Francis Drake, now followed in the wake of Diaz and da Gama and, in the very year when Portugal became annexed to Spain, sailed round the Cape of Good Hope. A few years later James Lancaster, another Englishman, landed at Table Bay. Then in 1595 a Dutch squadron rounded the Cape en route for Java and, three years after that, some twenty Dutch ships passed by on their way to India.

The long struggle for supremacy between Spain, Holland and England had brought about the development of the English and Dutch fleets at the very moment when the interests of Portugal's possessions in Africa and the East were, by reason of her annexation to Spain, to become subjugated to those of the Spanish empire in the Americas. Worse still for the Portuguese, Spain's enemies had become theirs and the hand of every Englishman, Dutchman and Frenchman was now against them. And when Philip of Spain closed the port of Lisbon to Dutch ships, after William of Orange had renounced his allegiance to Spain, the Dutch were driven to seek their own trade in the East and were thus forced into competition with the Portuguese. Nor was this the only way in which Spanish policy helped, albeit indirectly, to promote Dutch rivalry. In the fifteenth century Spanish persecution of the Jews had caused an exodus to Portugal with great consequential benefits to Portuguese education in geography, astronomy and other sciences which contributed to exploration. Now, with Portugal under Spanish rule, the Jews moved on—to Holland among other places. And from this new exodus, Amsterdam became the banking centre of Western Europe and the financial mainstay of Dutch trade with the East. From this development the Dutch East India Company was formed in 1602, two years after its English counterpart, with a royal charter which granted to it sovereign powers of administration and a monopoly of all Dutch trade.

Thus at the outset of the seventeenth century the Portuguese were to see their trading monopoly in the East shattered, some of their prized possessions, such as the Moluccas, seized and their African settlements in Angola and Mozambique threatened by their new Dutch rivals. And fifty years later, possibly their greatest mistake was brought home to them when Jan van Riebeeck founded the Dutch East India Company's settlement at the Cape of Good Hope. In 1510, Francesco D'Almeida, Portugal's Viceroy in India, to whose credit lay the conquest of the East African coast, had been murdered with sixty-five of his followers in a quarrel with the natives after he had landed at Table Bay on his way back to Portugal. From then onwards, the Portuguese gave the Cape a wide berth, preferring to use St. Helena as a staging-post for their east-bound ships. And even after the reverses which they suffered in East and West Africa towards the end of the previous century, they still clung to the foetid coastal swamps of Mozambique and Angola, ignoring the high and healthy plateaus which lay behind the Cape, only a short distance from the scene of D'Almeida's martyrdom.

Here, in these temperate highlands, there would have been scope for the descendants of those pioneers from Portugal who had brought from China, the Indies and Brazil almost every product which grows in southern Africa today, from maize to tobacco, from sugar-cane to sweet-potatoes, from citrus trees to wheat, together with rice, manioc, chilis, tomatoes and many other fruits. But, after their initial expectations of gold and silver in the lands of Monomatopa had been disappointed, Portuguese interest in Africa centred almost exclusively on the slave-trade. And since their West African possessions were able, at least for the time being, to supply the overseas demand for slaves, small regard was had for maintaining, let alone for expanding, Portuguese possessions in other parts of Africa. In fact, by 1698, when Mombasa fell to the invading Arabs from Oman, little remained of D'Almeida's conquests. Portugal had been driven from the Persian Gulf and the Red Sea, while in East Africa every fortress north of Mozambique had been abandoned either to the Arabs or to native insurgents. And at the start of the eighteenth century, the Emirs of Oman laid the foundations for the great Sultanate of Zanzibar by inducing the Portuguese to surrender, without a fight, all their claims and possessions from Mogadishu down to Cape Delgado.

No doubt the dead hand of Spanish dominion would have discouraged any Portuguese initiative in the empty acres of South Africa, had it been attempted. Spain had only a marginal interest in African conquest. But, even after Portugal regained her independence under her first Braganza King in 1640, she still made no move to occupy any part of the coast beyond her remaining possessions. And twelve years later she lost finally and forever the opportunity which a century and a half of prior settlement in southern Africa had held out to her. In 1652 the Dutch East India Company established at the Cape a half-way house between Amsterdam and Batavia, the capital of the Dutch East Indies. Portugal was confined to her coastal stations in tropical Africa and, like the other European powers that came to barter guns and cloth for slaves and gold and ivory along the West and East African shores, she had neither reason nor resources to penetrate into an unknown interior.

Thus the Portuguese settlements of Angola and Mozambique remained cut off from each other, isolated on their respective coasts. In the early seventeenth century a half-hearted effort was made to link these two settlements with a belt of territory stretching across the continent. But the attempt was frustrated by the King of Congo who, embittered by the abuses of Portuguese slave-traders and by the diminution of his kingdom as a result of rebellions among his vassals incited by Portuguese agents, barred the way to the interior. Nearly two hundred years later, England's seizure of the Cape from the Dutch during the Napoleonic Wars was to lead the far-sighted Portuguese Governor of East Africa, Dr. Lacerda, to warn Lisbon that before long there would be a British dominion in South Africa stretching northwards from the Cape and driving a wedge between Angola and Mozambique. But Lisbon failed to heed this timely prediction and, although the Portuguese continued to lay claim to the lands which lay between their West and East African colonies, it was not until the end of the nineteenth century that any real attempt was made to substantiate this claim.

But by this time it was too late. Britain and, more particularly, Rhodes' British South Africa Company had by then appeared on the scene, bent on establishing British sovereignty in and beyond the valley of the Zambezi. And under threat of a British ultimatum, Portugal was pinned back in the east and in the west. Denied her claim to a trans-African belt linking Mozambique with Angola, she became the loser in the scramble for southern Africa, as she had earlier been in her struggle with the Dutch for the Indies' trade. The Portuguese had been the first of the Europeans to discover and to colonise Africa: they had dotted its coasts with Portuguese names such as Sierra Leone, Calabar, Gabon, Angra Pequena and the Mascarene Islands. Yet when the map of Africa was finally divided and parcelled out between the European powers, their share was less than one tenth of the total area and, due to the economic ruin which followed the abolition of the slave-trade, a poverty-stricken tenth at that.

2 Dutch and English at the Cape

UNLIKE the Portuguese, the Dutch entry into Africa sprang from strictly commercial motives, unconnected with evangelical ambitions to overthrow Ottoman Sultans or to convert Moslems or heathen Africans to Christianity. A few years after they had thrown off the yoke of Spain, the Dutch made their first trading voyage to the Guinea coast in 1595. And within the next fifty years, on the pretext that Portugal formed part of the Spanish Empire with which they were at war, they took possession of a number of Portuguese settlements both on and off the coast of Africa, in addition to seizing some of the wealthier Portuguese possessions in the East. Mauritius, which had been for many decades a Portuguese port of call, fell to them in 1598 and, in due course, they took over the island of Goree off the Senegalese coast, Elmina on the Gold Coast and, for a brief period, Luanda, the capital of Angola. In 1645, the Dutch took St. Helena from the Portuguese and, spreading outwards from their new conquest at Elmina, they constructed sixteen forts along the Gold Coast where, by plundering the indigenous Fanti and Ashanti tribes, they contributed to a prodigious increase in the slave trade, sending over the next two hundred years literally millions of negro slaves to service the developing plantations of North and South America and the West Indies.

Also, during the first half of the seventeenth century, the Dutch several times threatened Mozambique. A hundred years later they actually occupied Delagoa Bay—after it had

Second British Occupation of the Cape

The Great Trek

been temporarily abandoned by the Portuguese—but they were subsequently forced to withdraw after an epidemic of fever had killed off most of their garrison of German mercenaries. In the East, Dutch traders and adventurers went further than the Portuguese. Java was taken and made the headquarters of the Dutch East India Company. Formosa was occupied in order to gain control of the China tea-trade and, when the Company were forced to withdraw from the island by Chinese pirates, an alternative base was established in Ceylon. One Dutch mariner, named Tasman, penetrated as far as Australia where, more than a hundred years before Captain Cook made his epic voyage, he discovered the island which bears his name.

But although Dutch ships had been rounding the Cape of Good Hope for several decades after the formation of the Dutch East India Company, their captains had shown little desire to make of this natural half-way house to the East anything more than a place of shelter in stormy weather. The Cape was not, so first reports had it, a good source of supplies for the Company's ships; St. Helena was much better equipped; and the native Hottentots—so-called from the Dutch words, 'hotteren' and 'tateren', which described their clicking, or stuttering, speech—were dismissed as a 'faithless rabble'. Then in 1647, a Dutch East Indiaman, the *Haarlem*, was wrecked in Table Bay. Her crew scrambled to the shore where they lived for the next twelve months, bartering with the natives and growing their own food, until they were picked up by a company fleet returning from the East Indies. On returning to Holland, the ship's captain reported so favourably on the prospects of the Cape that the Company decided to establish a victualling station there in place of St. Helena which, a few years later was transferred to British ownership. Thus in April 1652, Jan van Riebeeck, a ship's surgeon who had visited South Africa on a previous voyage, stepped ashore at Table Bay to claim Dutch sovereignty over the Cape, where he and his successors were to rule for the next one hundred and forty-three years under the supreme authority of the Council of Seventeen—the Company's board of directors in Amsterdam—and subject to the 'local' direction of the Governor-General in Batavia, three month's voyage away to the east.

At this point Company policy was firmly against colonisation, whether in the East Indies or in Africa; and the Cape was intended for use as a victualling station and nothing else. The Dutch wanted trade, not empire. The experience which their West India Company had learned from the recalcitrant settlers of New Amsterdam and New England, with their fractious petitions to Governor Stuyvesant for autonomy, had taught them to eschew settlements in Africa and the East. Their policy was therefore to concentrate on trying to gain and hold a monopoly in the trade of the East Indies and to eliminate all rivals—even if this meant antagonising British and French, as well as native, traders.

Yet, however much the Council of Seventeen might set their faces against more Dutch colonies overseas, it soon became clear that, if the Cape was to fulfil its appointed task, a limited degree of settlement was essential. To supply meat, wheat and wine to the Company's ships required labour and raw materials. And to satisfy these requirements, both Dutch immigrants and slave labour from outside the country had to be imported. For, during at least the first twenty-five years of Dutch occupation, the Hottentots not only declined to trade either their cattle or their services, but from time to time made war against the Company's properties and personnel. Van Riebeeck's instructions prevented him from seizing the Hottentot cattle and sending their owners to slavery overseas, as he would have liked to do. And since, towards the end of the first decade of its existence, the settlement's adult European population numbered only forty-six, with a garrison of around three hundred soldiers, it was deemed necessary to introduce European settlers, together with slaves from Madagascar and the East Indies and convict labour from India—the forefathers of the Cape Coloureds of today—and, with this added population, to allow a limited experiment in farming in the green valleys behind the little fortress village that was to become Cape Town. Thus it may be said that the concept of 'Boer', or farmer, settlement—from which sprang the first colonisation of South Africa—originated in large part with the need of the Dutch East India Company's ships for fresh meat which the natives, regarding their cattle as the inalienable symbol of their tribal status, refused to supply.

There was, however, another reason which led the Council of Seventeen to relax their resistance to colonisation—fear of France, against whom the Dutch were currently conducting a long drawn-out war. If the new Cape station was to be held against a possible French invasion, its fortifications and garrison had to be strengthened and this meant more labour and more mouths to feed. And to meet all these originally unforeseen needs, towards the turn of the century the Company adopted a policy of assisted migration for Dutch settlers and also for Germans and those French Huguenots who, following Louis XIV's revocation of the Edict of Nantes, took refuge in Holland and other Protestant countries.

By the census of 1707 the new policy had succeeded in raising the European adult population of 'free burghers', as distinct from Company employees, to 803. The garrison was increased to some 500 men and the numbers of imported slaves to nearly 1,200. Thus in fifty years, the European population of the Cape station had been more than trebled: the colony had arrived.

But, if the Company had changed their views on colonisation, they remained firmly attached to the monopoly principle and claimed first call on the burghers' cattle, corn and wine. Already many of the free burghers, to distinguish themselves from the Hollander officials of the Company's administration, had begun to call themselves 'Afrikaners' and looked upon themselves as sons of the soil and therefore its rightful owners. And it was not long before friction began to arise over the monopoly and price-fixing systems practised by the administration and over its methods of granting trading and property leases, especially when it became known that officials, sometimes including the Governor himself, were breaking their own laws to line their pockets.

Some farmers began to move further inland to escape from this atmosphere of corruption and restriction and to take their chance as frontier Boers, living in reed huts and trek-wagons, ranching their cattle and trading and bartering privately with the Hottentots—a practice strictly forbidden by Company regulations. Others soon followed and, although the Great Trek that was to carry the Boers beyond the Orange and Vaal rivers did not take place until the next century, the sturdy individualism of the free burghers had already begun to manifest itself. Resentful of the interference and of the abuses of colonial authority, the Trek-Boer was on the move.

Unlike the British when they faced the same problem a hundred years later, the Dutch East India Company made little or no effort to restrain or overtake these dissident elements, beyond issuing edicts bidding them to stop. For one thing the Cape garrison was still so small that, if serious fighting broke out with the Bushmen or Hottentots, it had to be supplemented by a commando system recruited from the free burghers. Defence and law enforcement on the frontiers were far beyond the Company's reach and had to be left to the frontier Boers themselves. Added to these problems, the Cape in 1713 suffered an outbreak of smallpox which wiped out nearly a quarter of its inhabitants, including hundreds of slaves and Hottentots. And on top of everything else, the Cape administration was in serious financial straits, with expenditure running annually at a figure of almost three times that of the revenue.

So serious, in fact, had the financial situation become in the early eighteenth century that the Council of Seventeen decided henceforth to halt any further colonisation and to put an end to the system of assisted migration. From then on, the Cape had to rely on slave labour and to abandon all hope of Company-sponsored development. And apart from a small continuing flow of voluntary migrants from Europe, among whom women were seldom more than a quarter of the total, the further expansion of the Colony's population depended to no small extent upon mixed marriages which the Dutch, like the Portuguese before them, but in stark contrast to the apartheid system of today, then permitted as a natural, inevitable, and even necessary corollary of colonisation.

Holland's Golden Age was fading fast and with it the fortunes of the Dutch East India Company were going into decline. While Britain had been tearing herself apart in the Civil War between Cromwell and the Stuarts, and while France and Spain were locked in the struggle of the Thirty Years War, Holland had profited from an absence of serious rivals. But by the start of the eighteenth century these conflicts had ceased: Britain and France became powers to be reckoned with: naval supremacy passed from Holland to England: Amsterdam gave way to London as the financial centre of Western Europe. And before the century ended, Holland was again stretched on the rack, with her native soil invaded by French forces, her trade monopoly in the East broken and her most prized colonial possessions seized. Now as she stood still, as if waiting for the blow that was to fell her, with the States-General paralysed by a growing republican threat to the Dutch monarchy, her imperial resolution faltered. Little more than sixty years after it started, Dutch development at the Cape had ground to a halt. And although, for the rest of the Company's tenure, Cape Town was to be known as the 'Tavern of the Seas' among the many ships' crews who called there en route to the East, the Colony was to languish in a state of inertia until the coming of the British gave it a new management and a fresh purpose nearly a hundred years later.

Like many other empires, that of the Dutch declined only slowly. And for all but a few years of the eighteenth century, the Dutch East India Company lingered on, recklessly paying dividends with no real profits to back them. But the writing on the wall spelled bankruptcy, and long before the end their policies, or lack of them, had reduced their Colony at the Cape to stagnation. With no further assisted migration, the numbers of European immigrants fell to such small proportions that, in all the century and a half of the Company's rule, the records show that little more than two thousand adults—nearly half of whom were Germans—emigrated to the Cape from Europe. And when the Dutch occupation came to an end in 1795, the burgher population numbered under 14,000, who were served by some 17,000 slaves.

With its market restricted by a shortage of population, trade at the Cape entered a long period of depression. Largely dependent on Dutch and other ships calling at Cape Town, the numbers of which even in the last quarter of the century did not average more than 120 a year, the colony's prosperity was further limited by the strict application of Holland's Navigation Acts which prescribed that trade to and from Dutch ports should be carried only in Dutch ships and therefore forbade any foreign vessel to trade with the Cape.

These restrictions inevitably caused great ill feeling among the Cape colonists. But what made them still more angry was the continued corruption of the Company's officials. From time to time complaints would reach the Council of Seventeen. Commissions of Enquiry would then be sent out to investigate; reforms would be recommended and occasionally a Governor would be dismissed. Thereafter for a brief while, a new broom would sweep clean at the castle. But, in the end, the venal would always get the better of the upright and, entrenching themselves behind the Company's monopoly, would revive the old ways of corruption. And as in the past, so in all the remaining years of Company rule, the disgust of the settlers found expression in a continuing Boer exodus towards the hinterlands of the north and the east. By the middle of the century, one of the Trek-Boers had crossed the Kei river into Tembuland and, in 1760, another of their number crossed the Orange river. Fifteen years later, these migrants could fairly claim to have settled in roughly a half of today's Cape Province, albeit to a density of no more than one man per five square miles. And in 1795 the Boers in the Graaf Reinet area of the eastern Cape went so far as to set up a Republic, which they declared to be independent of Cape Town.

The Company could do nothing to stop these migrations beyond indulging the feeble gesture of planting beacons to mark a boundary at the Fish river, which the Trek-Boers had long since left behind them, and forbidding anyone to go beyond this point. Nor, since a second smallpox epidemic had almost wiped out the Cape Hottentots, was there any effective native resistance to such movements. The Trek-Boers, therefore, had nothing to stop them and everything to encourage them to move out—a corrupt and greedy government to escape from and a land of green valleys and good pastures to escape to. And by the end of the eighteenth century, the Colony had grown from a

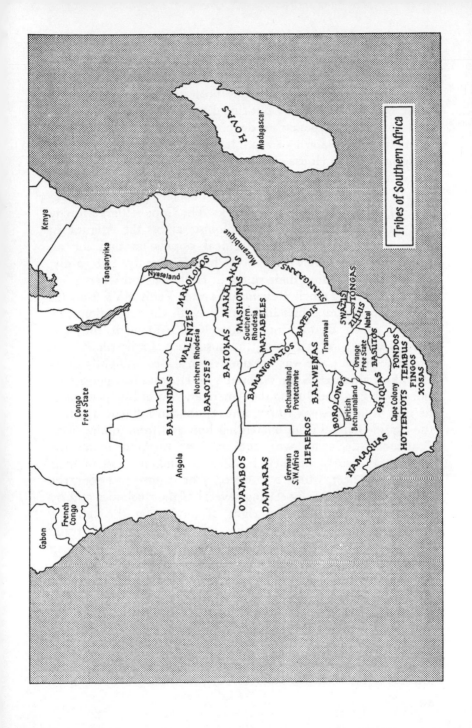

Tribes of Southern Africa

victualling station to an area half again as large as Britain.

But the Trek-Boers were not the only dissenters among the Company's 'subjects'. True, they protested more openly than those who stayed behind; but this did not mean that the infection had failed to penetrate deeply among the whole burgher population. The spirit of republicanism, which was currently undermining the House of Orange in Holland, found a menacing echo at the Cape, especially when the American colonists rose in rebellion against England and declared their independence of George III and all his works. The Cape settlers strongly sympathised with their fellow colonists across the Atlantic in their struggle against monarchical oppression and for an autonomy which they themselves had frequently, but vainly, sought by petitioning their rulers in Holland. And when a few years later the French Revolution swept Louis XVI from his throne, their sympathies likewise lay with the revolutionaries.

Thus when Britain found herself at war with the new republican regime in France, the possibility of a hostile French presence at the Cape was not one which she could lightly overlook. For, although King William V of Holland had personally sided with England during the American War of Independence, he had been too weak to prevent republican influences within the States-General from overruling him and from joining with France in declaring war against her. England made the Dutch pay dearly for their hostility by sinking most of their commercial fleet, which a hundred years before had been the largest in the world, by seizing several of their colonies and by forcing them to cede the right of navigation through the Moluccas, which destroyed once and for all the Dutch trade monopoly in the East Indies. But these reprisals only served to make the States-General the more embittered towards England. Moreover, they still further weakened Holland's ability to withstand French pressures, as was shown in 1781, when French troops arrived at Cape Town and, defying the threats of a British naval squadron, virtually occupied the place for the next three years.

Up to this point in time, England had not shown much interest in southern Africa. Her African trading stations were confined to the west coast—to Gambia, Sierra Leone, the Gold Coast and Dahomey—whence English merchants had carried on a lucrative trade from the sixteenth century onwards under royal charters which conferred on them the traditional commercial monopolies and exhorted them to expand the slave trade by all possible means. English ships bound for India had used the old Portuguese route up the East African coast and English interests had not been threatened by the Dutch presence at the Cape. But when the Dutch republicans joined the French in opposing England's efforts to crush the American colonists and still more when the revolutionary regime in France declared war in 1793, England was forced to view South Africa in a different light. For the occupation of Cape Town in the 1780s was not by any means the only manifestation of French interest in those parts of Africa which lay along England's line of communications with India and the East. Since the seventeenth century when the 'Company of the East' was formed under the patronage of Cardinal Richelieu, the French had nursed ambitions of colonising Madagascar, or 'New France', as it was then called. In 1643 they had established themselves on the nearby island of Bourbon, later to be called Reunion. And although the French East India Company, which took over the Madagascar concession in 1664, had suffered grievous setbacks from native insurrections and attacks by pirates, they had only recently started a further attempt to colonise the island. Added to this, the French had taken Mauritius from the Dutch in 1715 for use as a base to strengthen their hand in the East Indies trade.

Given this powerful French interest and presence in the Indian Ocean, it was inevitable that, on the outbreak of war, England should anticipate an early French move to take over the Cape from the Dutch and so to command the sea-lanes to the East. Her fears in this direction waxed stronger than ever when the French invaded Holland, captured the Dutch fleet in the frozen Texel river with the aid of a cavalry charge across the ice, and forced William V to flee into exile in England. And when the subsequent formation of the Batavian Republic, in place of the House of Orange and in alliance with revolutionary

France, was hailed with joy by the dissident Cape burghers, England could ignore no longer this incipient threat to her imperial communications. To make matters worse, at this very moment when England's links with her newly won empire in the east were menaced by a Franco-Dutch alliance, the Dutch East India Company were forced finally and solemnly to declare the bankruptcy which had threatened them for so long.

With no company to rule the Cape and moderate the pro-French ardour of the republican burghers and with not even a feeble friend on the throne in Holland, the challenge to English interests was clear and conclusive. And on June 11, 1795, nine English men-of-war anchored in False Bay and landed a small force of redcoats with an order, signed by Holland's refugee King, bidding the Dutch garrison to allow them to occupy the Cape. At first the royal command was disregarded and the garrison put up a brave show of resistance, hoping to gain time for reinforcements to arrive from France or Holland. But after three months of fighting withdrawal, the Dutch burghers and German mercenaries were forced to abandon the struggle and to surrender as prisoners of war under an armistice which was signed in September. The first British occupation of the Cape had begun.

It was to prove an unhappy and unsuccessful experiment for all concerned. Lord Macartney, the first English Governor, instituted certain reforms limiting the severity of the punishments meted out to slaves and native inhabitants. But apart from this and a few minor changes in the judicial and administrative systems, little was done to remedy the grievances of the local population. Due to the continuing state of war between England, France and Holland, trade recovered very slowly. And the new British administration was no more successful than the Dutch East India Company had been in seeking to contain the diaspora of the Boers beyond the official boundaries of Cape Colony. In fact, for most of the eight years of their first occupation, the British had to contend with an almost constant state of rebellion in the Graaf Reinet area of the eastern Cape, where the local Boers had earlier declared themselves independent of the Dutch East India Company. And when, in 1803, peace was restored with France and the Batavian Republic by the Treaty of Amiens, it was with considerable relief on the part of British officials on the spot that Cape Colony was handed back to Holland, together with the Dutch settlements in the West Indies which had become forfeit when the Batavian Republic joined hands with the French.

There was relief too for the Cape burghers when a new Dutch regime took control under a business-like Commissioner-General, Jacob de Mist, who radically reformed the administration, created an independent judiciary and generally tried to sweep away the corruption and abuses which had become common practice under the Company's rule. But he was gravely handicapped in his liberalising efforts by shortage of money, troops and skilled labour—the heritage of the Company's policies of retrenchment. And he was no more successful than his predecessors in his attempts to pacify the Colony's eastern frontier, where twenty years before the first battles of what was to become a long series of Kaffir wars had been fought by the colonists against Bantu tribes migrating from the northeast in search of land to graze their cattle. On top of this, within a few months of the establishment of the Dutch colonial regime at the Cape, hostilities were resumed between the French and the English and the Batavian Republic found itself once more at war with England, as an ally of Napoleon Buonaparte.

To the Dutch, the Cape was expendable by comparison with their richer possessions in the East Indies and de Mist had to sacrifice his best soldiers to strengthen the defences of Java. It was, therefore, only a matter of time before the English would return and retake the Cape, if only to forestall their enemies. And in January 1806, three months after Nelson had smashed Napoleon's fleet off Cape Trafalgar, English troops duly landed for the second time at the Cape where, outnumbering the burgher militia by three to one, they took possession of the Colony in the name of George III. The second and final British occupation had been established. Eight years later, after the House of Orange had been restored to the throne of Holland, the peace settlement of 1814 gave back to the Dutch all but two of the colonies which had been seized from them during the

Napoleonic Wars. The strategic importance of the Cape made it one of these two exceptions. And by the terms of the peace settlement, British sovereignty was confirmed over this former Dutch domain, in return for £5,000,000 compensation to enable Holland to strengthen the defences of her frontiers, which had been considerably extended by the inclusion of Belgium.

One of the first actions of the new English administration was to apply to the Cape the general prohibition of slave-trading in all Britain's dominions decreed in the Abolition Act of 1807. Only some thirty years before this initiative spelled the beginning of the end of the European slave-trade out of Africa, the institution of slave-ownership had been declared illegal in England. The French revolutionaries then went a stage further by abolishing slavery in the French colonies. But when the newly emancipated slaves of Haiti rose against French rule under the self-styled Negro 'General' Toussaint de L'Ouverture, a reaction set in and Napoleon repealed the abolition decree. For the next fifteen years, the West Indian traders and planters were, therefore, able to resist the anti-slavery campaign of such humanitarian crusaders as Granville Sharp, Thomas Clarkson and William Wilberforce by pleading that political tranquillity as well as economic necessity required the continuation of slavery and the slave-trade in the colonies. And it was not until that staunch champion of human rights, Charles James Fox, lent his weight to the abolitionist cause that Parliament was finally shamed into decreeing that the slave-trade was illegal in all His Britannic Majesty's possessions across the seas. Even then English traders continued in business surreptitiously, despite the watchful patrols of the Royal Navy, until in 1823 a breach of the Abolition Act became punishable by death and the profits no longer matched the risks.

Slavery at the Cape did not, of course, compare either in cruelty or in scale with the barbarous trade in suffering humanity from the West coast by which the Europeans supplied their plantations in the Americas with labour, for which the native inhabitants were either too fierce, too feeble or too few to be suitable. Nor did it bear any semblance to the horrors of the Arab slave trade in East Africa. Between them, the Europeans and the Arabs destroyed, or at least decimated, whole communities through the forcible abduction of literally millions of the fittest and ablest of their people. In the eighteenth century, as the American and West Indian plantations expanded, over two million negro slaves were imported from Africa. From the Congo Kingdom alone, some 15,000 slaves were shipped annually throughout the seventeenth century to the flourishing slave-markets of Lisbon and the New World: and in all, by the time this noxious trade was finally stopped in the nineteenth century, thirteen and a quarter millions of Congolese had been dragged from their homeland and sold into slavery in Europe and the Americas. By comparison with their brothers across the Atlantic, slaves in Cape Colony were generally well treated by their Dutch masters and manumissions were fairly frequent. No slaves were exported from the Cape, where at all times since the arrival of the Dutch there had been a continual shortage of labour. And although punishments were severe, at least it could not be said that the institution of slavery had caused any decrease in the African population.

The Colony had of course come to depend on slave labour for all of the past hundred years since the Company's retrenchment policy had put an end to assisted migration of European labour. And while the British Abolition Act did not interfere with the rights of existing slave-owners over their 'property', but only forbade any future buying or selling of slaves, nevertheless the Cape burghers resented this reform, along with a number of other changes wrought by the new British administration, as a threat to the Colony's economy and an unwarrantable attempt to change their traditional way of life. For, while the burghers might seem somewhat advanced in their republican sympathies with American colonists or French sansculottes rebelling against imperial and monarchical authority, their attitude towards the African native showed that they still lived in the seventeenth century, and had in no way progressed from the modes and customs of the time when their forbears cast themselves adrift from their native land. And the reforms carried out by de Mist during the brief interregnum between the British occupations owed their popularity to the fact that they were directed ex-

45

clusively towards making life easier for the colonists, while the natives' lot was improved not at all.

Thus, when de Mist's brief reign gave way to a new regime of English autocrats, who took it upon themselves to tell the burghers how many lashes they could give to a recalcitrant slave, the Boer settlers soon read into the 1807 Act an eventual threat to the owners of slaves, as well as to the slave-traders. Then to their even greater alarm, soon after British sovereignty had been permanently established in the peace settlement with Holland, a veritable flood of missionaries, with dangerous ideas about the equality of all men in the sight of God, poured into Cape Colony and spread out towards, and even beyond, its frontiers to the east and the north. The Moravian Brethren, followed by the London Missionary Society, had been first in the field in the last years of the eighteenth century. Now they were joined by the Wesleyans and the Church Missionary Society and other groups from England, Scotland and Holland. And it was not long before the mission stations began to arouse the wrath of the settlers who complained that they offered asylum to shiftless natives and so attracted labour away from hard-pressed farmers. When the missionaries retorted that the Boers should treat their employees better if they wanted to attract labour to their farms, relations became more than ever embittered between the sons of the soil and the men of God; and the Government who admitted the missionaries became the target for yet more resentment on the part of the settlers.

But it was in their attempts to bring English law and order to that area of constant disturbance—the eastern frontier—that the administration was to cause the first irreparable breach with their Dutch subjects by an act of savage repression which the Boers were to remember with a bitter burning hatred for almost all of the next hundred years. Since the days of de Mist's regime, the Xosas had claimed a large slice of the Colony's territory, known as the Zuurveld, which lay to the west of the Fish river boundary, and as an earnest of their claim had occupied parts of the area. De Mist having failed to evict them, it was not until 1812 that a combined force of British troops and Dutch burghers managed to clear the Zuurveld for European settlement, and to secure the Fish river frontier against further Bantu incursions. But any gratitude which the Boers might have felt for the assistance of their new rulers in reclaiming this area was soon dispersed when district officers and judges arrived to establish British rule over a territory which, in the days of the Dutch East India Company, had enjoyed almost complete autonomy. And when two years later a Boer settler was killed by a British patrol sent to bring him to court on a charge of cruelty to a Hottentot servant, his relatives and friends raised a rebellion, vowed to evict the British from the eastern Cape and declare a Republic, and even sought the aid of the Xosa chief, Gaika, to achieve their ends.

The rebellion was quickly suppressed: all but a few of the rebels were captured at Slachter's Nek and tried for treason. The majority were banished from the eastern frontier, but six rebels were sentenced to death. Of these one was reprieved by the newly appointed Governor, Lord Charles Somerset; the other five were hanged in particularly incompetent and brutal fashion. And with their execution, all the pent-up resentments of the Boers against their new masters coagulated in a curdle of cold imperishable rage. The long running fight had begun between Briton and Boer that was to last for the next ninety years. The first martyrs had been created in the struggle for which the rallying cry of the Dutch settlers would henceforth be the place-name of their martyrdom—Slachter's Nek.

Having suppressed this first Boer rebellion, Somerset's next task was to deal with a further outbreak of trouble with the natives on the eastern frontier. Here he was soon to learn some of the lessons which the Bantu border tribes—Xosas, Tembus and Pondos to the east and the Hereros and Bakwenas in the north—had been teaching the Trek-Boers for the past hundred years. He was, for instance, to discover in his dealings with the Xosas that a treaty made with a tribal chief was not necessarily regarded as binding his fellow chiefs or the tribe as a whole. He was also to learn that a concession of tribal land, which a European would regard as an outright sale, was considered by the Bantu as no more than a tenuous leasehold, which they could reclaim whenever they wished. Hence when he finally managed to drive the Xosas investing the frontier back beyond the Keiskamma river and forced Gaika to agree that the territory between the Fish river and the Keiskamma should be neutral ground belonging neither to white men nor to natives, Somerset's experience told him that the Xosa chief's word would not be an adequate guarantee of this buffer zone. Only a strong white settler population backed by troops on the Colony's side of the border could protect the area against further Bantu violations.

Yet, at this very moment, far from becoming more populous, the frontier lands were emptying of Boers who were drifting away to the north-east, partly in outraged protest against the Slachter's Nek hangings, partly because the grass was always greener on the other side of the next river. Although Somerset offered the burghers land-grants as an inducement to stay put, nothing could arrest the continuing dispersal of the Dutch colonists. Only an infusion of English settlers could fill the vacuum; and to this end, Somerset persuaded the British Government to follow the example of the Dutch East India Company in earlier times and adopt a policy of assisted migration. Impressed by the Governor's glowing account of the prospects for white settlement in South Africa, Parliament duly obliged with a grant of £50,000 to launch the scheme. And early in 1820, some five thousand Britishers—who were to be known as 'the 1820 settlers'—turned their backs on the depression that had followed in the wake of the Napoleonic Wars and set out for the Cape to claim the hundred acre land-lots which the Colony was offering to each of these new migrants.

No longer was the Cape to remain a Dutch community ruled by British officials. The first active, conscious step had been taken towards the creation of a British dominion in South Africa.

3 The Voortrekker Republics

THE next fifteen years did little to improve relations between Briton and Boer. In certain spheres the Cape's Governors showed willing to appease Dutch opinion, but their efforts were all too often vitiated by the dictates of their superiors in London. With the aid of the school-teachers introduced from Scotland, an expanded programme of education was set on foot, which included religious instruction in Dutch; and following Somerset's departure, freedom of the press, in the English and Dutch languages, was conceded. Also a certain degree of autonomy was given to the eastern districts of the Colony, where recent events had sharpened separatist sentiment. In reforming the legal system, it was decided to change to English law only in criminal cases and to allow Roman-Dutch law to obtain as before in the civil courts. But when the burghers began to agitate for some form of representative institutions, they were firmly told that there were not nearly enough qualified men in the Colony to form an elected Assembly. And when the agitation continued unabated, the dissidents were threatened with deportation and a ban was placed on public meetings.

In due course, these restrictions were lifted by the Imperial Government, acting in the spirit of the 1832 Reform Bill. But the cheers which greeted this concession to democracy were soon to be silenced. For a few months later, in 1833, the British Parliament decreed the emancipation of slaves in all Britain's dominions overseas, which for the Cape meant the immediate

49

liberation of a slave population which had by now grown to some 39,000. As a sop to the colonists, it was also decided to set up a nominated Assembly, consisting of five local citizens and the five official members of the Executive Council, which would legislate under the presidency of the Governor. But this was considered to be poor comfort for the slave-owning burghers, who wanted an Assembly of elected members who would represent to their British rulers the essential need for slaves to maintain the labour force. And when it became known that the compensation promised to the slave-owners had been cut by imperial decree by more than 50 per cent, which spelled ruin for many farms and the foreclosing of mortgages, the fury of the colonists knew no bounds.

Coming on top of a recent government decision to make Crown lands subject to sale by auction which had hitherto been granted freely, the Imperial Government's decision to halve the compensation to the slave-owners was bound to widen still further the gulf of discord between them and their Dutch subjects at the Cape. There were ominous rumblings portending a mass exodus of Boers. Leading colonists talked of a major trek to the interior and reconnaissance parties were despatched to Natal and beyond the Vaal river to explore the possibilities of large-scale Boer settlement beyond the reach of British rule. But before these scouts could return with radiant reports of high and healthy plateaus almost empty of inhabitants, the eastern frontier was set ablaze by a fresh Xosa invasion and the remaining Dutch population found themselves engaged alongside the new British settlers in yet another Kaffir War.

For two weeks the Xosas ran amok across the Zuurveld until the combined fire-power of the British garrison and the Boer commandos under Pieter Retief—who was later to lead the Great Trek—stayed their onslaught and drove them back beyond the Kei river. The settlers' losses were severe—one hundred dead, including Hottentot servants, hundreds of farms destroyed and thousands of horses, cattle and sheep taken as war booty—a total amounting to some £300,000 worth of property. The new Governor of the Cape, Sir Benjamin D'Urban, was determined to make the Xosas pay for the damage they had done. And as soon as the invaders withdrew, he proclaimed that the territory between the Keiskamma and the Kei—the neutral buffer zone in the 1819 treaty with Gaika—would become part of Cape Colony under the name of Queen Adelaide Province and declared that the Xosas, in addition to paying compensation for all stolen cattle, must henceforth keep to the other side of the Kei.

For the first time since the establishment of British rule, the Boers felt that, perhaps after all, they now had a Governor who understood their problems. But D'Urban, a professional soldier by trade and inclination, had neither the experience nor the temperament necessary to carry the day against determined political opposition at home. A cavalry officer who held the rank of Major-General in the British and Portuguese armies, he served with great distinction in the struggle against Napoleon and, after the Peninsular War had ended, stayed on to organise the Portuguese forces. But his only encounter with colonial problems before coming to the Cape stemmed from a spell during the 1820s as Lieutenant-Governor in British Guiana and Barbados. Not unnaturally therefore he, and the Boers too, in thinking that the new annexations would be confirmed by Whitehall and the Bantu threat to the Cape's eastern frontier would now be greatly allayed, failed to take account of the influence of the humanitarian societies in Britain, with their belief in the white man's responsibility for protecting and civilising the African native. In particular, he reckoned without such missionaries as Dr. John Philip, the superintendent of the London Missionary Society in the Colony. Philip, an unbending Nonconformist prelate who invariably took the side of the natives in any disputation with the colonists or the Cape Government, promptly raised an outcry against D'Urban's settlement, which he termed an attempt to exterminate the Bantu on the eastern frontier. The Secretary of State for War and Colonies, Lord Glenelg, who was greatly influenced by the growing humanitarian lobby in Parliament and in the press, paid more attention to Philip's hyperbole than to D'Urban's rational explanations. Within a few months, he bowed to these pressures and wrote to the Governor to warn him that his new frontier would have to be given up, since the Xosas had suffered grievous wrongs in the past and should not be made to suffer for their recent actions.

The unhappy D'Urban could therefore only temporise in the faint hope that different counsels might prevail. But the colonists soon drew their own conclusions from his failure to issue land grants or build forts in the newly annexed territory in fulfilment of his proclamation. Scenting another betrayal by the Imperial Government, the advance parties of the Great Trek— the culmination of the century-old drift of Boers northwards from the Cape—set off in the early autumn of 1836 to find and occupy the lands which their scouts had described in such glowing terms two years before. Whereupon D'Urban, antici- pating his final instructions from London, and concluding that there could be little further purpose in holding onto the new territory, ordered its immediate evacuation. Queen Adelaide Province was abandoned to the Xosas; and four months later, in February 1837, the main body of the Voortrekkers, led by Pieter Retief, moved out of the Colony and away to the north, armed with rifles and bibles, a bitter sense of grievance against their rulers and a supreme faith in God and their own capacity for survival.

By September of that same year which was to mark the beginning of the Victorian era, some 2,000 Dutch colonists had crossed the Orange river, to seek the Promised Land that was theirs for the taking and where they could resume their seven- teenth-century style of living and escape from British officialdom with its exasperating self-appointed trusteeship for the Bantu as equals of the Europeans. The first major step had been taken towards the division of South Africa into two irreconcilable systems—Boer and British.

Another, and at the time unforeseen, result of the Great Trek was to set in motion the chain of events which led to the estab- lishment of a British Colony in Natal. In 1824 two Britishers, Francis Farewell and James King, who were authorised by Somerset to trade with Natal, had bought some 30,000 square miles of land around Port Natal from Chaka, the dreaded Zulu chief who had forged from a small and insignificant tribe a dis- ciplined force of warriors whose name spelled terror and desolation from Lake Nyasa to the Drakensberg Mountains. These two pioneers were soon joined by other British traders and, ten years after the settlement had been founded, the small British community petitioned the Cape Governor to establish British rule at Port Natal. The Imperial Government refused their request on the grounds of expense, just as they had earlier declined to accept the cession of the southern half of Delagoa Bay which an enterprising Royal Navy Officer, Captain Owen, had obtained by treaties with certain tribal chiefs who claimed to be beyond the ambit of Portuguese rule.

Nevertheless, in 1836, the colonists returned to the charge, having renamed Port Natal after Governor D'Urban and having secured from Dingaan, Chaka's successor by right of assassination, a promise that the southern half of Natal would be ceded to them. But again the British Government rejected the Natal colonists' demand for annexation by the Cape, even though D'Urban recommended that it be supported. All that they would concede was the appointment by the Cape of a resident magistrate in Durban. However strategically important and climatically desirable Cape Colony might have been, in these early days Whitehall had little use for Natal, or for Delagoa Bay. Lacking the Cape's advantages for colonial settlement and separated from the nearest British territory by many miles of uncharted and presumably hostile territory, it was then felt that to annexe these areas would overstretch the available military and administrative resources of the Cape with no compensating benefit to British interests.

The Great Trek was to transform this attitude. Not only did the trekkers open up the uncharted hinterland; but, as they poured into Natal, a new threat presented itself to Britain's recently established supremacy in southern Africa. It was bad enough that the Cape Boers should move out beyond the Orange river to escape from British rule. But an independent Voortrekker Republic with access to the coast was something which no British Government wished to see.

Retief was the moving spirit behind this ominous development. Named as Commandant-General of the Voortrekkers, he led one of the main Boer groups across the Drakensberg

Mountains to Durban, while the others under Hendrik Potgieter went northwards to spread themselves in scattered communities from the Orange river to the Zoutpansberg plateau south of the Limpopo. Retief's arrival in Natal in October 1837 was welcomed by the English settlers who had given up hoping for British recognition and protection. But their gratification for this European addition to their settlement was short-lived. For, in the following year, when Retief went to Dingaan's kraal to accept the cession of southern Natal which the Zulus had promised, he and his followers were treacherously murdered. The Zulu impis thereupon swarmed down upon the coast, slaughtering over three hundred of the trekkers and thirteen English settlers and threatening to seize Durban itself.

Faced with the possibility of a wholesale massacre of Europeans in Natal, Sir George Napier, who had meanwhile succeeded D'Urban as Cape Governor, acted swiftly. With a background of professional soldiering which was a carbon-copy of his predecessor's, except for the fact that he had no colonial experience at all, Napier felt that only a rapid show of force could save Natal and its settlers from being overrun by Dingaan's men. With the reluctant approval of Glenelg he therefore despatched a force of Cape troops to help in holding the Zulu advance. The arrival of Napier's men, even though they only numbered one hundred, turned the tide and soon afterwards the settlers regained the initiative. Andries Pretorius, Retief's successor, led his commandos deep into Zulu territory to avenge Retief's murder with a decisive victory over Dingaan's impis at the battle of Blood River. The Zulus were forced to cede Natal to their conquerors, together with that part of Zululand to the north which gave access to St. Lucia Bay. Dingaan died a few months later, killed by his brother, Panda, with whom Pretorius had made a separate compact to show that treachery was not a monopoly of the Zulus.

With the Zulu threat to Natal now dispersed, Napier was instructed by London to withdraw. For a while he held on for fear of precipitating a Boer take-over by pulling out too soon. But in the end he was forced to yield to Whitehall's insistence that Cape forces should not be used to establish a British Colony in Natal. Lacking the experience to argue the toss with his superiors, he sent orders for the troops to return. Whereupon, as the British garrison sailed away in December 1839, the flag of the Voortrekkers was hoisted over Durban.

When this unwelcome news reached London, the Imperial Government ordered Napier to reoccupy Durban. But, being unable to gauge the situation precisely at a distance of six thousand miles, they left the timing of this move to his discretion. And with the artful Pretorius contriving to postpone the return of the redcoats by conducting a lengthy correspondence with Napier about guarantees of Natal's independence, it was not until May 1842, after a long march delayed by rains and by harassing attacks from Boer commandos, that a British force under Sir Harry Smith—later to be Governor of Cape Colony—finally advanced into Natal and reoccupied Durban. The Volksraad, the Parliament of the infant Republic, bowed to force-majeure and submitted to British control. The Boer state was broken up and, as the bulk of the Voortrekkers drifted away to seek their independence elsewhere, Natal was formally annexed as a district of Cape Colony in August 1845. British dominion had caught up with the Boers: but, more important still for the history of South Africa, it had cut them off from the sea.

A similar clash between Boer and Bantu was also to help bring about the annexation by Britain of the so-called Winburg Republic, where a group of Voortrekkers had settled in scattered communities between the Orange and the Vaal rivers and made their capital at Winburg in the centre of this extensive territory. Here a confused situation reigned with the Boers engaged in constant affrays—mostly caused by cattle thieving and conflicting land claims—with the principal Bantu tribes in the area, the Griquas in the south-west and the Basutos on the mountainous eastern boundary. Napier had made treaties with their respective tribal chiefs, Adam Kok and Moshesh, by which he undertook to subsidise and protect them, not merely for their own sakes, but also to avoid their being driven by the Boers across the borders into the Colony's territory, where it was British policy, as far as possible, to maintain segregation and to

55

prevent Bantu infiltrations. With only a limited number of troops at his disposal, Napier preferred to protect himself by maintaining these Bantu territories beyond the Orange River as buffer states, rather than by annexing areas which he could not properly police.

But, in the circumstances of the day, such a tenuous arrangement could not long endure. Both Boers and Bantu needed the same things—land and cattle—and a head-on collision between these two conflicting migrations was clearly inevitable. In 1845 a major clash was avoided by the timely despatch of a British force. But skirmishing continued until, two years later, the appointment of the purposeful Sir Harry Smith as Governor of the Cape, together with the arrival of British troop reinforcements, proclaimed that the Imperial Government were now beginning to look beyond the Kei and Orange rivers and thinking in terms of expanding Britain's influence and frontiers in South Africa.

For one thing, Smith was appointed not only as Governor of Cape Colony, but also as High Commissioner 'for settling and adjustment of the affairs of the territories . . . adjacent or contiguous to the . . . frontier.' For another, he was by nature an empire-builder and a man of action. A seasoned veteran of the Peninsular War, this son of an East Anglian surgeon had packed a variety of experience into his life as a fighting soldier which included among other things taking part in the Anglo-American War of 1812, where he witnessed the burning of Washington by British troops, and in the final destruction of Napoleon's armies at Waterloo. In 1828, he had been seconded to serve with the British forces in Cape Colony, in which capacity he saw his share of fighting in the Kaffir Wars, in addition to preparing the way for Britain's annexation of Natal.

Smith was therefore not the man to rest content with the status quo, the more so since his terms of reference specifically entrusted him with the safeguarding of British interests beyond the Cape's borders. Within a few days of taking up his new appointment, he therefore left Cape Town for the eastern frontier where a fresh outbreak of fighting with the Xosas and Tembus from beyond the Kei had recently occurred. Not hesitating for a moment, he annexed the former Queen Adelaide Province which D'Urban had been compelled to abandon and renamed it British Kaffraria. At the same time he proclaimed as Cape Colony territory all of a huge copper-bearing section of Namaqualand south of the Orange river as far as the Atlantic. Then, hastening northwards, he crossed the Orange river and made for Natal, intent on arresting the final departure of the Boers, which was threatening to depopulate this newly annexed 'province' of the Cape, as well as to put the Voortrekkers even further beyond the reach of British rule.

Meeting the Boers among the Drakensberg Mountains, he offered them large holdings of land if they would return to Natal. But his efforts had little success: only a few turned back and the majority trekked on. Some followed Pretorius to Potchefstroom beyond the Vaal where Potgieter's trekkers had established the capital of a loose federation of the Zoutpansberg and Winburg Republics and had claimed possession of all territory up to the Limpopo river. Others stopped short, preferring to create a miniature Republic independent of the rest across the Buffalo river boundary of Natal, which they named the Republic of Utrecht. Thus finding himself foiled in his efforts to induce the Voortrekkers to go back to Natal and settle down under British rule, Smith now switched to more coercive methods. In February 1848, he proclaimed as British territory the entire area between the Orange and Vaal rivers, under the title of the Orange River Sovereignty. And when Pretorius led his commandos across the Vaal in an attempt to throw the British out and recreate the Winburg Republic, Smith met him and thrashed him at Boomplatts south of Bloemfontein.

In the space of eleven years since Pieter Retief had led the Great Trek out of Cape Colony in February 1837, a vast change had been worked in southern Africa. By the extensions of Cape Colony westwards to the Orange river estuary and eastwards to the Kei, the former British policy of territorial segregation had been abandoned; and such Bantu tribes as the Namaquas, the Tembus and the Xosas—including not only the amenable western group of Gaika Xosas, but also their more sullen eastern cousins, the Galekas—had been brought under permanent British rule. In short, the total acreage of British dominion had been more than doubled and now encompassed all the territory from the Cape to the Vaal and the Tugela rivers, save for the Basuto and Griqua enclaves on the borders of Natal and Cape Colony.

All that was now left of Boer independence was to be found north of the Vaal; and a shaky independence it was at that. For, in their efforts to found a republican state, the Voortrekkers were seriously handicapped by a fierce rivalry for the leadership which had developed between Potgieter in the Zoutpansberg and Pretorius at Potchefstroom. Worse still for the future viability of any Transvaal independence, they were cut off from the sea by the British in Natal, by the Portuguese in Mozambique and by the Zulus and Swazis in between. West of the Republics lay the forbidding Kalahari Desert and to the north were the Matabele kraals of Msilikazi, a Zulu chief who had broken with Chaka and, after crossing swords with Potgieter's trekkers in the south-west of the Transvaal, had settled beyond the Limpopo.

On all sides, therefore, the Boers were surrounded by hostile people and inhospitable country, while within their own ranks the rifts and rivalries grew deeper. Pretorius accused Potgieter of failing to support him against the British at Boomplatts and of seeking to set himself up as a dictator. Potgieter in his turn refused to cooperate in the nomination of a Volksraad to represent all the Transvaal Boers. And when a Volksraad was nevertheless established in 1851 at the instigation of Pretorius and his followers from Potchefstroom, its members failed to resolve the dispute over the leadership and had to accept that the Transvaal 'state' should be divided into three small separate Republics—Potchefstroom, later to be called the South African Republic, under Pretorius, Zoutpansberg under Potgieter; and Lydenburg, on the Swazi border, under another Voortrekker leader, Willem Joubert.

Within three years of Britain imposing her rule up to the Vaal, the Transvaal Boers were in a state of fragmented disarray, ripe for the picking as their brothers had been in Natal and the Orange River Sovereignty, perhaps even riper. But now as suddenly as it had begun, the British advance was halted. Instead of sweeping the Transvaal Boers into the imperial fold, the British Government, to Smith's great dismay, elected to grant and guarantee their independence. Then, two years later, they not only halted their advance but actually reversed it by handing over the reins of government to the Boers of the Orange River Sovereignty.

After less than a decade of extending Britain's frontiers in Africa, the Imperial Government's attentions had been diverted by the crisis in Europe which culminated in the Crimean War; and British political thinking was entering upon a new phase of Liberal reaction against colonial adventures. In fact, even as Smith was busily doubling the area of British territory in South Africa, the Whig Government of Lord John Russell had foreshadowed this new trend by agreeing to confirm his proclamation of the Orange River Sovereignty on the strict understanding that this new acquisition would be financially self-supporting and would impose no burden on the Imperial Treasury. By 1852, after four years of British rule, it had become clear that this condition could not be fulfilled. By this time, too, the British taxpayer was having to pay £10 per white settler for Cape Colony's defences and had just been presented with yet another hefty bill of £2,000,000 for a further round of fighting on the eastern frontier—the eighth in the series of Kaffir Wars. Far from contemplating any extension of British rule beyond the Vaal, where the Boers were well out of reach, Whitehall's thoughts now began to turn towards policies which would reduce imperial expenditure and put the responsibility of administering the South African colonies onto the colonists themselves.

To these ends, the Cape was given an elected Legislative Council, for which all adult male subjects of the King, 'without distinction of class or colour', were entitled to vote; and four years later, Natal received the same treatment. As for the three Transvaal Republics, by the Sand River Convention of 1852, the British Government guaranteed their freedom to run their own affairs, on their undertaking not to engage in slavery and not to interfere south of the Vaal. Smith was recalled two months later and returned home a broken-hearted man. And in 1854, the Imperial Government bowed to the growing agitation for independence by the Boers beyond the Orange and, in the Bloemfontein Convention, signed over the independence of the Sovereignty, which now became the Orange Free State.

In an almost complete reversal of the policy of following up the Boers after the Great Trek, Britain had now conceded independence to all of their five republics between the Orange and the Limpopo rivers—the Orange Free State, the South African Republic, Zoutpansberg, Lydenburg and Utrecht. For fourteen of the next twenty years until the formation of Disraeli's Government in 1874, Liberal Governments held sway over Britain's fortunes at home and abroad. And during this period, the guiding principle of British policy overseas was the doctrine laid down by Lord Palmerston—himself Prime Minister for eight of these years—that Britain had no need of vast imperial possessions 'any more than any rational man with an estate in the North of England and a residence in the South would have wished to possess all the inns on the North Road', when all that he needed was 'that the inns should be well kept, always accessible and furnishing him, when he came, with mutton chops and post-horses'. Even Disraeli at that time echoed the prevailing view that 'these wretched colonies . . . are a millstone around our necks'. And although, paradoxically, the British Government decided at this same moment to establish a separate State Secretaryship for the Colonies which had hitherto been an adjunct of the War Office, the Palmerstonian doctrine was to obtain until the discovery of gold and diamonds some twenty years later aroused a fresh interest in imperial expansion in South Africa.

In one crucial respect, however, British policy had not changed, and would not change, whatever Palmerston and his disciples might prescribe. The Boers could have their freedom to govern themselves, but they were not to be allowed access to the sea. Natal, with its handful of 8,000 European inhabitants, remained British and in 1856, on being detached from the Cape, was created a Crown Colony. Likewise in the sixties when Pretorius, in search of an independent outlet to the Indian

Ocean, proclaimed the annexation of the Maputo river valley, a Liberal Government in Britain lost no time in obliging him to withdraw.

In part, this determination to keep the Republics away from the coast arose from a desire to maintain the flow of customs revenues to the Colonial treasuries, without which the financial burden of administering the Cape and Natal would have borne too heavily on the British taxpayer. But there was another reason as well. Not even the most zealous retrenchers of the Palmerstonian era could afford to ignore altogether the constant stream of rumours from the Republics that Holland was about to come to their aid or that France was about to renew her former alliance with Boer republicanism.

The talk of Dutch support might be pure wishful thinking by the Boers, since Holland was no longer in a position to intervene effectively. But the French were another matter and, as their Algerian adventure in 1830 had shown, a weak French monarchy was not above indulging in imperial side-shows as a means of diverting and rallying public opinion. True, the French had not yet been able to regain their supremacy in Madagascar, following Britain's restoration of the island to France in the settlement of 1814, because the paramount Hova tribe, under a frenetically xenophobic Queen, had evicted all foreigners from the island—traders, missionaries and officials. But far from the French threat to South-East Africa being diminished by these reverses, reports reaching London in the 1840s of sinister French intrigues with Boer emissaries in Natal suggested that France might well be seeking compensation for her losses in Madagascar on the African mainland in collusion with the Voortrekkers. No doubt these suspicions of England's traditional enemy were exaggerated, if not altogether unfounded, at this point in time. But they existed all the same and, since it was at all times established British policy to prevent any foreign power making common cause with the Boers, the merest suggestion of French manoeuvres in southern Africa was enough to determine that Natal should be firmly held and the ring around the Republics tightly secured.

4 The Rise of Colonialism

THE fact that the prevailing opinion of governments in Britain in the 1850s was opposed to further imperial ventures did not mean that in other quarters all thought of extending British dominion had equally subsided. On the contrary, during this period of retreat and retrenchment on the Imperial Government's part, a new element made its appearance among the British community in South Africa. Colonialism began to take over where imperialism had, temporarily, halted its advance. If the political gentlemen abed in England were too afraid or too parsimonious to protect British interests and extend British influence, then the colonists would do these things themselves. So ran a growing feeling in the Cape which, as it developed over the next twenty years, was to lead the Colony to take British Kaffraria under its spreading wings, to annex Basutoland and to attain self-governing status for its own citizens.

This development, so significant for the future of South Africa, was to no small extent promoted by the two men who, from 1854 to 1870, presided over the fortunes of Cape Colony and its neighbouring territories from the office of Cape Governor and High Commissioner—Sir George Grey and Sir Philip Wodehouse. Prior to Grey's appointment, in all the forty years since Britain formally acquired possession of the Cape, during which period all British colonies were administered by a department of the War Office, the Cape Governorship had been held by a succession of Regular Army officers frequently with no colonial training or background whatever. But with the creation of an independent Whitehall ministry for colonial affairs, this practice ceased and Grey was the first Cape Governor to be equipped with all the necessary qualifications and experience for this difficult and delicate appointment. Born the son of an infantry Colonel who had been killed in the Peninsular War, Grey too had begun his career as a regimental officer. But, preferring to see the world as an explorer rather than as a soldier, he retired from the army with the rank of Captain in his twenties and set off to survey the Australian coast on behalf of the Royal Geographical Society. At the tender age of twenty-nine, he was appointed Governor of South Australia and, four years later, was transferred to New Zealand, where he distinguished himself in bringing law and order to a country then threatened with native rebellion and anarchy.

Thus, unlike his predecessors whose qualifications consisted largely of a lifetime of campaigning and who, with few exceptions, had no experience whatever of colonial administration, Grey was able from an early age to acquire a deep understanding of the attitudes and idiosyncrasies of European settlers beset with native problems. And when he came to the Cape at the end of 1854, it was to begin a truly remarkable governorship. Far more than anyone who came before or after him, Grey set out to bridge the gulf between Briton and Boer both within and without Cape Colony. And to him above all others was due the harmony which developed between the Cape Dutch and the British until Cecil Rhodes, Joseph Chamberlain and Alfred Milner between them tore it asunder in the last tumultuous decade before the Boer War.

Yet Grey was no mere appeaser of Boerdom, content to sit out his years at the Cape making soothing noises to the Afrikaners in the Colony and conducting polite correspondence with their independent cousins across the Orange and the Vaal. He believed in, and persuaded the home government to continue, the policy of assisted migration of settlers from Britain. When he took office the mixed European population of Cape Colony was 140,000 and of Natal 8,000, most of whom were British. At the next census, in 1865, the Cape's white population had risen by fifty per cent to 210,000 and Natal's to 15,000.

Most important of all, Grey pioneered the concept of confederation, which he devoutedly believed to be the best way to make out of the disparate states of southern Africa a power which would be of benefit to the whole continent. He had helped to make it work in New Zealand and he was certain that some form of federal union should be applied to the problem of bringing the British and Boer communities together from the Cape to the Limpopo. There was, he found, considerable support for the idea in the Orange Free State, not by any means confined to the British minority, provided that provincial autonomy could be maintained. And Grey felt that, if Natal, the Free State and the Cape were to band together, the Boers of the Transvaal in their fragmented Republics would soon be drawn in as well. Besides, he saw in confederation a large part of the answer to the native problem. Especially would it help to overcome the everlasting troubles of the Cape's eastern frontier, where his idea was to join British Kaffraria with Natal, to fill up the intervening territory—Tembuland and Pondoland—with British settlers and friendly tribes, and to make the whole agglomeration a province of the union.

In all, or most, of these directions Grey's policy was out of tune with prevailing political thinking at home. In many respects too it went beyond what the more jealously independent Afrikaners beyond the Orange might have wished from a British Governor at the Cape. But, to begin with at least, Grey had a much freer hand than any of his predecessors; and in its impact on the Boers, his idea of including them in a confederation, albeit under British rule, was not nearly so noxious at this juncture as it was to become twenty years later after Britain had outraged Afrikaner opinion by annexing the Transvaal. For one thing, there was a feeling among the scattered Republics that they might do a lot worse than to place themselves under some such umbrella, if only as protection against the hostile Bantu within and without their borders. For another, there was at this time more jealousy than unity among the Boers. Considerable resentment had been created in the Free State when, following the

Sir George Grey

Moshesh

British withdrawal in 1854, Potchefstroom tried to impress their neighbours south of the Vaal into an Afrikaner union with the so-called South African Republic. And although the Transvaal Boers were in due course to resolve their differences and form themselves into one Republic, a lingering suspicion continued for many years to keep the Free Staters at arm's length from the Transvaalers and conversely to sustain a special relationship between them and their neighbours in Cape Colony.

But the secret of Grey's success with the Afrikaners lay in the fact that they judged him not so much by his attitude towards federation as by his handling of the native question. For, at this period, by far the most intractable issue for the Boers, as indeed for all white men in the frontier-lands of South Africa, was the problem of living alongside the migratory Bantu tribes whose constant quest for land brought them into continual conflict with each other, and still more with the Voortrekkers. At an earlier stage the Bushmen and Hottentots of the Cape, and even the Xosas and other better organised tribes beyond the frontiers, had offered little serious resistance against the greatly superior armaments of the white man. But by the 1850s, the balance had become more even. The Bantu, especially the Zulus and the Basutos, had by then learned more modern methods of waging war, profiting from the experience gained in fighting the colonists. They had, too, acquired guns from European traders and, according to Boer reports, even from certain missionaries. And with equipment every bit as modern as that of their white adversaries, the Bantu had become a serious threat to the Boers across the Orange and in the Zoutpansberg and to the British in the eastern Cape and Natal.

Grey—and later Wodehouse too—saw all too clearly the dangers inherent in the mounting clash between the two conflicting migrations, white and black. He knew that this clash, if unchecked, would lead to disaster whichever way the outcome might lie. For a wholesale extermination or enslavement of the natives by the Boers was as unthinkable as was the prospect of a Bantu flood submerging the territories beyond the Orange and overflowing into Cape Colony and Natal. For the moment, the balance of power lay more with the Bantu than with the still

65

weak and divided Republics. The Kaffir Wars on the Cape's eastern borders had given solid and significant proof of their dogged determination, if not to evict the white man altogether, at least to prevent him from encroaching on their preserves. Nor were the tribes lacking in cunning, as had been well demonstrated by the Basutos when, during a recent Kaffir War, they had waited until the British garrison was sent to the Cape's eastern frontier before provoking the Boers to take the offensive. Then, having worsted their attackers, they had helped themselves to the Boers' cattle and another sizeable slice of their lands. At the same time, whenever the Boers were victorious, they had shown all too clearly what sort of treatment the Bantu should expect in defeat by 'apprenticing' their orphaned children and imposing on subject tribes a 'labour tax', which systems were little more than slavery under another name.

Grey therefore found himself walking a tightrope between the rival interests of native and European inhabitants. If ever a man had responsibility without power, it was he—at least in the early stages of his governorship. Four under-strength battalions, a small frontier police force and the Cape Mounted Rifles were all that he had to enforce his laws and secure the defences of a territory bigger than England and France put together. In Natal, where a Bantu population of 150,000, mostly Zulus, outnumbered the whites by nearly twenty to one, there was but one British battalion. And north of the Orange, where Britain had a vital interest and Grey, therefore, an inescapable responsibility to see that Boer and Bantu kept the peace, the Imperial Government had renounced all effective means of controlling the situation.

Grey's first task on taking office was to secure his own base in the Cape. To plug the gaps in his defences, he wrung from the Cape Legislature an annual grant of £10,000 towards the upkeep of the garrison, an increase in the police force and authority to raise further locally recruited regiments to supplement the Cape Mounted Rifles. Then, when the Crimean War ended, he induced the Imperial Government to double the number of British battalions. But even these reinforcements might not have been enough to relieve the pressure on the

Colony, had it not been for an extraordinary self-inflicted disaster, which overtook the Xosas on the eastern frontier and which was to shatter the military power of this warrior nation for a generation.

In the closing weeks of 1856, prophets among the Xosas proclaimed that, if the tribesmen killed all their cattle and refrained from cultivating any crops, the spirits of their dead heroes would arise and drive the white man from the land and that thereafter there would be cattle and crops in abundance for the native African to enjoy, free from the menace of white settlement. Blindly trusting in these soothsayers, the Xosas obeyed instructions to the letter and, when the day appointed for their deliverance from the white man had come and gone without a murmur from the spirits, they died like flies before succour could reach them. The total number of dead east of the Kei is not recorded; but on the west side, in British Kaffraria, a Bantu population of over 100,000 was suddenly reduced to 37,000.

But if Cape Colony could breathe more easily now with the Xosa threat diminished, there was no relief for the Orange Free State in its struggle with Moshesh, the founding-father of the Basuto confederation. Starting from the humble background of a small tribe in the Drakensberg mountains, Moshesh had used his extraordinary powers of leadership to fashion this formidable nation from the scattered remnants of several other tribes which had become the victims of the recent Zulu, Matabele and Griqua migrations. A consummate diplomatist of considerable intellect and political skill, who entertained missionaries to tea with sponge cake and delighted in attending civic banquets in Bloemfontein, resplendently attired in the uniform of a French general, Moshesh successfully contrived to play the Boers off against each other and against the Cape Government. With diabolical cunning he had sent messengers to encourage the Xosas in their suicidal obedience to their prophets, hoping that, after they had killed themselves off, the Cape colonists would be too busy occupying the resulting vacuum to be able to defend the Free Staters, when he moved in to seize their lands. For Moshesh's ambitions lay far beyond the Drakensberg and its western foothills, where the Basuto nation had been forged in the white heat of war with Dingaan's marauding impis. In fact, his claims stretched northwards as far as the Vaal and westwards along the valley of the Caledon river down to its junction with the Orange.

All of these lands were also claimed and partly occupied by the Boer colonists of the Free State. But at this time the Free Staters were so weakened by divisions among themselves that it seemed highly unlikely that they could withstand much longer the pressures for union with the Transvaal Boers and the constant land-grabbing of the Basutos. In the first five years of the Republic's existence, two Presidents had been forced out of office and Bantu invasions from every point of the compass had driven the Free Staters to seek aid from across the Vaal in a desperate attempt to save their lands. Even this joint defensive effort had failed to bring definitive relief and in a treaty with Moshesh, signed in 1858, they had been obliged to concede substantial territorial gains to the Basutos between the Caledon and Orange rivers in order to buy a brief respite.

What then was Grey to do to stop Moshesh eventually mopping up the entire territory between the Orange and the Vaal and, as his appetite grew with conquest, later advancing on Cape Colony itself? Grey had shown much sympathy with the Free Staters in their struggle for survival and had refused to comply with Moshesh's request for a British representative to be appointed to his capital at Thaba Bosigo, for fear of encouraging the Basutos to further violence and so weakening still more the government in Bloemfontein. And his view that it was the weakness and division of the various settler states in South Africa which had prompted the Bantu to harry the white man was shared and appreciated by Europeans of every origin north of the Orange. But the fact that Grey identified with Free State thinking and recognised the menace of Moshesh did not solve the problem of containing the Basutos. Nobody knew this better than Grey himself. Nor was anyone more alive to the fact that the only effective solution was for Britain to arrest the drift towards 'disorder and barbarism' and accept responsibility for holding the ring between colonist and native at least in the Orange Free State. But when he gave vent to these ideas and, in response to a Colonial Office request for specific proposals, suggested the creation of a union of the British Colonies and Boer Republics, he caused convulsions at home.

Wilful, courageous and self-confident, Grey was a persuasive talker and orator; but, on paper, he lacked the ability to produce incisive, analytical arguments to defend his policies. It was once said of him, 'the mark was often missed but the aim was always high'. With confederation, the aim was high indeed, but Grey's arguments missed the mark with his superiors at home. Palmerston and his colleagues were ready to accept a federal union of the three British colonies—Cape Colony, Natal and British Kaffraria—but they were aghast at the suggestion that Britain should resume responsibility for any of the Boer Republics. Much to the regret of Briton and Boer alike, Grey was duly recalled and the confederation policy was pigeon-holed until the return of Disraeli's Conservative Government in 1874 brought about its revival.

Had it been applied in Grey's time, confederation might well have worked, the Afrikaner and British communities might have grown together and not apart, and two bitter bloody wars might have been avoided. There was then much support for this concept among the Boers between the Orange and the Vaal, and the fragmented Transvaal Republics might well have found the attractions of such a union irresistible. But it was not to be. In terms of his own countrymen's thinking, Grey was way ahead of his time. And when, in the next decade, the lure of newly discovered riches brought the Imperial Government to resuscitate the idea, it was already too late. During the twenty-year interlude of British non-intervention north of the Orange, the Boers were to make their own way and set their own house in order. By the end of the 1860s, these tasks had been achieved both in the Free State and, albeit after much civil strife, among the 15,000 cattle-ranchers north of the Vaal. Thus, when the Imperial Government was to lift its gaze once more beyond the frontiers of Cape Colony and Natal, the Afrikaner Republics were no longer so weak and divided; and what they might have considered as a welcome offer of protection twenty years earlier had come to be viewed as an intolerable threat to their independence.

The movement towards a closer union of the Boer states beyond the Vaal had started painfully but progressively in the middle fifties after the British withdrew behind the Orange river. And in 1860, the first united Volksraad met in Pretoria, which had been named after Andries Pretorius and chosen to serve as the capital of a united Transvaal state. But these early appearances of harmony were deceptive. For beneath the paper union of this first Transvaal Parliament there still lay a deep schism which had its origins in the early rivalry between Pretorius and Potgieter. Seven years before, in 1853, these two Boer leaders had died; but the feud was kept alive by their sons, Martinus Wessel Pretorius—later to become the first President of the Transvaal Republic—and Piet Potgieter. And although the latter died in the following year, the quarrel, far from waning, was carried on by Stephanus Schoeman who married Potgieter's widow and became Commandant-General of the Zoutpansberg Republic.

Nor did the younger Pretorius exactly help to smooth the ruffled feathers of the Zoutpansbergers. For, having failed in an attempt to coerce the Orange Free State at its birth into joining his South African Republic, this scion of the Potchefstroom faction set about trying to unify the Transvaal Boers by exasperatingly high-handed methods. Backed by his own Volksraad, he had himself 'elected' President under a constitution, which provided for the unification of all four Transvaal Republics and then invited their representatives to Potchefstroom to confirm his appointment. The Zoutpansbergers concurred in the arrangement, although only under protest and with the crucially important exception of Schoeman, their future Commandant-General. But the Lydenburgers would have nothing to do with Pretorius' union and, having declared their independence, shortly afterwards merged with their southern neighbours, the Utrecht Republic.

Thus was kindled the flame of open conflict between Boer and Boer. By his arbitrary actions, Pretorius had exacerbated the feud with the disciples of Hendrik Potgieter, now led by

Schoeman. But Pretorius was far too much concerned with furthering his plans for an Afrikaner union to weigh the risks of a collision with Potgieter's heir. And when, in 1859, the second Free State President in five years threw in his hand and retired to Natal, following the failure of the combined Boer forces to crush the marauding Basutos, he saw and seized his chance to bring about the union across the Vaal which he had failed to achieve five years before. Now in desperate straits, and with no one to lead them, the Free Staters pocketed their resentment over Pretorius' earlier high-handedness, elected him as President and voted for union with Potchefstroom. Simultaneously the Lydenburg-Utrecht combination decided to hold out no longer for a lonely and unviable independence and threw in their lot with Pretorius' wider union.

For a brief moment it seemed that the final unification of all the Boer Republics on both sides of the Vaal was at hand and that Schoeman would have to toe the line and abandon the feud with Potchefstroom. But the union of the Transvaal Republics was as yet no more than theoretical and the union with the Free State, although conceived, had not been born. Moreover, when the Volksraad of the new Transvaal Republic met in Pretoria in July 1860, one of its first decisions was to declare that nobody could be President of more than one Republic and that, while Pretorius presided in Bloemfontein, he could exercise no authority north of the Vaal. With no other option open to him, Pretorius bowed to this edict and resigned his Transvaal presidency. But, fearing that in his absence Schoeman would intrigue against him, he appointed a deputy to act in his stead, while he occupied himself with containing Moshesh's Basutos and acting as mid-wife for the birth of his brain-child, the union of the Free State with the new Transvaal Republic.

Schoeman, however, was not to be denied by his rival's attempt to keep his seat warm in Pretoria, while he presided over the Free State. Appealing to the people over the heads of the Volksraad, he dismissed Pretorius' deputy and declared himself as Acting President. As luck would have it, a boundary dispute now broke out between the Free Staters and their Transvaal neighbours and Moshesh cunningly chose this moment to renounce his 1858 treaty with the Free State. Pretorius was therefore pinned down by his responsibilities south of the Vaal and could do little to counter Schoeman's coup d'état. All he could do was to call for fresh elections for a new Volksraad in Pretoria to decide who should be President. But when, following the elections, the new Volksraad nominated a neutral candidate, Willem van Rensburg, as Acting President, Schoeman simply dug himself in at Pretoria, refused to recognise van Rensburg's election and defied the Government to evict him.

It was civil war and Pretorius, as he crossed the Vaal to rally his supporters in Potchefstroom, knew that he would have to fight it out to the end. But before Schoeman could be brought to book, the harassed Free State President was called back to Bloemfontein to deal with another serious Basuto incursion. In his absence the Transvaal Government's forces managed after three months of fighting to crush Schoeman's rebellion. But his rival's defeat brought small comfort to Pretorius. For, in the subsequent presidential ballot, by a vote which scarcely constituted a quorum, the Pretoria Volksraad proceeded to elect van Rensburg as President of the Transvaal.

Now it was Pretorius' turn to rebel against the authority of an elected Parliament. Resigning his presidency in Bloemfontein, he crossed the Vaal and, claiming with some justification that the election had been unconstitutional, seized Potchefstroom with the aid of his supporters. The Government's troops dealt with his challenge even more speedily than they had with Schoeman's and, after a month of further fighting, they won the day. Yet another Volksraad ballot was held; but this time the parliamentarians' choice reverted to the founder of their union and, with no more preoccupations in Bloemfontein to disqualify him, Pretorius was duly elected as President of a united Transvaal.

The civil war was over; the fragmented Transvaal Republics had found cohesion at last. But if the divisions among the Boers had been healed, the seeds of a far deadlier and more destructive conflict were now to be sown. For the constitution of the united Transvaal had laid down as an inalienable article of Afrikaner faith that there could be no equality between white and black inhabitants either in church or state. Which prescription was to bring the new Republic into a head-on collision with the very principles on which the social, religious and political systems of British South Africa were based. Worse still, it was to alienate many liberal and humanitarian thinkers in Britain to whom, in different circumstances, the Boers might have looked to bridle the aggressive expansionism with which later British Governments and their colonial henchmen in South Africa sought to subjugate the Afrikaner Republics.

Yet another casualty of the civil war in the Transvaal was Pretorius' project for a union across the Vaal with the Orange Free State. In the confusion of those turbulent months of 1863 this scheme had lapsed and, although in future years President Kruger was to seek its revival, the Free State and the Transvaal were henceforth to develop as separate states. Yet, if the Free Staters lost from the miscarriage of the union which they had supported, they soon found compensation in the person of a new leader, Jan Hendrik Brand, who in February 1864 took over the office of President which he was to hold without a break for all of the next twenty-four years.

Brand, the son of the Cape Assembly's Speaker, had been called to the English Bar in 1849 but had returned almost immediately to his native Cape Town, where he practised as a barrister for a few years before entering the first Cape Parliament in 1854. Ten years later, after Pretorius had relinquished his presidency in Bloemfontein and returned whence he came, the Free State Volksraad, casting around for a candidate to fill this uninviting office, made Brand their choice. Not even the most far-sighted optimist among them could then have known how well they had chosen or with what infinite care and devotion their new President would from now on set about the twin tasks of nursing the Free State from a weak and sickly childhood to a prosperous maturity and developing the relationship with his neighbours and former compatriots in the Cape.

Paradoxically this happy result was greatly helped by the fact that, unlike the Transvaal, the Orange Free State never possessed the kind of mineral wealth that attracted the covetous

73

. gaze of governments and speculators from outside. Instead, with a rich agricultural potential and expanding markets in Cape Colony—later to be supplemented by the revenues of a growing transit traffic by rail between the Cape and the Transvaal—it was able to develop slowly but surely as a pastoral state, free from the social stresses and strains which were to afflict its northern neighbours when the discovery of gold brought a veritable flood of foreign immigrants into the Transvaal. Thus, unlike his counterpart in Pretoria, Brand never had to wrestle with the problem of how to enfranchise a large community of foreign residents without virtually handing over to them the reins of government. Consequently at a time when the Transvaalers found it necessary to protect their independence by making it progressively more difficult for an ever-increasing influx of foreigners to obtain the vote, he was able to pursue an altogether more liberal policy. At an early stage of his regime full burgher rights, including the right to elect the President and the Volksraad, were granted to all settlers who had either been born in the territory of the Free State or had lived there for one year and owned £150 worth of land or for three years without owning any property. And although the Free State franchise, unlike that of Cape Colony, was limited to the European inhabitants, by comparison with the restrictions which were to be imposed on the non-Boer population of the Transvaal, it was to stand out as a landmark of democratic enlightenment and to create an exemplary harmony in the relations between Boers and British from the Orange to the Vaal. In fact, such was the state of tranquillity brought about by Brand's stewardship that, during the latter half of his presidency, the Free State was to fade almost completely from the unfolding drama of South African history and became a kind of political vacuum immured from the conflicts and controversies that raged about its borders.

But before this idyllic insulation could be achieved, several major problems had to be resolved, of which the most pressing —the Basuto question—had become more threatening than ever during the years of civil war in the Transvaal. Profiting from the vacuum caused by Pretorius' departure in 1863,

Moshesh had pressed his claims to the Vaal river boundary and, digging deeper than ever into Free State territory, had occupied a large slice of the Winburg area. Brand's first act as President was therefore to call on Wodehouse, as Grey's successor, to help in repelling this further Bantu invasion. Wodehouse did not hesitate to take the Basuto bull by the horns. Used to such experiences as being stoned by mobs of rioting negroes during a recent spell of eight years as Governor of British Guiana, he now hastened to the scene of the trouble and, having investigated the rival claims, laid down a frontier which gave the Basutos a small part of what they had seized, but which otherwise followed the lines of the 1858 treaty. Then he issued a stern warning to the Basutos not to press their claims beyond what he had awarded them; and as Moshesh began to withdraw behind the new frontier, he returned to the Cape with the grateful thanks of Brand and his Free Staters.

For a year or so the Basutos continued to observe the terms of Wodehouse's award. Meanwhile the Free Staters lost no time in improving their fighting skills and re-equipping their commandos. But for Moshesh—or rather for his sons who, as the old man approached his eightieth year, were taking over from their ailing father—the Basutos' compliance with Wodehouse's injunction was no more than a strategic withdrawal. At the first opportunity, therefore, the young and headstrong Basuto chiefs induced the Free Staters to attack them. On the classical pretext of a frontier incident, the Basuto impis swept back into Free State territory and even raided parts of northern Natal. To start with, they carried all before them. But in due course, the Free State commandos, now better organised and more experienced than before, managed to regain the initiative. And as they pushed the invaders back behind their boundaries, Bloemfontein proclaimed the annexation of all the pasture lands between the Caledon and Orange rivers.

Wodehouse saw all too clearly that the Free Staters, having drunk at last the heady wine of victory, were now determined to crush and destroy the Basuto confederation once and for all. He also saw from the direction of their new annexations that they were intent on opening up a corridor between Cape territory and Basutoland through which they might gain access to the sea on the coast of Pondoland. And to add to his worries, now that the broken Basuto armies were in full retreat before the advancing Boers, a general clamour for war against them arose from every side. The Transvaal, Natal, and the Zulus too, were out for the blood, the land and the cattle of these marauders who had plundered their neighbours for so long with impunity and were now reeling under a defeat which they had brought upon themselves. Abruptly and violently the pendulum had swung; and as the Transvaalers moved in to loot their fill of Basuto spoils and the Free Staters seized the verdant foothills of Moshesh's mountain homeland, what had once been a threat of black exterminating white was suddenly reversed. From preventing the Basutos overruning the Boers, Wodehouse's task was now to protect the Basutos from being themselves destroyed.

In April 1866, in a desperate attempt to save his people, Moshesh signed a treaty in which he accepted the Free State's annexations. But guerilla warfare continued, with the Free State commandos burning Basuto crops allegedly as a reprisal for Basuto raids on the newly annexed territories. And Wodehouse knew that the day was fast approaching when his invocations to President Brand and the Natal colonists to desist from a general war would no longer prevail and he would be forced to take Basutoland under British protection, as indeed the sons of Moshesh were now begging him to do. But Whitehall still hesitated again to extend its commitments beyond the Orange. And it was not until early in 1868 that a reluctant Colonial Secretary conceded that negotiations be undertaken with Moshesh for the annexation of Basutoland, although by Natal rather than the Cape.

Natal was, however, very far from Wodehouse's ideal as a protector of native tribes. For one thing, the Natalians were among those who had been baying for war against Moshesh. For another, they were suffering from the current economic blight which had overtaken all southern Africa. The brief boom which had followed the introduction of sugar-cane from India had given way to a series of deficits and droughts, aggravated by a credit squeeze, and to make ends meet the Natal Government

were seeking to impose a poll-tax on their own native population, all of which suggested that they were unlikely to be very
beneficient rulers for the Basutos. In the circumstances, Wodehouse decided to take the law into his own hands; and in March
1868, he annexed Basutoland to Cape Colony and sent in the
Cape Police.

Immediately he was assailed on all sides. The Colonial
Secretary reproved him for disregarding his instructions;
Natal was offended; there was opposition in the Cape Parliament; and the Free State protested furiously. In the past,
when the war had been going against them, the Free Staters
had been ready to accept anything which would have got the
Basutos off their backs; some had even talked of the Cape
annexing their own Republic. But now, with the tables turned
in their favour, they felt baulked of their prey and loudly
avowed that Wodehouse's action was a breach of the Bloemfontein Convention by which Britain undertook not to make
treaties with native tribes north of the Orange river.

Wodehouse, however, stood firm against all these reproaches
and, in due course, the Imperial Government swallowed its
objections and allowed his annexation to stand. A few months
later, Brand accepted the fait accompli in Basutoland and
agreed to sign a treaty which, while confirming the Boers'
gains in the Caledon-Orange river triangle, effectively quashed
the project for a Free State corridor to the Pondoland coast.
Basutoland had become and was to remain a possession of Cape
Colony for the next fifteen years. Wodehouse, as his critics in
London and Cape Town had been forced to accept, had
managed to steer a clear course between the two unthinkable
alternatives of expulsion of the whites and extermination of the
Basutos. More than this, he had done as Napier did before him
in Natal and had blocked another Boer access route to the sea.

During his eight years in office at Cape Town, the longest
governorship since Somerset retired in 1826, Wodehouse represented something of a paradox. An autocrat by nature, he
differed completely from his gentle-mannered predecessor.
Unlike Grey, he had no sympathy with those colonists who
wanted self-government for the Cape, perhaps because he had

77

not had Grey's experience of governing predominantly British communities overseas, having spent all his colonial service in Ceylon and the West Indies. Yet, while he might tell the colonists that they were not fit to rule themselves, he gave them —indeed he virtually forced on them—a taste for expansion by annexing large areas of native territory in their name and by brooking no opposition to his actions, whether locally or from home. Basutoland was a case in point: another was British Kaffraria which, in 1866, was taken under the Colony's wing on being handed over by an Imperial Government which had shown an ever decreasing interest in maintaining it. It had been Grey's ambition, after his confederation proposals had been rejected in London, to join British Kaffraria with Natal by subjugating and colonising the intervening Transkei territories of Tembuland and Pondoland. Wodehouse too had had similar thoughts to begin with. But he later discarded the idea out of fear of driving the remaining Xosas into the arms of the hostile inhabitants of Pondoland on the borders of Natal. Instead he invited the Cape Parliament to take over the responsibility for the Kaffraria territory which, due to imperial neglect, was rapidly falling into decay, and in which the mixed British-Bantu population was daily becoming poorer and more insecure.

The immediate reaction of the Colony's legislators was unfavourable. Faced by droughts and a mounting colonial debt, they were not disposed to add yet more burdens to their sorely pressed constituents. But, as with Basutoland, Wodehouse was not to be deterred by adverse first reactions. And at the second attempt, he persuaded the Cape Parliament to vote for annexing British Kaffraria. The Cape's frontiers were thus extended to the Kei. But for the time being they were to reach no further towards Natal. The idea, first mooted by Grey, of colonising the Transkei had lapsed, and all that Whitehall would sanction in this direction was a small addition of territory to the southern border of Natal—the Alfred District lying to the north-east of the Pondo Kingdom.

In the spring of 1870 Wodehouse left the Cape to become Governor of Bombay, a few weeks after the death of the old

Basuto chief, Moshesh. In their different ways no two men had done more to influence the future of South Africa. Through their combined impact on political thought in London and Cape Town, British rule had returned north of the Orange river, never to be withdrawn again. And through Wodehouse's own influence over Cape opinion, the Colony had advanced, while the Imperial Government still held back. Against the prevailing trend of Palmerstonian doctrine at home, a new brand of expansionist thinking was beginning to make itself felt at the Cape as the colonists came to shoulder their new responsibilities under the prodding insistence of their Governor. Colonialism had taken root and was beginning to exercise an influence over British policy in South Africa, which in the course of the next twenty-five years was to develop into the tail that wagged the Whitehall dog.

5 Annexation of the Transvaal

THE decade which followed the departure of Wodehouse as Cape Governor in 1870 undoubtedly marked the most significant turning point in South African history since the arrival of the 1820 settlers heralded the era of British colonisation. For it was during this period that Britain abandoned the Palmerstonian doctrine of imperial economy and economic imperialism in favour of a 'forward policy' designed to advance Britain's frontiers northwards from the Cape. In 1871, the discovery of diamonds at the junction of the Orange and Vaal rivers brought even Gladstone's diffident Cabinet to sanction British annexation of the territory known as Griqualand West. And in the following years, the Imperial Government's adoption of the confederation policy, which Grey had vainly advocated against the prevailing ride of Palmerstonian retrenchment in the fifties, led to the attempt to expand British rule and influence still further by the annexation of the Transvaal in 1877. True, within three years of their being annexed to the Empire, the Transvaalers were to throw off the British yoke and regain their independence. True, too, the humiliations suffered by British arms at the hands of Boer sharpshooters at Majuba Hill and of Cetewayo's Zulus at Isandhlwana were to bring about a further pause in the spread of British imperial and colonial rule in southern Africa. But it was only a matter of a few years before the advances initiated in the seventies were resumed. For such was the momentum of expansion from this most eventful decade that not even the most resolute "Little Englander" influences in Whitehall and Westminster could long withstand its thrust.

For the colonists at the Cape the seventies began on an auspicious note with the achievement of self-government, or 'Responsible Government' as it was then called. Ever since the 1820s when Somerset and his successors had refused to allow representative institutions, the movement among the settlers for autonomy had been gaining ground. At first largely dominated by the Cape Dutch, it had later been joined by the English element and in 1854 had won the right to an elected Assembly. At this point the leadership passed to a rising young politician of Milanese origins, John Molteno. Born in London in 1814, Molteno had come to South Africa at the age of seventeen to work in the public library at Cape Town. At twenty-three years of age he started an export business. But this venture proved unsuccessful and, in 1841, he turned his hand to ranching sheep and growing wool on a property near Beaufort West, where for the next eleven years he enjoyed a life of isolation and simplicity among the Cape Dutch farmers of the Great Karoo plains. During this period he fought in the Kaffir War of 1846 and, from his experiences in combat, he formed strong opinions as to the unsuitability of British imperial troops for such warfare. He also grew deeply to resent the dictatorial ways in which the British officers engaged in the Kaffir Wars treated the Cape colonists. Which views were to shape much of his political outlook when, following the Imperial Government's decision to concede representative institutions to the Colony, he became the Member for Beaufort West in the Cape Assembly and a strong supporter of Grey's sympathetic method of handling his colonial subjects.

Encouraged by Grey, Molteno took up the cause of 'Responsible Government' for the Cape. Now in his forties, he had become a man of considerable wealth with a commanding presence which bore witness to a great strength of character and physique. He was therefore a natural choice to preside over the committee of the Cape Assembly which, in the middle fifties, reported in favour of autonomy. But at that time, such recommendations were considered to be somewhat premature and over-ambitious by the majority of his parliamentary colleagues, who felt that the Colony was not yet ready to undertake the responsibilities of self-government.

The project was therefore shelved for the time being. But Molteno and his friends merely went to work all the harder to convert opinion in the Cape Assembly to their cause. By the middle sixties they had achieved considerable success, only to find that their way was now blocked by Wodehouse. For, while he had not hesitated to add territories such as Basutoland and Kaffraria to the area of the Colony's responsibilities, Wodehouse had been firmly of the opinion that the final say in the administration of these territories should remain with himself as the Governor and representative of the Imperial Government's supreme authority. As he wrote to Lord Granville, the Colonial Secretary, he did not consider that the Cape colonists could yet be entrusted with the 'uncontrolled management' of large native populations and were therefore 'unsuited for independence'.

But with the arrival in 1870 of the new Governor and High Commissioner, Sir Henry Barkly, a radical change in this outlook came about. Barkly had much personal sympathy with the idea of colonial autonomy. Indeed it would have been difficult to find a man better suited by experience and attitude to succeed an imperialist like Wodehouse. Born in the year of Waterloo the son of a West India merchant, Barkly had started life in business and for a brief spell had sat in the House of Commons as a strong supporter of Sir Robert Peel's free trade policies. But in his early thirties he had abandoned politics to take up a career as a Colonial Governor, serving in British Guiana, where he owned estates, in Jamaica, in Australia and in Mauritius. In the first two of these posts he acquired a considerable reputation as a peace-maker between the administration and the members of the legislature who, in both cases, he found on his arrival were up in arms over the Government's failure to concede certain reforms. Then, having brought peace and harmony to his West Indian charges, he was transferred to the other side of the world to take over as Governor of Victoria in Australia, where he acquired the further valuable experience of presiding over the introduction of self-government in the Colony.

In every way therefore Barkly seemed to be the right choice for the important and delicate mission now assigned to him. Besides, his superiors at home were beginning to toy with the idea of some kind of confederation in South Africa, in which a self-governing Cape Colony would in the nature of things play an essential part. The Cape's European population of 236,000 was nearly three times that of the Boer Republics and Natal put together. It therefore seemed only logical that a grouping of South African states would strengthen the whole and that the leadership of such a grouping should devolve upon Cape Colony with its overwhelming preponderance of white settlers. And if the Cape could be persuaded to take over such responsibilities, both within and beyond its own borders, then the Imperial Government would be able to cut expenditure, reduce their garrisons and delegate authority without sacrificing British paramountcy. But the essential first step to these ends was for the Cape itself to gain experience in managing its own affairs. The new Governor, therefore, immediately set about the task of persuading the more conservative elements in the Assembly to accept greater responsibilities. And within the next two years, his efforts were rewarded when, at the end of 1872, John Molteno was elected by his peers as the first Prime Minister of a self-governing Cape Colony.

Alas for Barkly, this was to be his sole contribution to the peaceful evolution of confederation. For the rest, whether acting on his own initiative or on orders from Whitehall, he was doomed to defeat his purpose at almost every turn. At the very outset of his term of office he found himself engulfed in the beginnings of the scramble for the mineral wealth of South Africa which had been discovered hard by the frontiers of the Boer Republics. And driven by the fear that possession of such wealth would disincline the Boers to throw in their lot with the Cape and Natal, he ended by so alienating Boer sympathies as to render any hope of achieving confederation impossible, save by force of arms.

Three years before Barkly began his governorship, the first recorded discovery of diamonds had taken place on the Cape's northern frontier. In the following year, a few more stones were found on Griqua territory at the junction of the Vaal and Harts rivers. But in neither case were the finds in sufficient quantities to excite the interest of more than a few prospectors from the Cape and Natal. In fact, at this point, the simultaneous discovery of gold at Tati on the border of Matabeleland and Bechuanaland and in Mashonaland away to the north-east seemed to be a more significant development. Pretorius certainly thought so and, promptly laying claim to the Tati area in the name of the Transvaal, he annexed a large slice of territory stretching as far as Lake Ngami, several hundreds of miles north-west of the Republic. At the same time, in an effort to open up a route to the sea, he proclaimed as republican territory a strip of land a mile in width on either side of the Maputo river down to Delagoa Bay, which he and his followers had long regarded as the natural outlet of the Transvaal Republic.

On both counts Pretorius was to find himself thwarted. Portugal objected that his annexation of the Maputo strip infringed her rights as the sovereign power in Mozambique, despite the fact that the writ of the Portuguese Governor at the pest-ridden collection of decayed forts and grass huts that was called Lourenço Marques ran no further than he could see from the windows of his mansion. Britain likewise insisted that the Transvaal's annexations be withdrawn. For the Imperial Government were determined not only to keep the Boers away from the sea, but also to prevent them from penetrating into Bechuanaland. Through this vast territory ran the Missionaries' Road which Dr. Livingstone had insisted back in the fifties must never be allowed to fall under the control of the anti-missionary Boers. Besides, it had become known in the Cape that the tsetse belt in the Limpopo valley was an almost impassable barrier and that the best, if not the only, route to the north lay through Bechuanaland. And Pretorius' move suggested that, in addition to looking for gold, he was contemplating expansion into what the colonialists in the Cape had begun to regard as a British preserve.

Faced with these objections by Britain and Portugal, Pretorius backed down and withdrew his annexations. But almost at this very moment, in 1869, the world-famous diamond, the 'Star of Africa', was found in Griqualand West. Pretorius promptly tried again. Anxious to augment the revenues of his Republic which were recovering only slowly from the general depression of the sixties, he obtained Volksraad sanction for a Transvaal diamond monopoly in Griqualand West. Simultaneously from Bloemfontein President Brand proclaimed the sovereignty of the Orange Free State over some two-thirds of the Griquas' territory including, of course, the areas where diamonds were known to exist. Yet another element in the competition for the diamond fields consisted of the newly arrived diggers and prospectors, mostly British and Australian from the Cape and Natal, who had already staked out their claims and were not going to be dispossessed by anybody. And before the Free Staters or anyone else could impose their title, the diggers proclaimed their own Republic under the 'presidency' of a former British naval rating, Stafford Parker.

These various claims and counter-claims, however, ignored one important fact. The land belonged neither to the Transvaal, nor to the neighbouring Free State, nor even to the diggers who were working the ground, but to Nicolaas Waterboer, successor of Andries Waterboer, who had founded the Hottentot state of Griqualand West in 1813. In the 1850s this chieftain had been recognised by the first Free State President, J. P. Hoffman, as sovereign ruler of the territory and now, fearing to lose his lands to the rival claimants of the diamond fields, Waterboer asked for British protection. President Brand thereupon requested that the issue be submitted to foreign arbitration. But Barkly, in his capacity as High Commissioner, objected to this idea no less than to the prospect of the Free State, or the Transvaal, owning the diamond fields of Griqualand West. For, as he saw it, it would be as dangerous to British interests that a foreign power should be invited to adjudicate in a British sphere of influence, as it would be to allow the Boer Republics to enrich themselves from the diamond fields and so to stand aside from any British-ruled confederation in South Africa.

Barkly, therefore, decided in favour of a British arbitrator and persuaded Pretorius and all other claimants, save Brand, to accept as umpire the Lieutenant-Governor of Natal, Robert

85

Keate. Pretorius later went back on his agreement and supported Brand in a last-minute appeal to London to agree to foreign arbitration. But these pleadings were to no avail. Keate quickly decided against the Boer claims and in October 1871, the Diggers' Republic came to an end when Barkly sent up the Cape police to hoist the British flag.

Griqualand West and its diamonds had been annexed under the very noses of the Afrikaner Republics. But while Britain's economic interests were to gain from this new acquisition, relations with the Boers were greatly to suffer. Coming on top of Wodehouse's Basuto settlement, this new move brought threats from Bloemfontein to go to war rather than submit to this arbitrary award. As for reactions in Pretoria, such was the anger of the Volksraad that Pretorius was driven to resign from the presidency. Nor, for a while, was there any great rejoicing in the Cape over this latest acquisition to the British Empire. The Cape Parliament had earlier agreed to annexe Basutoland in response to Whitehall's requests that the colonists should undertake a greater share of the responsibilities of administering British South Africa. And while the Griqualand issue was being discussed, they had further agreed to allow the Governor to administer Waterboer's lands in the Cape's name. But now many members felt that the Keate Award and Barkly's precipitate annexation had caused needless aggravation to the Free State and they were averse to saddling the Cape with responsibility for a territory which was the subject of a bitter dispute with their northern neighbours. Moreover, for the first two or three years, the diamond fields—except for the area later to be named Kimberley after Gladstone's Colonial Secretary— failed to live up to initial expectations and rising costs threatened to make the smaller holdings uneconomic. Thus, when they were asked to confirm Barkly's annexation and to add Griqualand West to Cape territory, the Assembly withheld its cooperation; and the territory became a Crown Colony under the governorship of Richard Southey, an 1820 settler and one of the leaders of the new expansionist school of Cape politicians who dreamed of a British dominion from Cape Town to the Zambezi.

Nearly five years later, the Griqualand dispute with the Free State was finally settled by a paltry cash payment of £90,000 by the Imperial Government together with the offer of a further £15,000, if the Free State would undertake to build a railway to link up with the Cape lines then slowly inching their way from the coast to Kimberley. And in 1877, as the diamond fields began to prosper, the Cape Parliament agreed to take over the territory. But the damage had been done. Annexation had struck the first of several mortal blows at the Imperial Government's own project for a South African confederation. By seizing the diamond fields and so denying this new wealth to the Boers, Barkly had largely defeated his own object. For his action showed all too clearly that Britain saw confederation first and foremost as a means of enriching herself and her colonists and that the stability and prosperity of the Boer states which she was said to be anxious to promote played an altogether secondary part in her thinking.

Indeed, at this point, the Boers had every reason to conclude that their interests had no place whatever in British policy and that confederation was no more than a trap to subject them permanently to British rule. For not only had Britain annexed Basutoland and Griqualand West; she had also denied the Free State access to the Pondo coast; she had refused to sanction Transvaal expansion towards the north-west, so as to keep the Missionaries' Road free for British expansion beyond the Limpopo; and not content that the Portuguese should have warned Pretorius off the Mozambique coast, she had weighed in with her own claim to the southern half of Delagoa Bay. True, Britain was denied this claim when, in 1875, France's President MacMahon, as the appointed arbitrator, awarded Delagoa Bay to Portugal. But this brought little comfort to the Boers. For one thing, they were still denied a seaport of their own. For another, Britain, realising that the arbitration was likely to go against her and believing that the Transvaal was secretly trying to buy the area from the Portuguese, made a deal with Lisbon which gave her a preemptive right to acquire the territory, should Portugal ever decide to dispose of it. Thus a double barrier was placed between the Republic and the coast. And all that the

Transvaalers got by way of consolation was a treaty of peace and commerce with Portugal, in return for which they had to recognise Portuguese sovereignty over Delagoa Bay.

Barkly knew only too well how much all this had injured the prospects of confederation. With a keen understanding of colonial susceptibilities, he had gone to South Africa hoping not only to sell self-government and added responsibilities to the Cape colonists, but also to win over the Boers to accepting a British dominion. His own hasty action over the diamond fields had therefore been a deviation from his normal methods, dictated by an obsessive fear that possession of these riches would make the Republics more than ever determined to steer clear of any union with the Cape. And during the latter part of his governorship, he tried hard to make amends for this aberration. But to no avail. For, with the departure of Gladstone's Government in 1874, Barkly's superiors threw caution to the winds, determined to force the issue of confederation in South Africa against all the odds.

The Palmerstonian era had passed into history and for the next six years, Disraeli, now converted to a thorough-going imperialism, reigned in Downing Street with Lord Carnarvon as his Colonial Secretary. Carnarvon had held this same office in Lord Derby's second ministry during the sixties, in which capacity he had steered through Parliament the British North America Act, whereby Canada became a self-governing confederation under the Crown. And flushed with this success, he now sought to apply his Canadian formula to South Africa, regardless of the differences between the two countries and of the deep distrust which had so recently been sown among the Boers.

To prepare the ground for his ideas, Carnarvon instructed Barkly to summon a conference of the British Colonies and Boer Republics to consider a common native policy as a first step to confederation. At the same time, he despatched Sir Garnet Wolseley, currently Britain's most distinguished soldier and a veteran of the Ashanti wars in the Gold Coast, to Natal with orders to reform the colonial constitution and to devise a native policy which would prevent a war between the races in the

Colony and so enable Natal to join a South African union as a state at peace with itself. Finally, to lobby for confederation, he sent to the Cape a Mr. James Froude, a historian with neither the experience nor the aptitude to handle this delicate mission. Froude's intervention was, in many respects, highly unfortunate. While winning some support for Carnarvon's policy among the British colonists, he stirred up many of the old antagonisms between them and the Cape Dutch and, by his high-handed and tactless approach, made a number of influential enemies. Barkly advised the Colonial Office that their emissary was going the wrong way about his business, but in vain. Molteno, in particular, was incensed by Froude's approach. From the years which he had spent and the ties which he had formed with the Cape Dutch settlers in the Karoo, he felt deeply that, if confederation were to succeed, it had to develop from within South Africa and could not be imposed by the Imperial Government. And all his experience had taught him that any attempt by the Imperial Government to enforce such a policy, in the present state of relations between Britain and the Republics, would meet with fierce opposition from Boers everywhere, including those in the Cape. Besides, Molteno and his colleagues were not exactly drawn to the idea of joining up with Natal and the Transvaal at this point for fear that it would involve the Cape in the native problems of the two states. The Basutos and the tribes beyond the Kei were already more than enough of a responsibility. And while they might wish to keep their options open for expansion in Bechuanaland and points north, Cape leaders had no desire at this stage to add the burden of governing Zulus to their many other problems.

For all these reasons, Molteno refused to act as Carnarvon's stalking-horse and held firmly aloof from what he called the 'agitation of the Imperial Government' for confederation. Nevertheless, Froude achieved some success by appealing, much to Barkly's and Molteno's annoyance, to the growing body of colonialist opinion in the Colony over the head of its conservative Premier. The Cape Parliament, having initially supported Molteno's stand, was eventually persuaded to vote in favour of Carnarvon's South African conference and the Natalians needed little prodding from Wolseley to add their own endorsement. President Brand personally saw no objection to discussing the possibility of confederation. And when Pretorius' successor in the Transvaal presidency, Thomas Burgers, also agreed to attend a conference—in the then somewhat over-ambitious belief that it might lead to a union under Boer, rather than British, leadership—Carnarvon decided to summon the parties to meet in London, with himself in the chair.

In August 1876, the conference duly met. It could hardly have been a greater flop. Molteno refused to attend and, as it turned out, confederation could not even be discussed, because the Free State Volksraad, still smarting from Britain's annexation of the diamond fields, insisted that Brand should withdraw, if the issue were raised. But Carnarvon was not to be diverted from his purpose by such opposition from Bloemfontein and Cape Town. And without any further attempt to secure the agreement of the assembled delegates, he proceeded to draw up a scheme of his own for presentation to Parliament and to the Governments concerned. This was to provide for a federation of Natal, Griqualand West and the Transvaal, which extraordinary project he was convinced would force the recalcitrant Cape Government and the embittered parliamentarians of the Free State to come to terms and join a union of all South Africa.

To say the least, it is extremely unlikely that such a lopsided arrangement as this attempt by Carnarvon to make the lesser include the greater would ever have come to fruition, even supposing the Transvaal Boers had been willing to join in it. Had it been put to the test Molteno's Government at the Cape would not have needed to stand aloof for any length of time to bring this union of the fringe states to a speedy collapse. But Carnarvon's project was never put to the test. For, within a few weeks of having circulated his draft proposals to the various Governments, this most mercurial of Ministers decided instead to impose his confederation policy upon the Transvaal on the first available pretext.

Nor did he have long to wait before such an opportunity arose. Towards the end of 1876, a dispute had arisen between the Pretoria Government and the Bapedi chief, Sekukuni. The cause of the row was Sekukuni's refusal to pay taxes, to return cattle which his tribesmen had stolen from the Boers, or to permit the Republic to build a railway to Delagoa Bay through his territory, which the Transvaalers claimed had been ceded to them by a thirty-year old agreement with the paramount Swazi chief. The railway project was particularly dear to the heart of President Burgers and his followers. Although in many ways, Burgers' ideas were too newfangled and liberal to suit the eighteenth-century attitudes of his electors, this was one modern development on which all Transvaalers were ready to support him. Having been denied access to their own seaport, the Boers were determined to build a railway to Delagoa Bay as far as the limits of their sovereignty allowed, even if they had to pay usurious rates of interest to raise the necessary loans in Europe. And they were not going to let the Bapedis stand in their way. Besides, they had had more than enough of native rebellions in the Zoutpansberg, whence they had been ousted from all but one of their original settlements during the 1860s. And in Pretoria it was strongly felt that, with Cetewayo's Zulus threatening the south-eastern border, this was no time to show weakness in face of Bantu defiance.

Burgers accordingly led the Boer commandos in person against the Bapedi army. But although he won an initial victory, he failed to follow it up and the commandos, disgusted with his irresolute leadership, abandoned the field to Sekukuni. Nor was his popularity enhanced, when he called upon the Volksraad to raise a special tax to pay for the war which he had failed to win. The burghers objected that, if the state's coffers were empty, so were their own pockets. And in their desperation and fear that the Zulus would now set upon the Transvaal, some of them began to talk of linking up with the Cape or Natal as a lesser evil than pursuing a bankrupt independence at the mercy of the Bantu within and without their borders.

Carnarvon needed no further encouragement. Promptly he made up his mind to annexe the Transvaal on the pretext of protecting it from Zulu invasion and rescuing it from insolvency. Disraeli had certain misgivings about embarking on this venture at a time when an Eastern crisis was boiling up and the Russians were threatening to move into the Middle East. But Carnarvon made annexation sound so easy that he got his own way. Sir Bartle Frere was sent to replace the unhappy Barkly with orders to press on with the new forward policy, and Sir Theophilus Shepstone, the Natal Government's representative with the Bantu tribes, was commissioned to perform the act of annexation.

Early in 1877, Shepstone arrived in Pretoria to size up the situation. His visit had a mixed reception. Burgers welcomed him at first as a friendly adviser, come to help the Transvaalers to set their house in order. On the other hand, the members of the Volksraad were less inclined to treat with him on such terms and quickly showed their disapproval of Carnarvon's union project. However, when news later reached them that not only an imperial force but also a Zulu impi was moving towards the Transvaal's borders, the Volksraad became more amenable to the idea of treating with the Imperial Government's delegate and, in the hope of being left to run their own affairs, adopted some of Shepstone's suggested reforms which they had initially rejected. But it was too late. Shepstone ignored their second thoughts and, on April 12, 1877, he proclaimed the annexation of the Transvaal. Burgers retired to the Cape on a pension of £500 a year granted by the Colonial Office and Rider Haggard, the novelist who was then serving on Shepstone's staff, hoisted the Union Jack over Pretoria.

Britain was launched once more upon a policy of outright expansion. With a British Administrator installed in Pretoria, she could now claim paramountcy as far as the Limpopo. The road to the north lay open; and, for a while at least, the Boers of the Transvaal sullenly accepted their vassalage, too shocked by the sudden ending of their bid for independence to offer any resistance to the paramount power.

But if things were temporarily quiet in the Transvaal, the situation elsewhere was anything but easy. Annexation had deeply embittered the Free Staters who resolved more firmly than ever to resist any idea of confederation. And in the Cape, J. H. Hofmeyr, the leader of the Dutch community, who had been working for a union of the Colonies and Republics in the hope that it might help to bind Briton and Boer together in a 'South African patriotism', felt that Carnarvon's action had struck at the roots of his conception.

Still worse was to come with the arrival at Cape Town of Sir Bartle Frere, who took up his post a fortnight before the annexation of the Transvaal. Frere was an almost unmitigated disaster. Having spent up to this point almost all of his adult life in India where he rose from the ranks of the Bombay Civil Service to become Governor of the province, his only experience of Africa had been gained when, in 1872, he had gone to Zanzibar to negotiate an agreement for the abolition of slavery in the Sultan's dominions and, three years later, he had accompanied the Prince of Wales on a visit to Egypt. But none of his postings had equipped him for the delicate task of handling self-governing communities of British colonists, let alone of Boers. His zeal in reforming the systems of land tenure and the sanitary conditions of village life in Bombay might have been highly commended by his superiors; and his courage in helping to suppress the Indian Mutiny might have won him special mention in two parliamentary votes of thanks. But as he showed from the very beginning of his governorship, he was hopelessly miscast in South Africa. Disregarding all advice to hasten slowly with confederation, he was soon at loggerheads with Molteno and his other Ministers whom he treated like junior officials.

Soon after his arrival at Cape Town, in a misguided attempt to intervene in a dispute between the Galeka Xosas and their neighbours, the Fingos, he drifted into yet another Kaffir War— the last of the long series. With reckless daring he crossed the Kei river and, at great personal risk, spent several weeks trying to seek out Kreli, the Galekas' paramount chief, and talk him into submitting to Cape rule. Then, when this bid failed to bring Kreli to book, he declared him to be deposed and sent troops to do battle with the Galekas, which actions only succeeded in uniting the tribes of the Transkei against the white invaders. Molteno, drawing on his own experience as a commando fighter in the forties and making no attempt to disguise his disapproval of Frere's methods, promptly suggested that,

93

since a further Kaffir War was now inevitable, the commander of the Frontier Police should be given a free hand to conduct the campaign rather than the G.O.C. British troops, whose understanding of native warfare was inadequate for the task. Whereupon Frere, completely disregarding his Premier's highly successful record over the past six years, dismissed him from office and summoned an untried yes-man, Gordon Sprigg, to form a Government.

It was a most unfortunate decision. For one thing, Molteno henceforth withdrew from active politics and, save for a brief interval in 1881, after Frere had departed the scene, when he served in Thomas Scanlen's Government, the Cape was to lose the services of probably its most efficient administrative Premier and certainly the man most revered by the Cape Dutch. For another, the new combination of Governor and Premier could hardly have been more dangerous. To the foolhardiness of Frere was now added the capriciousness of Sprigg, a former supporter of Molteno during the agitation for self-government who had turned to attacking his leader after Molteno's Government had failed to accept the findings of a committee set up under his chairmanship to investigate the defences of the eastern frontier. Younger son of a Baptist Minister in Ipswich, Sprigg was as volatile in his political attitudes as he was lacking in humour in the company of his fellows. Yet this earnest and industrious parliamentarian, who assiduously attended every debate in the Cape Assembly, possessed an unshakable confidence in the wisdom and rectitude of whatever purpose he happened for the moment to be pursuing. And since at this juncture he had recently switched from opposing to supporting confederation and had roundly attacked Molteno for his opposition to Carnarvon, he seemed to Frere to be a natural ally and helpmate in the tasks that lay ahead.

Certainly Sprigg raised no objection to imperial officers conducting the campaign beyond the Kei, despite the fact that their inexperience helped to prolong the fighting for almost a year and required the summoning of reinforcements from Britain before the Transkei tribes could be forced to submit. Then when the war was finally brought to an end in June

94

1878, he readily joined with Frere in insisting that, to obviate any further repetition of trouble on the Cape's eastern frontier, the Xosas should be disarmed. Orders to this effect were issued and were duly carried out by the Cape Police. Whereupon Frere, flushed by his success in finally bringing to an end the Bantu threat across the Kei, decided in the autumn of the same year, in his capacity as High Commissioner, to try similar conclusions with Cetewayo's Zulus, whom he blamed for all the native troubles in South Africa and who he insisted must be disarmed if their neighbours were ever to live in peace.

This reckless decision was his worst and most fateful blunder. The Zulus were the last in the line of native migrations into South Africa, which had begun with the Hereros now settled in the south-west. And ever since Chaka's day, they had been of all the Bantu groups the most feared by white and black alike—as indeed is still the case today. Chaka had boasted, not without some justification, that he was 'King of all the blacks', while his 'brother', King George of England, having defeated his 'rival' Napoleon, was 'King of all the whites'. Cruel to an almost unimaginable degree, he had tried to eliminate all possible rivals to his own throne by murdering his brother, all his mother's relatives and even his own sons. Imposing on his warriors a truly terrifying discipline—whole regiments would be put to death as a punishment for defeat in battle—he had greatly expanded his territories and had overrun and absorbed some fifty or more independent Zulu tribes. In the end he was assassinated, after he had overstepped the mark by ordering the slaughter of some two thousand wives of a defeated regiment. But under Chaka's successors—Dingaan, Panda and Cetewayo —the Zulus lost none of their ferocity, discipline or self-esteem. Grouped in regiments, bearing such names as 'crocodiles', 'wanderers', 'snakes', 'seers of evil', 'slaughterers' and 'invincibles', their armies numbered more than half a million warriors. And armed with their spears and their shields of red, white and black ox-hides, with their kilts of cow-tails, monkey, leopard and wild-cat skins topped by long plumed head-dresses, they presented an awesome sight as they gathered for battle in their ox-horn formation, with two racing wings to encircle their enemy, while the main force closed in from the centre, hissing through their teeth and beating time with their feet to simulate the sound of wind and storm.

The only weakness which the Zulu confederacy had developed since the days of Chaka was a chronic tendency to civil strife. It was this weakness which had cost them a sizeable slice of territory on their north-western border with the Transvaal—known as the Blood River Territory—when in 1865 Cetewayo, set about by rival claimants to his throne, had been obliged to buy peace and recognition from the Transvaal by ceding the area for Boer settlement. But in the seventies as the Transvaal Republic grew poorer and feebler, the Zulus began to count the days when they would 'wash their spears' in the blood of those who had dispossessed them and, carrying all before them, advance into the fertile highlands beyond the Vaal. Their hopes were dashed by Britain's annexation of the Transvaal, which confronted them in the north, as well as the south, with an imperial barrier. And just as they were contemplating this frustrating development, Frere arrived in Natal and decided to impose upon the Zulus the policy of disarmament which he had applied to the Xosas on the Cape's eastern border.

Warnings promptly issued from Whitehall that the Imperial Government were too preoccupied with the Eastern Question to be able to send troop reinforcements to deal with the Zulus and they hoped that, through prudent diplomacy, peace would be preserved with Cetewayo. But Frere was scarcely a 'prudent diplomat'. Insisting that British prestige demanded strong action, he charged ahead with his ultimatum to the Zulu chief. However, as he was soon to discover, the Zulus were not like any other Bantu tribe. The Galekas might hand over their weapons to the Cape Police, but not the Zulus. Frere might as well have ordered the rivers to stop running, as to have issued such an ultimatum to Cetewayo. And when a British force moved across the Natal border into Zululand in January 1879 to enforce his demands, it was virtually wiped out at Isandlhwana, while another column of redcoats barely escaped a similar fate at Rorke's Drift, a few miles to the west on the Buffalo river. Revenge came six months later, when Cetewayo was defeated

Sir Bartle Frere

M. W. Pretorius

and taken prisoner at Ulundi. But Isandlhwana had dealt a crippling blow to British prestige throughout South Africa. And the fact that an imperial force could be destroyed by black savages was not lost upon the Boers of the Transvaal.

There, nearly two years after annexation, the first numbed reaction had begun to wear off and such compensating advantages of vassalage as an enlarged market for Transvaal produce had failed to make up for the loss of freedom. A new spirit was emerging among the Boers who were beginning to agitate for a return to independence. And behind this agitation loomed the figure of Paul Kruger—the man whose black-coated, burly frame, melancholy countenance and double-bass voice were to embody over the next two decades all the stubborn, uncompromising resolution of an embattled and exclusive Afrikanerdom.

Kruger's ancestors had lived in South Africa since the early eighteenth century as strict adherents of the Dopper sect of the Dutch Reformed Church, so called because of its members' ceaseless determination to extinguish all new thinking, as a 'Dop' snuffed out a candle. Raised on the Holy Scriptures, which were daily read aloud at lunch and supper and had to be memorised under pain of punishment, the young Kruger was trained in an austere school and, though he survived to see the dawn of the twentieth century, he remained for all his life a creature of eighteenth-century Calvinism and regarded the Bible not merely as a Holy book but as his life's guide and companion. Indeed, the Scriptures were almost his only form of learning. For in the rough and simple conditions of existence on the open veldt, the sum total of schooling which he and his fellows enjoyed was no more than three months with a travelling teacher—which accounts perhaps for his insistence in later life, even in the presence of the famous circumnavigator, Captain Slocum, that the world was not round but flat!

The Boers had few skilled men among them in those days and such building as they did in each of their early settlements consisted of humble mud and reed houses and a large church. Schools had no place in their plans; and for literature there was the Bible and little else. Thus the young Kruger was taught to

97

shoot straight, sooner than he learned to read and write. And at the tender age of ten, after he and his family had joined Potgieter's advance guard of the Great Trek, he fought his first battle along with his elders when repelling a native raid on the trekkers' laager at Vegkop. Two years later, he crossed the Vaal to settle first at Potchefstroom and then, following his first marriage at the age of twenty-two, near Rustenberg, in a wild, beautiful and fertile land, some seventy miles west of Pretoria. Here he acquired an early fame as a hunter of lions and elephants and took part as a field-cornet in commando operations against the Bapedis in the Zoutpansberg and the Bakwenas on the Bechuanaland border of the Republic.

Inevitably the Great Trek left an idelible mark upon Kruger. Reared upon the bitter, burning memory of Slachter's Nek, the hazards and heartaches endured by the trekkers in their bid to escape from colonial rule intensified his resentment against the British. The constant harassments of Boer laagers by Bantu impis sharpened his antagonism towards the African natives and their missionary apologists who insisted, against the Bible as he read it, that black and white were equal in the sight of God. 'Cursed by Canaan. A servant of servants shall he be . . .', was Kruger's view of the Bantu, who as 'savages must be kept within bounds' and should be taught that they were second-class citizens who must obey and learn. And the defence of that birthright of every Boer—the soil that he occupied and settled—against the enemy, whether Bantu or British, man or beast required a constant vigilance and preparedness. Just as each trek-waggon had been a self-contained fighting unit, its women and children as able as their menfolk to shoot down marauding natives or wild beasts and equipped with the knowledge and resources to make bullets as readily as to bake bread, so each and every Boer farm had to be its own fortress and its owners had to obey instantly any summons to band together in a commando formation when a major danger threatened. These rules he applied with determined vigour when, towards the end of the Civil War in the Transvaal, he became Commandant-General and, supported by commandos loyal to the constitution, forced the rebellious Schoeman to abandon his rebellion. And both in this post and later as President of the South African Republic, he maintained the same rigid discipline, insisting that his burghers must remain alert and ready for any eventuality.

It was this alertness to opportunity which, following the defeat of British arms at Isandlhwana, suggested to the Transvaal Boers that the time was ripening for a coup de main to recover their independence. Argument and protests to the Imperial Government that annexation was a violation of the Sand River Convention had got them nowhere. Kruger, as Vice-President under Burgers at the time of the annexation, led two deputations to London, but each time he returned empty-handed. On the first occasion, Carnarvon insisted that the annexation must stand and rejected Kruger's suggestion of a plebiscite to determine the people's will. All he would concede was the use of Dutch as an official language in the new administration. 'Isolated independence' as demanded by the Transvaalers would not, Carnarvon said, ensure their peace or security. And to go back on annexation would, he contended, not be in the best interests of the Transvaal where all was now quiet, the natives were happy and the commercial community and property owners had come to recognise the benefits of British rule. Nor, on his second visit to London, did Kruger fare much better with Hicks-Beach, who became Colonial Secretary after Carnarvon had resigned over Disraeli's eastern policy. Hicks-Beach offered no more than self-government under the Crown and Kruger came home once more a disappointed man whose only enjoyable experience on his travels had been a balloon ride above the streets of Paris.

The new Colonial Secretary was scarcely any more skilful than his blustering predecessor at dealing with the likes of Kruger. No doubt Cecil Rhodes was exaggerating when he described him as 'unfit to be Treasurer of a Parish Council', but Hicks-Beach was certainly unsuited to the Colonial Office. A dour, bad-tempered man who had little sympathy for the Boers, or for that matter even for British colonials, he was known by his colleagues in Parliament as 'Black Michael' and was said by a contemporary to be 'the only man I know who habitually thinks angrily'. He was not, therefore, the man to reverse the annexation policy; and Kruger, returning once more to Pretoria empty-handed, knew well that the Boers would have to fight to regain their independence. With this aim in view, he promptly called a conference of his countrymen at which a solemn vow was made to resist annexation by every possible means.

It was at this point that the news of the imperial forces' defeat at Isandlhwana reached Pretoria. The effect on the Boers was dramatic. And when, coincidentally, Frere crossed the Transvaal border on a visit of inspection to his new imperial acquisition, he was met by hundreds of burghers, armed and in menacing mood. Nevertheless he insisted that the independence movement was the work of a few Boer malcontents acting under some sinister foreign influences and ordered his Administrator, Colonel Lanyon, who understood the Boers no better than he did, to impose on the Transvaal the Imperial Government's already rejected offer of autonomy under British sovereignty. Finally, he returned to Cape Town without even bothering to visit Bloemfontein, or in any way to try to calm the rising indignation of the Free Staters over the treatment of their brothers beyond the Vaal.

In fact so disastrous had been Frere's handling of his functions over the past few months especially in relation to the Zulus, that the irascible Hicks-Beach soon began to realise what a liability he had become. Frere was therefore censured by Whitehall and was relieved of his responsibilities for the Transvaal and for Natal and Zululand, which were now entrusted to Wolseley as Special High Commissioner for South-East Africa.

Alas, the transfer brought no improvement. Wolseley refused even to permit the Transvaalers the autonomy under the Crown which Hicks-Beach had offered and Frere had sought to impose. Instead, he decided to deal with them as he had done with the defeated Ashanti and to subject them to a rigid colonial rule, saying that the Vaal river would flow backwards before the Transvaal regained independence. He then marched against the Bapedis; and incredibly enough at a time when the Boers were vowing to fight annexation to the last bullet, after he had forced

Sekukuni to surrender, he began to send the imperial troops home. Kruger's followers promptly held a further meeting, at which they hoisted the Vierkleur, demanded that the old Volksraad should be summoned and resolved to withdraw all further cooperation with the British occupation. Yet, despite these ominous reactions, Wolseley blandly proclaimed his colonial constitution for the Transvaal and in the spring of 1880 sailed home, leaving General Sir George Colley to watch the fuse which he had lighted burn its inexorable way to the waiting barrel of gunpowder.

A few months after Wolseley's withdrawal, South Africa's other Jonah departed the scene. For in April 1880, the Liberal Party were returned to office once again, following Gladstone's famous Midlothian campaign. Whig pressures in the Cabinet quickly saw to it that there would be no going back on annexation of the Transvaal. But Gladstone was nevertheless determined to get rid of Frere whom he had gone out of his way to attack publicly for condoning atrocities which he alleged had been committed by imperial troops in the recent Zulu war. In September of that same year, therefore, Frere was duly recalled —but not before he and his Cape Premier had embarked on yet another ill-timed and unnecessary contest with the Bantu which was destined, indirectly at least, to be the spark which finally ignited the Transvaalers' revolt.

Unheeding of the lessons of the campaign against the Zulus, Frere and Sprigg decided to call upon the Basutos to hand over their arms to the Cape Police. But the successors of Moshesh were no less determined to keep their guns than were the followers of Cetewayo. Although Sprigg assured Frere that disarmament would pass without any disturbance, the Basutos in fact gave almost as good an account of themselves as the Zulus. And when the Cape forces moved on their kraals, more than 20,000 well-mounted and well-armed warriors poured down from their mountain strongholds and forced their British adversaries to withdraw.

To the watchful Transvaalers everything now indicated that the moment of truth had arrived. Cape forces were heavily involved in another Bantu war, the independence movement had acquired considerable quantities of arms from overseas via the Free State and the 3,500 troops who, thanks to Wolseley's decision to withdraw, were all that remained of the British garrison in South Africa were deeply demoralised by their experiences in Zululand. Also, as Kruger had discovered when he visited the Cape a few months earlier to drum up support for Transvaal independence and opposition to confederation, there was much sympathy for the cause of Boer republicanism among most of the Cape Dutch population. So, with every omen beckoning them to strike without delay, the Volksraad met, proclaimed the restoration of the Republic and appointed a triumvirate of Kruger, Pretorius and Joubert, the Commandant-General, to carry out the functions of the presidency. And on December 16, 1880, Commandant Pieter Cronje attacked the British garrisons at Potchefstroom and Pretoria. The war of independence had begun.

From the outset it could hardly have gone worse for the imperial forces. Despite the evidence of their inadequacies which the encounter with Cetewayo had exposed, Colley and his staff nevertheless clung to a dangerously exaggerated idea of the superiority of their own troops over any adversary. Perhaps they did not know that Boer marksmanship had been sharpened to a point of near perfection by the knowledge that ammunition was in such short supply that the commandos could seldom issue more than fifteen rounds per man and the bullets used to kill an enemy or a beast had to be cut out and used again. But if they did not know this, they and their troops were soon to pay a bitter price for so grossly underestimating their enemies. For, within a few weeks, they had received such a drubbing from the Boers that the Colonial Secretary, Lord Kimberley, offered terms, if the Transvaalers would lay down their arms. Kruger, however, retorted that he would discuss a settlement only if British forces were meanwhile withdrawn from Transvaal territory. And since this was too much for Gladstone's Whig colleagues to swallow, fighting continued until February 1881 when, with the war only ten weeks old, there came the final rout of the redcoats at Majuba Hill, with Colley himself among the many British dead.

In England there was an immediate outcry and demands for vengeance came from the Horse Guards Headquarters of the Army and from the public at large. An arrogant jibe attributed to Kruger that 200 burghers were a match for 12,000 British troops added insult to injury; and the coercionists in the Cabinet demanded that reinforcements be sent to wipe out this stain on Britain's record. But this time they did not have it all their own way, for their clamour was matched by the insistence of the Radicals that annexation had been a mistake and it was now time to correct it. And Gladstone, who personally had all along favoured conciliation, was now less afraid of the coercionists' pressures than of his Radical colleagues' threats to resign if negotiations for a settlement were not immediately started. Thus the conciliators won the day and retrocession of the Transvaal was agreed, but with a formula which provided for continuing British 'suzerainty', which the previous Tory government claimed had existed ever since the signature of the Sand River Convention in 1852. And when the issue was settled by the signature of the Pretoria Convention in July 1881, the Transvaalers were granted within defined boundaries, 'complete self-government, subject to the suzerainty of Her Majesty' in their dealings with foreign powers and with the tribes to the west and east of the Republic.

Such a settlement left far too many loose ends to be satisfactory. At best it was a poor, patched-up compromise between the demands of the Boers for complete independence and the determination of the Imperial Government to rescue some symbol of political paramountcy from the debris of military defeat. As such, it was bitterly attacked in the Pretoria Volksraad and Kruger, who had fought hard to persuade Gladstone to drop the 'suzerainty' clause, had to use all his influence to persuade the burghers to agree to these terms. Better, he argued, to accept this half-loaf for the time being than to resume the fighting. For he feared that to prolong the war would not only oblige Britain to send massive reinforcements against the Transvaalers, but would also give the restless and resentful Zulus an opportunity to 'wash their spears' in Boer blood.

On the strength of these arguments, the Volksraad agreed to

ratify the Pretoria Convention while making it clear that they regarded this 'unsatisfactory state document' as binding the Republic only 'provisionally'. Which qualification proved to be more than a mere face-saving device when, three years later, the settlement was modified in favour of the Boers. But even after these changes had been agreed, the errors and omissions of this hastily concocted treaty continued to bedevil Anglo-Boer relations and to provide a pretext for continued British intervention in the affairs of the Transvaal. For one thing, the peacemakers failed to include in the treaty any provisions for governing the franchise, which enabled Kruger to favour his burghers at the expense of other residents. For another, the reference to suzerainty set a precedent for subsequent British Governments to persist in the claim to paramountcy beyond the Vaal. Thus, either way the Imperial Government were presented with the necessary pretext when, as in the 1890s, they resumed their efforts to coerce the Transvaalers into submitting to British dominion. And when they found that, by invoking sovereignty, they upset the liberal conscience of the nation, they were able to switch their attack and mobilise support by pointing to the unfair discriminations in the franchise against British subjects residing in Kruger's Republic.

6 The London Convention

THE fiasco of Majuba was followed by a further brief pause in the advance of British rule and influence in South Africa. For one thing, Gladstone was not slow in exploiting British reactions to the failure of confederation in order to gain the upper hand over the Whig coercionists on the Government benches and so to reverse the policy of his Tory predecessors. For another, the Government's attentions were becoming increasingly preoccupied by the rising agitation for Home Rule in Ireland. On top of this, in 1882, Gladstone and his colleagues found themselves reluctantly obliged to dispatch an expeditionary force under the ubiquitous Wolseley to crush a nationalist rebellion in Egypt against the authority of the Ottoman Sultan, to whom Britain looked for the physical protection of that life-line of her empire, the Suez Canal.

Moreover with a serious economic depression descending on South Africa in the early eighties, the European population at the Cape became for the next few years too involved in their own problems to concern themselves with expansion. Apart from the influential minority group of chauvinists who had banded together under the title of the Imperial League to demand vengeance for Majuba, the British colonists now joined with the Cape Dutch in opposing further imperial intervention or advance. Sprigg had met with a decisive rebuff at the hands of the Cape Assembly when he tried, at Frere's bidding, to obtain parliamentary endorsement of the Carnarvon policy.

Kruger had descended in person upon the Colony to mobilise opposition among the Cape Dutch and the Assembly had refused to be dragooned by the High Commissioner and his Premier. Then, following the recall of Frere, Sprigg's Government fell in May 1881, after a series of failures had culminated in the inconclusive disarmament war with the Basutos. Confederation had died of the wounds inflicted on it by Boer and Bantu alike; and it only remained for Gladstone and his Colonial Secretary, Lord Kimberley, to perform the funeral rites by enjoining upon Frere's successor, Sir Hercules Robinson, never to raise this dangerous and unpopular issue again.

For the time being it seemed as if the momentum created by the growth of an expansionist colonialism in the previous decade would give way permanently to the introspective mood which descended upon the Cape Government and Parliament at the start of the eighties. Indeed had it not been for the pervasive influence of the chauvinists and, more particularly, the intervention of Germany in establishing a Protectorate in South-West Africa in 1884, the colonists, of British as well as Dutch origin, might have been content to keep to their own back-yard, disregarding those areas beyond the Cape's northern borders which the Palmerstonians had left empty.

Had they done so, they might have broken down the barriers of mutual suspicion between the Afrikaners and their British fellows and have lived at peace among themselves and, still more, with the Boer Republics. For at this point, a bold and imaginative effort was being made to create in place of these divisions a new and abiding unity of the European races. In 1879 Jan Hendrik Hofmeyr, a prominent Cape journalist and a member of the Cape Parliament, had formed out of a Boer farmers' association a political group known as the Afrikaner Bond. Hofmeyr's object was to sweep away the barriers of nationality between the British and the Dutch and to create a new Afrikaner nationalism, which would recognise South Africa rather than England or Holland as the homeland, but which would preserve close ties with the British Empire in such matters as arrangements for mutual defence. Membership of the Bond was open to all, regardless of national origins or political associations, and anyone who had made his home and sought his livelihood in South Africa was welcome to join.

However, since its primary aim was to protect the interests of agriculture and to help in bringing education to the rural areas and since 85 per cent of the agricultural community in the Cape were of Dutch origin, the Bond inevitably appealed far more to the Boer than to the British elements of the population. Contrary to Hofmeyr's hopes, its membership therefore became in practice overwhelmingly Dutch, which fact, taken together with the proclaimed aim of its founder to propagate a new non-British and South African patriotism in a British Colony, was enough to make every British chauvinist condemn the Bond as a mutinous cabal dedicated to undermining imperial influence in South Africa. Frere certainly never understood that Hofmeyr's object was not to create an anti-British pressure group but to unite the nationalities of South Africa. Nor, even if he had, would he have approved of it. He had no use for the Bond's qualified acceptance of confederation, on condition that the flag should be South African and not British; and he deplored Hofmeyr's support for the cause of Transvaal independence, which he claimed showed that the Bond's real purpose was to prepare the ground for a South African union under Boer leadership. And although his successor showed a comparatively refreshing understanding of Hofmeyr's problems and aspirations, there were still those at the Cape who thought like Frere.

Thus, from the outset, Hofmeyr's imaginative intentions were frustrated and the Bond, not unnaturally, grew up in the image which Frere and his like had created for it. Hence, after a slow start, its first big uplift came with the success of the Transvaalers' fight to regain their independence. From 1881 onwards, branches began to spread not only throughout the Cape, but beyond the Orange and the Vaal as well. Which developments, needless to say, served only to intensify British anxieties about the Bond's associations. True, Hofmeyr was in due course to succeed in moderating the early anti-British prejudices of his followers and later to become Cecil Rhodes' principal political ally. Yet for all the rest of its existence, the Bond was as a red rag to a bull for the Imperial League and similar groups in the

Colony who never ceased to suspect it and every other manifestation of Afrikaner thinking as disloyal and even treasonable.

Apart from the impact of the Afrikaner Bond upon race relationships in South Africa, the early eighties produced a host of domestic problems for the Cape Government. For one thing, in 1882, an economic depression no less serious than that of the 1860s descended upon the Colony. The wine farmers were hit by a severe epidemic of phylloxera, the vine disease which had ravaged the vineyards of France in the previous decade. Drought and cattle disease followed. Nor was the depression confined to the rural areas. In Griqualand West which, when it finally became incorporated in Cape Colony in 1880, Rhodes had called 'the richest community in the world for its size', rising production costs were now threatening to put many diamond companies out of business. The banks were refusing credit and diamond shares were falling by up to 50 per cent. Railway development had slowed to a snail's pace, adding yet one more contributory cause to the downfall of Sprigg's Government; and there seemed to be small immediate hope of a rail link between the diamond fields and the Cape, let alone of any extension beyond.

Worst of all, the Basutos were becoming completely unmanageable. Soon after his arrival at the Cape, Robinson had reversed the disastrous disarmament policy adopted by Frere and Sprigg, which punished loyal Basutos alike with rebels; and he had allowed those who were loyal to the Cape Government to keep their guns on payment of a licence fee. But this distinction merely caused a civil war between the two rival chiefs—Letsea, the eldest son and heir of Moshesh, who professed loyalty to the Cape, and Masupha, a younger son and leader of the rebellious faction. To end the strife, a Basuto pitso was called. But in the ensuing debate, Letsea was defeated and the Basutos voted to reject Cape rule. Whereupon the Cape Cabinet, now under Thomas Scanlen, decided to wash their hands of the whole affair and despatched a senior Minister, John Merriman, to London to persuade Gladstone to relieve the Colony of its Basuto burden.

Scanlen, the first Cape Premier to have been born in South

Africa, was temperamentally well suited to the role which circumstances had created for him. A barrister by profession, he only served in one Government—that which he himself headed after the fall of Sprigg in 1881. Although he sat in the Cape Assembly for all of twenty-six years, he seemed as lacking in ambition to further his own political career as he was to advance the Colony's frontiers. Thus at a time when the Cape was faced with a series of pressing native and economic problems, Scanlen's inclination was to reduce wherever possible the area of the Colony's responsibilities and, concentrating on domestic issues, to reverse the trend towards expansion. Even when, in the latter part of 1882, Boer freebooters, acting in defiance of the Pretoria Convention, moved into Bechuana territory and set up two Republics, under the names of Stellaland and Goshen, on the Transvaal border between the Molopo river and the northern frontier of Griqualand West, he and his colleagues seemed to be relatively unmoved.

Robinson informed London that tribes which were firm friends and allies of Britain were in danger of extinction by gangs of Boer marauders from what he called these 'robber republics'. He also warned the Pretoria Government that they would be in breach of the 1881 Convention, if they made any attempt to include Stellaland and Goshen in the Transvaal. And Cecil Rhodes, the Member for Griqualand West in the Cape Assembly, strongly urged Scanlen's Government to intervene in response to the pleas of the anti-Boer tribes in Stellaland for British protection. But at this time Gladstone was no more willing than Scanlen to become involved in a dispute over the Boers' claim to some westward extension of their borders, whatever the Pretoria Convention might have said. The Transvaalers had been casting longing glances in this direction ever since the sixties. Although Pretorius had at that time been forced to withdraw his annexations of Bechuana territory when faced with British objections, they remained determined to extend their writ into this area, if only to put a stop to the continual harassments of their settlers by the tribes along the Transvaal's western frontier. And to make the Boers abandon the two new satellite Republics would require considerable pressure and a substantial imperial force, neither of which Gladstone was prepared to sanction. Robinson's and Rhodes' pleas therefore went unanswered and the tribes were, for the time being, left to make their own peace with their new Boer rulers.

Apart from these considerations, Gladstone's Government were about to negotiate a revision of the Pretoria Convention. At the very moment when Robinson and Rhodes were pressing for action to restrain the freebooters, Kruger was on his way to London to present the Transvaal case for a new treaty, having just been elected—by a three to one majority—for the first of his four terms as President of the Republic. At such a time, the Liberal leader and his colleagues, who were still striving to preserve a somewhat tarnished anti-imperialist image, scarcely wanted to pick a quarrel over a piece of territory which the new Colonial Secretary, Lord Derby, had pronounced as completely valueless to Britain. And, with Scanlen's Government at the Cape showing relatively little concern about the freebooters' activities, Gladstone was resolved to do all that he could to win Kruger's goodwill and, without trying to force the issue over Stellaland and Goshen, to negotiate with him a more permanent settlement which would safeguard British and Boer interests.

Certainly Derby went out of his way to iron out the difficulties and to bring the discussions to a successful conclusion. And although Kruger did not get all the concessions he wanted and at one point almost came to blows with Robinson, the Colonial Secretary met him more than half-way and the resulting agreement, which was signed in London in February 1884, represented a substantial advance for the Transvaalers. At Kruger's absolute insistence, all references to 'suzerainty' were omitted from the new text. The Boers were no longer subject to a British veto in respect of their native policy and they were to be freed of all interference by the British Resident in Pretoria in their internal affairs. As for the 'Freebooter Republics', it was agreed that a part of both Stellaland and Goshen should be formally included in the Transvaal, which was henceforth officially recognised under the title of the 'South African Republic'.

Against this the Transvaalers were still to be hemmed in from the sea. They were not to be allowed to make treaties with foreign powers or with native tribes to the east or west of their borders without the consent of the Imperial Government. And by way of double-locking the door, their claims to extend westwards to the Missionaries' Road were firmly rejected, while any possible outlet to the eastern seaboard was blocked by a clause guaranteeing the independence of the intervening territory of Swaziland. Finally provision was made for civil rights to be accorded to all Europeans in the Transvaal and for a fair deal for the importation of British colonial goods.

Taken all round, the new London Convention offered a reasonable compromise which, had it been left to reasonable men to work out, could have created a lasting *modus vivendi* between Briton and Boer. Alas, this was not to be and, as events were all too soon to show, the embers of conflict were far from having been extinguished. For, just as the Transvaalers were to fail in their obligations to grant civil rights to the non-Boer residents of their land, so equally Britain, acting under renewed imperialist impulses, was to insist that the suzerainty conferred by the Pretoria Convention had not been abrogated by the later treaty.

For the moment, however, such controversies were muted and Gladstone and Derby could congratulate themselves on having temporarily at any rate, laid the ghosts of Majuba. Back in Pretoria, Kruger could loudly proclaim—without at the time any contradiction from Britain—that under the London Convention suzerainty had 'ceased to exist'. True, he was obliged to concede to certain of his critics in the Volksraad that, by the limitations imposed on the Republic's power to make treaties, England had still only repaid fifteen shillings of the twenty she had stolen at the time of annexation. But in London he had got enough to make sure of ratification and so to consolidate the substantial gains that he had made for his country.

Opinion in the Cape also shared in the general feeling of relief that a détente in Anglo-Boer relations had, apparently, been achieved. A month later, Cape Ministers were still further gratified to learn that the Imperial Government had agreed to relieve them of their responsibilities towards Basutoland. During the negotiations for the London Convention, Gladstone and

Derby had been under severe pressure from Radical opinion in general, and the Anti-Slavery Society in particular, not to allow the reactionary Boers to extend their authority any further over native tribes. Thus, while the last thing the Liberal leaders wanted was to extend their own authority in South Africa, in the case of the Basutos they had really no option. In the first place, Merriman had served notice on them that the Cape Government could no longer sustain this burden. Secondly, Letsea had issued a moving plea to Queen Victoria not to withdraw British protection from his country, saying 'Listen, Queen, to my earnest prayer, abandon me not, for abandonment means our complete destruction'. And since, if the Cape withdrew, the only alternative to a British Protectorate was to 'abandon' Letsea's people to the not so tender mercies of their Boer neighbours at a time when the tribes had been fatally weakened by civil war, Gladstone agreed in March 1884 that the Imperial Government should henceforth exercise direct rule over Basutoland.

But even as Scanlen and his colleagues were rejoicing over this welcome alleviation of their responsibilities, a development was taking shape which was to direct their gaze once more beyond the Cape's borders. This was the establishment of a German settlement at Angra Pequena in Namaqualand less than two hundred miles beyond the mouth of the Orange river. Germany's interest in South-West Africa stemmed from the presence of several Rhenish missions which had established themselves in Damaraland in the 1820s and had later been joined by a handful of German merchants drawn by the prospects of a lucrative trade in ivory. In 1868, this German presence was threatened by an outbreak of inter-tribal war; and Bismarck, then with no thought of acquiring this or any other African territory had asked the British Government if they would be prepared to safeguard the lives and property of the missionaries. But, although these areas had long been considered unofficially as forming a hinterland sphere of influence for the Cape, both this and a further request made in similar circumstances twelve years later received a non-committal reply from London and the Germans in South-West Africa were left to fend for themselves. Then at the end of 1882, after the formation of the African and Colonial Societies in Germany had begun to popularise the idea of not merely trading but also colonising in Africa, a Bremen merchant, Franz Luderitz, bought some 240 square miles of territory around Angra Pequena on the Namaqualand coast and, inspired by the German Colonial Society, asked his government for protection. Bismarck, who viewed the prospect with little enthusiasm, decided to renew his suggestion that Britain might care to undertake the necessary Protectorate. But beyond being told that the Cape must be consulted, London's reaction was no more forthcoming than before.

The British Government saw no advantage for themselves in claiming South-West Africa, despite periodical assertions from the Cape that the area contained rich deposits of copper and silver. In 1878, solely because it offered the only good harbour in the area, Disraeli's Cabinet had agreed to annexe Walvis Bay —'three houses and a store'—situated on the Damaraland coast half-way between the Angola frontier and the Orange river border of Cape Colony. But two years later the British Resident had been withdrawn after tribal strife had made his position untenable, since when Britain had more or less turned her back on South-West Africa. Apart from titular possession of Walvis Bay, all that then remained of British interests was a Cape Town company at Angra Pequena which was engaged in prospecting for minerals.

In the spring of 1883, having thus waited in vain for eight months for an answer to Bismarck's enquiry, Luderitz took possession of Angra Pequena's harbour and hoisted the German flag. There was an immediate outburst at the Cape. Even the complacent Scanlen was now obliged to turn from his domestic preoccupations to convey a stern warning to London of the grave consequences, which would ensue if a foreign power established itself in South-West Africa, and to suggest that Britain should immediately preempt every unclaimed space from the southern border of Angola round to Delagoa Bay. Apart from the challenge it would offer in a traditionally British sphere of influence, Scanlen pointed out that an alien administration so near to Cape territory would be an active threat to the Colony. It would, for instance, be impossible to control the import and sale of arms to the Namaqua and Damara tribes who might, either of their own volition or at the bidding of their German rulers, turn their rifles on the Cape settlers on the Orange river frontier. And when Bismarck, anxious not to upset British imperial or colonial interests for a territorial gain of such marginal value, asked yet again whether Britain would not prefer to establish her own Protectorate at Angra Pequena, the Cape Government renewed their pressures on London to accept the proferred role. Merriman too weighed in to urge on the Imperial Government the need for 'annexation to the Empire of the remainder of the coast from the Portuguese possessions to the Orange River'. Merriman had once described this area from personal observation as a 'treeless, waterless waste with an atmosphere like a blast furnace, full of mountains and bare stone . . . without a scrap of soil and composed of granite'. But, however useless it might be economically, he and his Government colleagues were convinced that in German hands it would represent a serious threat to the Cape; and they made it clear that, if Britain would not preempt the area, they would do so themselves in the name of the Colony.

However, Gladstone and Derby continued to hesitate, unable to return a definite answer to Bismarck's repeated enquiries and unwilling to take over the territory themselves. At which point, Scanlen elected to lay down the burden of office. The actual pretext for his departure was a vote in the Cape Assembly censuring the measures taken by his Government to combat the phylloxera epidemic. But the real reason was his determination, against the majority of his parliamentary colleagues, to rid himself of responsibility not only for Basutoland but also for the Transkei territories annexed to the Cape at the end of the seventies and to hand over their administration to the Imperial Government. A coalition headed by Sprigg, Hofmeyr and a relative newcomer to Cape politics, Thomas Upington, opposed Scanlen on this issue at a General Election and, when the new Parliament assembled, he was only too happy to bow out on the minor issue of import restrictions to protect the Colony's vineyards.

In May 1884, therefore, a new Government took office in the Cape under the leadership of Upington, who had acted as chief Opposition spokesman during Scanlen's premiership. Apart from also being a barrister, the new Premier was in marked contrast to his predecessor. Born in Ireland of Roman Catholic parents, Upington had settled in Cape Colony in 1874 after a brief spell at the Irish Bar. Four years later he was elected to the Assembly and was immediately brought into Sprigg's Government as Attorney-General, in which capacity he showed himself to be an ardent imperialist and supporter of Carnarvon's and Frere's confederation policy. In due course he was to become considerably less enthusiastic about the advantages of imperial intervention; but for the moment he was prepared to bring every possible pressure to bear on Whitehall to prevent the Germans installing themselves on the Colony's borders.

On taking office, Upington lost no time in informing London that, in the absence of any action by the Imperial Government, he intended to ask the Cape Parliament for authority to annexe all the coast of South-West Africa from Walvis Bay to the Orange river, which would include Angra Pequena. But his efforts were too late to avail. In face of the rising tide of German imperialism, even Bismarck was now no longer able to lower the flag at Angra Pequena. And after further desultory discussions with Berlin, the Imperial Government decided in the following July to overrule Cape Ministers and to tell all concerned that Britain would recognise a German Protectorate over those areas of South-West Africa not under British jurisdiction. In other words, Germany could have all the coast from Angola to the Orange river, except for Walvis Bay.

The Cape Government protested vigorously at this decision, complaining bitterly that South-West Africa should at least have been reserved until some final agreement with Germany about African spheres of influence had been concluded. They even dug up an alleged claim by Wodehouse, when Governor of the Cape, to British jurisdiction over Angra Pequena. But the deed was done, and Gladstone was not going to undo it, even though at this very same moment Germany was also establishing herself in Togoland and the Cameroons on both sides of the

British position in the Niger delta. The Cape might complain of the 'crippling effect' of a German presence on its borders. But, if only because he needed Bismarck's support in other parts of the world and more particularly for Britain's new role as the protector of Egypt, Gladstone could not afford to quarrel with Germany over a 'waterless waste' in South-West Africa.

But, if Gladstone's Liberal Government at home were still too concerned with the problems of ruling Egypt and of letting the Irish rule themselves to risk any further imperial ventures in South Africa, British opinion at the Cape was again firmly and irrevocably set on the path of expansion. And with the Germans established beyond the Colony's Orange river frontier and, more threatening still, planning to build a railway into the interior in the direction of Bechuanaland, the attitude of Cape Ministers towards the Republics of Stellaland and Goshen had undergone a rapid change. Whereas originally Scanlen had regarded these freebooter states as a logical, if not legitimate, reaction by the Transvaalers to the harassments which they had suffered for many years from the Bechuana tribes on their borders, the two Republics now suggested a threat to the Cape's hinterland, which called for speedy intervention to protect the road to the north and keep it safe from German and/or Boer encroachments.

This reorientation of Cape thinking was in no small way the work of that young rising star of South African industry and politics, Cecil Rhodes. Many months before the Cape Parliament came to accept the need for preemptive action in Bechuanaland, Rhodes had been urging that these wide open spaces should be annexed in the Colony's name. And after Luderitz had hoisted his flag at Angra Pequena, he did not rest until he had induced the Cape Government to intervene to prevent the Germans linking up with Kruger's Republic to block the road to the north, the 'Suez Canal' of southern Africa's trade routes, as he called it. Which auspicious achievement was to launch Rhodes as the leader and folk-hero of colonialism at the Cape, who for the next ten tumultuous years was to play the lead opposite Paul Kruger in the unfolding drama of South Africa's history.

In an era not exactly lacking in notable and notorious

figures, there was certainly none more extraordinary than this Hertfordshire parson's son who grew from a physical weakling to be hailed by his admirers as 'the Collossus' and damned by his enemies as 'the curse of Africa'. Descended from yeoman English stock, Rhodes in his youth had been too delicate in health to go as his brothers had done to a public boarding school and, after doctors had advised his parents that the state of his lungs required a change to a warm climate, he came to South Africa in 1870 at the age of seventeen. At this point in his life, he regarded himself as destined for Holy Orders; but after a year spent working his eldest brother's cotton plantation in Natal, he was lured to the diamond fields of Griqualand West, where his ambitions became somewhat less spiritual. South Africa had cast its spell upon him and, with its new-found riches added to its natural beauties and near perfect climate, it seemed to be the natural place to found another British dominion across the seas. As this vision grew in his adolescent mind, an even greater concept began to develop—a federation of empire of which a British South Africa would form part and which, together with Germany and the United States of America, would keep the peace and preserve order throughout the world. But, even in his teens, Rhodes realised that, as he later told General Gordon, 'it is no use having big ideas if you have not the cash to carry them out.' Thus, if only as a means to realise his dreams, he resolved to make his fortune in the new diggings at Kimberley.

He felt somewhat the same about the need for a first-class education, which belief later prompted him to provide in his will for the famous scheme of Oxford scholarships, that bore his name. And, since his own poor health had obliged him to settle for what he regarded as the second-class education of a day boy at Bishops Stortford Grammar School, he decided when at Kimberley to read for a degree at Oxford University. For the next eight years, therefore, Rhodes kept his terms at Oriel College, Oxford, at such intermittent intervals as his diamond mining interests would allow. And in 1881, he obtained his degree, having spent nearly £10,000 in doing so, including some £2,000 on steamer fares alone.

In this achievement in adult education he had been greatly

helped by the man who was to become one of his closest partners both in his diamond enterprises and in his later ventures beyond the Limpopo—Charles Dunnell Rudd. Rhodes met Rudd in 1872 when the two young prospectors were working adjoining claims in the Kimberley diamond fields. Rudd, who was then twenty-eight, nine years older than Rhodes, had come to South Africa in the middle sixties from Trinity College, Cambridge, where he had distinguished himself as a fine athlete, but had broken down in health due to over-training. Realising how much a university degree meant to his younger friend, he had looked after Rhodes' diamond interests to enable him to keep his terms at Oxford. More important still, he became a partner in the first big gamble which was to lay the foundations of Rhodes' extraordinary business empire.

In 1875, a paralysing slump had hit the diamond fields when the yellow ground where the earlier diamonds had been discovered gave way to blue soil which was harder to work and much less productive. The early diggings had never been a very economic proposition. Situated on a hot, dust-ridden, waterless and treeless plain and consisting of a vast honeycomb of pitted ground with each pit representing an individual claim only a few yards square but often going as deep as 200 feet, the diamond mines quickly became dangerous and often unworkable quarries. The roadways between the claims had become tight-rope walks and accidents were frequent as men, mules and trolleys tumbled into the pits. Subsidence of the pit walls occurred equally often and, with the added hazards of a prevalence of rainwater and primitive hauling gear, native workers were crushed to death so frequently by land-slides that the newspapers tired of reporting such disasters.

Added to this, there were constant disturbances over such issues as the right of native Africans to hold claims; and during an outbreak of violence in 1874, the Jolly Roger had been hoisted by a group of prospectors who were members of the Fenian Brotherhood of Irish revolutionaries. Illicit diamond selling by the workers grew apace as the temptation to supplement low wages became irresistible. And claim-holders responded by incarcerating their employees in compounds surrounded by high walls, which denied them all access to the outside world, and by dosing workers suspected of swallowing diamonds with cathartic. Yet Kimberley's crime rate continued to escalate to such staggering proportions that the Diamond Laws Commission was obliged to report in 1888 no less than 11,000 criminal convictions for a total population of under 30,000. Hundreds of workers died of drink in an area where bars, bearing such homely names as the Black Horse and the Pig and Whistle, sprang up so fast that there was one for every sixteen inhabitants. Well might Merriman describe the diamond fields as 'a seething mass of opulent iniquity'.

In these conditions the striking of the hard blue ground seemed to be the last straw. And in the near panic which followed, many diggers, as well as the banks who had become claim-holders by foreclosing on loans to prospectors, became only too anxious to get rid of their claims even at knock-down prices. Rhodes and Rudd saw their chance. Convinced that the ultimate future of the industry was assured, because, as Rhodes put it, every man who became engaged would wish to give his future wife a diamond, they took a gamble and bought large numbers of claims, including the De Beers mine—so called after the De Beer brothers who had formerly owned the farm on its site—which they pooled with their own holdings to form in 1880 the De Beers Mining Company. They also bought and leased modern pumps and invested in an ice-making machine which provided the vast chain of Kimberley saloons with the novelty of cold drinks. The profits from these enterprises were then ploughed back into the company.

With the aid of more modern equipment the blue soil barrier was duly overcome and the return of prosperity, needless to say, enormously enriched the De Beers Company with their now extensive holdings. But still this was not enough for Rhodes whose incipient megalomania was leading him to think that the best hope for the diamond industry lay in an amalgamation of all the various interests, which would give him control over a virtual diamond monopoly at Kimberley. Following his final departure from Oxford, Rhodes therefore set about persuading the rugged individualists who made up the diamond industry to join with him and Rudd in a vast amalgamated concern. It was a long struggle but after nearly seven years of argument and ruthless nerve-racking beggar-my-neighbour methods, helped by a £1,000,000 loan from Rothschilds Bank, Rhodes' absolute determination won the day. A new corporation was formed under the name of De Beers Consolidated Mines and, as an indication of Rhodes' ultimate aims, was given a Trust Deed which entitled the directors to use its resources to create a new British dominion in the territory to the north of the Transvaal and Bechuanaland.

His most difficult and intractable opponent had been the son of a small Jewish shopkeeper in London's East End—Barnett Isaacs, locally known as Barney Barnato, who controlled the Kimberley mine which produced diamonds of better quality and more cheaply than any of Rhodes' holdings. Rhodes set about 'squaring' Barnato by a combination of flattery and pressure, which was to become typical of all his doings and dealings in commerce and later in politics. First he outraged the class and race-conscious members of the Kimberley Club by proposing Barnato for membership. Then he nominated him as Member of Parliament for one of the Kimberley constituencies. At the same time Rhodes set about loosening Barnato's control of the Kimberley mine by buying all its available shares in association with another of his partners, Alfred Beit, who was the agent of a German firm of diamond merchants. By these methods the share values were inflated to a point where Barnato's associates could no longer resist the temptation to cash in on their profits.

Yet still Barnato himself held out against amalgamation, largely out of his intense dislike of the terms of the new corporation's Trust Deed which, as a businessman interested only in making money, he felt would involve him and his share-holders in political adventures, wars against natives and Boers, and a mass of imponderable risks for little or no commercial purpose or financial reward. But Rhodes' tenacity forced him finally to surrender after a meeting lasting eighteen hours in the house of a Scottish doctor, Leander Starr Jameson, who, like Rhodes and Rudd, had come to South Africa to recover his health, overstrained during his years of medical training, and who was to become one of Rhodes' closest associates and his principal agent in the Jameson Raid conspiracy. At four o'clock in the morning a weary Barnato gave in saying, 'You have a fancy for making an empire. Well, I suppose I must give it to you.'

By this coup Rhodes and his associates became the virtual dictators of the diamond fields. And he was yet another step nearer to gathering the 'cash' to realise his 'big ideas' for the north and, who could tell, perhaps in even wider and more distant realms. For Rhodes' dreams were not limited to Africa alone. In a will which he had made ten years earlier when he was only twenty-four and still had to make his fortune, he directed that his estate was to be devoted to establishing a 'secret society for the extension of British rule throughout the world', for promoting emigration and colonisation by British subjects and 'especially the occupation by British settlers of the entire continent of Africa, the Holy Land, the valley of the Euphrates, the islands of Cyprus and Candia, the whole of South America, the islands of the Pacific . . . the Malay Archipelago, the seaboard of China and Japan, the ultimate recovery of the United States of America as an integral part of the British Empire . . .' all of which would be welded into a federated power 'so great . . . as to hereafter render wars impossible. . . .'

From any other man such a will would have seemed as the romantic reveries of a schoolboy or some idiotic practical joke. But Rhodes was no schoolboy and as for making practical jokes, he is said to have so lacked humour that, if anyone said something funny during a discussion at which he was present, he would wait poker-faced until the laughter had subsided and then carry on with the discussion as if nothing had happened. He therefore meant what he wrote in his will and, as his career was to demonstrate with brutal clarity, he would do anything and everything to achieve his ends whatever means might have to be employed. For Rhodes, therefore, the arrival of the Germans on the South African scene in the middle eighties could not have been more opportune, providing as it did the perfect bogey with which he could scare all concerned, even including the diffident Gladstone, into resuming the advance of British rule and influence outwards from the Cape.

7 Annexation of Bechuanaland

THE indifference with which London and Cape Town had viewed the idea of a German presence in South-West Africa during the early eighties might, with the advantage of hindsight, seem strange, even for such colonially unambitious leaders as Gladstone and Scanlen. But at the time it had no doubt never really occurred to either the Imperial or the Cape Government that any foreign power would encroach upon the Colony's hinterland and the road to the north. For up to this point, save very recently in Egypt, Britain had had to contend with virtually no competition from other European states in any part of Africa. By the 1870s the Danes had gone, having sold their remaining trading stations on the Gold Coast to Britain in the middle of the century. The Dutch Government had lost interest when the slave-trade was abolished and had retired from all but a few fortresses on the Gold Coast, which in 1872 were exchanged for the cession of British claims in Sumatra. The Portuguese were asleep; and the Italians and Germans were busy consolidating a national unity still less than ten years old. In 1872 Bismarck told the British Ambassador that for Germany colonies would be a source of weakness. And nine years later he was still vowing that, 'We shall have no colonial policy so long as I am Chancellor. We have a navy that cannot sail and we must have no vulnerable points in other parts of the world.' As for the Belgians, they had only gained their independence in 1830 and, preoccupied with the problem of finding their feet, were showing no interest in seeking colonies in Africa or elsewhere. Even in France, the imperialist drive had come to a standstill, following nearly two centuries of exhausting wars and devastating defeats at the hands of England and, most recently, of Germany, which had left France with little inclination for colonial expansion.

But it was too much to expect that this situation, so convenient for Britain's imperial designs, would continue indefinitely. For all Bismarck's refusals to hazard his Pomeranian Grenadiers in overseas adventures, it was but a question of time before Germany would be drawn into a general scramble for colonial possessions and for the vacant African territories in particular, if only for reasons of national pride and status. Likewise the Italians and the King, if not the people, of Belgium were certain to follow the international fashion and, in due course, to become owners of African estates. The Portuguese, too, had in the end to wake up and claim their own, even though their improvident omission previously to occupy the territories in question was to invalidate most of their claims. As for France, overseas conquest and colonisation had been part of French tradition for more than a thousand years. In the immediate aftermath of the war of 1870, imperialism might for a time be regarded as a treasonable negation of France's overriding national interest—the recovery of Alsace and Lorraine from the Germans. But it was in the nature of things that the French would be bound ultimately to resume their long-interrupted quest for empire.

The French race had been conquering and colonising the world ever since the Gauls overran Greece, the Normans took Sicily and the Crusaders set themselves up as the 'colons' of the Holy Land. And in the seventeenth century, Richelieu and Colbert had set out to create the first French Empire in the Indies and India, in Canada and Louisiana, and had instituted, under the name of the 'Pacte Coloniale', a system of rigid trading monopolies for a network of French chartered companies in France's overseas settlements. To further these imperial designs, the Cardinal and his successors embarked on a large-scale programme of naval building and, following the example of the Portuguese and Dutch, established a chain of bases to serve as victualling stations for the conquest of India in such places as Madagascar and the Mascarene Islands, as well as at various points on the West African coast between Senegal and Gabon.

Thanks to these endeavours, the French fleet soon outgrew its Dutch and Spanish rivals, Senegal was colonised and Goree Island seized from the Dutch. French companies blossomed in all directions, carrying on trade in Africa; and under French naval protection, the Compagnie des Indes Orientales supplanted the Dutch in India. But then in the eighteenth century, the first French Empire began to crumble. Following a series of shattering conflicts with England, France was stripped of her overseas territories. And when the last of these struggles, the Napoleonic War, had ended, she had lost every major possession, including Canada, India and Louisiana, and was left with a few scattered settlements unwanted by the victors, such as Senegal, Guinea and Madagascar in Africa, plus a handful of islands in the West Indies and the Pacific Ocean.

With the demoralisation of defeat added to the legacy of anti-imperialism handed down by the Revolution, France now appeared to have turned her back on colonial expansion. Her West African trading posts, although they continued to be maintained by French companies, received no official support during most of the first half of the nineteenth century. True, in 1830, Algiers was plucked from the Ottoman Empire by a punitive expedition sent to exact retribution for an insult to the French Consul. Also, in 1855, General Faidherbe, as Governor of Senegal, set out to open up the interior, which had for long been barred to European colonisation by the powerful empire of the fanatically Moslem Tokolors. But these French advances were isolated moves, not part of any concerted plan to resume imperial expansion. Neither in Algeria, nor in Senegal was any attempt made to follow through. The Orleanist regime of Louis Philippe and, despite its lofty title, the Second Empire of Louis Napoleon gave scant encouragement to overseas ventures. And following the débâcle of 1870 and the loss of Alsace-Lorraine, anti-imperialist sentiment became, if anything, even more intense. For the next decade the eyes of every true French patriot became fixed on the 'blue line of the Vosges' and any Frenchman who dared to advocate imperial expansion was branded a 'traitor to France on the Rhine'.

Thus throughout the first three-quarters of the nineteenth century, France presented no threat to British expansion or settlement on the African continent. Indeed, far from contemplating any extension of French possessions overseas, both before and after her defeat by Prussia, France was actually trying to rid herself of some of her African settlements, or at least to rearrange them so as to reduce the risk of a clash with British interests. On no less than five occasions between 1866 and 1879, the French Government offered to trade various West African possessions if Britain would allow them to join together the two parts of Senegal which were separated by the tiny British settlement along the Gambia river. This area had become a Tom Tiddler's ground for every bandit fleeing from French justice and every rebel against French rule. And since it was the policy of the Second Empire and, to begin with, of the Third Republic, to improve relations with Britain, the French were prepared to pay a high price to remove any cause of friction such as inevitably arose with the British authorities when French patrols followed fugitives across the Gambia border.

In 1866 they offered to trade the Ivory Coast in exchange for Gambia and, in the following year, they added Gabon as well. Britain's response was to ask instead for the Mellacourie area of the Guinea coast. And although this was France's most highly prized trading centre in West Africa, the French Government were considering its cession when the war of 1870 brought the discussions to a halt. For a while no more was heard of the Gambia exchange. But in 1874 the French raised the matter again with an offer to trade the Ivory Coast and the Mellacourie, only to be told that Britain would settle for no less than the cession of all French settlements from Guinea to Gabon.

Once more the French agreed, albeit reluctantly. But since the House of Commons was currently engaged in debating the Bill of Mr. Plimsoll, M.P., to improve safety measures for British merchant seamen, there was no time for Parliament to enact, the necessary legislation to give effect to the Gambia exchange before the annual recess. And by the time that Parliament was reconvened, the project had come under such heavy attack from the British merchants in Gambia and the French in Guinea and elsewhere that neither Government thought it politic to pursue the matter for the time being.

Nevertheless, in 1876, the French came back and offered to trade everything from Guinea to Gabon, subject only to their having the right to continue operating French tariffs on the Dahomey coast. The area in question measured only a few miles in length. But the French proviso was nevertheless made a breaking point by Britain's Colonial Secretary, Lord Carnarvon; and France was told to forget the whole arrangement. And although the French made one further attempt three years later to exchange the Mellacourie for Gambia, Disraeli's Cabinet were no more attracted by this suggestion than their predecessors had been by previous offers. For as the seventies drew to a close, Britain's attentions were being drawn to other parts of Africa— to the South with its promise of untold wealth beneath the soil, and to Egypt, where the new short route to India via the Suez Canal commanded her presence and protection and averted her gaze from the strategically unimportant and climatically insupportable colonies in the West.

Then in the 1880s the inevitable happened. France recovered from the shock of her defeat by Germany, reverted to her empire-building role and resumed her colonial advance, drawn by the need to supply her expanding industries with raw materials and overseas markets. The anti-imperialist wave receded and, as her Foreign Minister, Gabriel Hanotaux, put it, France realised that she could no longer 'turn her back on the magnificent promise in the world that was opening before her, thinking only of the provinces seized from her'. Confronted by British claims and British expeditions from the Congo to the Red Sea and from the Niger to the Nile, and observing other European powers, such as Germany, Italy and Portugal preparing to press forward in Africa, the French decided not to wait 'until these imminent rivals were able to veto our every move', but instead 'to move ahead of them and follow our own course in every sphere'. And from the standstill of the past eight decades, France now launched out on a policy of simultaneous expansion in North, West and Central Africa, in Madagascar and in Indo-China. Tunisia became a French protectorate. French colonial forces under General Gallieni punched their way eastwards from Senegal into the Upper and Middle Niger valley and into the hinterlands of Sierra Leone and the Gold Coast. The French presence was consolidated along the coast from Guinea to Gabon. And from the Congo, de Brazza pushed northwards up the Ubangui river to Lake Chad, bent on his design to create in Central Africa a turn-table on French soil from which the routes of French expansion would radiate in all directions.

Britain's interests and influence in West Africa now came under serious pressure. The very existence of British traders from Gambia to the Niger delta seemed to be menaced, with only the courage and determination of such men as Sir George Goldie of the Royal Niger Company and Captain (afterwards Lord) Lugard, who commanded the Company's tiny native force, to stand between them and eviction. But far worse than these threats was to come out of the imperialist revival in France. At least in Whitehall, the West African colonies had always been in the last resort expendable, objects to be bartered for concessions in strategically more important areas. But the new French 'génération coloniale', inspired by the dictum of the new high-priest of French imperialism, Jules Ferry, that 'colonial policy is the child of industrial policy', were looking towards wider horizons than West Africa. Believing with Ferry that 'the arrival of the most recent industrial powers—the United States, Germany and Switzerland—has drawn the whole western world onto a slope which it will not be able to reclimb', Frenchmen had begun to dream of a belt of French influence and occupation stretching across Africa from the Niger to the Nile and joining Senegal to French Somaliland, which grandiose project struck at the very existence of Britain's position in Egypt as guardian of the Suez Canal.

In the middle eighties the scramble for Africa thus began in earnest. From a position in which no serious rival to British preeminence existed up to a few years before, Britain suddenly seemed to be beset with competitors. For as the French began the advance that was to make them the largest land-owners on the African continent, so other European powers followed their suit. Following the eviction of the Egyptians from the Sudan by the Mahdi, the Italians moved into Somaliland and Eritrea; the King of the Belgians established his personal estate in the Congo; and in this same momentous decade the Germans hoisted their flag in the Cameroons and Togoland in West Africa, in Tanganyika on the east coast and at Angra Pequena in South-West Africa.

In many respects Britain had only herself to blame for the pressures which now menaced her position as the paramount European power in Africa. In the west, by preferring to retain the Gambia wedge against repeated offers by France to trade her claims from Guinea to Gabon, she enabled French forces to move in from the coast and link up with their compatriots pushing eastwards from Senegal. As a result, every British possession from Gambia to the Niger delta was shortly to become encircled by French-held territory. On the Congo, Britain's rejection of H. M. Stanley's offer to claim his new discovery in Queen Victoria's name let in King Leopold, and in turn precipitated de Brazza to plant the tricolour of France on the north bank at Stanley Pool—the site of modern Brazzaville. In the Cameroons, Britain was hoping to persuade the chiefs to cede sovereignty over their territories. But the Germans got in first when the celebrated African traveller, Dr. Nachtigal, induced the local paramount chief, King Bell, for the price of £1,000, to accept a German Protectorate, while the would-be British treaty maker, Consul Hewett—thereafter to be known as 'Too-late Hewett'—was slowly making his way along the coast.

Nachtigal's visit to the Cameroons had been announced as being designed solely to report on the state of German commerce in the area. And since German companies had been trading with West Africa from the seventeenth century onwards, there had seemed to be no reason to conclude that his journey concealed any ulterior purpose. Nor were British suspicions aroused when in 1884 Dr. Karl Peters and a couple of henchmen arrived at

Cetewayo

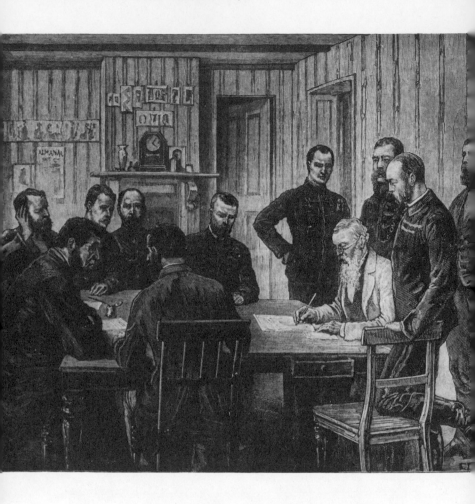

Transvaal War—Signature of the Armistice

Zanzibar. For in the same way Hamburg merchants had recently established a flourishing trade in the Sultan's domains and Germans were by no means an unusual sight in these parts. Once again therefore Britain was taken by surprise when Peters, after spending a few weeks in the interior of Tanganyika, reappeared with enough treaties to give Germany a claim to 60,000 square miles of territory, later to be expanded by right of purchase from the Sultan to include the entire coast from Cape Delgado, which marked the border with Mozambique, to within a hundred miles of Mombasa.

This last German acquisition might not of itself have caused great concern to London or Cape Town. For it was not until the end of the eighties when Karl Peters began to challenge British interests in the area of Lake Victoria and so to threaten the source of the Nile that the Imperial Government began seriously to interest themselves in East Africa. However, at the Cape, and shortly afterwards in Britain too, the German move into Tanganyika was not seen as an isolated action, but rather as part of a concerted plan to throw a German barrier across southern Africa from Dar-es-Salaam to Angra Pequena.

In fact, neither in this nor in any other direction did the Germans aspire to threaten any legitimate British designs. But as, during the mid-eighties, Britain's possessions and interests in other parts of Africa came under increasing pressure from French expansion, the mere existence of yet another potential European rival in Tanganyika and Angra Pequena, in a position to make common cause with the Boers, became enough to turn the scales finally in favour of a forward policy in South Africa. Not only did these events seem to confirm the warnings of Whig and Tory imperialists that British interests were being exposed to a serious threat; but, because they were seen to portend an ever-increasing extension of Boer control over native tribes, they also brought prominent Radicals such as Joseph Chamberlain as well as the humanitarian societies to join the clamour for the preemption of South African territories which, if left unclaimed, were liable to fall into unwelcome and unfriendly hands.

The scramble for Africa had created a perfect bogey-man for the expansionists at home and in the Cape; and in consequence, even under Gladstone, let alone under his Tory successor, Lord Salisbury, Britain proceeded to embark on a series of annexations in all directions. Over the next three years, on the pretext of preventing a German-Boer link-up and of forestalling any further German encroachments, the Imperial and Cape Governments between them annexed Bechuanaland, Zululand, St. Lucia Bay on the Tonga coast and the territories of the Pondos, Galekas and Tembus in the vacant area between Cape Colony and Natal. And when all these blank spaces had been filled and the last of the new Protectorates had been proclaimed in 1887, a British 'Monroe Doctrine' was in operation along the whole coast from the mouth of the Orange to the border of Mozambique. The only exception was a narrow strip of Tonga territory which gave onto the Indian Ocean at Kosi Bay, although even this small gap in the ring fence was proclaimed a British sphere of influence by virtue of a treaty between Natal and the Tonga Queen. Inland, too, the vast sweep of the Bechuana plains, stretching from the northern borders of the Cape to the Upper Zambezi valley, was taken over to serve as a British wedge between the Germans and the Boers. More significant still, in 1888, the road to the north was secured for exclusive British use by the conclusion of a treaty with the Matabele King, Lobengula, by which all his domains between the Limpopo and the Zambezi—the territory known today as Rhodesia—became a British sphere of influence.

The annexation of Bechuanaland came as the culmination of a determined campaign by Rhodes, begun during Scanlen's premiership in response to the establishment of the Stellaland and Goshen Republics and continued with even greater intensity after the proclamation of the German Protectorate in South-West Africa. Shortly after the annexation of the Transvaal in 1877, Rhodes had heard that the Germans were thinking of establishing in Matabeleland a colony where Boers might find escape from British interference alongside kindred souls from Germany. These rumours, taken together with reports that Kruger was currently saying that he infinitely preferred German encroachments to British, had deeply disturbed him. For, not content with amassing a large fortune from his De Beers diamond holdings at Kimberley, Rhodes had already begun to dream dreams about 'my North' and the vast Eldorado of gold and other minerals which, he claimed, lay buried in the land of King Solomon's mines. And although he greatly admired Germany and had, in fact, long advocated her inclusion in a 'Pax Teutonica' with the United States of America and a federated British Empire, he was not going to allow his African dreams to be shattered by a German alliance with the Boers.

Therefore, directly Luderitz hoisted his flag at Angra Pequena, Rhodes seized the opportunity to urge that immediate steps be taken to forestall the Germans in Bechuanaland. Scanlen, although shocked by the German action, hesitated to undertake such a far-reaching commitment at a time of grave economic depression in the Colony. But Robinson, the new Governor and High Commissioner, had less qualms and, on his authority, Rhodes was permitted to try his hand at negotiating with the two freebooter states some arrangement to protect the security of the Cape and its hinterland.

This mission was to have a mixed result. In the case of Stellaland, Rhodes succeeded in coming to terms with the Boers' leader, van Niekerk, and managed to persuade the Stellalanders to accept Cape rule on the promise that they would be allowed to keep those lands which had been conceded to them freely and without duress by the tribes who favoured the Boers. But in Goshen it was a very different story. Here the freebooters were an altogether more intractable crowd and, while Rhodes was busy negotiating in Stellaland, they succeeded with the help of a personal intervention by the Transvaal's Vice-President, General Joubert, in browbeating friends and foes alike among the tribes into submitting to the rule of their so-called Republic. The Goshenites were therefore in a strong position to refuse any dealings with the Cape and, when Joubert returned to Pretoria, they demonstrated their independence of British influence by hoisting the Vierkleur and proclaiming their allegiance to the Transvaal.

This defiant gesture, no less than Rhodes' dealings with van Niekerk in Stellaland, created a state of some confusion. For whatever preferences the Goshenites and Stellalanders might have expressed in determining their own future, the fact remained that the future had been already arranged for them by the terms of the London Convention which gave a part of both Republics to the Transvaal. Confronted, therefore, with a situation in which, contrary to the Convention, one of the Republics had opted to be attached to the Transvaal and the other had agreed to be ruled from the Cape, Kruger decided to bring matters to a head by proclaiming the Goshen Republic as annexed to the Transvaal, subject to the consent of Whitehall.

His action was to prove a cardinal blunder. True, amid the ensuing outcry from the Cape and Britain, he hastened to withdraw his proclamation and told the Goshenites to lower the Vierkleur and await a final decision on the partition lines to be drawn in accordance with the London Convention. But the damage had been done, however swiftly Kruger might have sought to undo it. He could shout from the housetops that his only purpose had been to bring the Imperial Government to clarify the situation and that he never intended to proceed with the annexation of Goshen if Britain objected to it. But he did not carry conviction with those in power in London and Cape Town, who now began to suspect that, in spite of the concessions which the Imperial Government had so recently made to them, the Transvaalers were in league with the Germans in a devilish plot to throw a barrier across southern Africa which would cut the Cape off from its hinterland.

Rhodes certainly lost no time in exploiting these suspicions. Pointing to the vast vacuum in Bechuanaland where there was nothing but the Kalahari Desert between the Germans in South West Africa and the Boers in the Transvaal, he urged Upington to take immediate steps to forestall any attempt to block the road to the north. In particular, he argued that the Cape Government should endorse his arrangements with the Stellalanders and should use whatever force was necessary to expel the Goshenites altogether and send them packing back to the Transvaal. Moreover, he insisted that the necessary action should be taken by and in the name of the Colony, rather than the Colonial Office, for which agency he had developed a profound aversion as being altogether too slow and clumsy in reacting to colonial requirements and too exigent in prescribing the conditions for its assistance.

But Upington, much as he agreed that forceful action was necessary, lacked the resources to mount a colonial expedition of sufficient strength. Besides, as a supporter of Carnarvon and Frere in the era of confederation, he had yet to become disenchanted with the idea of imperial intervention. To Rhodes' dismay, he therefore responded to the call for action by invoking the British Government's aid and, through Robinson, sending a stern warning to London that long and extensive hostilities against the freebooters would be inevitable unless prompt and effective steps were taken to remove this threat to the Cape's hinterland. This time the response in Whitehall was swift and positive. Roused by Kruger's attempt to annex Goshen, the Imperial Government now reacted forcefully to the Colony's invocation. And in October 1884 they decided to send a force of 5,000 British troops, under the command of General Sir Charles Warren, to maintain order, to establish the London Convention boundaries and to take and hold Bechuanaland for the Crown until its ultimate future might be decided.

Warren had had several years of recent experience in South Africa, where he had commanded the Diamond Fields Horse, served on the Griqualand-Bechuanaland Boundary Commission and, in 1879, briefly acted as Administrator of Griqualand West, prior to its incorporation in Cape Colony. But for all his experience, he had not acquired the temperament for dealing with the Boers. Hot-tempered, conceited and autocratic in his relations with Afrikaners, he all too readily mistook geniality for personal admiration and friendliness for submissive meekness. But if Warren was an unsuitable choice for the task of winning over Boer freebooters to a British allegiance, his own decision to select as his assistant the Rev. John Mackenzie of the London Missionary Society was an even greater error. Bitterly anti-Boer and deeply suspicious of the Transvaalers' every motive, in a score of years spent as a missionary among the Bamangwato in the north of Bechuanaland, Mackenzie had become an uncompromising imperialist who had urged Frere

to extend British rule all the way from the Cape to the Zambezi.
(In Pretoria he was known as the 'imperio-maniac'!) Following
the establishment of the freebooter states, he had been appointed
as British Agent for Bechuanaland to hold a watching brief over
British interests in the area. But he had used this office to try to
force the Imperial Government to intervene and evict every
Boer settler in Stellaland and Goshen and he had exceeded his
instructions in refusing to recognise the land titles which the
Boers held, even where these had been voluntarily granted by
the pro-Boer tribes. Without any proper authority he had
declared these lands to be under British imperial protection and
hoisted the Union Jack. And when he encountered a natural
reluctance on the part of the more reputable settlers to serve
him, he had appointed a group of men as guardians of the peace,
some of whom were no better than cattle-thieves and crooks.

Robinson, in his capacity as High Commissioner, had recalled
Mackenzie, after he had alienated every Boer in the area,
whereupon Rhodes had been sent to make his deal with van
Niekerk. But now, as Warren's chief adviser, Mackenzie saw his
opportunity to get his own back on the freebooters and to annul
Rhodes' agreement about land holdings; and fired by these
vindictive aims, he advanced with Warren into Bechuanaland in gleeful anticipation of the prospects before him. Rhodes
accompanied the expedition at the request of Robinson, who
felt it necessary to have someone to watch Warren carefully
and, if possible, to keep him in check. But his presence was to no
avail. For, as soon as Warren reached Stellaland, he took
Mackenzie's view about land titles, ignoring Rhodes' counsel;
and on this and every other issue, Rhodes found himself unable
to exercise any control over this high-handed pair.

Having thus rearoused the enmity of every Boer in the freebooter States, Warren marched on early in 1885, with Rhodes
and Mackenzie in tow, to hold a meeting with Kruger at Fourteen Streams on the Vaal river which was to settle the partition
lines. Whatever suspicions the Boers might have aroused by
their earlier attempts to move into Bechuanaland, Warren's
boorish behaviour at this encounter was inexcusable. Ever
since Kruger had withdrawn his annexation of Goshen, he and

his Government had genuinely tried to quieten the situation. When fighting had broken out between pro-Boer and pro-British tribes, he had enjoined on the Boers not to join in; and to those settlers whose lands lay outside the areas which the London Convention had awarded to the Transvaal, he had made it plain that no help or protection could now be expected from Pretoria. Indeed, once he saw that no further extension of his frontier in that direction would be admitted, he had actually urged the Cape Government to move in and annex all of Bechuanaland outside the Convention boundaries.

But Warren disregarded these substantial gestures, preferring to be guided by the prejudiced advice of the 'imperiomaniac', Mackenzie, whose very presence was an affront to the Boers, after his behaviour in Stellaland and Goshen. Also, despite an assurance from Kruger that there would be 'no collision', he arrived at the meeting with a powerful escort of imperial troops, thereby suggesting to the Boers that he either doubted Kruger's word and expected treachery or was hoping to cow them by a demonstration of armed force. According to Dr. Leyds who was present as Kruger's State Attorney, Warren's language during the conference was no less uncalled for than his actions beforehand. With dire threats he insisted that the South African Republic must prevent not only its burghers but also its natives from crossing into Bechuana territory because he had no land to offer them. Goshen, he insisted, must be cleared of Boers beyond the demarcation line and any Boer who stayed there after the boundaries had been drawn would be treated as a rebel. With even greater stupidity, when Kruger pointed out that some Goshenites, including their leader van Pittius, were not under Pretoria's jurisdiction as they were not citizens of the Transvaal, Warren retorted that any inhabitant of Goshen who was not either a Transvaaler or a British subject must be a robber.

In spite of this brutish behaviour by Britain's delegate, the Fourteen Streams Conference succeeded in establishing the boundaries of those portions of the two Republics which were to be included in the Transvaal under the London Convention. Agreement was also reached to invite President Brand to act as arbitrator in any future frontier disputes. But as if nothing had been settled, Warren hurried back to Stellaland and Goshen to declare martial law and demanded reinforcements of up to a thousand Cape police, on the grounds that bands of rebel Boers were conspiring against him in secret meetings and that he was in imminent danger of attack from the Transvaal. When Upington's Government refused to comply with this requisition, saying that there were scarcely that number of police in all of the Colony, he protested that his efforts to maintain law and order were being frustrated by Cape Ministers who favoured the 'rebels'. Then in a crowning act of idiocy and injustice he ordered the arrest of the Stellalanders' leader, van Niekerk, for the murder of a cattle-thief on such flimsy evidence that even Mackenzie was obliged to admit that there was no case against the man and that Warren's real purpose was to discourage the enemies of the Imperial Government from plotting against British supremacy.

This was the last straw for Upington and his colleagues, who now declared to Robinson that they could no longer attach any weight to Warren's statements or accept any responsibility for his actions. Likewise Rhodes threw in his hand and resigned his office as Deputy Commissioner for Bechuanaland. Never one to take kindly to serving under anyone else and filled with resentment that his demands for action by the colonial government to protect the road to the north had brought about this calamitous intervention of what he contemptuously called the 'Imperial Factor', he protested to the High Commissioner that his every promise to the Stellalanders had been broken and that Warren's actions, such as van Niekerk's arrest, had been as imbecile as they were illegal. Robinson, in his turn, reported to the Colonial Secretary that his emissary was causing widespread distrust and resentment among all the Dutch inhabitants of South Africa. He had ordered that Warren's proclamation of martial law be revoked. But, until the man was withdrawn, he could not, as High Commissioner, be held responsible for the consequences to Britain's relations with the Governments of the Transvaal, the Orange Free State, or even Cape Colony. Whether or not actual fighting would result from the current explosive situation,

Robinson concluded that Warren's activities meant that a large British force would have to be kept in Bechuanaland, which would impede annexation to the Cape and leave the Imperial Government with a costly and troublesome Protectorate.

Derby, indecisive as always, now seemed as unable to stop the imperial juggernaut as he had once been unwilling to start it. As Merriman had reported during his discussions in London about the future of Basutoland, Derby found the utmost difficulty in making decisions about South Africa, which he 'dreaded as a child dreads scalding water'. Unable therefore to bring himself to act on his High Commissioner's advice and recall Warren, he merely instructed him to consult Robinson whenever possible on questions of policy. But this turbulent officer was not to be checked by so light a rein. Charging northwards across the Molopo, he set about collecting concessions and making treaties with the Bechuana tribes right up to the Matabeleland border. Claiming that Khama, chief of the Bamangwato in the north of the territory, had offered him 80,000 square miles of land —including the Tati goldfields, which happened to be in Lobengula's domains—he declared a Protectorate over the whole of Bechuanaland, from which he insisted that all Boer colonists be excluded. Then, in a triumphant report to London, he proclaimed that he had pacified South Africa, crushed the seditious elements and rescued the Bechuana natives from oppression by Boer freebooters.

In fact, as the record in the Cape Archives shows, Warren's discussions with the Bechuana tribes were in marked contrast to his claim to have been greeted everywhere as a saviour of the Bantu. The octogenarian chief of the Bakwenas, Sechele, might have been converted to Christianity when Livingstone visited his kraal in the 1840s. But the arrival of this overbearing imperial officer aroused in him and his followers grave anxiety that those who had earlier redeemed his soul now coveted his lands. Sebele, his son and heir, went straight to the point, asking why Britain proposed to take the Bakwenas' country away from them. Warren answered that he was not trying to take away their country but was offering them the Queen's protection. 'What are we to be protected against?' asked Sebele. Against the Boer freebooters who had taken the Borolongs' lands down south, came the reply. To which the Bakwena chiefs rejoined that, unlike the Borolongs, they could protect themselves, provided they had powder and guns; and so long as they could protect themselves, they had no desire 'to become Britain's vassals as others have become vassals of the Transvaal, paying tribute.' But Warren was in no mood to listen to logical arguments, whether from Boer or Bantu lips. Brusquely retorting that the Bakwena chiefs talked too much and that it was nonsense to say that they needed no protection, he brought the discussion to a close. And a month later the Bakwenas, along with the other tribes beyond the Molopo, were willy-nilly brought under British protection.

All these proceedings caused a deplorable impression at the Cape, not only among the Bond and Cape Dutch, but also within the British community. Yet it was not until ten months after Warren had started on his rampage that the Imperial Government were finally persuaded to recall their high-handed emissary. Meanwhile, the Cape Assembly, from having only a few months earlier eagerly desired to advance the Colony's northern frontier, if only to protect its hinterland, had begun to fight shy of accepting any responsibility for governing the deeply embittered Boers of Bechuanaland. Upington too had become thoroughly disillusioned by the outcome of his appeal for imperial assistance. More significantly still for the future of South Africa, Warren's antics had converted Robinson to an aversion for the 'Imperial Factor' almost as profound as that of Rhodes himself.

Against such opposition the Imperial Government now urged in vain that the Colony should annexe what was left of the Stellaland and Goshen Republics. The Cape Government and Parliament would not hear of it. Whitehall should clear up irs own mess, they maintained, and not ask the Colony to do so. Thus, in September 1885, the Imperial Government were obliged to take on direct responsibility for the protection and administration of Bechuanaland, claiming the London Convention as their authority for so doing. On Robinson's advice, this huge territory was divided into two separate regions. The area lying to the south of the Molopo river—including those parts of Stellaland and Goshen which fell outside the boundaries agreed between Kruger and Warren—was proclaimed a Crown Colony with a resident Administrator, Judge Sidney Shippard, acting under the orders of the High Commissioner as 'Governor of British Bechuanaland'. The northern part from the Molopo to the Matabele border, but excluding the Tati area, was declared a British Protectorate and placed under the surveillance of Judge Shippard, with a resident 'Assistant Commissioner' in the person of the Rev. John Moffatt, whose father, the celebrated missionary, Dr. James Moffatt of Kuruman, had been the first European ever to visit Bechuanaland. These officials were, however, to hold little more than a watching brief and the Bechuana chiefs in the Protectorate were to be left to govern their tribes in their own fashion. For as Robinson recommended to Whitehall, this vast and largely desert area, with scarcely any surface water and no known minerals, held only one interest for Britain—the fact that it contained the road to the north which had to be protected against 'filibusters of foreign powers'.

Abandoned by Pretoria, the Boers of Goshen whom the London Convention had left outside the Transvaal's jurisdiction now returned whence they had come. But in Stellaland, where even Mackenzie once admitted that the freebooters were law-abiding and useful citizens who had in many cases acquired their lands legitimately, quite a number of them stayed and settled down under British rule. In fact, three years later, the situation in the areas embraced by the Crown Colony was to calm down to a point where the Cape Government, prompted by Rhodes, became converted to the idea of annexation. But, since humanitarian opinion in England insisted that, for the time being, direct rule would be more likely to ensure a fair deal for the natives than a colonial administration, it was not until 1895 that Rhodes, as Cape Premier, succeeded in obtaining the transfer of this territory to Cape Colony.

While the frontiers of British influence were thus being extended north of Cape Colony's borders, the Imperial and Cape Governments had been busily preempting territory in several other directions. For ever since Kruger, with more haste than judgement, had proclaimed the annexation of Goshen to the Transvaal, it had become an axiom of British policy to suspect every action of the Transvaalers, especially if it involved any dealings with Germany. The fact that in 1884, following the signature of the London Convention, Kruger had visited Germany and been fêted by the Emperor Wilhelm and his Chancellor, Bismarck, was now recalled as a highly sinister development. So was his decision to offer to a Dutch-German syndicate, the Netherlands Railway Company, a concession to build the Transvaal section of the Delagoa Bay railway. So too was the establishment, two months before the Germans took South-West Africa, of the so-called New Republic on Zulu territory with a claim to a frontier extending to the sea at St. Lucia Bay, the finest anchorage between Durban and Lourenço Marques.

As in the case of the Boer freebooters in Stellaland and Goshen, the territory acquired for the New Republic had been granted to Boer volunteers who had joined in internecine fighting between rival Zulu chieftains, on the promise of land from their protégé once he had defeated his opponent. Following the defeat and capture of Cetewayo, Zululand had been divided by its British conquerors into some thirteen different regions under semi-independent chiefs, in an attempt to deny any possibility of the Zulus recovering the unity which they had enjoyed in Chaka's day. In the event, the chaos and strife which this policy of balkanisation brought in its wake were so serious that the Imperial Government were obliged to restore Cetewayo to his throne. But even this move failed to produce peace and, as intertribal warring continued, several hundred Boers from the Transvaal, under one Lukas Meyer, moved in to take the pickings offered by the state of general confusion. And, in May 1884, Meyer and his followers established in the western areas of the Zulus' domains the so-called New Republic.

To begin with, apart from the Natal colonists who had designs on Zululand as a dumping ground for unwanted and undesirable Bantu from their own territory, scarcely a single British eyebrow was raised over Lukas Meyer's action. The Imperial Government saw no profit in opposing it, or for that matter in annexing Zululand with all its internecine troubles; and their views were shared by those in authority at the Cape. Even the Boers' claim to St. Lucia Bay was not at first taken seriously, having regard to the distance from the New Republic's frontiers to the coast and the fact that any access route would have to traverse large tracts of territory in the possession of Zulu factions still hostile to Boer encroachments. But within four months this state of untroubled apathy was transformed by Kruger's actions in Goshen. From then on, with the threat of the Boers from the Transvaal and the Germans from South-West Africa making common cause against British interests, the New Republic's claims appeared in an altogether more sinister light. And it was only a matter of weeks before suspicion ripened into certainty with the discovery that a German officer in the service of the South African Republic had obtained from a son of Cetewayo a large concession of land in the vicinity of St. Lucia Bay. The resemblance between this move and the tactics of Luderitz at Angra Pequena, leading to the German Protectorate over South-West Africa, was not lost on the Cape. Nor was it ignored in London, where the new Radical-Imperialist alliance was swinging into action bent on pushing Gladstone's Government into expanding Britain's frontiers in South Africa at almost any cost.

Derby now came under mounting pressure from these parliamentary forces to make a stand in South Africa. For a brief while, Gladstone continued to mutter that he welcomed the Germans 'as our neighbours in South Africa or even as the neighbours of the Transvaal'; and Derby declined a request for British protection from the Hereros beyond the Orange as involving Britain in a commitment too near to German territory to be 'in accordance with international comity'. But opinion at home and in the Cape was not long to be gainsaid; and in December 1884, amid loud but unavailing protests from the New Republic, the Imperial Government annexed St. Lucia Bay, by virtue of a treaty signed in the forties by the Zulu King, Panda. Then in the following month, they declared a Protectorate over the coast of Pondoland, where German officers had been reported to be seeking concessions from the native chiefs;

and the Cape Government played their part by annexing to the Colony the rest of the 'vacant' Transkei territories—Galekaland and Tembuland—and by taking over full responsibility for Walvis Bay. Two years later, Britain finished the job by annexing the remains of Zululand and handing it over to Natal; and by way of a consolation prize for the Boers, who had once more been shut off from the sea, official British recognition was conferred on the land-locked New Republic.

So it came about that, in the middle eighties, a Liberal Government put aside their dislike of imperial ventures and launched Britain on a course of expansion in southern Africa from which there was to be no more turning back. By the start of 1887, the vacant spaces on the coast from the Orange river estuary round to Delagoa Bay had been filled; a wedge had been driven between the Germans in South-West Africa and the Boers of Kruger's Republic; the road to the north had been secured; and the way was open for Britain, through the agency of Cecil Rhodes, to stake her claims up to and even beyond the Zambezi. Well might Robinson have remarked on the irony that Gladstone's Government, having been elected on a 'platform of curtailing imperial responsibilities', had added 'more to them than any previous Ministry in the present century'.

But if the cause, or at least the pretext, for all this expansion had been the suspicion engendered in British hearts by the actions of Kruger and the Germans, the manner in which it had been achieved was to leave an indelible mark upon the Transvaalers and, more particularly, upon their stubborn and suspicious President. Kruger might have started the sequence of events by his unwise and untimely decision to annexe Goshen to the Transvaal. But by ignoring or distorting his subsequent efforts to prevent his citizens causing trouble for the British or the Bantu beyond his borders and by brushing aside the Transvaalers' legitimate rights in order to advance Britain's frontiers, the Imperial Government and their agents had reopened the wounds of Slachter's Nek. The patchwork surgery of the London Convention had been in vain, and deep in their hearts the Boers now knew that ere long they would have to fight once again to keep their independence.

8 Gold and the Rise of the Rand

THE rush of events which accompanied Britain's great leap forward in the middle eighties was to transform the scene in South Africa. From then on the pace quickened immeasurably as changes in the economic balance of power whetted the appetites and hardened the attitudes of the protagonists. Preeminent in this momentous catalogue were the discovery of gold in huge abundance in the Transvaal and the emergence of Cecil Rhodes as the paramount influence in Cape politics.

Few political figures can have achieved their ascendancy by more methodical planning and systematic thrust than Rhodes. From his election to the Cape Assembly in 1881 onwards, he used his prodigious fortune to advance his political prospects with the same determined drive that won him his diamond monopoly at Kimberley. Opponents, actual or potential, were bought off with share offers in his various enterprises; others were won over by the grandeur of his schemes; and to ensure adequate advertisement for his political views and his expansionist designs he bought a controlling share in no less than six newspapers of the *Cape Argus* group. But perhaps the cleverest of all his preparations was to be found in the selection of his political allies, of whom the three most important and influential were Robinson and his deputy, Commander Graham Bower, who held the post of Imperial Secretary to the High Commissioner, and Jan Hofmeyr, the founder and leader of the Afrikaner Bond.

As Rhodes knew full well, Robinson and Bower were essential to his plans, because of the key positions which they occupied at the Cape and because, with Bechuanaland and the road to the north under the Imperial Government's protection, he had to secure their approval for his designs in the lands that lay beyond. More important still, both of these men were in sympathy with Rhodes' partiality for using colonial agencies to expand British rule in South Africa and shared his distaste for intervention by the 'Imperial Factor'. Robinson's career as a colonial administrator had taken him to the West Indies, Hong Kong, Malaya and Ceylon, after which it had followed much the same lines as that of Sir George Grey, in that before coming to the Cape he had for eight years served as Governor of New South Wales and, more briefly, of New Zealand. Like Grey, his kindly and unpompous nature had led him to a warm understanding of the sensibilities of colonial settlers and it did not need Warren's antics in Bechuanaland to convince him that imperial intervention all too often did more harm than good.

Indeed, so much did Robinson seem to some people at Westminster and in Whitehall to favour colonial interests and Rhodes' schemes at the expense of imperial designs that, had he not been succeeded by a thorough-going imperialist, the offices of Cape Governor and High Commissioner for South Africa might well have been separated after his departure, leaving future Governors confined in the squat white mansion beside the avenue of van Riebeeck's oaks to performing such mundane duties as opening and proroguing Parliament and commuting or confirming sentences on convicted criminals. For, towards the end of Robinson's reign, a powerful movement grew up in England in favour of divorcing the High Commissioner from the influence of those who ran the self-governing Colony and who, so long as this office was combined with the governorship, would be liable to make their will prevail not only in the Cape, but in the domains beyond for which the High Commissioner was responsible. To guard against this risk and to ensure that the interests of the Crown in southern Africa would not go by default, an all-party 'South Africa Committee' was formed, which influential group included among its leading lights no less of a budding imperialist than Joseph Chamberlain, along with a number of other prominent political figures.

Rhodes' other essential ally was J. H. Hofmeyr, the founder and leader of the Afrikaner Bond. With the English party in the Cape currently divided between moderates and chauvinists, Liberals and Imperial Leaguers, Rhodes saw the Bond as a compact and homogeneous body led by the most effective politician in South Africa who, for all his talk of creating a new Afrikaner patriotism, wanted to maintain South Africa's connections with Britain, if only because she held the command of the seas. Rhodes saw something else as well in the Bond's political programme which he could turn to his own advantage. Hofmeyr was a dedicated protectionist whose main interest was to shield the Dutch farmers and wine-growers in the Cape against foreign competition. Here therefore were all the makings of a bargain between these two aspiring politicians; and as always quick to seize his opportunities, Rhodes made a deal with Hofmeyr by which each undertook to support the other's policies. Rhodes pledged his backing for a protectionist tariff, while Hofmeyr promised to put no obstacle in the way of Rhodes' plans for expansion in the north.

For Hofmeyr such an undertaking represented a remarkable volte-face. Only a short while before, he had opposed Rhodes' efforts to bring the Stellalanders under Cape rule, because he regarded Bechuanaland as an area into which the Transvaalers had every right to expand. Yet now he was prepared to take on trust Rhodes' protestations of friendship for the Afrikaner, little knowing that, even as their alliance was taking shape, Rhodes was writing to tell his friends in England that, far from having become 'pro-Boer', his pact with Hofmeyr merely meant that he wanted to get the Cape Dutch onto his side for as long as he needed their support for his designs in the north. For Rhodes had convinced him that his brand of colonialism was, to say the least, preferable to the overbearing behaviour of the Imperial Government as had been shown by such men as Carnarvon, Frere and Warren.

But whatever Hofmeyr might himself believe, he was not going to persuade anyone in Pretoria to share his trust in

Rhodes. Recent events in Bechuanaland had rearoused too much suspicion of all that Britain represented and few, if any, Transvaalers were prepared to draw fine distinctions between colonialism and imperialism. Inevitably, therefore, Hofmeyr's compact cost him the friendship and trust of the Transvaal Boers, and especially of Kruger who, with more prescience than the Bond's leader, had decided that Rhodes, for all his obvious distaste for Warren's high-handed behaviour at Fourteen Streams, was at heart no friend of the Republics. Nevertheless, greatly to his credit, Hofmeyr ignored his Transvaal critics and kept to his bargain for all of ten years, until the dire duplicity of the Jameson Raid finally tore away the veil and revealed his partner as a double-dealing megalomaniac, whose real purpose was not only to grab the north, but also to force the Boer Republics by subversion and conquest into a British-ruled South Africa.

For the moment, therefore, Rhodes could feel sure of the support of Hofmeyr who controlled the Cape Dutch vote and of the High Commissioner and his principal lieutenant who controlled the road to Eldorado. What he now needed was to secure the necessary concessions beyond the Limpopo and to persuade the Imperial Government to issue a formal charter which would enable him to annex and govern the northern territories on which he had set his sights. But even as he was contemplating this next move, an event occurred in the heart of the Transvaal which was to transform the balance of economic power in South Africa—the discovery of the gold fields of the Witwatersrand—or, as it came to be called, the 'Rand'—a few miles to the south of Pretoria.

This was not the first time that gold had been found in the Transvaal. But on each previous occasion, after the inevitable rush, accompanied by a minor Stock Exchange boom, the supply had in due course petered out and the speculators and prospectors had drifted away, disconsolate and impoverished. The first of these discoveries had occurred in the Lydenburg area in the seventies, some four years after the first diamonds had been found at Kimberley. A rush of diggers, mostly Australians and New Zealanders, had followed from Natal.

But their most significant achievement had been to make themselves so thoroughly objectionable to the Boer authorities, with their threats to take over the area and put it under the British flag, that Kruger was forever afterwards to distrust all prospectors regardless of their origins and character.

Ten years later another and more promising find had been made at what was to become the township of Barberton, near the Swaziland border. A new rush followed, claims were pegged, companies were floated and thousands of shares printed. A local Stock Exchange was established and investors in Britain fell over themselves to buy the shares, many of them in the belief that they were investing in the newly re-discovered mines of King Solomon. But initial hopes soon proved illusory. Only five of the Barberton mines made any real profit and, as the boom collapsed, most of the shares became valueless. In fact Barberton became such a dirty word that for several years to come British investors treated all so-called gold mines with the utmost circumspection.

Thus when the new discovery of gold on the Rand was first announced, the news was greeted with little enthusiasm by those who had already burned their fingers in earlier speculations. But one man in Kimberley, J. B. Robinson, who had been squeezed out of the diamond business by Rhodes' amalgamation project, decided to retrieve his fortunes in gold. Forming a partnership with Alfred Beit, under the name of the Robinson Syndicate, he became the first large-scale investor in the new gold fields. Rhodes, at this stage, held aloof, as did many other British investors. For one thing, he preferred to concentrate on the bird in the hand that was the Kimberley diamond industry. For another, he was convinced that the riches of the Rand would prove as illusory as those of earlier finds and that the real Eldorado lay to the north in Lobengula's country.

Robinson, therefore, obtained first choice of the ground, an opening which he exploited with such skill and foresight that, before long, he had made a fortune worth several million pounds. And when Rhodes sought to retrieve his lost opportunity by proposing an amalgamation of the gold mines similar to that of the diamond fields of Kimberley, Robinson held most of the trump cards and was well able to fend him off. Hard as Rhodes tried, through their mutual partner, Beit, to bring his rival to terms, Robinson held out, secure in the knowledge that he had two shares for every one owned by Beit. For once in his life, therefore, Rhodes found himself unable to buy out a competitor and had to be content with forming his own company— the Goldfields of South Africa, later to become the Consolidated Goldfields—which he endowed with the same powers to annexe and govern territory that were written into the Trust Deeds of his De Beers Company.

But whatever opportunities Rhodes might personally have missed, the Rand gold fields had come to stay; and nothing would ever be quite the same again in South Africa. From a state of chronic semi-bankruptcy, the Transvaal was henceforth to become the richest country of the entire continent, let alone of South Africa; and as the centre of gravity shifted to Kruger's Republic, Cape Colony was slowly but surely to lose its claim to unrivalled paramountcy.

Formerly the Transvaal had been a pastoral state with an exclusively Afrikaner population consisting almost entirely of 'sons of the soil'. So simple and insular was the outlook of most of its peasantry that, although many of them had for long known from casual finds—such as veins of gold in the stonework of a Rand farm-house or gold-bearing pebbles lying out on the veldt—that their lands contained rich mineral deposits, they had for as long as possible kept this knowledge to themselves, for fear of attracting undesirable foreigners to their country. Now, however, there was no disguising the wealth of the Rand. A new influx of foreign prospectors, speculators and miners moved in from Kimberley, the Cape, Natal and, as confidence grew with increasing discoveries, from England, America, Australia, Germany and other lands across the seas. The 'Uitlanders', as these newcomers were called, had arrived. And with their arrival the new township of Johannesburg began to sprout as a hideous tin shanty-town, perched on a bleak plateau 6,000 feet above sea level, an eyesore of squalor, intersected by latrine trenches and infested by gangs of 'bummers' seeking to trap the unwary into buying dud claims. Bars sprang up almost as fast as houses, accompanied by a rash of brothels, as prostitutes moved in to garner the pickings of the new gold rush. The few hotels were so crowded that many of their guests had to sleep on tables or the floor. 'Worse than Kimberley', was Merriman's outraged comment, 'yes, a great deal worse . . . a loafing, drinking, scheming lot . . . a society (which) would corrupt an archangel or at any rate knock a good deal of the bloom off its wings', and which, judged by the never-ending talk of investments, seemed to be composed 'exclusively of millionaires . . . seedy individuals talking glibly of thousands of pounds in a little shanty that would not be considered a decent place for a stable.'

In fact, among all the riff-raff which the Rand was to lure from the far corners of the globe, there were also many decent straight-dealing citizens who cared for more than just a quick and easy profit. But if a Cape Liberal like Merriman felt as he did about the new influx of Uitlanders, it is hardly surprising that Kruger should have been as suspicious of their presence as he was outraged by their worship of Mammon. At heart a typical peasant, he never really understood and certainly never liked the gold mining community. Johannesburg was for him an evil place full of evil people and he judged the Uitlanders as a whole by the conduct of their worst elements. With the memory still fresh of the diggers from Natal with their threats against the Boer authorities in Lydenburg, he regarded this new influx of foreigners to the Rand as a flock of vultures—'aasvoels'—who had no rights to the same status as his burghers. And in a famous speech uttered a few years later, he minced no words in emphasising the distinction which he drew between the Afrikaners and these new alien residents. 'People of the Lord, you old people of the country', he said by way of greeting the burghers in his audience; and then turning to the Uitlanders, he burst out, 'You foreigners, you newcomers, yes, even you thieves and murderers'. Likewise, he was wont to say, prophetically enough, that every ounce of gold would have to be weighed in 'rivers of tears' and that the blood of thousands of Boers would be spilled to defend their soil 'from the lust of others yearning for its abundant yellow metal.'

Nevertheless Kruger was not so unworldly that he failed to

appreciate that, whatever 'thieves and murderers' it had brought to the Rand, the discovery of gold had come at a highly opportune moment for the economy of his Republic. At the beginning of 1885 the treasury was virtually empty, the government's credit with the Standard Bank was exhausted and further advances had been refused. The rigid system of protection imposed since the War of Independence had failed to create a thriving home industry and economy. On the contrary, a veritable rash of small uneconomic industries had resulted from a system which failed to benefit the people of the Transvaal and only irritated their neighbour states. Likewise, the Government's scheme of granting special concessions for the import of certain unfinished goods and for other things such as the manufacture of dynamite had proved expensive and counter-productive. The concession holders abused their privileges by importing virtually finished goods and maintaining artificially high prices by a vicious system of monopolies; and although the scheme helped the authorities to maintain revenue without raising taxes, it became thoroughly detested by producers and consumers alike.

Added to this, the introduction of Dutchmen direct from Holland, and even Germans, to staff the higher echelons of the Government had caused much popular criticism. Soon after the Transvaal regained its independence, Kruger came to realise that he could not run his administration solely with the aid of his burghers, whose simple patriotism and peasant background were not equal to the complex tasks of governing the adolescent Republic. Unlike Brand in the Orange Free State, he refused to bring in men from the Cape, however qualified they might be. For Cape men were all suspect in Kruger's eyes as agents of a power with evil designs upon the Transvaal. And in the circumstances, it seemed only logical to employ Hollanders, such as Dr. Leyds who was brought to Pretoria in 1883 to be State Attorney at the age of twenty-four. But such logic had little appeal for the burghers who felt slighted by the preferment of these outsiders from Europe who, with no roots in the soil, could never really understand the people whom they were called upon to govern.

Worst of all the problems of Kruger's Republic in the middle eighties was the financial predicament which was threatening to extinguish the one slender hope of making a reality of the independence which the Boers had won. For want of money, the Netherlands Railway Company had not been able to make a start on the Transvaal section of the Delagoa Bay railway; and to make matters even more depressing, the concessionaire, to whom the Portuguese had entrusted on a 99-year lease the construction and operation of the Mozambique section of the line, a dubious American company promoter called Colonel Edward McMurdo, had failed to advance more than a few miles from Lourenço Marques. Indeed, with the Transvaal Government unable to raise a loan for as little as £5,000, it had seemed at the beginning of 1886 that there would be no hope of avoiding almost total dependence on the Cape or Natal for an outlet for the trade of the Republic. This would have been an intolerable subservience at any time. At this moment, when Kruger had decided in the light of recent British actions in Bechuanaland to order quantities of arms from Europe, for the defence of the Republic, it would be to offer virtual surrender.

Nevertheless, there was no escaping the fact that, while the Transvaal had not started building its railway to the sea, both the Cape and Natal rail systems were inching ever closer to the Republics. The Cape railways had reached Kimberley and Aliwal North on the western and southern borders of the Free State; and the Natalians, fearing that a Transvaal-Delagoa Bay line would spell ruin for the port of Durban, had for the last ten years been striving to build a railway to link Natal with Bloemfontein and Pretoria. Moreover, the attitude of Bloemfontein was in these matters more encouraging to the Cape than to Kruger. The Free Staters might not want to let down their kinsmen across the Vaal. But at the same time they could not afford to fall out with Cape Colony, on whose ports and railways the economic life of their state depended, least of all at a time when the Transvaalers had no alternative railway facilities to offer, still less any outlet to the sea.

At that point, Kruger had therefore had no option but to throw himself on the mercies of the Cape; and in January 1886, he informed Upington's Government that he was ready to join a customs union and to agree to the extension of the Kimberley line to Pretoria. Brand promptly suggested that thought be given to developing Kruger's offer into a general tariff agreement for South Africa, hoping to reconcile the Free State's divergences with the Transvaal in some such wider economic union. Rhodes too urged the Cape Government to accept what he saw as a chance to lay the foundations of a South African federation under Cape leadership. But Upington dithered and, in doing so, cast aside a unique opportunity. For, before his successor, Sprigg, could take up Kruger's proposal, towards the end of the same year the Rand had revealed its new wealth and the Transvaalers' hopes of building their own railway to Delagoa Bay were splendidly reborn. With the gold boom at full blast, the Netherlands Railway Company now bent to their task and even the dilatory McMurdo became momentarily galvanised into activity at the Mozambique end of the line.

Hofmeyr promptly appealed to Kruger not to withdraw what was an essentially sensible proposal for a customs union simply because he was no longer obliged to put it forward by the indigent state of his treasury. But Kruger was in no mood to listen to such advice. Circumstances had changed; and he now had no need to beg favours from the Cape. With the revenues from the gold fields he would be able to build his railway to Delagoa Bay and so to gain at least a semi-independent outlet to the sea. He would not therefore revive his offer of a customs union until he was in a position to make his own conditions. In fact, far from hearkening to appeals to join with the British Colonies in creating a wider unity in South Africa, Kruger soon set about trying to detach the Free Staters from their ties with the Cape. In October 1887, at a meeting with the Free State President, he offered to conclude a military alliance and tried to persuade Brand not to admit any rail extensions from the Cape onto Free State territory for at least another ten years, in return for financial compensation for any losses suffered by retaliation from the Colony.

These advances were, however, somewhat premature. Brand refused to be drawn into such an exclusive relationship with

Kruger's Republic. He had taken exception to the behaviour of some of the freebooters in Goshen and he had no desire to ally himself too closely with a regime which countenanced such potential trouble-makers. Nor did he see any gain in antagonising opinion at the Cape where, he was satisfied, the combination of Robinson, Hofmeyr and the Bond could be relied upon to act as a counter-weight to the more violent chauvinist and anti-Boer influences in the Colony. Therefore disregarding Kruger's overtures, he persuaded his Volksraad to sanction the extension of the Cape railway system as far as Bloemfontein. More than this, he proposed a commercial conference with the Cape and Natal which resulted early in 1888 in a customs union of the Free State and Cape Colony.

But a few months afterwards, Brand died and was succeeded by Francis Reitz, an Afrikaner whose nationalist views inclined him to look more to Pretoria than to Cape Town for support. Quickly sensing his opportunity, Kruger resurrected the proposals which Brand had turned down and, in March 1889, he persuaded the newly installed Free State President to sign a military alliance with the Transvaal. He also induced Reitz to allow Pretoria the right to veto any extension of the Cape Railway beyond Bloemfontein until such time as the Delagoa Bay Railway had reached within two hundred miles of the Transvaal capital.

Kruger had secured his southern flank; and with his treasury beginning to swell with the revenues from the gold fields, he now felt strong enough to state his terms to Britain. First and foremost, he made it clear that he had to have a seaport of his own. Given such an outlet for his Republic, which would enable him to talk on level terms with the British Colonies in South Africa, he would be prepared to enter a customs union with the Cape. But so long as he remained hemmed in 'as it were in a kraal', he would make no such concession. As for rail extensions from the Cape, once the Delagoa Bay line was within two hundred miles of Pretoria and his independent access to the coast was assured, he would admit the railway from Bloemfontein, but not before. For good measure, he said he would also allow the Cape the benefits of free trade with the Transvaal.

If such terms had been suggested a few years earlier, they would have been totally and immediately dismissed by both the Cape and the Imperial Governments acting upon the absolute and unquestionable rule that the Boers must be kept from the coast. But by the late eighties the situation had changed in two important respects. For one thing, the Transvaal was now clearly strong enough to set its own conditions for making a deal with the Cape. For another, the waxing political influence of Rhodes had brought about a significant change of British tactics in dealing with the Boer Republics. Political paramountcy remained the overriding aim. But as a means to this end, a new concept of an economic union of South Africa had come to the fore, in place of the old Carnarvon policy of an imposed political federation, *tout court*. Hence Rhodes' urgent plea that Upington should close with Kruger when, three years earlier, the Transvaal President had unconditionally offered to join a customs union and to admit the Cape railway to Pretoria. And although Kruger's newly acquired wealth and power had saved him from having tamely to surrender his Republic's independence, Rhodes remained dedicated to the new tactic of inveigling the Boers into a customs and railway agreement. Indeed the Rand's new-found prosperity had if anything, made him keener than ever on the idea. For, as he saw it, within such an arrangement, the Transvaal would offer new markets and opportunities for investment for the Cape and Natal, whereas if it remained outside, Kruger's Republic might swiftly become a threat to British paramountcy in South Africa.

To this view Rhodes was able without much difficulty to convert both the High Commissioner and Hofmeyr, while Sprigg, as in most things, was happy to follow suit. And in his turn Robinson succeeded in winning the support of the new Conservative Colonial Secretary, Lord Knutsford, a man of considerable experience of colonial affairs who had served under Carnarvon as a departmental official before entering politics. Knutsford readily saw the advantages of bringing the South African Republic into an economic union with the Cape. Certainly he much preferred this idea to the expense of having to buy the Mozambique section of the Delagoa Bay railway, which

Sprigg's representative in London had recently suggested as an alternative means of bringing pressure to bear on Kruger. Besides, Britain's trade with South Africa had risen from £2,000,000 a year in the 1850s to £14,000,000 in 1887, and closer economic ties within the area would presumably lead to an even greater increase.

Thus when Kruger put forward his terms in April 1889, Robinson and Rhodes promptly applied their minds to the possibilities of making a deal with him which would bring an economic federation into being, while conceding the minimum of additional independence to the Transvaal. One such method was to come to some agreement about Swaziland. The independence of the Swazis had been guaranteed by the London Convention. Yet, if Kruger were to gain access to the sea, there was only one possible route for him to take. Now that the Portuguese had made good their claims to the Mozambique coast down to Delagoa Bay and the British had annexed all Zululand up to the Tonga border, that route lay through Swaziland and Tongaland to Kosi Bay. Kruger had had his eye on Kosi Bay for some considerable time. But, while this valuable natural harbour and its Tonga hinterland were as yet unannexed by either Portugal or Britain, he was still bound by the London Convention to secure British permission before he could negotiate for any concessions with the native tribes to the east of the Transvaal. Besides, Tongaland was now a British sphere of influence. On more than one count, therefore, the Imperial Government could veto any move by the Boers to induce the Swazis and Tongas to grant them access to Kosi Bay; and while Kruger, thanks to the revenues of the Rand, was now in a much stronger position to bargain with Britain than before, he was still very far from holding all the trumps.

Moreover, even as Kruger was making his bid for a seaport, yet another delay occurred in the construction of the Mozambique section of the Delagoa Bay line. The ostensible reason was an abnormally heavy rainfall which gave rise to serious floods. But in fact, it was becoming progressively more obvious that McMurdo was more interested in trading his concession than in building a railway; and since the Mozambique section of the line comprised seven-eighths of the total stretch from Pretoria to Delagoa Bay, this new delay boded ill for the Transvaal. To speed things up, Kruger tried to buy out McMurdo's company for a million pounds. But his manoeuvre was thwarted by a temporary recession of the gold boom on the Rand which brought with it another credit squeeze.

The situation was somewhat eased when, a few months later, the Portuguese Government lost patience with McMurdo, revoked his concession and took over the construction of the Mozambique line. But, even with a new sense of urgency in Lourenço Marques, it was bound to take time for any substantial progress on the railway to materialise. Meanwhile the Transvaal's negotiating position would not be improved. Nevertheless Kruger still held one valuable card in his hand. This was the right of the Transvaal to expand towards the north which the London Convention had omitted to make subject to British approval. Unlike on the east and west of the Transvaal's borders, the Boers could engage in making treaties and seeking concessions from the native tribes north of the Limpopo, without first having to obtain Britain's approval.

Kruger had, in fact, already exercised his rights in this area by despatching Piet Grobler in July 1887 to negotiate a treaty with Lobengula, which Grobler claimed had resulted in the King happily agreeing that burghers from the Transvaal should be allowed to settle north of the Limpopo, under the jurisdiction of a Consul of the South African Republic who would reside at the Matabele capital. At the same time, it was no secret that Rhodes had set his sights on Matabeleland and Mashonaland, convinced that he would find there the 'New Rand' which would far outshine the gold fields of the Transvaal in wealth and so prevent the centre of economic gravity in South Africa from shifting to Kruger's Republic. True, Robinson had not at first shown much concern over the Grobler treaty and had, in fact, announced that the Transvaal had a right to have a window open to the north. But Kruger knew all too well that the High Commissioner was very susceptible to Rhodes' influence and it therefore came as no surprise to him when subsequently a British emissary was sent to pledge Lobengula not to cede any part of his kingdom without the sanction of the Imperial Government.

Nor was this British move any real disappointment to Kruger's plans. For while he had thought it wise to establish his right to make treaties in this area, in fact, the north was the last direction in which he wished to see his Republic expand. The Matabeles, as the trekkers had found out many years earlier when they had met them in the Transvaal, were no less tough and hostile than their Zulu cousins in the east. And although there were some Boers like Joubert who were prepared to risk the dangers of Boer settlement in the north, Kruger personally preferred that his burghers should confine themselves to hunting expeditions and he certainly had no wish to establish sovereignty there. For, having driven the Matabeles beyond the Limpopo in 1837, any suggestion that the Boers were threatening to displace them yet again would, he feared, drive them to desperate and dangerous retaliations. Besides, when signing over his country as a British sphere of influence, Lobengula had seen fit to repudiate the Grobler treaty, even denying its very existence. Also, to clinch the argument against Boer settlement in the north, there was the barrier of the tsetse belt in the Limpopo valley which meant that to reach Matabeleland and Mashonaland from the Transvaal with certainty and safety, let alone to maintain regular communications, it would be necessary to approach via Bechuana territory on the west, which was now a British Protectorate.

Kruger, therefore, knew that, in offering to renounce his right to expand northwards and so to leave the way clear for Rhodes, he had a concession, which it would cost him little or nothing to make, but which the British might want seriously enough to give him in exchange a road through Swaziland to the sea. Moreover, when he duly played this card in May 1889, the reaction of the High Commissioner suggested that it might well gain him the trick. Robinson considered access to Kosi Bay a fair and reasonable exchange for the renunciation of the north. Nor was he greatly concerned about letting the Boers into Swaziland to build their railway to the coast. Although the Natal colonists had repeatedly suggested that Swaziland be annexed, he had poohpoohed the idea, saying that the country was in any case totally inaccessible to British troops. The only approach to the territory which did not involve crossing one of the Transvaal's boundaries lay across the fever-stricken marshes of Tongaland and a series of mountain passes with no roads.

Robinson had in fact suggested to London two years before that the Swazi King, Umbandine, who had created appalling confusion in his kingdom by granting concessions right, left and centre to unscrupulous speculators and prospectors from the Transvaal and Natal, would be well advised to 'place himself under the Government of the South African Republic', whose proffered assurances for the protection of native interests seemed perfectly satisfactory. Unlike the Zulus, the Swazis had no coastline and were separated from the sea by many square miles of territory under different rulers. Access to Swaziland would therefore give the Boers no automatic passport to the coast and, to build their railway to Kosi Bay, they would still require the agreement of the Tonga Queen and of two extremely independent chieftains, Zambaan and Umbigesa, whose territories lay across their route.

Besides, Britain had recognised the New Republic to the south of the Swaziland border, even though it owed its inception very largely to the activities of Boer freebooters who had joined in the civil war between rival Zulu factions; and the Imperial Government had raised no objection when soon afterwards Lukas Meyer's creation was incorporated in the Transvaal. True, certain Zulu chiefs had protested against the establishment of this alien enclave and, claiming to be 'brave and loyal friends of the English Government', had asked for British protection. But Derby, as the reigning Colonial Secretary, had refused to intervene. And it was only when Lukas Meyer was reported to be seeking an arrangement with Cetewayo's successors to extend his territory as far as the coast that the Imperial Government had finally bowed to parliamentary pressures from Natal and annexed Zululand in 1887.

Apart from all this, the Boers could fairly claim, ever since 1846, to have been the protectors of the Swazis against their Bantu neighbours. As recently as the early seventies, they had entertained Swazi appeals for help against the ravages of Cetewayo. Kruger even contended that in 1875, on the death of the founding father, Umswazi, his son and heir, Umbandine, had confirmed at his coronation that the Swazi people were subjects of the Transvaal, though with full autonomy in internal affairs. Moreover, the Boer farmers who had established themselves in Swaziland had behaved in exemplary fashion, had not taken any unfair advantage of the tribes and had utilised the country's green hill-pastures in accordance with properly agreed leaseholds which allowed them to graze their herds during the winter months when the high veldt of the Transvaal was dry and arid. All things considered, there was some justification for the Boers to argue that, far from making trouble in the area, they had in fact 'put an end to the internal disturbances by which the Swazis would have exterminated themselves'. Kruger no doubt overstated his case when he said that prior to 1881, Swaziland had belonged to the Republic. But, historically speaking, the Transvaal had more right than anyone else to make Swaziland a Protectorate, and could certainly claim the right to make it a staging-post for a route to the sea.

Nevertheless, things were to go by no means as easily for Kruger as the first reactions from Cape Town seemed to suggest. For one thing, Robinson, now ageing and anxious for retirement, was on the point of departure from South Africa; and although it was generally hoped that he would eventually return after a well-earned respite, he deliberately put paid to any extension of his governorship by publicly condemning the intervention of the 'Imperial Factor' in South African affairs as soon as he reached home. Apart from this, there was the opposition of Natal to Boer expansion in this area to be taken into account. The Natalians had never really accepted Britain's recognition of Lukas Meyer's New Republic; and they still wanted to see Swaziland annexed as British territory. This aspiration had been denied them by the steadfast refusal of the Imperial Government to add the Swazis to their growing list of responsibilities. But in 1887 in the same year as Zululand was annexed, the Governor of Natal, Sir Arthur Havelock, was authorised to sign a treaty with Queen Zambili of Tongaland, after she had appealed for British help against Portuguese encroachments on her northern borders. By this compact the Tongas were bound not to have dealings with the Boers without Britain's consent. True, the treaty had not been followed up by any British move to annexe Tongaland, Queen Zambili having made it clear that she had no wish for a formal Protectorate. But since Kosi Bay provided Tongaland's main outlet to the sea, Havelock's action had put yet another obstacle between the Transvaalers and the coast.

Moreover, at this point, a fresh complication arose to thwart Kruger's plans for a seaport of his own. Umbandine, hoping to win favours on both sides, decided to play a double game. When, for instance, he was confronted with a British remonstrance for having received a representative of the Transvaal at his kraal, he would pretend that he had been led to believe that his visitor was an official of the Natal Government. And after a poll of Europeans in his country had shown a majority of three to one in favour of Transvaal rule, he was to be found simultaneously assuring the Boers that he wanted their protection and complaining to the British of his treatment by the Boers.

Inevitably these complaints stirred protests in England against any idea of the Transvaal having a right of way through Swaziland and encouraged the Natalians ever more vigorously to campaign for annexation. A few months later, the Swazi King's death—probably from alcoholic poisoning—put an end to this duplicity. But by that time the damage had been done; Robinson had left South Africa; and the Imperial Government found themselves faced with mounting pressures against allowing the Boers to rule over any more tribal areas. The Transvaal, it was said, had conspired with the Portuguese to carve up the Swazi Kingdom between them under a secret treaty in 1869 and had later tried to take over the country by buying off Umbandine with a pension of £2,000 a year. Wherefore the Pretoria Convention had specifically ruled out Transvaal sovereignty. Moreover, the humanitarians and imperialists argued, the Swazis had shown their friendship for Britain by helping Sir Garnet Wolseley finally to dispose of Sekukuni and it was unthinkable that they should be handed over to the Boers, even

C. J. Rhodes

Jan Hofmeyr

as part of a bargain to gain undisputed access to the north.

Opinion at the Cape, on the other hand, was currently a lot less dogmatic about these issues. Strongly influenced by Rhodes, there was a growing feeling that, in return for renouncing Boer claims to the north and agreeing to join a customs union, Kruger should be allowed to negotiate with the tribes concerned the necessary cessions of territory to build his railway to Kosi Bay and that the Transvaal should govern the Europeans in Swaziland in keeping with their expressed desires. The all-important thing, according to this school of thought, was for Britain to secure 'unhampered' control beyond the Limpopo, not to cling to 'doubtful possession' of a territory of so little profit or accessibility as Swaziland. As for Kosi Bay, it was argued that, contrary to traditional doctrine, a seaport in the hands of the Boers could, in effect, be a tactical asset, in that it would enable Britain to 'coerce them cheaply if necessary and . . . would pave the way for the ultimate establishment of a virtual dominion of South Africa under the British flag'.

Not unnaturally, however, Knutsford was more susceptible to the pressures of Westminster than he was to the arguments of Cape politicians. Faced with the protests of the humanitarian-imperialist alliance in Parliament and the press, he could not bring himself to accept Kruger's proposals or to concede exclusive Boer control over any aspect of the administration of Swaziland however many warranties Pretoria might offer that native interests would remain unaffected. At the same time, realising the importance of gaining unimpeded access to the north, the Colonial Secretary hesitated to reject such terms out of hand. As a temporising device he therefore agreed to establish an Anglo-Boer Commission to enquire into the situation and determine the real desires of the Swazi people. But with the Europeans in Swaziland persisting in their determination to be governed solely by the Transvaal, the best that the Commission could do was to suggest that they be placed under joint rule, pending a final settlement.

In December 1889, Britain and the Transvaal agreed to put the Commission's recommendation into effect. But no sooner had the Swazi problem been shelved by the establishment of the

Anglo-Boer administration than another issue arose to add to British suspicions of Boer motives. For, at this point, a Transvaaler of British origins, named Bowler, announced that he intended to lead a Boer trek across the Limpopo into Mashonaland. For Rhodes, this was the very type of threat to the north which he had hoped to exclude by giving Kruger his own way in Swaziland. In a state of great apprehension he therefore hastened to tell the High Commissioner's office that at all costs the Bowler trek had to be prevented. 'You cannot', he said, 'allow a single Boer to settle across the Limpopo until our position in the north is secure'.

His appeal put the new High Commissioner, Sir Henry Loch, in a somewhat awkward position. Loch's duty was to uphold Britain's, and Rhodes', claims beyond the Limpopo. Yet, with Knutsford unwilling or unable to concede Kruger's terms for turning his back on the north, he had nothing with which to bargain. All that he could do was to try to bluff the Transvaal leader into stopping the trek. With a directness in keeping with his Indian cavalry background, Loch therefore told Kruger that, to show his good faith, he should forbid Bowler's project and solemnly warned him that, if he failed to do so and the trek went forward, the Transvaal Government would be held responsible for any collision or injury to British interests beyond the Limpopo.

Astonishingly enough, Kruger's reaction to this piece of bluster was to submit without demur. Obsessed with his need for a seaport of his own, he saw the Bowler trek only as an obstacle to the necessary agreement with the British, not as a threat which he might hold over their heads to secure better terms. Without a moment's hesitation he therefore forbade the trek and, hoping to have thus ingratiated himself with the Imperial Government, he invited the High Commissioner to meet him at Blignaut's Pont, on the Vaal, to try and reach some agreement on the crucial issues of Swaziland and Kosi Bay. Loch accepted the invitation; and, in March 1890, accompanied by Rhodes, he duly met Kruger and his State Secretary, Leyds, for the first time.

On Knutsford's instructions, Loch made it clear that he had

not come to bargain. The Transvaal, he said, must abandon its claims in the north unconditionally before there could be any discussion of Swaziland or Kosi Bay. Kruger promptly objected to such a procedure, pointing out that his claims in Lobengula's domains were 'superior' to Britain's, since the Grobler treaty preceded Rhodes' concession. But, when he saw that the High Commissioner was adamant, he again gave way, even though he must have known that, by doing so, he was finally throwing away what was by far his strongest card.

However, if Kruger hoped by this major concession to sweeten the atmosphere of the negotiations, he was soon to be disappointed. For when the discussion turned to Swaziland, Loch bluntly told him that he must accept an indefinite continuation of the joint government there. The British Parliament, he said, would never agree to the Boers governing the Europeans in Swaziland on their own, for fear of prejudicing the independence of the Swazi people. Nor could Britain admit Boer sovereignty over any Tonga territory. But if the Transvaal would accept such limitations, Kruger could have Kosi Bay and build a railway to it through the intervening territories.

Kruger protested that he was being asked to give up everything. He had withdrawn from Bechuanaland six years earlier in face of British pressures; he had just unconditionally renounced the north; and now he was told he must abandon Swaziland and any hope of sovereign control over the railway to the sea. The British Parliament might have its opinions, but so did the Volksraad, who would certainly never entertain such a proposition. Besides, he said, the joint government of Europeans in Swaziland would never work. 'How can two great farmers live together in the same house?' Nor was it enough to say that he could build a railway to Kosi Bay. 'How could I protect my interests in the railway if I get no land besides?' In the past St. Lucia Bay had been Boer property, but Britain had taken it to serve her interests. At the very least he must have a strip of land through the intervening territories to safeguard his railway and his port. It was no good Loch saying that Britain would protect Kosi Bay. He must insist that the Transvaal should have the right and the means to do so for itself.

As the conference adjourned for the day Kruger grasped the High Commissioner's hand and said, 'I wish to hold firmly to the hand of England . . . it is the wish of my heart to be England's friend'. But whether he meant it or not, there was no disguising the fact that the talks would reach a complete deadlock, unless one or other party were prepared to give way. In the event it was Loch, acting on Rhodes' advice, who made the necessary gesture, subject to the approval of his superiors in Whitehall. Rhodes was no less disturbed than Kruger by the prospect of the talks breaking down. For he knew that if this were to happen, Kruger could not in fact be held to his promise not to press his claims beyond the Limpopo, however unconditionally it might have been made; and at this point nothing mattered to Rhodes so much as to make sure that this promise would be kept.

On the following day, therefore, Loch opened the discussion by saying that, in order to secure an agreement, he was prepared to use his good offices to persuade the tribes to allow the Transvaal Government to build their railway to the coast. He also undertook to recommend to London that Kruger's Republic should be allowed to negotiate with the tribes for sovereign rights over the railway strip from Swaziland right through to Kosi Bay. In return, he expected Kruger to agree to join a customs union, concede free trade for British imports, admit the Kimberley rail extension to Pretoria and the Rand and, finally, agree not to part with Kosi Bay to any third party.

On this understanding, Kruger agreed, not with any great enthusiasm, to recommend Loch's offer to his Executive Council. But on his return to Pretoria, such were the reactions of his ministerial colleagues that he did not dare to put the proposition to the Volksraad. Clearly they felt as Loch did in reporting home, that Kruger had been offered 'an almost worthless concession for very material advantages'. Yet, incredibly enough, the Imperial Government also looked askance at the Blignaut's Pont terms. Fearing repercussions from the humanitarian societies, they jibbed at the idea of placing tribal areas, even if these were only railway strips, under Boer jurisdiction. The Boers, they said, could have no sovereign rights,

164

whether in Swaziland or in the other territories which lay between them and the sea.

Once again a deadlock seemed inevitable. But Loch, not to be denied, resorted to a combination of pressure and persuasion. By way of pressure, he sent to Kruger on a take-it-or-leave-it basis the draft of a convention which allowed for a rail outlet to Kosi Bay without any sovereign rights in the intervening territories. Simultaneously, he began to assemble a police force to take over Swaziland and install a British Administrator, if the Volksraad should reject these terms. By way of persuasion, he got Hofmeyr to hasten to Pretoria and tell Kruger that, if he would sign the convention without asking for any amendments, the Imperial Government would be prepared to consider favourably all outstanding issues, once the joint administration of the Swaziland Europeans had been set up on a permanent basis.

The ensuing encounter between the two Afrikaner leaders was not a happy one. Kruger distrusted Hofmeyr for his alliance with Rhodes and he deeply resented his lending himself to these British manoeuvres. During one of several heated exchanges, he completely lost his temper and angrily thrust at the Bond's leader, 'You are a traitor and you come here as a traitor'.

Yet, in spite of this bitter dialogue, Loch's tactics of pressure and persuasion won Kruger's agreement to his terms. Kruger might resent having a pistol put to his head and he might dislike the High Commissioner's choice of emissary. But he attached the greatest importance to the pledge which Hofmeyr conveyed on the authority of the Imperial Government. For, although nobody explained exactly what this ambiguous undertaking involved, Kruger certainly took it to mean that, given a little time to overcome the objections of the jingos and do-gooders at home, Knutsford and his colleagues would be prepared to concede his requests for sovereign control at least over the railway. The terms of Loch's convention were indisputably worse than those which the Transvaal Government had rejected after Kruger had returned from the Blignaut's Pont negotiations. But they gave him the all-important requirement of a railway to the sea; and with the addition of Hofmeyr's pledge, Kruger felt that he had enough to persuade his Cabinet and the Volksraad to accept the bird-in-the-hand, in the confident hope of gaining better terms in the not too distant future.

Thus, to gain access to Kosi Bay, Kruger agreed to trust to the good faith of the Imperial Government on the strength of a promise which could mean anything or nothing. And in August 1890, in what was to become known as the First Swaziland Convention, he conceded every requirement that Loch had put before him.

Even though he had fatally weakened his hand by unconditionally waiving his claims beyond the Limpopo, it still seems extraordinary that Kruger and his fellow Boers should have accepted such a one-sided arrangement with so little objection. Admittedly, the Volksraad ratified it as they had done with the Pretoria Convention in 1881, as a temporary measure. But that they and their President should have made no further attempt to gain concessions from Britain can only be explained by their blind determination to secure, at all costs, a route to the sea and by an equally unseeing belief on their part that the Imperial Government would honour what Loch had authorised Hofmeyr to promise on their behalf. Little did these guileless burghers know, as they cast their votes to ratify the agreement, that five years later Britain would cut the route to the sea by annexing Tongaland and therefore Kosi Bay, together with the intervening territories. Likewise, little did they suspect that Rhodes would repay them for giving him unchallenged access to the north by attempting to overthrow the Republic by force in collusion with the Uitlanders on the Rand.

9 The Road to the North

THE relative ease with which Rhodes won from Kruger the right to colonise the north unchallenged by the Transvaal Boers was in marked contrast to the opposition which he encountered from rival European claimants, from Lobengula and even from his own Government at home. In fact, it is fair to say that, had the office of High Commissioner then been held by anyone but Robinson, with his strong personal preference for the colonial as opposed to the 'Imperial Factor', Rhodes' dreams would in all probability have perished. For, during the years 1888-9 it was frequently touch and go for him in Matabeleland. First, the Imperial Government refused to ratify the concession obtained from Lobengula which gave him a monopoly of prospecting rights in the Matabele realms; then the Portuguese threatened to bar the way to the north; and when these menaces had been disposed of, the Matabele King repudiated his undertakings with an insouciance, astonishing even by Bantu standards, at the bidding of rival European prospectors gathered at his Bulawayo court. And it was only Robinson's patience and persistence that won over the doubters in Whitehall, warned off every European challenger and, in the end, persuaded Lobengula to abide by the concession granted to Rhodes in the name of the Matabele people.

Of these three achievements the last proved the most difficult to accomplish. For to do so, Robinson and his agents had to overcome the traditional jealousy and suspicion with which

167

every Bantu tribe guarded its lands and kept all concession-hunters at bay. Even those relatively 'tame' chiefs on the borders of the Transvaal and Zululand, who had been induced to seek British protection out of fear of Boer freebooters or Cetewayo's marauders, had insisted that tribal lands were not for sale to anyone and that, being 'not baffled' in the government of their own people, as the Bamangwatos' Khama put it, they should continue to enjoy full autonomy. The Matabeles were no exception to this rule; and what is more, they neither needed nor sought protection against anybody. On the contrary, it was their neighbours who needed protection against them.

For these ferocious Zulu offshoots were a law unto themselves. Their royal capital had a ring of terror about its name—Bulawayo, the 'place of slaughter'—which was exemplified by the ever-present stench of putrescent flesh, by the litter of hides and heads of oxen slaughtered for the King's feasts and by the vultures constantly circling overhead in waiting, like the crocodiles in the nearby river, for the latest victims of the witch-doctor's malice and the executioner's garrotte. Following Zulu custom, the Matabeles were organised as a warrior nation. The young men were enrolled in impis—the Bantu term for regiments—lived on a diet of beef and beer and were not allowed to marry until their thirty-fifth year. Each impi lived in a separate kraal, whence from time to time one or more would be despatched to remind some vassal tribe of its vassalage by burning its villages, looting its cattle, destroying the crops and carrying off the children to be brought up as warriors or slaves in the service of the Matabele realm. Ever since the 1820s when Msilikazi had led his ten thousand warriors and their families northwards in the breakaway from Chaka, the Matabeles had played havoc with every tribe with whom they came in contact. The Makalakas and Mashonas to the north-east had been made their vassals or, as they put it, their 'dogs'. The Barotses on the north-west beyond the Zambezi had frequently suffered their onslaughts. The Bamangwatos under Khama's father, Sechome, had been driven to take refuge in the mountains about Shoshong; and it was not until after the advent of the British Protectorate that Khama could safely move his capital back to the plains of Palapye, on the line of the advancing railway from Kimberley to Matabeleland. Even then the Matabeles claimed a large slice of territory on the Bechuanaland border between the Shashi and Macloutsie rivers, which was henceforth known as the 'Disputed Territory'. And overall their claims to sovereignty comprised the entire area between the Limpopo and the Zambezi as far east as Tete, the Mazoe valley and the mountains east of the Sabi river.

In 1868 Msilikazi had died, riddled with disease and crippled with gout and was buried according to Zulu custom. His body, sewn up in the freshly flayed hides of two black bulls and guarded by twelve of his widows until it was all but decomposed, was taken in a large tented wagon drawn by sixteen black oxen to the Matopos Hills, south of Bulawayo, there to be immured in a cave, while another fifty black bullocks were slaughtered to provide for the traditional two days' sacrificial feast for the Matabele impis. But for all the ritual ceremony of his funeral, Msilikazi left no titular heir. For, like Chaka, he had done away with any members of his family who, he thought, might have threatened his throne. There was, however, one survivor—a son called Lobengula, whose name meant 'driven by the wind', to recall what happened to the tribe at the time of his birth as they were being continually chivvied northwards first by Chaka's avenging armies and later by the Transvaal Boers. Lobengula had been spirited away by his mother to protect him from the fate of his brothers at the hands of their suspicious father and, according to legend, had been brought up by witch-doctors living in the Matopos Hills. From here he was sought out by the induna—the Bantu equivalent of Minister—who had become Regent on the death of the King; and much against his will, for he feared retribution from rival claimants to the throne, Lobengula was installed as Msilikazi's successor in March 1870.

Standing over six feet tall with a stately gait and fierce countenance, his great naked bulk clad only in a kilt of monkey skins, with a head-ring of parakeet feathers in his hair and quaffing huge draughts of beer in the company of a selection from his more than sixty wives, Lobengula presented the complete picture of a legendary tribal monarch. Moreover, due perhaps to his unorthodox upbringing, he was a much more astute man than his father, with an awareness of the outside world which Msilikazi neither possessed nor thought necessary. Yet, for all his imposing presence and comparative intelligence, Lobengula lacked the ability of his father to control his people and throughout his reign there were constant rumours of incipient insurrections in those kraals which had never really accepted as their king this outsider who, for all his royal blood, had not been reared as a true son of Msilikazi.

Much of this disaffection has been caused by the influx of white men, following the discovery of gold in Mashonaland by the German traveller, Dr. Mauch, and his English companion, Mr. Hartley, in 1866. Although Msilikazi had allowed prospectors to dig at Tati on the edge of the Disputed Territory, no concessions had been granted elsewhere. Nevertheless, after his death, many Europeans kept on coming to Bulawayo to ask permission to prospect. When they had been refused, a number of them had, under the guise of hunting for game, abused Lobengula's hospitality to conduct illicit diggings, which misbehaviour had aroused the wrath of the impis who craved an opportunity to wash their spears in the blood of these foreigners.

Khama, with his more docile Bamangwatos, could afford to grant mining concessions, as he had done to the Bechuanaland Exploration Company. But Lobengula dared not risk arousing his people; and although the King's word was law, he found it increasingly difficult to restrain his young warriors, who claimed the traditional right to protect their lands against foreign incursions and who turned a deaf ear to his reminders of what had befallen other Bantu tribes, such as the Basutos, who made the mistake of trying conclusions with the white men. His father had been able to keep the Europeans outside his gates by means of treaties of peace and friendship signed in the eighteen-thirties and fifties with the Cape Governor and the Transvaal President of the day. But, in his father's reign, gold diggers had not haunted the King's kraal as they were now doing; and apart from a few men of God and a handful of traders, who had married native girls and adopted the Matabele way of life, there had then been no foreigners around to whet the appetites of the Matabeles for blood.

In this dilemma Lobengula turned increasingly to the missionaries who since 1859 had been permitted to practise in Matabeleland, and more especially to John Moffatt, whose father had been a trusted friend of Msilikazi and had founded the first mission station in the country at Inyati, where Lobengula, like his father before him, frequently attended church services. John Moffatt, whom Lobengula called 'Joni', knew the country well, having spent six years in charge of the Inyati mission in such total isolation from the outside world that for twelve months at a stretch he and his wife received no word or letter from anyone. And with one so knowledgeable and understanding of Matabele ways, it was natural that Lobengula, in his desperate need for someone to confide in, should have made this remarkable missionary his close friend and adviser. For almost every other European at his court had an axe to grind or a concession to seek and was therefore suspect in his eyes. Only Moffatt, only his friend Joni, would give him disinterested advice, whenever he needed it.

Nothing could have been more fortunate for British designs, or more accurately for Rhodes' ambitions, beyond the Limpopo than this special relationship between Moffatt and Lobengula. For, in the late eighties, several developments occurred which caused Britain and Rhodes, considerable anxiety. The first of these was the conclusion of a treaty in 1886 between Portugal and Germany which claimed to delimit the two countries' spheres of influence in southern Africa. By this treaty Portugal laid claim to a belt of territory along the Zambezi valley linking Mozambique to Angola and including in the Portuguese sphere of influence the whole centre of the continent between the Zambezi and the Limpopo rivers, which claim would have effectively shut Britain out from all of Central Africa. Also, in the early eighties, reports had reached the Colonial Office which suggested that the Portuguese were helping the Germans to establish a foothold in the area of Delagoa Bay and were planning to admit German settlers to the hinterland of Lourenço Marques. Added to this, McMurdo had visited Berlin in 1884 to tout his railway concession and to discuss plans for introducing German traders and manufacturers to Mozambique. And not long after that, rumours reached the High Commissioner in Cape Town of German intrigues in Tongaland.

Coming so soon after Bismarck's move into South-West Africa, these reports created alarm in British quarters, where it was felt that Portugal and Germany might be in league to cut Britain off from the north, with Germany adopting the guise of the Transvaal's protector and perhaps taking over the Delagoa Bay railway from McMurdo. Accordingly, the Imperial Government protested in Lisbon in vehement terms against the 1886 treaty. The Portuguese Government was reminded that, along with the other European colonial powers, they had only recently agreed that territorial claims could only be recognised where effective occupation existed—and there was at this time no proper garrison outside of Mozambique and Angola. Portugal was also asked for an assurance that the agreement of 1875 following the MacMahon Award would be honoured and that Delagoa Bay would revert to Britain if the Portuguese ever decided to part with it.

Lisbon duly gave the required assurance and, although Portugal continued to lay claim to Mashonaland by virtue of what she termed her ancient rights and refused to recognise Lobengula's palpable dominion over the area, the issue was not pressed any further. The Colonial Office took comfort in the supposition that the Portuguese would be unlikely to take any early steps to establish an effective occupation and the 1886 treaty was allowed to die a natural death. Yet no sooner had this crisis passed than a second threat to Rhodes' designs materialised. In the following year, Piet Grobler appeared at Lobengula's kraal with the commission of the South African Republic to renew the treaty made between Msilikazi and Pretorius in 1857. After a brief stay at Bulawayo, Grobler left with the agreement which, among other things, recognised him as Kruger's Consul at the King's court with jurisdiction over such Transvaal citizens as Lobengula might allow to hunt and trade in his domains.

This was altogether too much for Rhodes, who had himself

been trying to obtain a concession from Lobengula and whose agent, Fry, had earlier in that same year left Bulawayo empty-handed. Directly he heard the news of the Grobler treaty, Rhodes sought out the High Commissioner and urged him to claim the area between the Limpopo and the Zambezi for England, and hence for himself. There was not a moment to lose, he told Robinson. If the Boers once got a foothold in Lobengula's country, it would be lost forever. Convinced that in the north lay what he called the 'New Rand', which would far excel the wealth of Johannesburg, Rhodes made it clear to Robinson that his ambitions lay even beyond the Zambezi; and when the High Commissioner asked where he would stop, he pointed on the map to the southern boundary of Tanganyika. For all these reasons, he contended, it was imperative for Britain to forestall the Boers and all other claimants by declaring a Protectorate over Lobengula's territories, as had been done in the case of Bechuanaland beyond the Molopo.

Robinson was somewhat aghast at all this. Much as he sympathised with Rhodes' concept of colonialist expansion in Africa, he jibbed at the extent of his ambitions. Besides, he could not see the Colonial Office taking kindly to the idea of a Protectorate over Matabeleland and Mashonaland. True, they had recently taken Bechuanaland under their wing. But this, he felt, would probably make them all the more hesitant to rush into extending their responsibilities as far as the Zambezi. The Portuguese threat had little, if any, substance; and while Lobengula might have accepted Boer traders and hunters and even a Boer Consul, he could be relied on not to give away his country to anyone. In fact, he might well resent a British Protectorate no less hotly than he did the claims of the Portuguese to his territory and the constant solicitations of European concession hunters. Nevertheless, Robinson did agree to instruct Moffatt to take leave of absence from his post as Assistant Commissioner of the Bechuanaland Protectorate to visit his friend Lobengula and to inform him of Britain's desire to renew 'the friendly relations which were instituted by the treaty entered into by Sir Benjamin D'Urban and his father, Msilikazi, fifty-two years ago'. If this approach were well received, Moffatt was told that he would have authority to pay periodical visits to Bulawayo 'to further . . . the extension of British influence and trade throughout Matabele and Mashonaland.'

Robinson's instructions could hardly have been more tentative. Yet when Moffatt emerged from a lengthy stay at Lobengula's kraal in February 1888, he did so with a treaty of peace by which Britain claimed an exclusive sphere of influence over all the Matabele domains and Lobengula undertook not to enter 'into any correspondence or treaty with any foreign state or power' or to sell or cede any part of his country without the sanction of the High Commissioner. As to the Grobler treaty, Lobengula laughed so uproariously that he nearly collapsed his throne, when Moffatt asked if he had accepted Boer protection. He wanted no dealings, he said, with the Boers who wished to steal his country, as they had stolen his father's at the time when the Matabeles first came to rest in Transvaal territory.

Clearly Rhodes had lost no time in putting his own gloss on the High Commissioner's instructions to Moffatt who, although an utterably honourable man, was among the many who could not resist the patriotic fervour and overwhelming charm with which Rhodes so often managed to cloak his vainglorious ambitions. Certainly, for the next year or so, until Rhodes' new Colony became established beyond the Limpopo, Moffatt found himself working as much for Rhodes in Bulawayo as for the Imperial Government in Bechuanaland. And as further proof that Rhodes scarcely ever failed to get the man whom he wanted to work for him, in the next critical months he became for Rhodes' purpose as essential an intermediary with Lobengula as was Robinson with the Imperial Government.

Still Rhodes had to wait some eight months before he could follow up this break through and stake his prodigious claims in Lobengula's country. For one thing, the wheels of government at home took until the summer to grind out a ratification of Moffatt's treaty. Portugal and Kruger both protested the deed. Portugal claimed that the lands of the Mashonas and the Makalakas had never belonged to the Matabeles and were therefore within the Portuguese sphere of influence. Kruger, for his part, contended that Britain could not claim Lobengula's country as her sphere of influence, because the London Convention gave the right of expansion in the north to the Transvaal and because Grobler's treaty preceded Moffatt's. Besides, as Leyds put it, 'it was the Boers who first taught Lobengula the superior power of the white race, not the English'. Kruger's protest was made the more bitter by the fact that Grobler, returning to the Transvaal to collect his wife, had been killed in the Disputed Territory in a skirmish with a troop of Khama's Bamangwatos. For he was convinced that the blame for his emissary's death lay with Khama's British protectors, and in particular with Rhodes, whom he accused of seeking to avenge himself on the man who had beaten him to the punch by his treaty with Lobengula.

Kruger was, in due course, to waive his claim to sweeten the negotiations over Swaziland. And Salisbury was induced by the Colonial Office to reject the Portuguese protests. But he was not to be hurried into doing so. Rhodes did not at this point wield anything like the influence that he later had with the British Cabinet, or with the Colonial Office. Indeed Knutsford did not then even know who he was and Salisbury did not want to give unnecessary offence to Portugal for fear of antagonising her German friends whose diplomatic support he needed to sustain Britain's paramountcy in Egypt.

Apart from all this, soon after the signature of Moffatt's treaty, the local attitude towards the Europeans in Matabeleland had hardened perceptibly. And as the year 1888 progressed and ever more British and Boer traders and prospectors poured into Bulawayo to seek the King's favour, so the young warriors of Lobengula's impis became increasingly restless and resentful. What made matters worse, and infinitely more dangerous for these Europeans, was the fact that almost every one amongst them, in order to gain his own ends, would fill the King's ear with malicious stories about his fellows. Frenetically jealous and suspicious of each other, the idea of uniting their claims and so negotiating from strength was totally foreign to them. Thus, the King's kraal became a centre of sordid intrigue and, not unnaturally, Lobengula was given to believe that, with the exception of the missionaries and a few traders and other residents of long standing, all Europeans who wished to do business with him were crooks and adventurers without even honour or respect for one another. Accordingly he became ever more convinced that the only course for him to pursue, if he was to avoid trouble and bloodshed in his kingdom, was to continue steadfastly to refuse all requests to prospect for gold.

These were scarcely very encouraging conditions for Rhodes to make his bid for mineral concessions in Lobengula's country. Well might he pause, as these gloomy reports kept on coming from Moffatt every time he visited Bulawayo. Yet Rhodes knew too that, if his dreams of opening up the north were ever to see the light of day, he had to have the gold of Mashonaland. For without such a prospect he could never attract enough investment to finance his grandiose designs. He might have given himself, under the Trust Deeds of the De Beers and Consolidated Goldfields Companies, the power to spend shareholder's money on colonial expansion and development. But great as it was, the combined wealth of these two enterprises would not take him anywhere near the frontier of Tanganyika. His designs could only be realised by a vast new enterprise financed by British investors and authorised in its appointed tasks by the Imperial Government—in other words, a Chartered Company. 'Philanthropy plus five per cent' had become his motto—philanthropy to secure the support of Government and Parliament at home and to mollify the humanitarians, five per cent to attract the investors. And the surest way to secure that five per cent was to get the mineral concession for Mashonaland.

Thus, after much careful thought, Rhodes decided to dare all and ask Lobengula for what he wanted. Moffatt would help somehow to persuade the Matabele King that he was not like the other Europeans who were haunting his kraal. Moffatt had the King's ear and was enthralled by the visionary aim of opening up the north. Moffatt would induce Lobengula to send the other claimants packing and do business only with Rhodes. And so it was, just as Rhodes had calculated, that when his emissaries reached Bulawayo in September 1888, Moffatt was there to present them without delay to Lobengula seated in his bath chair beneath the tree that marked the traditional conference site with a gold-fringed umbrella above his head.

Rhodes himself was not present and the party which was led by his associate since the old Kimberley days, Charles Rudd, also included Rochfort Maguire, a brilliant Irish lawyer whom Rhodes had met at Oxford, and a well-known South African traveller, 'Matabele' Thompson, with the Rev. C. F. Helm, the London Missionary Society's resident representative at Bulawayo, acting as interpreter. Rudd opened the proceedings by handing over a greeting gift of a hundred sovereigns and, although the negotiations were constantly interrupted by Lobengula making medicine—and taking it too for his gout—the talks made rapid progress, largely thanks to the way in which Moffatt had prepared the ground for the delegation. With the courageous support of one of the Matabele indunas and some judicious interpreting by Helm, Rudd and his companions soon succeeded in persuading the King that the best way of resolving all the arguments with the Europeans would be to do business with them as representatives of the strongest group of applicants. Indeed, it seemed that Lobengula was only too ready to clinch matters with them, provided they were prepared to give him plenty of guns and ammunition, which Rudd was perfectly ready to do, in contrast to Kruger who had only sent the Matabele King two sporting rifles as a sweetener for the Grobler treaty. But when word came that Judge Shippard was on his way to Bulawayo to investigate the killing of Grobler, the King took the advice of his indunas and decided to await the decision of the Great White Queen's representative as to whether or not he should give these Britishers sole rights to dig in his country.

In the middle of October Shippard arrived, accompanied by his A.D.C., Major Goold-Adams, and dressed more suitably for a Buckingham Palace levee than for a tribal indaba, with his short pot-bellied frame encased in a black frock-coat to which was pinned the insignia of the Order of St. Michael and St. George. To add to the curiosity of the Matabeles about their new visitor, a messenger, who had seen Shippard taking a bath in the course of his journey, reported that this 'powerful wizard' had taken off all his clothes and, sitting in a bowl of boiling water, had 'rubbed his body all over with a terrible white frothing medicine and then squeezed boiling water over himself with some strange vegetable'.

In his consultations with the King, Shippard had no hesitation in recommending Rhodes' claims, for he too had succumbed to the irresistible appeal of this young empire-builder ever since he had heard him telling the High Commissioner that his ambitions lay as far north as the Tanganyika border. Thus, as Shippard departed, Lobengula decided to accept the advice of the Great White Queen's emissary and it only remained for Maguire to draw up the necessary document. This he did in such terms as gave Rhodes and his associates ' the complete and exclusive charge over all metals and minerals situated and contained in his (Lobengula's) kingdom, principalities and dominions, together with full power to do all things that they may deem necessary to win and procure the same (and) to take all necessary and lawful steps to exclude from his kingdom, principalities and dominions all persons seeking land, metals or minerals or mining rights therein. . . .' Lobengula also undertook to help in excluding these 'persons' and promised 'to grant no concessions of land or mining rights' after the date of signature of Rudd's concession. In return, Lobengula was to receive one hundred pounds a month, a thousand rifles and ten thousand rounds of ammunition, plus a steam gunboat for use on the Zambezi river. After a brief further discussion in which Lotje, the induna who had supported Rudd's case from the start, confirmed that his royal master would be wise to sign these terms, Lobengula put his mark upon the concession. Then, when Rudd, Maguire and Thompson had also signed it, the royal elephant seal was attached. Four hours later, Rudd was on his way to Kimberley, determined to give the Matabele King no chance of changing his mind.

Rhodes had got what he wanted—a monopoly right to prospect in Matabeleland and Mashonaland. And in the following month a notice in Lobengula's name appeared in the *Cape Times* stating that all the mining rights had been disposed of in his domains and that 'all concession-seekers and speculators are warned that their presence in Matabeleland is obnoxious to the

Chief and the people'. But it was still far from plain sailing for Rhodes. For one thing, the precious concession was very nearly lost when Rudd, returning south, became separated from his escort and, after wandering aimlessly in the desert for several days without water, decided that his end had come. Before delirium set in, he had just enough strength and presence of mind to bury the concession in a hole next to a tree, to which he fixed a piece of paper describing what he had done. But a short while afterwards, he was found and revived by a party of Bushmen who, when he had retrieved the concession, helped him on his way to Kimberley.

More serious still, when London learned of the terms of the Rudd concession, the Imperial Government loudly protested that, by promising to supply arms to a Bantu tribe, it ran counter to the undertakings subscribed by Britain at a recent international conference on slavery in Central Africa. Rhodes assured them through the High Commissioner that, in fact, the Matabeles were less dangerous with rifles than with assegais, because they were convinced that the higher they raised the sights of the rifle, the further the bullet would travel, whereas with the assegai their aim was deadly. However, the Colonial Office were still not happy. The concession, they said, conferred a monopoly and, only three years before at the Berlin Conference, they had urged the other imperial powers to oppose monopolies and support free trade. In the light of Sir George Goldie's commercial monopoly on the Niger, it was a somewhat disingenuous argument. But disingenuous or not, the Under-Secretary of State for the Colonies had no hesitation in telling the House of Commons that the Government would advise Lobengula to grant no concession without careful consideration and to permit nobody to exercise a monopoly in his kingdom.

Following this pronouncement, Robinson leapt into the breach on Rhodes' behalf with an emphatic recommendation that the Colonial Secretary should recognise the Rudd concession and accept it as the best way to deal with the problem of developing Matabeleland and Mashonaland. Did Knutsford, he asked, really want to see in these territories a repetition of the chaos and confusion which Umbandine had brought upon his

Swazi kingdom by giving out concessions to all and sundry for grazing and mining, for railways, post offices, telegraphs and banks? In Matabeleland, such a situation would lead to serious trouble and bloodshed. Lobengula could never govern the large number of Europeans, including British, who were seeking admission; his impis would soon get out of hand and Britain would then be obliged to take the highly expensive course of annexing the territory to protect her subjects. Surely a monopoly such as was offered in the Rudd concession, with the possibility of its developing into a Royal Charter, was infinitely preferable to annexation. Apart from anything else, he estimated that it would save the British taxpayer a quarter of a million pounds a year. And in a final dig at the 'Imperial Factor', he concluded by saying that British Bechuanaland, 'as regards its prisons, hospitals, public buildings, roads and civil servants generally', was a poor example of the benefits of annexation to the Crown, 'a forcible illustration of the effect of attempting to administer a Crown Colony—if I may be permitted to use the expression—"on the cheap".'

Needless to say, Moffatt was writing in similar vein as the man-on-the-spot to warn Whitehall that, so long as 'irresponsible persons, with little or nothing to lose, are at liberty to come and put a match into the highly inflammable materials around, no advance will be made towards a gold-mining industry'. And faced with such weighty advice from the High Commissioner and his peripatetic representative at Lobengula's court, Knutsford finally relented and agreed to support the Rudd concession.

No doubt Rhodes had also helped to lubricate the Imperial Government's conversion by offering to finance the development of the Bechuanaland Protectorate, in which territory he was to conclude an amalgamation deal with the Exploration Company who owned the rights to prospect for minerals in Khama's part of the territory. To the intense relief of the Colonial Office, who were beginning to find that Warren's Protectorate was an unmitigated white elephant, he offered to spend over £700,000 in Bechuanaland. Of this sum, £500,000 would be for building the railway from Kimberley to Bulawayo, £30,000 to install a telegraph line and £200,000 for general development of the Protectorate. Apart from this, he proposed to pay £4,000 a year towards the expenses of maintaining a British Resident at Bulawayo. And since no Government could afford to turn down such an offer, least of all in the era of Victorian economics, Rhodes could now count on the support of 'Grandmama'—as he was wont to call Whitehall—and hence on the unfettered patronage of the High Commissioner, the Administrator of British Bechuanaland and the Assistant Commissioner for the Bechuanaland Protectorate, who was also Lobengula's most trusted counsellor.

Rhodes' conquest of 'Grandmama' could not have been more timely. For within three months of granting the Rudd concession and before Knutsford had been won over, Lobengula had begun to renege on his agreement. Although Maguire and Thompson had stayed behind at Bulawayo to guard against any backsliding, they had been unable to hold the King to his bargain or to drown the voices of those aggrieved by Rudd's success, as they poured their poison into the royal ear.

The most persuasive of these voices belonged to Edward Maund, an employee of the Bechuanaland Exploration Company and a former British army officer, who had first visited Lobengula in 1885 to assure him on Warren's behalf that the British Protectorate over Bechuanaland would not be directed against him. Maund claimed to have persuaded the King to let him prospect in the Mazoe valley area of Mashonaland; and when Rhodes' representative contended that, if true, this would be a breach of the Rudd concession, Lobengula called a meeting which was attended by Moffatt and Maund, together with other European claimants. But the meeting only served still further to confuse the King's mind. Rhodes' emissaries had made out that they had the backing of the British Government and the Great White Queen. Yet now he was told that this was not so and that these favours were enjoyed by others. Some people had even assured him that there was no British Government and that the Great White Queen was only a myth; and he was beginning to think that perhaps they were right.

Maund then proposed that, to clarify matters, Lobengula should send two trusted indunas to London to act as his 'eyes and ears', to ascertain that Queen Victoria did in fact exist and to take to her a message from himself. The King jumped at the proposal and, as Maund had clearly intended, suggested that he should accompany the delegation. Early in 1889, therefore, two Matabele indunas, with Maund in attendance, left Bulawayo for Cape Town en route for England. They took with them two documents. The first rehearsed Lobengula's territorial claims and disputed the Portuguese claim to Mashonaland. The second stated Lobengula's desire 'to know that there is a Queen' and, if so, to seek her advice and help, 'as he is much troubled by white men who come into his country and ask to dig gold'. There was, he said, no one with him whom he could trust and he hoped the Queen would 'send someone from herself'.

This message was duly delivered to Queen Victoria who personally received the indunas in audience, so that they might see for themselves and for their chief that she was a living being. In answer to Lobengula's message she promised that a considered reply would shortly be conveyed by her own 'induna' charged with colonial responsibilities, Lord Knutsford, and to confirm the evidence of her existence, she agreed to enclose in it a photograph of herself. The reply when it came must have delighted Maund as much as it horrified Rhodes. Voicing the initial opposition of the Colonial Office to Rhodes' intended monopoly, Knutsford virtually advised the King to renounce the Rudd concession. It was not wise, he said, to put too much power into the hands of some applicants and to exclude other deserving people. 'The Queen advises Lobengula not to grant hastily concessions of land, or leave to dig, but to consider all applications very carefully. . . . A king gives a stranger an ox, not his whole herd of cattle.'

Rhodes managed to get a sight of Knutsford's message before it was delivered to Bulawayo. Seeing in it the potential destruction of all his plans, he tried to persuade the High Commissioner's office to modify it and, when this attempt failed, he suggested that it be said to have been 'lost at sea'! All to no avail. The Imperial Government had spoken and their word had to be conveyed to Lobengula whatever might be the effect on the Rudd concession.

But even with the opposition of Whitehall to contend with, Rhodes was not lacking in devices to protect his interests. Ever since Maund had thrown down his challenge, he had been straining every nerve to enlist the support of Shippard whom he had warned that 'Lobengula may give away his whole country to bogus companies . . . and what is left will not be worth De Beers' while to pay the expenses of good government'. When Lobengula's delegation passed through Kimberley on their journey to England, he had tried to browbeat Maund into turning back, saying that the Rudd concession was unassailable and that any rival claimants were wasting their time. When this approach failed, he sought to bribe his challenger to work with him and leave the Bechuanaland Exploration Company which, he said, could not offer comparable inducements and would probably let him down in the end. But Maund had proved impervious to all arguments; and unable to win him over by direct threats or blandishments, Rhodes switched the attack to his employers. Here at last his persistence was rewarded. Pointing out that a £50,000 concern could not long stand up to the £13,000,000 of De Beers and Consolidated Goldfields, Rhodes bought his way into the Bechuanaland Exploration Company and persuaded the two principal directors to join the Board of the United Concessions Corporation—the predecessor of the British South Africa Company which was to finance Rhodes' schemes for the north. Without further ado, therefore, Maund was turned from a rival into a servant of Rhodes' enterprises.

Yet these commercial and financial intrigues, successful as they were in themselves, did not by any means solve all Rhodes' problems. For even before he received Knutsford's message, Lobengula under increasing pressure from his indunas and from rival claimants, decided openly to repudiate the Rudd concession. The induna who had advised him to deal solely with Rhodes, was put to death; and the King, while admitting that he 'had signed away the mineral rights of the whole country to Rudd and his friends', now told Robinson that his indunas had refused to ratify the concession. Four months later after his emissaries had returned to Bulawayo, bringing with

them Knutsford's oracular warning against monopolies, Lobengula not unnaturally thought that the Queen would support,
if not welcome, his action. Replying through Shippard, he
thanked her for her 'word' and assured her that he would not
give away his whole herd of cattle. And following a verbal inter-
polation by his indunas upon their conversations in London, he
announced that he would not let anyone dig for gold in his
country except 'as servants'.

Two further complications were now added to Rhodes'
problems. First, another letter was sent to Lobengula warning
him not to give away his property. This came from an English
humanitarian group, the Aborigines' Protection Society, acting
on the advice of the Reverend Mackenzie, who was still in South
Africa busily stirring up trouble for his old adversary, Rhodes.
Second, and more serious, both Maguire and Thompson left
Bulawayo, the former out of boredom with life at the King's
kraal and the latter in panic following warnings that Lobengula was about to have him executed. Rudd was ill at this point
and Rhodes, advised that it would be very unwise and probably
counter-productive for him to appear personally in Bulawayo
under existing conditions, turned to his friend, Dr. Jameson.
With that extraordinary capacity for inducing people to work
for him against their own better judgement, he overcame all
Jameson's objections to leaving his Kimberley practice and
persuaded him to take over as his representative with Lobengula. Perhaps it was the streak of the gambler in the dapper,
diminutive doctor—which six years later was to lead him to
defeat and disgrace in the abortive Jameson Raid—that made
him forsake his patients and undertake this hazardous mission.
At any rate he agreed and a few days later, in April 1889,
accompanied by Thompson and another young doctor, Rutherford Harris, later to become the Cape Town Secretary of
Rhodes' Chartered Company, Jameson set off for Bulawayo,
taking with him half the promised consignment of rifles and
ammunition.

Although Lobengula was at first greatly annoyed to see
Thompson back at his kraal and angrily called him a coward
for having fled from Bulawayo, Jameson soon managed to get

on terms with the King, whom he delighted by successfully treating his gout with pain-killing remedies. Lobengula was also much taken with the doctor's charm and sense of humour; and his apparent lack of any fear either of the King or of his warriors made a deep impression on those at the court who had grown used to seeing Europeans grovelling in the royal presence. In token of his admiration, Lobengula even made him an induna, named him 'Daketela' and presented him with a cloak of ostrich feathers to mark his rank.

Jameson was soon to need every iota of this esteem. For during his stay, the Imperial Government vouchsafed their reply to Lobengula's second message, in which he had assumed that the Great White Queen would support his repudiation of the Rudd concession. And since the Colonial Office had by now decided to accept the High Commissioner's advice and to up-hold Rhodes, the reply was, of course, an almost complete contradiction of their earlier cautionary advice. Apart from this, it was couched in the worst kind of official jargon which Jameson, on reading it through, considered highly inappropriate for communication to His Matabele Majesty. Nor did he think that the Imperial Government's gesture of sending their reply with an escort of two officers and two other ranks of the Royal Horse Guards in full-dress uniform would greatly help matters. They might present a colourful spectacle in the African bush; but they could scarcely help him to explain the Imperial Government's sudden volte-face.

By radically rewriting the Government's letter in more suitable terms, Jameson was able to avoid a major explosion on Lobengula's part. But there was no way of disguising the fact that this new message was a reversal of the Queen's previous advice. This alone made the King suspicious enough; but what irked him even more than to be told that he should now deal only with Rhodes and his associates was the proposal that these white men would make their own laws and would, therefore, not be under his jurisdiction. Lobengula might be fascinated by the Horse Guards in their blue and silver regalia; indeed he insisted on seeing them every day of their stay and would frequently refuse to talk business because 'I am still looking at

the Queen's servants'. But he could not understand why Her
Majesty's Ministers should now be recommending to him the
very people against whom they had earlier gone out of their way
to warn him. He trusted the Queen and her Ministers because
he trusted Moffatt and, he had become accustomed to the idea
of being 'protected' by the Crown. But he profoundly disliked
the idea, now apparently advocated by the Queen, of a 'Government' of prospectors, whether it be the single company headed
by Rhodes or some amalgam of the other European claimants
residing at Bulawayo. Even if he personally were to accept it,
such an arrangement would, he feared, be greatly resented by
his people. Only with difficulty had he been able to ensure that
the Great Dance—the chief festival of the year and a critical
time for white visitors because of the frenzy which it excited
among his people—passed off with only one minor demonstration of hostility towards the Europeans in his kraal. And he
feared that, if he were now to commend the Rudd concession
to his impis, he would be faced with an uncontrollable outburst
of indignation. Accordingly, he replied very coolly to the
Queen's latest message, simply noting the volte-face which it
contained and saying that he would think about the matter
further.

Jameson however refused to take no, or even maybe, for an
answer; and with the aid of the ever-present Moffatt, he
gradually managed to win over Lobengula. His first break-
through came when the King told him that he could dig 'one
hole' and suggested that he do so at Tati, where concession-
hunters had been sent in Msilikazi's day. Then, after Jameson's
prospectors returned from Tati to report that their searches in
this area had produced no gold to speak of, Lobengula finally
relented. He still would not allow Rhodes and his associates to
prospect in Matabeleland as being too close to the nerve centre
of Bulawayo. But he did agree that they should be 'given the
road' to Mashonaland, provided that they kept at a 'safe'
distance from the Matabele kraals and in every other way
refrained from exciting untoward repercussions among the
King's impis.

10 The Winning of Rhodesia

DURING all these comings and goings at Bulawayo, Rhodes was setting the wheels in motion to secure a Royal Charter for the great new enterprise with which he was going to 'open up the North'. As soon as he had eliminated or bought out all serious rivals, such as Maund and the Bechuanaland Exploration Company, he came to England and began to make the necessary approaches in London. Here he was hampered by the fact that he was not yet well known in political quarters and that most of those who did know about him were powerful opponents. The most important of these were members of that group of imperialist watchdogs, the South African Committee, such as Chamberlain, the Duke of Fife, who was a son-in-law of the Prince of Wales, and Lord Grey, a grandson of the Prime Minister who presided over the passage of the Reform Bill in the thirties. Added to this imposing array was a former Colonial Secretary, Henry Labouchere, who since his brief spell in office had become an implacable opponent of all British expansion overseas, whether by imperial or colonial agencies. And finally there was the Aborigines Protection Society, who, egged on by the Rev. MacKenzie, held that all colonials treated natives worse than animals.

Against such opposition Rhodes set about mustering some highly influential supporters. He managed to enthuse Lord Rothschild with his plans—a highly important catch since Rothschild was not only a most influential financier but also the father-in-law of that great Liberal Imperialist, Lord Rosebery, who five years later was to become Prime Minister. Also Sir Hercules Robinson, now back in England and a director of the B.S.A. Company, was very glad to help by putting in a word for his friend from the Cape with the Colonial Secretary and in other quarters where it mattered most. And added to this, Rhodes managed to win to his support no less a figure in the world of political journalism than W. T. Stead, the editor of the influential *Pall Mall Gazette*.

Another crucially important conquest was Sir Harry Johnston who had just been appointed British Consul-General in Mozambique, with responsibilities for overseeing British interests in Nyasaland, where the African Lakes Company, a largely philanthropic enterprise endowed by the Church of Scotland, together with a handful of missionaries, were said to be carrying on Livingstone's work with all too little money and not much governmental support. Johnston was important to Rhodes not only because of his posting to Portuguese East Africa but even more because he had, as few Foreign Office representatives abroad could claim, direct access to Lord Salisbury, who was currently both Prime Minister and Foreign Secretary. And Salisbury, with more pressing and important issues to weigh in the diplomatic scales than those involving southern Africa, was to Rhodes' way of thinking dangerously inclined to trade potential British spheres of influence in West or South Africa in order to gain concessions in other areas for which Rhodes cared not a rap. Moreover, Salisbury knew little of Rhodes who he thought was 'rather a pro-Boer M.P. in South Africa' and, until Johnston got to work on him, cared little for the empire building schemes of this upstart colonial which, even if they were desirable, should, he felt, be carried out by the Imperial Government and not entrusted to some commercial company.

But Johnston had ambitions not dissimilar to those of Rhodes. In particular, he wanted to 'save' Nyasaland which had little to offer apart from an over-abundant population and which had hence become a prey to the Arab and Portuguese slave-traders from Central Africa and Mozambique. He was also deeply worried by the evident wish of the Portuguese Government to extend their sphere of influence in this direction and by the covetous glances which the Germans in Tanganyika were said to be casting upon this beautiful land of green hills and valleys. Johnston dreamed too of connecting South and North Africa via Nyasaland and the Zambezi valley by a stretch of territory along the borders of the Congo Free State and Tanganyika. Indeed it was he who invented the 'Cape-to-Cairo' catchword, which Rhodes later made his slogan. But Salisbury, for all his respect and liking for his extraordinary Consul, who was wont to parade across the African continent holding aloft a white umbrella, termed this project a most 'inconvenient possession' and kept Johnston much too short of money to enable him to realise his dreams. Hence he was a relatively easy conquest for Rhodes who, on meeting him in London and discovering the similarity of their ambitions, promptly handed him a cheque for £2,000 to initiate their partnership.

Such a transaction between a prominent company director and a servant of the Crown would, of course, be considered highly irregular today. But in the nineteenth century it was not unusual for British consular officers to undertake other assignments outside their official employment, such as, for instance, the Consul at Khartoum in General Gordon's day who was also the *Times* correspondent. At any rate, Rhodes' cheque marked the beginning of an important, if brief, association by which Johnston became at one and the same time, Britain's and Rhodes' representative in Nyasaland. The partnership came to a bitter end, when Rhodes lost interest in the area, having failed to 'square' the African Lakes Company who wanted philanthropy, but without Rhodes' five per cent. But this was not before Johnston had served his purpose by helping to induce Salisbury to pocket his prejudice against empire-building by private enterprise and to support the application for a Royal Charter for the British South Africa Company.

Johnston's £2,000 was not the only cheque which Rhodes handed out at this crucial juncture in his fortunes. In the belief that the Irish M.P.s at Westminster might well hold the parliamentary balance between success and failure for the Charter, he gave their leader, Charles Parnell, £5,000 as a first instalment of a promise of double the amount. True, he made it a condition that, when the next Bill for Irish Home Rule should be introduced, Parnell would agree that Irish M.P.s should continue to sit in the House of Commons, so as to preserve intact the links of empire. But, whatever some of his biographers may assert, there can be little doubt that in this transaction Rhodes was more concerned to win added support for his Charter than to keep the Irish parliamentarians within the imperial fold. Indeed, even after he had obtained the Charter, he felt that there was a continuing need to 'square' opinion at Westminster. In 1890, he foresaw that the Liberals, who under Gladstone's continuing leadership were still a long way from adopting the imperialist policies of Rosebery and further still from supporting his own type of empire-building, might soon rule again in Whitehall. And acting on this assumption, he decided to hedge his bets with a substantial contribution to Liberal Party funds, with the proviso that, if the Liberals in office remained intent on 'breaking up the Empire', the money should be given instead to charity. He also insisted that the donation be kept secret, so as not to spoil his relations with those Tory Ministers with whom he was currently dealing.

By the end of April 1889, Rhodes felt that he had done all that he needed to prepare the ground. Accordingly, he applied on behalf of himself and his B.S.A. Company partners, Rudd, Beit and Gifford, for a Royal Charter which would give him imperial authority not only to do what his concession from Lobengula allowed him to do—to dig for minerals—but also to colonise, to trade and to build railways and erect telegraphs as well, even though Lobengula had not shown the slightest inclination to allow him to do any of these things. Knutsford recommended the application to the Prime Minister on the grounds that it would cost the Government nothing. Indeed, as Rhodes had made plain, it would actually save them money. Besides, Rhodes would probably go ahead with all or most of his plans, even if the Charter were refused, since there was nothing under existing British law to prevent him from doing so.

Salisbury duly agreed with his Colonial Secretary's submission, although not with any great enthusiasm. And Rhodes and his associates were told to draft the kind of Charter that they wanted, and to submit it for official approval. The Prime Minister's only spoken reservation concerned the Board of the proposed Chartered Company which he said should include prominent figures in British public life as well as men well versed and endowed in South African business matters such as the four applicants. The poachers were to have a few game-keepers to supervise them.

To meet this requirement, Rhodes typically decided to approach two of the leading lights of the South African Com-mittee, the Duke of Fife and Lord Grey. And to illustrate once again his extraordinary ability to 'square' his opponents and convert·them into partners, both these noblemen accepted his invitation to become London directors of the British South Africa Company. With the addition of the Duke of Abercorn, the composition of the Board was completed and in October 1889, Queen Victoria signed the Royal Charter. The Company, with its capital fixed at £1,000,000, was thereby authorised to operate in the Bechuanaland Protectorate and beyond the Limpopo to the west of Portuguese East Africa. Although at first Ministers sought to impose a northern limit at the valley of the Zambezi, Rhodes naturally held out against this and, in its final form, the Charter contained no limitations to the north. Within this enormous area, the Company could 'make treaties, promulgate laws, preserve the peace, maintain a police force and acquire new concessions . . . make roads, railways, harbours or undertake other public works, own or charter ships, engage in mining or any other industry, establish banks, make land grants and carry on any lawful commerce, trade, pursuit or business'. The only qualifications imposed were a limited right of super-vision by the Colonial Secretary, protection of native rights and a provision that the Charter could be revoked after twenty-five years or sooner, if the Company should fail to honour its obligations.

At the age of only thirty-six, Rhodes had created not merely a company but the foundations of a self-governing state in an area equal to that of the British Colonies and the Boer Republics in South Africa put together, and a state which was to last for thirty-three years until in 1923 the B.S.A. Company's rule was replaced north of the Zambezi by a Crown Colony and to the south by a self-governing dominion. In face of a fait accompli of such magnitude, opposition to Rhodes melted away, leaving only an implacable Labouchere to launch a few barbed shafts at the Treasury Bench in the House of Commons, supported by the grumblings of the humanitarian societies that it would all end in tears. In the event, these few Cassandras were to be proved all too right, but in the excitement of the moment nobody paid any attention to their gloomy forecasts.

Thus, when Loch arrived in South Africa at the end of 1889 to take up his duties as Governor and High Commissioner, Rhodes had secured his Charter and the question to be decided was when rather than whether he should despatch his Pioneer Column to claim his northern empire. To disarm criticism at home that he was trying to rush matters, and Lobengula in particular, Rhodes told Knutsford that he did 'not suppose much if anything would be done for two years'. He was, he said, most anxious not to hurry things in Matabeleland, but rather to gain the confidence and allay the anxieties of Lobengula. But the idea of Rhodes not being in a hurry was a contradiction in terms. Tomorrow, for him, was far too uncertain: everything must be done today. Besides, he knew that, with an imperialist such as Loch installed as High Commissioner, the sooner he moved, the better it would be for his designs. Before leaving England, Loch had made very clear to the Colonial Office his belief that the B.S.A. Company should be kept on as tight a rein as possible and that decisions on such matters as mining concessions and railway rates should be approved by the Colonial Secretary before they became enforceable under the Company's law. So Rhodes had been put on notice that he could not expect from the new High Commissioner the same complaisance and uncritical support that he had been able to count on with Robinson.

Apart from this, there was the Portuguese claim to the Zambezi valley and Mashonaland to be considered. Portugal's Consul in Cape Town had published a notice in the *Cape Argus* in December 1888 protesting against Lobengula's assertion of

Sir Harry Johnston

Zulu Warrior

sovereignty over the Mashonas, whose territory he contended lay within the area claimed by Portugal. And although up till that year there had been no effective Portuguese occupation in Mashonaland, an expedition had recently left Lisbon under Colonel Paiva D'Andrada, a former Portuguese Military Attaché in Paris now turned explorer and prospector of empty spaces, with the avowed intention of taking possession of the Zambezi valley in the name of the House of Braganza. Salisbury had promptly told the Portuguese Government that Lobengula was, in fact, master of Mashonaland, and would allow nobody to enter the territory without his permission. Therefore Britain could not recognise any Portuguese claims in the area. But D'Andrada had carried on unheeding of this warning diplomatic salvo. Aided by a half-caste lieutenant of Goanese descent, a notorious slave-trader called Ignazio di Manuel Antonio, more commonly known as Gouveia, he managed to talk certain chiefs in Zambezia into accepting the offer of the Portuguese flag and proclaimed that they had thereby agreed to become vassals of Portugal.

In some cases, D'Andrada's troops then withdrew, the flags were used to supplement the chiefs' wardrobes and all traces of Portuguese sovereignty were removed. But in July 1889, a Matabele patrol discovered a force of three hundred African troops under Portuguese command still encamped on the Unyati river in Mashonaland and engaged in building a fort. This disturbing news was shortly followed by news that certain chiefs in the Mazoe valley were refusing to pay tribute to Lobengula, contending that they were now under Portuguese protection. And to add to Rhodes' anxieties came a report in November from the famous African hunter and explorer, Frederick Selous, who is said to have inspired Rider Haggard's character, Allan Quartermaine, and whom Rhodes had recruited to serve as guide for the B.S.A. Company's Pioneers. Returning from a hunting safari and reconnaissance in Mashonaland via Tete and the Zambezi, Selous went straight to Rhodes and told him that he had not a moment to lose in securing his concession, since the Portuguese seemed suddenly to have taken on a new lease of life in the area. He also advised that the Pioneer Column should approach from the south and not, as had first been suggested, from the east up the Zambezi, and that their route should skirt Matabeleland and not cross it. This would eliminate the risk of fever in the Lower Zambezi and avoid having to traverse Portuguese territory. At the same time, it would steer clear of Lobengula's impis who might see a threat to their homeland in a march directly across Matabele territory. Given such precautions, Selous felt sure that Lobengula would not attempt to interfere with the Pioneer Column's advance.

With such arguments to support him, Rhodes had little difficulty in persuading Loch of the need for speed. Almost immediately after his arrival, the High Commissioner had written to Knutsford saying that, after all, 'the Portuguese appear likely to be a serious trouble'. Moreover, he pointed out that, under the terms of Lobengula's agreement with Rhodes, the King could call on the B.S.A. Company to help him evict the Portuguese from his lands. If Loch were to authorise them to comply with such a request, he would be 'authorising an act of war against a friendly country', whereas if he refused his sanction, he would be forcing the company to break faith with Lobengula and so would put them 'in a very dangerous position'. The situation was temporarily relieved when, at the very end of the year, Moffatt reported that the Portuguese had withdrawn from the Unyati, having run short of food and fearing attack from the Matabeles. But as they left, they had told the Mashonas that they would return in the following year when the mealies were ripe.

Thus there was no time to lose if the Pioneers were to forestall the Portuguese and so reduce the risk of an awkward and embarrassing collision. For although tactical reasons might have obliged the Portuguese to pull out from the Unyati for the time being, their Governor-General in Mozambique had as recently as November issued a proclamation creating a new district of Zumbo which included all the area in dispute as Portuguese territory. On top of this, on New Year's Day 1890, Bowler published in the Transvaal press details of his scheme for colonising Mashonaland on the strength of a concession which he alleged he had obtained three years earlier from a

Mashona chief named Mcheza. The announcement was quickly followed by confidential assurances from Pretoria to Cape Town that Kruger 'disapproved' of this scheme and would take steps to prevent it. But for the next month or so, the mere existence of such a project gave Rhodes an opportunity, of which he made full use, to play up the threat of the Bowler trek to British interests in the north. And while Loch thought it more likely that Kruger might try to use Bowler as a lever to obtain concessions in Swaziland and access to Kosi Bay, he could not altogether dismiss the possibility that, with or without the tacit consent of Pretoria, a Boer trek might succeed in forestalling a British presence in Mashonaland.

In January 1890, therefore, Loch called a meeting in Cape Town with Rhodes and Selous which was also attended by Shippard and General Carrington, a British army officer who had been designated as commander of the Pioneer Column's military and police escort. At this meeting, Rhodes unfolded his plan of action. This was to send an advance-party under Selous early in April to construct a wagon road along the fringes of Matabeleland and, on arrival in Mashonaland, to occupy and explore a portion of the territory in the area of Mount Hampden where the Company's first base was to be established. Thereafter the main column would set forth. Loch had no alternative but to agree to this plan, albeit in the somewhat negative terms that he could see nothing 'that would justify the exercise of his authority to delay the advance'. For he felt that, whatever the risks of allowing Rhodes to go ahead and chance a clash with the Matabeles—which would involve imperial forces in subsequent punitive action—the greater danger was that the north might be divided between the Portuguese and the Boers, and possibly the Germans as well, if the speediest possible steps were not taken to claim it for Britain.

Thus, despite his misgivings about the suitability of Rhodes and his private enterprise company to tackle such a difficult and delicate task, Loch gave his sanction for the Pioneer Column to make preparations for their advance. But a few weeks later a serious hitch occurred when Selous visited Lobengula to discuss plans for making the road to Mashonaland. Ignoring Rhodes' assurances that the Pioneers would keep at a constant distance of not less than a hundred miles from any Matabele kraals, Lobengula now pretended that he had not given permission for the Company to enter Mashonaland and refused to allow any road to be made. The King also said that he was tired of talking to Rhodes' emissaries and demanded that the 'big white Chief' himself should come and see him in order to settle their differences.

Rhodes, however, refused to go to Bulawayo and Jameson was sent back to argue with Lobengula. Hoping to persuade the King to look for protection to Rhodes and his associates, Jameson made much of the fact that Loch had sternly warned Kruger that, if he allowed the Bowler trek to proceed across the Limpopo, he would do so on pain of attack by British forces. But Lobengula was not to be fooled by such special pleading. 'I think', he grunted in reply, 'you are keeping the Boers out to have room for yourselves.' Nor was he much impressed by Jameson's talk about the Portuguese threat. For, as he had several times told Moffatt, he had great contempt for the Portuguese and felt that his impis would be well able to take care of any incursions from that quarter. Their withdrawal from the Unyati was proof of this. Thus, the most that the doctor could get from Lobengula was a statement that he did not refuse permission to dig in Mashonaland, but that Rhodes must 'Come and see me'.

Rhodes, somewhat typically, concluded from this that Lobengula was weakening and that all that was needed was for the Company to show that they were determined to move speedily, backed by the necessary show of force. It did not occur to him that Lobengula's further change of attitude had probably been brought about by rumours reaching Bulawayo of a recent exchange between Rhodes and Khama which had led the Bamangwato chief to suppose that the B.S.A. Company were planning to invade Matabeleland by force of arms and would look to Khama to support them in this action. Loch had sternly rebuked Rhodes for engaging in such unwarranted and improper discussions and had insisted that political relations with Khama and other chiefs must be conducted solely by the High

Commissioner and his officers. But he was too late to prevent Khama, who dearly wished to settle his scores with the Matabeles, from letting it be known that with Rhodes' help the moment of retribution would shortly be at hand.

No doubt these hints to Khama arose from a conspiracy, extraordinary even by Rhodes' standards, which was hatched between him and a former employee of the Bechuanaland Exploration Company, named Frank Johnson, two months after the Charter was issued. According to Johnson's own account, Rhodes and he entered into a secret agreement in December 1889 to overthrow Lobengula and seize Matabeleland by force. Johnson was to raise a group of five hundred men at the expense of the B.S.A. Company. As soon as a convenient pretext should occur such as the next Matabele incursion into the Disputed Territory between Matabeleland and Khama's country, this force was to 'carry by sudden assault all the principal strongholds of the Matabele nation and generally so to break the power of the Matabele as to . . . reduce the country to such a condition as to enable the . . . B.S.A. Company to conduct their operations in peace and safety.' Every man in Johnson's force was to have the right to a farm of 3,000 acres and to be allowed to prospect for gold in Matabeleland. Johnson was to get £150,000 if he succeeded and the Company was to take over the government of the country once the Matabeles' power had been broken.

Unfortunately for Rhodes, Johnson thought it necessary to inform his business partner, an Irishman called Heaney who was inclined to drink too much. Shortly after becoming privy to the plot, Heaney in his cups blurted out the story to one of the missionaries at Palapye who felt it his duty to inform Shippard. Despite his friendship and admiration for Rhodes, Shippard knew that this conspiracy must be prevented at all costs. The Imperial Government's message commending Rhodes and his associates to Lobengula had stressed that the Queen was satisfied that 'they are men who will fulfil their undertakings and who may be trusted to carry out the working for gold in the Chief's country without molesting his people, or in any way interfering with their kraals, gardens or cattle'. And the King was told that

197

he would therefore be 'acting wisely in carrying out his agree-ment with these persons'. Yet here was evidence that 'these persons' were plotting to attack the King and, having broken the power of the Matabeles, to seize his country in breach of their own pledges and of those given by Queen Victoria's Ministers on their behalf.

Shippard therefore hastened to inform the High Commis-sioner who promptly summoned Johnson to account for this extraordinary story. Johnson obeyed the summons but, on his way to see Loch, called on his fellow conspirator who had meanwhile learned from Shippard that the cat was out of the bag. When Johnson arrived, Rhodes blandly told him that he had denied all knowledge of the story and had informed Ship-pard that, if such a plot existed, it must have been concocted by Johnson himself. Moreover, he insisted that, when talking to Loch, Johnson should back him up and 'take everything on yourself'. And such was Rhodes' power over his associates, that Johnson duly took all the blame and exculpated his partner completely.

The conspiracy was thus frustrated and Rhodes had to wait three years before he was able to crush Lobengula and seize his country. But it is probable that, thanks to Heaney's indis-cretions, some word of this discreditable episode reached Bulawayo and caused the King's final volte-face. Nevertheless, the soothing influence of Moffatt, who was nowadays spending most of his time at Bulawayo, duly succeeded in calming Lobengula's suspicions; and in April 1890, Moffatt was able to report that 'the manner of the people . . . is far more favourable to the whites, especially towards the English'. Since the line of march would not approach within a hundred and fifty miles of the Matabele kraals, he did not now anticipate any great diffi-culty from Lobengula or his people. And on the strength of this reassuring intelligence, plans for the advance went ahead and officers were appointed to command the column and its police escort.

At this point Rhodes discovered, at a fortuitous re-encounter with Johnson at the Kimberley Club, that Carrington's estimate of a million pounds for a police escort of 2,500 men for the

Pioneers was quite unrealistic. Johnson, who knew Matabeleland and had served in the Bechuanaland Border Police, insisted that a tenth of this number of police could afford ample protection at a cost of less than £100,000. He was promptly invited to take over command of the expedition; and despite his earlier experience of Rhodes' methods, Johnson accepted the charge. Moffatt was appointed as the Company's Resident at Bulawayo. Carrington was transferred to the command of the Bechuanaland Border Police who, to deter Lobengula's impis, were to be stationed in strength near the Matabele frontier; and Lt.-Colonel Pennefather of the Inniskilling Dragoons, a veteran of the campaigns against the Zulus and the Boers, was appointed to command the police escort, with Selous acting as guide.

The Pioneers themselves, numbering some two hundred, came from a variety of backgrounds and were recruited from different parts of the British Colonies in South Africa and from the British communities in the Boer Republics. (One of them was Patrick Campbell, later to be killed in the Boer War, who was the husband of the famous actress and lady-friend of King Edward VII.) Each man was offered seven-and-sixpence pay a day, and was promised fifteen gold claims and 3,000 acres of farm land, although at this point Rhodes had no such land to offer to anyone. Supplies sufficient for four months were to accompany the expedition and Archibald Colquhoun, who had been designated as the first Company Administrator of Mashonaland, indented for champagne, caviar and pâté de foie gras 'in view of the considerable and probably increasing amount of entertaining that will have to be gone through'!

By the end of June, all was ready and Loch gave his final approval for the Pioneers and their police escort to start on their journey. Loch also took the precaution of sending a message to Lobengula, together with a further letter from Knutsford speaking in the Queen's name, to reassure him that the expedition boded no threat to his Kingdom. But at the last minute Lobengula again had second thoughts; and in a reply despatched with two indunas to Cape Town, as the Pioneers gathered on his borders, he asked 'Why do you send your impi?' Recalling that Rudd had told him that no more than ten men would be coming to dig in his country and would obey his laws and live with his people, he felt that so large a force could only mean that 'Rhodes wants to take my country by strength'. And in the course of discussions with the indunas in Cape Town, at which Rhodes was present, Loch was told 'Mr. Rhodes came to ask for permission to dig, and the Chief gave it; but now Rhodes wants to kill him.' Whether or not Lobengula was referring to reports of Rhodes' plot with Johnson, the indunas were not satisfied with the High Commissioner's assurances and insisted that the King's fears and suspicions should be relayed to the Queen.

Four days later the reply came from the Colonial Office once again assuring Lobengula in the Queen's name that he could place his faith in the B.S.A. Company whose purpose in his country was peaceful and who had come to him as friends with no intention of attacking him or stealing his country! But Rhodes did not wait for the Queen's soothing words to reach their destination. And well before the indunas returned to Bulawayo, the Pioneers were already on their way to Mashonaland. In spite of this, the King refrained from any hostile act or interference. At the start of their advance, he sent word that they should halt. But when they ignored his order and marched on, he took no further steps to impede their progress. No doubt the presence in strength of the Bechuanaland Border Police on his frontiers helped to stay his hand. But it was nevertheless due more to his wisdom and good faith than to any action or intention on the part of Rhodes that the Pioneers arrived at Mount Hampden and established the township of Fort Salisbury on September 12, 1890, after a march of seventy-seven days without a single casualty. For even after the Column had started, Rhodes was still toying with the idea of seizing Matabeleland by a surprise attack and was only dissuaded from the attempt by Selous' categorical refusal to have anything to do with so crazy and treacherous a scheme.

After nearly two years of cliff-hanging suspense, Rhodes had won through to secure what he believed to be the 'New Rand'. But if Rhodes had won, Lobengula was to lose. For, just as Kruger was rewarded for renouncing his claims in the North with the Jameson Raid and the Boer War, so the Matabeles were to pay a capital price for having put their trust in Rhodes. Within three years of letting the Pioneers into Mashonaland, the Matabele King was dead and his Kingdom destroyed. And all because Rhodes, using tactics horribly similar to those deployed in later years by Hitler and Mussolini in the Sudetenland and Abyssinia, had to indulge his insatiable appetite by grabbing all of Lobengula's domains.

In the interval it was, however, the Portuguese who were to be the first victims of this man's extraordinary hunger for territory. Apart from his schemes for the seizure of Matabeleland, Rhodes had never made any secret of the fact that his ambitions lay far beyond the limits of the Rudd concession. One of the many areas which he coveted was Manica, an allegedly gold-rich district east of Mashonaland ruled over by a chief named Umtasa, an alcohol addict who claimed to be independent both of Lobengula and of his southern neighbour, the Gazaland King, Gungunyana. Thus, on orders from Rhodes, a party of the Pioneer Column headed by Colquhoun broke away from the main advance soon after reaching the Mashona table-land to visit Umtasa and obtain mining concessions from him and, if possible, access to the Indian Ocean sea-board. Two days after the main body of Pioneers had planted their flag at Fort Salisbury, Colquhoun and his escort arrived at Umtasa's kraal, where the chief, arrayed for the occasion in a naval cocked hat and a leopard skin, was duly persuaded, largely out of fear of the Portuguese, to sign a treaty. By this deed he was recognised as 'Paramount Chief of the Manica nation', with a stipend of £100 per year, while the B.S.A. Company were granted the 'sole, absolute and perpetual right' to prospect in his territory. Umtasa undertook not to treat with any other power without the Company's consent and he assured Colquhoun that he had signed no treaty with the Portuguese, his only 'obligations' being a time-expired mining concession which he had granted to a Mr. Beningfield, whom he insisted on calling Mr. Diningbell!

Nor was Manica Rhodes' only attempt to extend the frontiers of his new-found empire at its inception. Away to the northwest, he had managed to recruit Francois Coillard, a French missionary in Barotseland across the Zambezi, to work on his behalf by helping his emissary, Frank Lochner, to sign up the Barotse chief, Lewanika. He had also despatched other agents deep into Angolan territory to secure concessions and make treaties with the tribes, while on the east coast of Africa, his representative in Gazaland, a Colonial Service doctor and explorer named Aurel Schulz, obtained an agreement with Gungunyana in the autumn of 1890 in similar terms to the Rudd concession—mineral rights in return for an annual subsidy and a supply of rifles and ammunition. Thus, in this incredible year 1890—during which, for good measure, he also became Prime Minister of Cape Colony—Rhodes could, by virtue of treaties concluded with tribal chiefs, lay claim to a belt of territory stretching almost the whole way across Africa, from Gazaland on the Indian Ocean westwards to the Cunene and Cubango river basins, two hundred miles from the Atlantic sea-board, and from the Limpopo northwards to the regions beyond the Zambezi. In due course the requirements of British foreign policy were to cut him back on either side of this vast area and to leave him with the territories now known as Zambia and Rhodesia. But at the time he might well claim, as he did, to have secured 'the balance of Africa'.

11 Portuguese Reawakening

NEEDLESS to say, Rhodes' far-reaching claims were soon to bring the B.S.A. Company into collision with the Portuguese. And for the first nine months after the occupation of Mashonaland, his and the Imperial Government's attentions were largely taken up with finding a solution to this conflict of interests, which would give the Company as much territory as the Portuguese could be bullied into conceding.

The scramble for Africa was now approaching its climax and Portugal had awoken from a long imperial slumber to make a desperate effort to assert what Britain and her other rivals often rudely termed her 'archaeological' claims in the southern part of Central Africa. But her attempt was doomed to failure from the start because, for all her prestige as the prior discoverer of these regions, Portugal was no match for the megalomania of Rhodes, and because she had failed to take the elementary and essential precaution of occupying the territories which she claimed. In the event, far from adding to her existing colonies in East and West Africa, she was lucky not to lose still more than she did in the final settlement.

As her treaty with Germany in 1886 showed, Portugal laid claim to a belt of territory across Africa from coast to coast linking Mozambique with Angola. By priority of exploration she assumed possession from the Zambezi valley to the estuary of the Congo river. But in all this vast area there was at the time very little sign of Portuguese influence, let alone of Portuguese occupation. Without any appreciable surplus population at home from which to draw settlers and colonists to run their African possessions, the Portuguese had almost from the beginning adopted the policy of assimilating the native Africans. Far from there being any colour bar, it was a punishable offence to insult a half-caste. Mixed marriages were encouraged and from the mid-eighteenth century, anyone who was not a slave and had been baptised and given a rudimentary education enjoyed full privileges before the law. Also, in order to encourage a settled population, a system of prazos—land settlements—had been developed for all loyal citizens and colonists. But over the years this system fell into decay and abuse, as the prazos passed by sale or extortion into the hands of unscrupulous half-breed slavers and their agents. Worse still, as the prazo holders grew richer and more powerful, so they began to defy the authorities and in most inland areas ended by substituting their rule for that of the Portuguese.

In East Africa, where the Portuguese had been installed on the island of Mozambique since 1507, and where they claimed sovereignty from Delagoa Bay as far north as Cape Delgado, their influence did not, in fact, extend for more than a few miles inland. And along the coast they were largely confined to their fortresses. From the great four-bastioned castle of San Sebastiao, for instance, their authority was limited to a few farms around the bay. At Angoche, south of Mozambique Island, the Governor lived in a thatched hut and his writ ran no further than the limits of his own garden. At Quelimane near the estuary of the Zambezi, the garrison numbered no more than a motley eighty-five native troops. And even at Lourenço Marques, the largest of their Mozambique settlements, the Portuguese scarcely ever ventured beyond the limits of the town which, though situated on the best natural harbour in all South-East Africa, was a poor and smelly place which had seen its best days during the slave-trade and consisted of a mass of grass huts, reed fences and decayed forts with rusty cannon, with a population of under five hundred of whom no more than a fifth were Europeans.

Inland from the coast lay Gazaland and Manica which the

Portuguese liked to think were their vassal states but which, until very recently had scarcely been touched by any European influence even in the earliest period of discovery and colonisation. Gazaland's King in the early 1880s was Umzila, a Zulu chief whose father, like Msilikazi, had broken with Chaka and led his Shangaan tribe northwards out of Zululand. Umzila claimed paramountcy over Manica as well as Gazaland and had married one of his daughters to Lobengula in a 'political' union designed to ensure Matabele support for his claims. He held the Portuguese in great contempt, referring to them disdainfully as 'women'; and he was greatly nettled by their claim to have made him their vassal when, in fact, the Portuguese paid him tribute and survived largely by his good will. Indeed, in 1870, he had decided to have no further dealings with Portugal and asked the Natal Government to accept him as an 'ally, friend and tributary'. But for fear of offending their own oldest ally at a time when the future of Delagoa Bay hung in the balance, the British Government had declined his offer.

At about this time, Colonel D'Andrada came to East Africa and, having surveyed the scene, formed a Franco-Portuguese company to which the Government in Lisbon granted a monopoly concession in the Zambezi basin in order to promote 'mining, commerce and industry based on free labour'. He also persuaded the Portuguese Government to send an expedition to Umzila to offer him protection and to find out what, if any, relations he had with the British. If the Chief should respond favourably, the expedition were to leave a garrison at his kraal and march on to Manica to repeat the treatment with Umtasa. But Umzila did not respond favourably: instead he sent the expedition packing and refused to allow them 'the road' to his Manica vassal.

In 1884, Umzila died and was succeeded by his son, Gungunyana, who the Portuguese Governor-General, Castilho, felt might be more amenable to the idea of Portuguese protection, as he was said to be a lesser man than his father and reputedly feared attack by his brother-in-law, Lobengula. Another expedition therefore set out from Lourenço Marques early in 1885 to offer the King terms which included a yearly subsidy and a Portuguese Colonel's rank and uniform. Gungunyana was no less suspicious of these overtures than his father had been. But he was sorely disturbed by reports of Warren's doings in Bechuanaland and of Boer designs beyond the Limpopo, as well as by constant rumours that Lobengula wished to add the Gazaland grazings to his empire. And feeling that in this situation he could not afford to ignore Castilho's offer, he sent envoys to Lisbon to conclude a treaty by which he undertook to receive a Portuguese Resident at his kraal, to accept a defined frontier—the Limpopo river—between his domains and Lourenço Marques, to let Manica live in peace and to permit D'Andrada to dig for minerals.

This achievement of Castilho's might have been a shrewd stroke on the part of the Portuguese. For by seeking mineral rights rather than territorial concessions, they had assuaged Gungunyana's worst suspicions. And by imposing their protection on Gazaland they were anticipating the kind of move by which Rhodes was later to try to encroach upon their position at Delagoa Bay. But Castilho soon spoiled his chances of turning the Gazalanders into real allies by contending that the treaty confined Gungunyana's sovereignty to the south of the Pungwe river, which meant that his writ did not run in Manica. Feeling that he had conceded enough in agreeing not to impose his rule on Manica by force, Gungunyana protested that his paramountcy still extended as far north as the Zambezi valley and therefore included Manica and Barue. But the Portuguese, who had had their own designs on Manica since D'Andrada had awakened them to its potential wealth, refuted his claims. Whereupon the Shangaan Chief appealed to the British and, like his father before him, despatched an embassy to Natal with a petition for a treaty and a huge ivory tusk for presentation to the Governor. The tusk proved too heavy to carry and was left on the road: but the messengers arrived and duly presented their petition.

Thus, a little more than a year after making Gungunyana their ally, the Portuguese had driven him to turn to Britain. Castilho therefore decided not to rush matters with Manica for fear of precipitating a similar reaction in this reputedly gold-rich territory and of still further alienating Gungunyana. Even when in May 1888 a deputation from Umtasa came to tell him that their chief wished to be under Portuguese protection and was ready to receive a Portuguese Resident, Castilho thought it advisable not to take up Umtasa's offer immediately.

Then at this point D'Andrada returned to East Africa, determined to extend Portuguese influence as far inland as possible with the aid of his Mozambique Company whose terms of reference, like those of Rhodes' B.S.A. Company, empowered him to 'promote and direct colonisation . . . (and) undertake any form of enterprise whatsoever, mineral, agricultural, industrial or commercial. . . .' With a subsidy and a flotilla of armed steamers provided by Lisbon, D'Andrada was able to convince the Shangaans of the futility of pressing their claims in Manica and Barue. And early in 1889, Gungunyana, after sending one final punitive expedition to show Umtasa what he thought of his flirting with the Portuguese, foreswore further gestures against his neighbours and moved his kraal and the bulk of his tribe down from the north of his territory to a site near Lourenço Marques, far from the Manica border. Umtasa's offer was then accepted, a Portuguese Protectorate was established over Manica, and D'Andrada moved further inland, bent on extending Portuguese authority up the Zambezi and into Mashonaland.

Here was undoubtedly the most chaotic of all Portugal's African 'possessions'. At Sena in the Zambezi valley, a state of almost total decay obtained with only four European residents, no trade to speak of and a military post manned by one soldier and consisting of four stone huts which housed the ornaments from a church which no longer existed. The only recent development undertaken by the colonial authorities had been the erection of a flag-pole! Further up river at Tete, things were hardly any better. Here a dilapidated fort and a few thatched huts housed a garrison with no European officers and a hundred or so soldiers, a few of whom were natives and the rest 'degredados', exiles from Portugal under order of banishment or criminals, who had elected to serve their sentences in some fever-ridden army post rather than in a Portuguese gaol. In Sofala there was not one Portuguese resident and not even a literate native. And at the extremity of Portugal's 'influence' on the Zambezi was Zumbo where a fort and barracks was commanded by a native captain—'capitao-mor'—with a garrison that varied in numbers from nought to twenty-one.

The main reason for all this chaos and decay was to be laid at the door of a rebel prazo holder, locally known as Bonga, whose real name was Antonio Vicente da Cruz. Like other prazo holders, Bonga had recruited a large private army. In the early seventies he had held the area from Sena to Tete in thrall under a reign of terror which neither the Portuguese nor any of his 'subjects' dared to try to break. Bonga had eventually come to terms with authority, but the ending of his rule in 1875 only led to a series of native rebellions against the prazo system. And the Portuguese, as always lacking the troops to restore order in such situations, were forced to rely on such unsavoury and undisciplined semi-bandits as Gouveia, who was no more loyal to Portugal than Bonga, to do the job for them. As the Governor of Sena remarked when Gouveia appeared with the rank of capitao-mor and a private army of ten thousand men which he had obtained after marrying the daughter of the King of Barue, 'All the robbers around here are appointed capitaes-mores'. But when he suggested to his superiors that steamers be sent up the Zambezi to reassert Portuguese authority, he was dismissed from his post for insubordination and mental derangement!

It was not until the late eighties that Castilho, newly appointed as Governor-General in East Africa, ventured to suggest that the Portuguese Government should do something about the state of affairs in the Zambezi valley. The power that Bonga represented had not been destroyed, he told Lisbon. Nor had Zambezia been pacified. And neither of these things could be achieved until the prazo system and the private armies that went with it had been abolished and the power of the war-lords who fed on these abuses had been crushed by determined Portuguese action. Like the unhappy Sena Governor, he demanded gun-boats to patrol the Zambezi and the construction of a road and railway to assist communications, which were still virtually non-existent.

Lisbon received these recommendations at a time when the

formation of the British Imperial East African Company, together with the news of Moffatt's treaty with Lobengula, had aroused much Portuguese anxiety for their possessions in this part of Africa. Thus, although they dreaded to tackle the prazo holders and their private armies, the Portuguese were quick to see the importance of putting steamers on the Zambezi and building a railway from the coast. And as D'Andrada appeared on the scene with his own near-equivalent of Rhodes' Royal Charter, a survey team was sent to Mozambique to explore the possibilities of a railway from Quelimane to Sena. But, for all D'Andrada's adventurous spirit and determination, he and the surveyors were already too late. For by this time, Rhodes had won his concession to dig for gold in Mashonaland and was about to challenge Portugal in the very area which she was now desperately striving to reclaim. The Portuguese might try to wean the Mashonas away from Lobengula; they might send an embassy to treat with Lewanika and the Barotses; and they might issue any number of proclamations asserting that Zumbo was the centre of a vast Portuguese district embracing the lands both north and south of the Zambezi river. But Rhodes was on his way to these selfsame areas with the British Government at his back and the ruthless driving force of his own ambition to spur him on. Thus an early collision was as inevitable as was the fact that, when it came, it would be Portugal who would have to give way.

This was to be no new experience for the Portuguese. Only a few years before they had been forced to yield on the west coast of Africa in the face of irresistible pressures from France and Germany in support of King Leopold's private empire in the Congo. In some respects, this defeat was an even bigger disappointment to their hopes than were their losses in the Zambezi valley. For one thing, they had hopes that Britain would back their claims in this part of Africa. For another, they had spent a great deal more money and energy in West Africa than in Mozambique, in spite of the serious recession which followed the general abolition of the slave-trade. And although Angola's exports of oil, ivory, coffee and copra had not proved a profitable substitute for the human cargoes which once left its shores, Luanda, Angola's capital, could still claim in the seventies to be the most beautiful city on the west coast, with an excellent harbour, fine buildings and other amenities.

Nevertheless the Portuguese hold over Angola was somewhat tenuous. The port of Ambriz to the north of Luanda was, for instance, approachable only from the sea, since the local tribes refused to allow any Europeans to cross their territory, for fear of losing it to white occupation and with it the carrier trade from the interior to the coast. In fact, ever since the excesses of the Portuguese slave-traders in the Congo had driven the tribes to rebellion and massacre in the sixteenth century the Portuguese had been, as in Mozambique, largely confined to the coast where for the past three hundred years they had been content to play the role of shippers and traders of slaves and other cargoes brought to them by the omnipresent middlemen of the Angolan interior. And it was not until King Leopold of the Belgians formed his International African Association with its designs on the Congo basin that they began to think of recovering their long-lost position in this area.

To this end, in 1877, Andrade Corvo, Portugal's Foreign Minister, announced to the Cortes—Portugal's Parliament— that the Congo was within the Portuguese sphere of influence and that Britain had recognised this fact, although she had been opposed to Portugal physically occupying the area. And, in keeping with their efforts to consolidate their claims in the east, the Portuguese Government followed up Corvo's proclamation by despatching Serpa Pinto, the most renowned of Portugal's colonial officers at this time, to survey the country between the Congo and the Zambezi valleys.

Portugal had felt grossly insulted by her exclusion from the 1876 Brussels Conference at which every other European country with colonial interests—Britain, France, Germany, Russia, Italy, Austria-Hungary and Belgium—was invited to agree to Leopold establishing his International African Association. And she was still further disturbed to hear that the celebrated explorer, H. M. Stanley, had been sent by the Association to lead an expedition to the Congo Basin with instructions to gather concessions from the tribes to establish 'a republican confederation of free negroes . . . to be independent, except that the King (Leopold) . . . reserved the right to appoint a President who should reside in Europe'. Nor was Lisbon any happier to learn that the French had sent their own man, Savorgnan de Brazza, hot-foot after Stanley to make sure that the north bank of the Congo should be reserved to France. And to add still further to Portugal's problems, the British Government, who had never recognised Portuguese claims in this area for fear of being accused of encouraging clandestine slave-trading, now felt bound to tell Corvo that he had got it wrong and that Britain could not support his claim to the Congo.

Despite this rebuff, the Portuguese remained determined to come to some arrangement with Britain over the Congo. Apart from their fears of Leopold and the French, they had heard rumours that Cape Colony had designs on Angola's southern borders. Lisbon therefore proposed that a comprehensive treaty be drawn up, which would divide all the west coast of Africa from the Congo to the Cape between Portugal and Britain. First reactions in London were however discouraging. Lord Salisbury, Disraeli's Foreign Secretary, decided that the offer of an unwanted empty space in South-West Africa was insufficient inducement for Britain to reverse her policy and approve Portugal's claims on the Congo; and accordingly he turned down Lisbon's proposal. But, after the change of government in 1880, Granville, as Salisbury's successor, took a different line. Believing that the greatest menace to British interests in West and Central Africa was France and that British trade might prosper from Portuguese occupation of Congo territory, he offered Portugal a package settlement. Britain would recognise Portuguese claims from Ambriz northwards to a point which would give them about a hundred miles of coast each side of the Congo mouth and all the lower reaches of the river itself. In return, Portugal had to guarantee free trade, cede to Britain her West African possessions at Whydah and in Dahomey, and ratify the agreement giving Britain first refusal of Delagoa Bay.

Immediately Leopold's Association protested that this agreement would hinder rather than help free trade and announced that they would oppose Portuguese occupation by force. France also proclaimed that she would not recognise Portuguese claims on the Congo. De Brazza, who had meanwhile hoisted the French tricolour at Stanley Pool on the site of what was to become Brazzaville, was despatched to the scene with an expedition, armed in such a way as to make it clear that it was aimed at European and not native opposition. And to back up this expedition, a French force was landed north of the Congo estuary on land claimed by the Portuguese.

Regardless of these threats and protests, however, Granville went ahead with the negotiations and after a few last-minute changes, a treaty was duly signed in February 1884. Uproar followed in France, Belgium and Britain and, to a lesser extent, even in Portugal as well. In Britain, violent opposition was expressed by the humanitarians, especially by the Baptist Missionary Association and the Anti-Slavery Society, that their elected leaders should have conceded such claims to the Portuguese, who had once so despoiled the Congo by their slave-trading, who had not proclaimed the liberation of slaves in their colonies until the late seventies and who were still said to be carrying on a clandestine slave-trade in East Africa. So vocal did the opposition prove that Granville's colleagues soon lost their nerve and decided to postpone presenting the treaty for Parliament's approval. In Portugal, there were protests against the cession of Whydah and the undertaking to grant free trade. But the Lisbon Government met these objections with a stern reminder that, if this treaty should fail, they would be left face to face with Leopold and the French, who would probably annexe all the north bank of the Congo and pin them back to the coast below the estuary.

French opposition centred on the fact that Portugal had dared to negotiate with Britain to the exclusion of France—a strange argument to put to those, who had themselves been excluded from the deliberations which gave birth to the International African Association. France, it was said, was not only willing but anxious to negotiate an arrangement with Lisbon defining frontiers north of the Congo estuary. But she would not tolerate an exclusive Anglo-Portuguese arrangement. Also she considered that, if Whydah should be ceded to anyone, it should be ceded to her. And in Belgium, Leopold's Association loudly protested that the treaty would limit their ability to bring civilisation to the Congo, which they claimed was the prime duty of their humanitarian and philanthropic enterprise.

Harry Johnston, returning from a visit to the Congo at this time, was able to shatter these disingenuous pretensions with a report on the treatment of the Congolese by the Association's officials which was almost as horrifying as that submitted two decades later by Sir Roger Casement as the local British Consul, which was to rally world public opinion to bring Leopold's private empire to an end and transfer it to the care of the Belgian Government. Incensed by what he saw as much as by Stanley's attempts to blacken the Portuguese with accusations of slave-trading, Johnston proclaimed that Leopold's agents treated their Congolese subjects no better than slaves. While pretending to end slavery as a native institution, they had created 'a gigantic commercial monopoly' and to this end were abusing native labour with disciplinary atrocities which included flogging fugitives or slackers to death with the sjambok.

But, for all this, the Association made some influential friends and allies for themselves. Duped by their pretensions to have ended slavery, the United States Senate agreed to recognise them as a sovereign state. And still more important, the French were won over by Leopold offering them the reversion of all the Association's possessions should they find it necessary to sell out, in return for which France agreed to recognise them and all their claims south of the Congo river. Stanley and de Brazza might still be deadly rivals in the field; but when it came to intervention by a third party such as Portugal, apparently in league with Britain, Leopold and the French had no hesitation in closing ranks to resist such a threat.

With this new alliance between Paris and Leopold added to the evident reluctance of the British Parliament to ratify the treaty, the Portuguese began to feel somewhat isolated. And in May 1884, they decided to put their case to an international conference which, in addition to their sworn opponents, would also consist of 'neutral' powers such as Germany, Italy, Austria-

Hungary, Holland and Spain. Britain was at first opposed to the idea, not wishing to be confronted at this stage by the French who might ask too many awkward questions about British trade monopolies on the Niger. Nevertheless Lisbon insisted on canvassing support for the project among the nations concerned.

Immediate approval was forthcoming from the German Chancellor who, as always thinking and planning ahead, had by now assumed that the Anglo-Portuguese treaty was a dead letter in view of the universal opposition which it had encountered. Bismarck liked the idea of a conference at which Germany would have a say in future arrangements in Central and West Africa; he had indeed just told the British Government that he expected to be consulted about any new treaty which might replace the now clearly defunct agreement of the previous February. For with the German flag now flying in South-West Africa and about to be hoisted in the Cameroons, Germany was beginning to think imperially, and the German Colonial Society was emerging as a new and influential political pressure group, which would not allow German interests to go by default in any agreements covering West Africa. Besides, Bismarck had been nettled by Granville's failure to respond to his hints that the cession of Heligoland to Germany might help to resolve any Anglo-German differences in Africa. And an international conference might make Britain more amenable by bringing her face to face with her rivals and critics; it might also help to straighten out the confusion into which the coming scramble for Africa threatened to plunge the powers concerned. The French supported the proposed conference for similar reasons. Whereupon Granville and his colleagues decided that, if only to secure German support for a British presence in Egypt, which was their overriding interest in Africa, they would do well to fall in with Bismarck and the French and agree to the proposed conference.

Seeing how their diplomatic initiative had miscarried, the Portuguese Government promptly despatched a former Foreign Minister, Serpa de Pimental, on a secret mission to Paris and Berlin in a desperate last-minute effort to save the Anglo-Portuguese treaty. But this manoeuvre met with no success in either capital, largely because the opposition to the treaty in France and Germany was based on suspicion and resentment of Britain rather than Portugal. The French suspected that Britain was intent on denying them the fruits of de Brazza's exploits; and Bismarck, who refused even to see Lisbon's emissary, thought that, for all Gladstone's assertions that he welcomed Germany as a neighbour in Africa, Britain in fact deeply resented the new German Protectorates.

As the luckless de Pimental returned empty-handed to Lisbon, Bismarck and Jules Ferry, the French Prime Minister, decided to take the initiative themselves and, in October 1884, they informed Granville that their two Governments felt that a regulation of trade in West Africa would be for the common good and that, to this end, a conference of the interested powers should be held in Berlin. Thus the 1884-5 Berlin Conference came about with all the colonial powers assembled and the British and the Portuguese eyeing each other warily across the table. The Portuguese strove bravely to salvage something from the wreckage of their ambitions. Contending that the International Association were not a fully recognised state and that any formalities which might be agreed for future occupations of Africa could not therefore apply to Leopold's private empire, they announced that they would guarantee free trade if their claims, as recognised in the Anglo-Portuguese treaty, were admitted. But their efforts were in vain, partly because of the opposition of the powers and partly due to a dramatic intervention by H. M. Stanley.

Stanley was bitterly opposed to the Portuguese. Ten years earlier, he had written to Harry Johnston to protest against the idea of Britain supporting Portugal's claims anywhere on the Congo. Together with its tributaries, he claimed that the Congo Basin offered over 4,000 miles of navigable water which, thanks to the expenditure of Anglo-American money, had been opened up to give access to civilisation in what had only recently been 'hopelessly impenetrable' jungle. 'Would you bestow all this', he asked, 'as a dower upon such people as the Portuguese who would seal it to the silence of the centuries? . . . If you deliver these people into the hands of the Portuguese, you deliver them soul and body to Hell and slavery. . . . Will you still vote that we sacrifice all this to a nation whose countrymen allowed the pearl of African rivers to lie idle for nearly four centuries? Bah! the very thought sickens me.' And since Stanley was still convinced that the worst fate that any international conference could impose on the Congolese would be to 'deliver' them into Portugal's hands, he now made a dash to England to warn that, if the International Association were not recognised as a state and allowed all that they claimed in the way of territory, there might be war on the Congo.

This crude piece of blackmail spelled final doom for the Anglo-Portuguese treaty and for Portugal's claims to the Congo. Granville had already made it clear to the Portuguese that Britain would not support them beyond the point where she might find herself in conflict with the other powers. Now, in face of the threat posed by Stanley as Leopold's principal henchman on the spot, he collapsed completely and, finally ditching his own treaty, he recognised the International Association as a state for the purposes of the partition of Central Africa. Portugal was offered as compensation recognition of her claims from Ambriz to the Congo mouth and up the estuary to a point five miles beyond the reach of ocean steamers—a mere fraction of what the treaty had allowed her—and even this small mercy was conditional on her reducing her colonial tariff.

Inevitably, the Portuguese Government rejected this offer as totally inadequate and pressed their claims at least as far as Noqui, one hundred miles up river together with a slice of territory on the north bank. But Leopold would have none of this and, for a while, it seemed that the conference would end in deadlock on the Congo issue. Then Bismarck, prompted by a conscience-stricken Granville, made Portugal an offer. He undertook to support her now reduced demands, if she would make certain commercial concessions to Germany in East Africa. But still the International Association would not yield; and although Portugal now looked to Bismarck as her only friend, he could not bind Leopold who, with French support, was beginning to scent the sweet smell of victory.

Deadlock therefore continued until, finally, the Portuguese

delegate was forced to recognise that his government must yield still further. At his suggestion, and in order to enable his government to persuade the Cortes that they must bow to force majeure, the British and French representatives together informed the Portuguese negotiators and Leopold's agents that they must come to an agreement between themselves. In this way the logjam was finally broken; and in February 1885, an agreement was reached by which Portugal secured the south bank as far as Noqui, together with an enclave between French and International Association territory at Kabinda on the coast north of the estuary, while Leopold took all the rest of the south bank, together with the north bank from Noqui to the mouth of the Congo. Leopold's empire was recognised by Portugal and the other powers under the title of the Congo Free State and the Cortes grudgingly accepted the settlement.

Portugal had paid the price of failing to occupy her claims in time to forestall her rivals and of relying on British support in an area where the Imperial Government were not prepared to challenge those powers whose hostility would embarrass them in Egypt. But, if the Portuguese had learned in the Congo not to look to Britain for help in regions which were of little interest to her, East Africa was to teach them that a collision in lands desired by the British would lead to an even worse defeat. For, as the eighties wore on, they had to contend not only with the ambitions of Rhodes, but also the suspicions of the Imperial Government that Germany, in league with the Boers and/or the Portuguese, intended to bar the way for British expansion north of the Limpopo.

Such suspicions had, of course, been considerably enhanced by the German Chancellor's suggestions at Berlin for commercial concessions in Portuguese East Africa. Coming on top of rumours that Germany was planning to take over a section of the Transvaal border as a Protectorate, Bismarck's proposal appeared in Whitehall and Cape Town as a thinly disguised request to Portugal for a German right of way from Delagoa Bay to Kruger's Republic. Nor were the Imperial Government's anxieties exactly allayed by persistent reports reaching the High Commissioner in Cape Town throughout 1887 that the Transvaal Boers, with encouragement from Berlin, were planning to seize Delagoa Bay from the Portuguese, and that only the fear of being brought into conflict with Britain had so far deterred Kruger from making the attempt.

The Colonial Office pressed for strong diplomatic action to forestall these alleged manoeuvres. Any threat to Delagoa Bay by ιa third party touched them on the raw. Together with successive Cape Governments, they had been anxiously and covetously watching this crucial area ever since the Portuguese failed to ratify an agreement, signed in 1879, which gave Britain the right in an emergency to use the Bay to send troops across Mozambique territory to the Transvaal, then under British annexation. Nevertheless, Salisbury, now back in control of Britain's international relations, refused to make any approach to the Portuguese. His Minister in Lisbon had assured him that, notwithstanding her parlous economic situation, Portugal would brook no pressures or propositions for Delagoa Bay, because the Government would not dare to face the public outcry which would follow if it were given up. And all that the Prime Minister would sanction in the way of precautionary measures in the area was to accept Queen Zambili's offer to place Tongaland under British protection and so to extend the application of Britain's 'Monroe Doctrine' against the Boers as far as the Mozambique frontier. But here, at least, he showed no sign of vacillation. For when Castilho threatened the Tongas with war, angrily protesting that the Queen was a Portuguese subject because a part of her territory lay within the area covered by the McMahon Award, Salisbury firmly refused to withdraw the British Protectorate and the Portuguese were obliged to haul down the flag which they had hoisted at Zambili's kraal.

Yet, for all the anxieties of the Colonial Office and of Cape Colony politicians on the subject of Delagoa Bay, it was not there but in Nyasaland that the inevitable collision between Britain and Portugal finally came about. Commercially speaking, Nyasaland was an unprofitable country. But, for this very reason, it had become a particular interest of the humanitarians in Britain. For with little to export save a constantly surplus population and with a natural system of communications through the chain of lakes, beginning with Lake Nyasa itself and extending via Lakes Tanganyika, Edward and Albert to the southern borders of the Sudan, it offered irresistible opportunities for Arab slave-traders from the north. Livingstone's explorations in the middle of the eighteenth century had shown that, despite their claims, the rule of the Portuguese did not extend to the Nyasa area. And at Livingstone's funeral in Westminster Abbey, James Stewart, a Free Churchman from Scotland who had worked and travelled with the great explorer, vowed that he would realise his mentor's dream and build a mission centre in Nyasaland. So in 1875 the first of the Scottish missionary pioneers set out from Britain and, ascending the Zambezi and its tributary the Shire, arrived in the Shire Highlands at the southern end of Lake Nyasa. In the following year, the Church of Scotland missionary settlement of Blantyre, so-called after Livingstone's birthplace in Scotland, was established mid-way between the lake and the Zambezi valley.

At this point in time there was, of course, no official British presence in the territory. But not long after the Blantyre mission had begun operations, a British trader, who had accompanied a group of missionary reinforcements to the area, suggested to the Foreign Office that the Nyasa region should be placed under British jurisdiction for its own good. Britain, he said, had a right to the country by reason of missionary occupation, even though Portugal might claim to have been the first to explore the area. What he does not appear to have said was that the Scottish missionaries had inherited all Livingstone's animosity towards Portuguese colonial methods and were encouraging the tribes to the south of Blantyre to defy, and even to attack, the Portuguese whenever they approached. But the British Minister in Lisbon did not fail to make the point when Salisbury asked him what he thought about Britain assuming a Protectorate over Nyasaland. He admitted that the Blantyre mission had done well in keeping a sharp look-out on the slave-trade from the north and introducing the natives to trade, as well as the gospels. But he thought that the missionaries would make serious trouble between Britain and Portugal unless some British authority were established in the area in the very near future. The Portuguese could not properly object to a British Protectorate, he said, because Lake Nyasa was as unknown to them in the nineteenth century as, according to their assertions, it had been known to them in the sixteenth. Besides, they too would benefit from the law and order which a Protectorate would establish.

In fact, not only were the missionaries antagonising the Portuguese, they were also treating the natives with a brutality scarcely in keeping with their professions of Christianity. Both at the Church of Scotland mission at Blantyre and, to a lesser extent, at the Free Church station at Livingstonia on Lake Nyasa, the most savage punishments were meted out for even minor offences. A hundred or more lashes was a frequent punishment for fornication or robbery. Trials were a travesty of justice, the lack of an alibi being considered adequate grounds for conviction, even in capital cases. One luckless individual died after receiving two hundred and seventy lashes for stealing some beads which later proved to have been removed by a European trader. And when it came to shooting people for crimes such as murder, the executioners were often so incompetent that it took many agonising minutes for the victims to die.

These atrocities eventually became public knowledge, despite the efforts of British Consular officers in Mozambique to hush them up for fear that the Portuguese would make capital of them. Thereupon the Church of Scotland appointed a commission of enquiry, dismissed the leaders at Blantyre and issued an edict reminding their missionaries that their purpose was to found a church, not a penal settlement. But still no action was taken by the Imperial Government to place Nyasaland under their protection. And although the Portuguese now began to penetrate up the Shire river towards Lake Nyasa and a collision was clearly approaching, Granville, on becoming Foreign Secretary, merely requested Lisbon to refrain from offensive operations and appointed a Consul, without any administrative powers to keep an eye on Nyasaland, its missionaries and its slave-traders. Portugal was asked to give this representative the necessary facilities and to cooperate generally in checking slave trading and developing legitimate trade in the area, which equest Lisbon was only too glad to concede, regarding it as an mplicit admission by Britain that the Shire was within the Portuguese sphere of influence.

But for the traders, who had followed their missionary brethren to Nyasaland, this was not good enough. Three of them—James Stevenson, the founder of the Livingstone Central Africa Company, and his associates, the brothers Moir—had set out to do more than merely substitute legitimate trade for the selling of slaves. Having merged with the larger African Lakes Company, they had also undertaken the task of building a road —the Stevenson Road, as it came to be called—from the north end of Lake Nyasa to Tanganyika. If the Cape-to-Cairo dream were ever to be realised, they said, it would be along this road. Sandwiched between marauding Arab slavers from the north and the Portuguese in the south, they felt that a Consul with merely supervisory functions could not give them sufficient support or protection to fulfil these far-reaching imperial needs, particularly while blood-thirsty cut-throats such as Gouveia boasted that they could invade and seize the Shire Highlands at any minute with an army of five to six thousand men.

Once more, therefore, the Imperial Government were asked to grant their protection to Nyasaland. But although the British Minister in Lisbon again supported the request, Granville turned it down, on the grounds that the African Lakes Company were not capable of achieving the tasks which they had set themselves. Nor was Salisbury any more sympathetic when he returned to the Foreign Office two years later. His lonely and helpless Consul was told that there would be no British Protectorate and that he must therefore fend for himself and do his best to check the slave trade and introduce civilisation in collaboration with the traders and missionaries.

No less impassive was Salisbury's reaction when, early in 1887, the Portuguese, on Castilho's initiative, drove the Zanzibar Sultan's men from their remaining toeholds on the coast south of Tanganyika and established the northern frontier of Mozambique at Cape Delgado at the mouth of the Rovuma river. These proceedings might interpose the Portuguese between Nyasaland and the sea, but they did not incline the Prime

Minister to intervene beyond urging Lisbon not to be too hard on Britain's friend and ally, the Sultan. Even when, in the following year, the Portuguese arrested the African Lake Company's steamer for an infringement of their regulations Salisbury continued to insist that the Imperial Governmen had no obligation to defend the Nyasa settlements. The Company had brought this penalty upon themselves, he contended And two months later he actually withdrew his Consul and abolished the post, on the grounds that it involved the Government in responsibility for the irresponsible acts of the Company without any power to prevent them.

However, when the Company found themselves in trouble with native uprisings and asked the Portuguese for transit rights to import arms to defend themselves, the Imperia Government did for once weigh in on their behalf. Castilho's initial refusal to concede the Company's request was termed an unfriendly act. And when Lisbon offered to waive Castilho's prohibition if Britain recognised Portuguese claims, Salisbury firmly retorted that the waiver must be unconditional, since Britain did not recognise that Portugal had any valid claims north of the junction of the Shire and Zambezi rivers. Lisbon duly gave way and the arms were allowed to pass through Mozambique to the Company's settlements.

Nevertheless, Salisbury was still determined, if possible, to avoid extending the area of British responsibility in southern Africa; and in an attempt to settle matters by diplomatic methods he now proposed a territorial agreement with Portugal. Knutsford at the Colonial Office was ready to settle for the Zambezi as the dividing line between the two spheres of influence. This would have satisfied Portugal's desire for a belt across Africa along the north bank of the Zambezi. At the same time it would have kept her out of Lobengula's lands which, by the Moffatt treaty, had been declared a British sphere of influence. In return, the Portuguese would be asked to concede free trade on the Zambezi and, to quieten the humanitarians in Britain with their fears of Portuguese slave-trading, while at the same time obviating the need for Britain to establish another Protectorate, they were to undertake not to occupy Nyasaland.

But when this proposition was put to Lisbon the response was not enthusiastic. For one thing, Castilho had not abandoned his ambitions in the area. For another, a Lieutenant Cardoso of the Portuguese Navy was at that very moment engaged in signing up chiefs at the southern end of Lake Nyasa as vassals of the King of Portugal, whose signed authority he bore. And the Portuguese, who were hoping for German support and had been greatly stimulated by Cardoso's progress in Nyasaland, countered by claiming the very territory which Moffatt had reserved for Britain. Denouncing the Rudd concession as an infringement of Portuguese rights, they insisted that Mashonaland was not within Lobengula's control and that the Matabele King had no authority to give, nor Rhodes to accept, concessions in an area which properly belonged to Portugal by right of prior discovery.

It was now becoming clear that the Portuguese were more interested in certain specific territories, such as Mashonaland and the Shire district, than in gaining a belt across Africa. And when Salisbury sent Harry Johnston to take over the negotiations in Lisbon, they were without difficulty persuaded to abandon the belt, provided they received compensation in Nyasaland. Such an arrangement would have well suited Johnston who eight months earlier, in August 1888, had first mooted his idea for a British belt from the Cape to Cairo in an article in the *Times*. His only concern was that Portugal wanted some two-thirds of the western shore of Lake Nyasa, whereas he felt that she should be satisfied with one-half. But apart from that, he was very ready to close with Portugal on the basis that, while she had the shadow of the flag, Britain would have the substance of such Nyasa trade as existed and, still more important, unimpeded access to the north beyond the Zambezi.

However, Salisbury would not hear of handing over the Nyasa settlements and people to the care of the Portuguese. He might not be prepared to spend the British taxpayers' money to protect them. But he bluntly asserted that he would rather have a row with Portugal than face the wrath of Scotland, where nearly eleven hundred Presbyterian ministers and other church dignitaries had signed a petition categorically refusing to commit their missions to Portuguese protection. Indeed, such was his fear of these indignant Scottish prelates that, on receiving their petition, he proclaimed without further hesitation that the Nyasa missions were British territory. The negotiations were broken off, and Johnston was sent to Mozambique as Consul-General, with orders to keep the Portuguese out of Nyasaland, although still without so much as a gun-boat to help him to do so.

Nothing could now prevent a collision between Britain and Portugal in the Shire district, particularly when, in defiance of Salisbury's proclamation, Serpa Pinto was despatched to join forces with Cardoso, with instructions to make Portuguese occupation south of Lake Nyasa effective. Johnston hurried after him to sign up the chiefs along the western shore of the lake, partly for the benefit of his other patron, Rhodes, partly in fulfilment of his commission from Salisbury. Encountering Pinto on his travels, Johnston, armed with little more than his white parasol, told him that he was trespassing on British territory and demanded that he should withdraw. Pinto disingenuously replied that his purpose was scientific, not political, that he was acting under the authority of the Governor-General of Mozambique and could not take orders from anyone else. Nevertheless, he decided, in the light of his encounter with Johnston, to return to base to seek further instructions. Then, as he journeyed south, his expedition was set upon by Makololo tribesmen, prompted by agents of the African Lakes Company. The Makololos were soundly defeated; whereupon Pinto, deciding to strike while the news of his victory still resounded in the Nyasa area, turned about and marched northwards again to subdue the tribes, some of which had only a few days before accepted British flags from Johnston.

In December 1889, Pinto returned to Mozambique triumphantly proclaiming that the Shire had been occupied, the Makololos had abandoned their allegiance to Britain and Portuguese authority had been established from the Zambezi valley to Lake Nyasa. Salisbury now became fully aroused, partly for fear of Scottish clerical reactions, partly because Pinto's 'triumph' happened to coincide with D'Andrada's claim to have

Lord Salisbury's ultimatum to Portugal (1890)

Major Serpa Pinto

subdued Gazaland and Manica. For not only did the Prime Minister dread the wrath of the Church of Scotland, but Rhodes was also beginning to assert his influence in London in no uncertain fashion, and Rhodes wanted all these territories for his own empire. Lisbon was therefore told that Mashonaland, the Shire and Nyasaland, together with the Luangwa valley between the Zambezi and the Tanganyika border, were British preserves and that Britain refused to recognise Portuguese claims in any of these areas. And when cables arrived from Rhodes saying that the Portuguese were building forts in Mashonaland, followed by reports from Blantyre that they were slaughtering the Makololos by the hundred with Gatling guns, Salisbury followed up with a demand to Lisbon that all these operations should cease and a guarantee be given that British settlements would be immune from attack. Meanwhile, to reinforce his remonstrance, British warships cruised ominously off the East African coast with orders to seize Mozambique Island, if the Portuguese rejected Britain's demands.

The Lisbon Government conceded the guarantee of immunity for the settlements, but contested Salisbury's other demands with the usual arguments claiming Portugal's right of prior discovery. At the same time, struck by the gravity of the Prime Minister's latest tone and by the naval threat to Mozambique, they also cast around Europe in search of support from the other powers. But none was forthcoming. All were sympathetic but, as with Britain over the Congo, none would risk a clash with Portugal's challenger. Lisbon was advised on all hands to settle with the British as soon as possible.

Encouraged by Portugal's failure to drum up support and spurred by Rhodes and the Church of Scotland, Salisbury now increased the pressure, describing the Portuguese case as a lot of 'irrelevant archaeological arguments' to justify an invasion of British rights based on British settlements. But Portugal had drawn her sword and, if only to satisfy the Cortes, she had to brandish it. Opinion might be hardening in Britain, but in Portugal it was becoming incensed. So D'Andrada pressed on in Manica and Mashonaland, Gouveia set out against Gungunyana, and Pinto mowed down more Makololos with his

Gatling gun, while Lisbon sought to maintain the pretence that none of these expeditions had any aggressive intentions, that Portugal wanted to settle her dispute with Britain by peaceful negotiation and that, if this was impossible, the Berlin Conference powers should be invited to arbitrate.

Then in January 1890, the African Lakes Company, following further arrests of their steamers by Portuguese river patrols, telegraphed the dramatic words, 'War is imminent'. Salisbury now committed to go all the way in support of British interests, decided that the time had come to issue an ultimatum. His Minister in Lisbon was instructed to demand from the Portuguese the withdrawal of all their forces from the Shire and from Mashonaland. If within twenty-four hours, he had not received a copy of the Portuguese Government's cable ordering Castilho to make these withdrawals, the Minister was to leave Lisbon aboard a British warship which was standing by for this purpose. Meanwhile, to add point to the ultimatum, the British squadron at Zanzibar was ordered to sail towards Lourenço Marques to reinforce the naval threat to Mozambique, while other warships from Gibraltar headed for the Tagus estuary, there to loom within easy range of Portugal's capital.

Salisbury's big stick succeeded where earlier arguments had failed. Lisbon gave way and, though still protesting and reserving Portuguese rights in Nyasaland and Mashonaland, agreed to send the required orders to Castilho in order to avoid 'an imminent rupture of relations with Great Britain'. Inevitably an outcry followed in Portugal. The British Consulate was stoned and its Royal coat of arms dragged through the streets by an angry mob. Again the Portuguese sought the support of the other European powers. But only the Austrian and Spanish Governments showed any zeal on their behalf. The United States had not recovered from their resentment over the seizure of the American Colonel McMurdo's railway company and would not lift a finger to help. France, Germany and Italy were no longer interested, although the Italian Foreign Minister, Francesco Crispi, expressed to Salisbury his fear that the Portuguese monarchy might fall, if no agreed settlement were reached and Portuguese public opinion were simply left to lick its wounds. But while Salisbury had no desire to quarrel with Portugal and was still ready to reach a diplomatic settlement with Lisbon, albeit on his own terms, the Portuguese themselves only succeeded in stiffening Whitehall's resistance by first insisting that the issue be submitted to arbitration and, when Salisbury retorted that there must be direct negotiations, by reverting to their old claim to a belt across Africa in addition to Nyasaland.

Stupefied by this proposition, Salisbury decided to allow time to moderate such vain and unrealistic demands. Treating Portugal's claim as ridiculous, he turned his attentions to negotiating the frontiers to be established between the British and German spheres of influence in East Africa. Here he faced an altogether different and more delicate problem. Egypt was his overriding concern in Africa and without German support in Egypt, the British position would be precarious, if not untenable. For, with France hostile to Britain for having usurped her former paramountcy in this area, Germany held the balance on the Committee of Control which supervised the Khedive's finances and regulated the expenditure of Egyptian money. Without the German vote on the Committee, Britain would have to spend her own money, if she was to maintain her garrison and her influence in Egypt. Therefore Germany had to be appeased in East Africa, even if it meant allowing her claims in Tanganyika to cut across the Cape-to-Cairo line. And in July 1890, a Convention on these lines was duly drawn up and signed by Britain and Germany.

Immediately after the terms of this agreement were made known, Lisbon took heart, hoping that Britain, having allowed Germany to block the Cape-to-Cairo project, might be less opposed to Portugal's claims to a transcontinental belt. In fact, the Anglo-German Convention produced exactly the opposite result. Under its terms, Britain had, for her part, consolidated her position in the north of Nyasaland and secured the Stevenson Road joining Lake Nyasa with Lake Tanganyika; and she was not going to let the Portuguese insert any wedges into these substantial and important gains. Rhodes would see to that, even if the Imperial Government's resolution were to falter. For not only was he about to advance into Mashonaland; he was also making a bid for the African Lakes Company in the Nyasa area, as well as despatching his agents far and wide into Mozambique and Angola to procure concessions from whatever chiefs could be induced to treat with him. Still more far-reaching, his gaze was firmly fixed to the north of the Zambezi, even as far as the Katanga, where the reported wealth of copper and gold was such as would pay for all the Company's administration and leave a handsome profit besides.

For over a year, Rhodes had been urging the Imperial Government not to 'give away' territory to Portugal which, while perhaps sweetening international relations, would cripple the development of the north. In particular he asked that, in any agreement with Lisbon, Britain should not recognise Portuguese sovereignty south of the Zambezi, except perhaps at Delagoa Bay, and so leave Gazaland and the Pungwe river route to the sea open to the B.S.A. Company. To 'checkmate the Portuguese' in the north, he sent Joseph Thomson, a famous African explorer, beyond the Zambezi to establish relations with the tribes from east of Lake Nyasa to the Katanga and Barotseland. During the negotiations with Germany, he had bombarded the Colonial Secretary with demands that Britain should hold on to the Stevenson Road, in which area Johnston had obtained a number of concessions for him. 'This highway must remain English', he insisted, 'I will not work for the Germans'. And he had never ceased to remind London how essential it was to retain control of the territory connecting Lake Tanganyika and Lake Nyasa, in order to 'direct the greater portion of the interior equatorial trade into British hands.' Likewise, he maintained that Manica should be taken and held by him. No Portuguese occupation existed in the area, he said, and there were as many English traders and prospectors there as Portuguese.

With such pressures gathering about him, Salisbury resumed negotiations with Lisbon in August 1890; and although he could not obtain all that Rhodes demanded, he nevertheless gained a handsome compromise, which gave Britain unimpeded access to the north, from Mashonaland through to the Katanga and Tanganyika. Portugal was allowed to keep most of Manica, the frontier being established at the Sabi river, and her sovereignty over Gazaland was confirmed. But in Nyasaland she was excluded from all but the Lower Shire, and for the rest the northern limit of her claims was set at the Zambezi. Also, of course, she had to abandon all claims to Mashonaland and to accept Zumbo as the western limit of her sphere of influence in Zambezia. On top of all this, she had to guarantee free trade and navigation on all waterways under her control, as well as agreeing not to transfer to a third power without Britain's consent any of the territory conceded to her.

As with Kruger over Swaziland, Britain had driven a hard bargain with Portugal. And as in the Swazi negotiations, so in the discussions leading to the Anglo-Portuguese Convention, it was Rhodes who called much of the British tune. Two years earlier in the days when Salisbury had refused to bestir himself over Nyasaland and Knutsford had been prepared to allow Portugal a belt north of the Zambezi joining Mozambique to Angola, Rhodes had not as yet been able to make his influence felt on imperial policy. But for the last several months, when the British attitude had stiffened, he had been leaning over the Imperial Government's shoulder, demanding more and more territory for his schemes and forcing Salisbury and his colleagues to listen to him.

Then, in July 1890, a month before the final negotiations started with Portugal, and after yet another Sprigg government in the Cape had fallen over yet another railway project, this unique merchant adventurer became Cape Colony's Premier. Thus to the enormous economic power which he wielded through his diamond monopoly in Kimberley, his gold interests on the Rand and most recently as founder of the British South Africa Company's empire in Mashonaland, Rhodes now added the crucially important political backing of the Cape Government—a mettlesome four-in-hand which, in all conscience, should have been enough to requite any man's ambitions. From Cape Town to the Zambezi, with options open beyond, he was now the uncrowned King. Yet, as events were soon to show, even these achievements did not satisfy him. For, as always with Rhodes, *l'appétit venait en mangeant.*

229

12 Collision with Portugal

When the Pioneer Column took off for Mashonaland in June 1890, the Anglo-Portuguese Convention had not been signed. Colquhoun was therefore unaware, as he concluded his treaty with Umtasa in Manica, that he was trespassing on ground which Britain had just recognised as Portuguese territory. Not that this made the slightest difference to Rhodes. For, when the news broke that, in the wider interests of British foreign policy, Portugal had been allowed to keep the larger share of Manica, he categorically refused to accept the frontiers which the Convention offered him. Regardless of whatever limitations might have been agreed by Salisbury for 'diplomatic' reasons, Rhodes' appetite had been whetted by Colquhoun's glowing accounts of the potential wealth and temperate climate of Manica and he was determined to take and hold all of these fertile highlands. The Colonial Office was notified accordingly and Colquhoun was instructed to stand fast upon his treaty with Umtasa and to defy the Portuguese to turn him out.

One of Rhodes' first acts on becoming Cape Premier had been to move a resolution in the Legislative Assembly condemning the Imperial Government for coming to terms with Germany over Central and East Africa without consulting the Cape Government. Rhodes' anger on reading the terms of the Anglo-Portuguese Convention was therefore greater than ever. Furious that Salisbury had not allowed his ultimatum to be the last word in the exchanges with Portugal and so ensured that 'bona-fide occupation' became the sole basis of any settlement, he protested bitterly to London at what he called the loss 'by the treaty of a large portion of our territories' to a lot of Portuguese 'half-breeds'. In Barotseland whose frontiers, he claimed, extended as far west as the Cunene river, 'one half of our valid sphere of influence' had been given away. And in the east, areas had been ceded, where no Portuguese presence or occupation existed, where even the Mozambique Company's concession-holders were almost all Englishmen and where the native inhabitants accepted 'the B.S.A. Company as the dominant power'.

Unable to resist reminding the Imperial Government of what his achievements had saved them, Rhodes added that 'without firing a single shot we have occupied probably the richest goldfield in the world, with the acquiescence of the natives, at a cost to the Company of something like £200,000'. But what was the use of all these efforts and expenditures if, after bona-fide occupation had been established, these lands were to be 'signed away' to pander to Portugal's 'prehistoric rights'. Rhodes also launched a bitter attack on Johnston, whom he held responsible for the loss of 'half the Barotse just ceded to me and the whole (sic) of Manica and Gazaland'. He would have nothing to do with this 'disgraceful treaty', he said. And accusing Johnston quite unfairly of being the principal architect of the Convention, he concluded, 'You have given away the whole west . . . you ought to be thoroughly ashamed of your work; but in spite of your desertion, I shall go on fighting and I have not the slightest intention of giving way to the Portuguese . . . . I am now occupying Manica and I do not think that even you and the Portuguese combined will turn me out. The least I can ask you to do is to repair the mischief you have done by getting the Portuguese treaty dropped.'

Even for Rhodes this was vigorous and threatening language. But come what might, he was utterly determined not to abandon his newest claims, especially in Manica. And when the Portuguese protested on the spot and in Cape Town that Umtasa was their vassal and that the Company were trespassing on their territory, he upheld Colquhoun in insisting on the validity of his treaty and of the concessions granted by Umtasa, whether or

231

not they lay within the Portuguese sphere as defined by the Convention. Nor did he stop there. For in almost the same breath, he authorised Jameson and Frank Johnson to advance through Mozambique to the coast to survey the possibilities of a rail, road and steamer route to Beira via the Pungwe valley. And when Colquhoun objected that such an infringement of Portuguese sovereignty might create a dangerous situation, Rhodes overruled his Administrator and told Jameson and Johnson to press ahead, speciously pointing out that the Anglo-Portuguese Convention, although signed, had not yet been ratified. All that he would concede to Colquhoun's objections was to instruct Jameson, if his advance should be challenged by any Portuguese authority, to pretend that the Company had no intention of calling in question Portugal's sovereignty on the Pungwe. In fact, Rhodes had no intention whatever of respecting Portuguese territory or of acting within the terms of the Convention, wherever these were to his disadvantage. For he was solely concerned to establish his nine points of the law before the Portuguese were able to move in and claim what Britain had conceded to them; and if the Imperial Government would not reserve him a route to the sea, as he had requested, he would simply grab it for himself.

But if Rhodes was up in arms against what the Convention purported to give to Portugal, the Cortes in Lisbon were no less aggrieved to learn what their Government had conceded to Britain and to Rhodes. So were the Portuguese soldiers and settlers in Mozambique, who had to be restrained by the new Governor-General, Brito Capelo, from mounting an expedition to seize the Maputo valley in Tongaland in revenge for their losses in Zambezia. But try as they did to persuade Salisbury to modify the agreement, the Portuguese Government only managed to get one small change. Instead of having to seek British approval of any concessions of territory to a third party, Salisbury agreed that Portugal should offer Britain first refusal.

Inevitably such a minor concession completely failed to mollify the outraged parliamentarians of Lisbon. And after attempts to persuade the Cortes to ratify the Convention had been met with uproar, the Government resigned in mid-

September. Salisbury promptly warned their successors that he would regard any undue delay over ratification as tantamount to rejection which would leave Britain a free hand. But heedless of these ominous words, the Cortes dug in their toes and adjourned in the following month without further debate or decision.

Needless to say, Rhodes was delighted by the Cortes' action. Immediately he telegraphed to Colquhoun that the hated Convention had fallen through, which gave the Company 'a free hand as far as the coast'. The Administrator was to act accordingly, to occupy at least as far eastwards as the Buzi valley and to resist and repel the expedition which was reported to be on its way under the command of D'Andrada to reclaim Manica. Rhodes also telegraphed to the Colonial Office to express his hope that the Imperial Government would now withdraw the Convention altogether and would put no obstacle in the way of his reaching the sea at Beira. To stiffen his London Board, in case the Government should put pressure on them to prevent a collision with the Portuguese, he cabled that the Pioneers who had settled themselves in Manica during the past few weeks would not move out, no matter what agreements Britain might make in the wider interests of foreign policy. And to the Pioneers and other prospectors the B.S.A. Company passed the word that all of Manica was now within their sphere of influence, although at this point the expedition under Captain Forbes that was to make it so had only just received their marching orders.

Meanwhile D'Andrada was making the most of his head-start over the Company's force. And early in November, accompanied by Gouveia, he reached Umtasa's kraal only to find that Colquhoun, who had become increasingly ill at ease in the role of empire-builder, had left the area to take up his duties as Administrator at Fort Salisbury. Seizing his opportunity, he ordered the Manica chief to hoist the Portuguese flag. Umtasa, who was already beginning to have doubts about the wisdom of treating with the Company, having been kept under virtual house arrest by Colquhoun to prevent him signing up with any potential rivals, now bowed to force majeure, accepted D'Andrada's demands and declared before representatives of the

Manica concession holders assembled to witness his submission that he and his territory were subject to the King of Portugal. But as the ceremony drew to a close, Forbes suddenly appeared on the scene with a party of Company troopers. D'Andrada and Gouveia were arrested for trespassing on Company concessions and were sent under escort to Fort Salisbury and thence to Cape Town, where amid furious protests from Lisbon and Mozambique at this high-handed act of piracy they were eventually released on orders from the Colonial Office. Forbes then pressed on into Manica, seized Macequece, the principal Portuguese base in the territory, and signed up the tribes between the Pungwe and Buzi rivers where, although the area was claimed by D'Andrada's Mozambique Company, there was no sign of Portuguese settlement or occupation.

In Rhodes' own words, the Company had now 'acquired mineral rights over the whole country south of the Zambezi with the exception of a narrow strip of coastline'. With such a swift and far-reaching coup to his credit, he not unnaturally concluded that he had got the Portuguese on the run and that with one more push he could establish his route to the sea. Thus, on the strength of a somewhat over-optimistic report from Jameson on the feasibility of the Pungwe route to the sea, in which the doctor made little of the prevalence of tsetse-fly in the marshy lower reaches of the river, he now gave orders for the immediate occupation of the Portuguese port of Beira. But this was too much for the Imperial Government and their High Commissioner. Salisbury might have told Lisbon that the failure of the Cortes to ratify the Convention had given Britain a free hand. Loch, too, might have supported the Company's claims in Barotseland and Manica and, in reporting to the Colonial Office, even excused the arrest of D'Andrada at Umtasa's kraal as a defensive action by the Company. But seizing a Portuguese port with the use of armed force could only be an act of war. However Rhodes might argue that goods could be sent from the Cape to Mashonaland via Beira for a seventh of what it would cost by the overland route, such commercial convenience could scarcely justify outright aggression. On Knutsford's orders, Loch therefore refused to sanction any further advance by Company forces; and Rhodes was told that his recent acquisitions of territory would not be allowed. He had jumped the gun and 'advanced too rapidly' into areas which, even if the Convention had lapsed, had long been recognised as Portuguese and could not now be declared British, save by another treaty.

Apart from his fear that Rhodes might put Britain in the wrong, Salisbury had decided that it was only prudent to allow Lisbon time either to persuade the Cortes to think again about the Convention or, if this failed, to negotiate a new agreement. After the fall of the Portuguese Government, King Carlos had appealed to Queen Victoria for a settlement that might help to strengthen the monarchy, which was threatened by popular clamour against conceding Portugal's colonial claims. And to help the House of Braganza in its hour of danger, in November 1890, Salisbury agreed to a standstill arrangement by which—without prejudice to any ultimate settlement—each side agreed not to make treaties or obtain concessions in areas ceded to the other in the Convention for the next six months. Rhodes was told that the standstill agreement must be rigorously observed, and to spell out what this involved, Loch gave explicit instructions that the Company's forces should halt their advance, refrain from any further offensive movements and return Macequece to the Portuguese.

Needless to say, Rhodes was furious with Salisbury for letting the Portuguese off the hook, instead of maintaining his right to a free hand. Determined to keep every inch of what he had gained in Manica and in Mozambique and in blatant defiance of Loch's edict, he therefore ordered his forces to hold on to Macequece; and when an emissary of the Governor-General of Mozambique arrived to take possession of the town for Portugal, he was arrested by Forbes' troopers. So certain was Rhodes of getting most of Mozambique and of its coastline, if he held out long enough, that when he learned that his London Directors were seeking to acquire financial control of the Mozambique Company, he told them to desist. For, as he put it, if there should be no settlement with Portugal, 'we shall acquire everything'.

Rhodes' optimism had been stimulated not only by Forbes' successes in the Pungwe and Buzi valleys, but still more by reports from his emissary in Gazaland, Dr. Schulz. Under the Convention Britain had recognised all Gazaland as Portuguese. But in October 1890, Gungunyana was professing to Schulz such hatred and contempt for the Portuguese—'they are only black men like myself'—that it seemed to Rhodes that, with a modicum of persistence, he could convert the Shangaans into enduring allies and make their territory into a permanent route to the sea.

Initially Gungunyana had received Schulz with some reserve and suspicion. Saying that he had been tricked so often by the Portuguese that he distrusted all Europeans, he at first refused to transact any business before receiving at least a first instalment of Schulz's proffered payment of 1,000 rifles, 20,000 rounds of ammunition, a bonus of £1,000 and a yearly stipend of £500. But in the end, he was induced to discuss terms, not so much by the persuasiveness of Schulz, as by the manner in which Almeida, the Portuguese representative in Gazaland, over-played his hand in trying to put him and his indunas against the B.S.A. Company. For even to Gungunyana's untutored mind, it seemed a little too much like special pleading for a Portuguese to say that the Company would treat him as they were planning to treat his brother-in-law, Lobengula, and would drive him out of his kingdom once they got a foothold in it. And when Almeida sought to clinch the argument by saying that, no matter what Gungunyana and Schulz might agree upon, the future of Gazaland would be decided between the Portuguese and British Governments, the Chief angrily flung at him, 'Not without consulting me, Gungunyana, will any question be settled concerning my affairs.'

Following this outburst, Gungunyana declared to Almeida that he did not regard himself as owing any allegiance to the Portuguese who, he claimed, paid tribute to him through the Mozambique Company. The fact that he was flying Portugal's flag, he said, was simply a matter of courtesy. And after further discussions with Schulz, he decided to summon his warriors and to proclaim before them and Almeida that he wished for British protection. The impis were duly gathered together, sporting the 'death plume' in token of a recently successful punitive expedition against one of Gungunyana's vassals; and before the assembled company, the King declared that he intended to 'become English'. Turning to Almeida, he said, 'You and your nation have always lied to me, my father and my grandfather'. Then pointing to Schulz, he declared, 'The English are my friends; that man is now my friend, but if his nation treats me like the Portuguese did, I will kill him. Now may the Queen of England take me by the hand and not let go'.

Such vehement assertions inevitably led Rhodes to believe that Gazaland had been won for the Company. In fact, this was far from being the case. For one thing, Gungunyana had steadfastly refused to sign any treaty with the Company until he received the promised payment of arms and money. And although his verbal assertions had been made prior to November 1890, in the absence of any written commitment, the standstill agreement favoured the Portuguese, and not Rhodes, in the case of Gazaland. For another, Gungunyana, like Umtasa and many of his own people, had become sadly demoralised by liquor, which Portuguese traders from Lourenço Marques were wont to sell in large quantities to the natives of the interior, partly for gain and partly with the deliberate intention of weakening their resistance. As a result, he was even more inclined than Lobengula to vacillate and to change his mind, especially when his suspicions were aroused. When, therefore, following his declaration of allegiance to Britain, the promised shipment of arms failed to materialise, Gungunyana began to suspect that the British, like the Portuguese, were going back on their word. Excuses about Portuguese controls on the coast were brushed aside with contempt. Had the English, he asked, suddenly become afraid to send a ship up the Limpopo because a 'petty race of half-caste traders' would not give permission?

Now the Company could do nothing right in Gungunyana's eyes. He even found cause to complain of discrimination when a report reached him that the Company had presented Lobengula with two 'white bulls' without offering him the same! And at the end of December in a fit of pique, probably aggravated by a

237

bout of excessive drinking, he called another indaba and announced that, after further consideration, he wished to declare his fidelity to Portugal. His previous proclamation in favour of Britain had, he explained, been made on the misunderstanding that the Portuguese had abandoned him and that Schulz was an emissary of Natal and not of the B.S.A. Company! For good measure, and at the prompting of the ever-present Almeida, who wanted to strengthen Portuguese claims to Manica, he added that his paramountcy stretched as far as the Zambezi and that, by dint of his new allegiance, Manica now fell within the area of Portuguese sovereignty.

However, as Almeida had correctly told Gungunyana, it did not lie with him or the B.S.A. Company to decide who should be the paramount power in his kingdom, still less in Manica. This question was to be settled by Britain and Portugal; and no matter whether Rhodes succeeded or failed to win the Chief's allegiance, there was little doubt that the ultimate settlement would favour Portugal. Having recognised Portuguese sovereignty in this area in no less than four different treaties since the start of the nineteenth century, Britain could hardly now support Rhodes' claim to Gazaland. Moreover, the Company had themselves accepted in their Charter that their sphere of operations would lie 'to the west of the Portuguese dominions', which presupposed Portugal's paramountcy in Gungunyana's territory. Thus, the utmost that Britain could ask of Portugal was that the two governments should jointly guarantee the independence of Gazaland, which would enable the Company to enjoy whatever mineral concessions they might be able to obtain there. But when this proposal was put to Lisbon at the beginning of 1891, the Portuguese rejected it as a 'perfidious suggestion of the South Africa Company', designed eventually to oust Portugal altogether from the coast. Likewise, a British offer to compensate Portugal north of the Zambezi, if she would cede the better part of Manica was rejected out of hand.

Rhodes' reaction to all this was to behave as if nothing had happened to upset his claims. Jameson was despatched to Gungunyana's kraal, there to do as he had done with Lobengula in the difficult period before the Pioneer Column's departure. And a small steamer, the *Countess of Carnarvon,* was chartered to carry the promised gift of rifles and ammunition to the changeable Chief, which cargo, in order to fool the Portuguese authorities on the coast, was stated to be for the use of the B.S.A. Company in Mashonaland. In the middle of February 1891, the steamer duly arrived in the Limpopo estuary, where she was met by Portuguese customs officials who requested that she heave to, while they sought instructions from their superiors. But when they failed to return the next day, her captain continued his journey up-river and, some twenty miles from the estuary and forty miles from Gungunyana's kraal, discharged his cargo which was stored in a native hut. Two days later a Portuguese patrol arrived and took possession of the hut and its contents, pending payment of the necessary duty. But on a written guarantee of £2,000 from the Company's agent, the cargo was released for onward transmission, 'to Mashonaland'. The steamer returned to Durban; and the agent arranged for porters to deliver the arms to their real destination.

With this much-desired present—which Jameson declared to the King came as a personal gift from Queen Victoria—Gungunyana was induced to change sides yet again and to confirm his vows to Schulz, although still no formal treaty was signed. But when the *Countess of Carnarvon* returned three weeks later to collect the Company's men, the Portuguese discovered that they had been tricked. The steamer, with Jameson and his men on board, was met by a Portuguese gun-boat, her captain was informed that he, his crew and his ship were under arrest for smuggling and, with an armed guard on board, he was forced to proceed to Delagoa Bay. Here Jameson and the other passengers were released, but the ship was detained.

Like other collisions between the Portuguese and the B.S.A. Company at this period, the arrest of the *Countess of Carnarvon* caused confusion and embarrassment in Whitehall. The Imperial Government could not overlook this insult to the British flag. Yet, at a time when both governments were trying to patch up the quarrels and smooth the ruffled feelings of the previous year, they did not want to make too much of the incident.

Besides, they were more irritated with the B.S.A. Company for putting themselves in the wrong by smuggling arms to Gungunyana than they were with the Portuguese for arresting a British steamer.

Indeed Salisbury, to his growing annoyance, was finding Rhodes an ever more disruptive influence. His persistent attempts to detach Gazaland from Portugal's sphere of influence in Africa, his refusal to observe the standstill agreement and his open defiance of Loch's orders, issued three months before, to evacuate Macequece could only deepen Lisbon's suspicions that he would not rest until he had driven the Portuguese from all of their East African possessions, or at least from the coast between Beira and Delagoa Bay. True, Portugal had also broken the standstill agreement by refusing to allow free passage up the Pungwe river for British steamers and cargoes. And they had recently arrested a Company officer, Sir John Willoughby, who was attempting to travel to Mashonaland via Beira. But whenever Salisbury remonstrated against the closing of the Pungwe, Lisbon retorted that the river would be opened as soon as the B.S.A. Company's forces withdrew from Macequece.

Salisbury, never having wanted a row with Portugal, with all its potential implications for British foreign policy, was anxious to settle the question of the Company's eastern frontiers as soon as possible. At the beginning of April, Rhodes was therefore told once and for all that his claim to Gazaland could not be upheld. The Imperial Government had decided to recognise Portuguese sovereignty in the realms of Gungunyana, who was to be left to drink his life away under the Portuguese flag hoisted daily by one of Almeida's soldiers at the royal kraal. As for Manica and the opening of the Pungwe, Salisbury knew that there could be no possibility of agreement until Macequece had been returned to the Portuguese. But, once this had been done, there was a good chance that the Company would be able to keep all or most of the Manica territory which they had occupied prior to the standstill agreement and which included decidedly more than the Portuguese had conceded in the 1890 Convention. Loch was therefore instructed to see that his original orders were now finally carried out and, accordingly, he sent his Military

Secretary, Major Sapte, to enforce the necessary disengagement and withdrawal of Company troops.

Sapte's mission could hardly have been more timely. For only two days before he reached Beira en route for Manica, a Company force, acting on orders from Rhodes, had engaged a troop of Portuguese attempting to reclaim Macequece and, after inflicting heavy casualties, had put them to flight. A furious reaction followed in Mozambique. Martial law was proclaimed throughout the Colony and a full expeditionary force was assembled with orders to retake Macequece at any cost. Thus, with the Portuguese effectively in a state of war against the B.S.A. Company, Sapte had to move swiftly to avoid a major clash which, whatever the outcome, could only imperil Salisbury's negotiations with Lisbon.

A desperate chase now took place across the fly-infested swamps of the Lower Pungwe, with Loch's emissary straining every nerve to overhaul the advancing Portuguese and to reach Manica before it would be too late to prevent a collision. Fortunately, Sapte had the advantage of being able to travel without large numbers of porters and pack animals liable to be struck down by the deadly tsetse. Reaching Macequece ahead of the Portuguese, he ordered the Company's forces, in the name of the High Commissioner, to withdraw without further delay and to inform Lourenço Marques that they had done so.

Portugal's prestige was thus redeemed and the peace preserved. More than that, the Company had been saved from the follies of their own overweening ambition. For with Macequece back in Portuguese hands, Lisbon could no longer put off coming to some final agreement with Britain. In vain she appealed once more to the other European powers to support her claims in the Zambezi valley; Germany alone responded and then only to the extent of cautioning Salisbury not to push his demands to the point of endangering the Portuguese monarchy. And with the standstill agreement about to expire at the end of its six months term, Portugal was obliged to give way over Manica, to open up the Pungwe and to release the arrested steamer.

In June 1891, an agreement was therefore finally reached

which allowed the B.S.A. Company to keep most of their conquests in Manica and certainly far more than they had gained under the 1890 Convention. The Portuguese obtained the compensation north of the Zambezi which they had refused earlier in the year; but the western limit of their possessions was set at Zumbo. Freedom of navigation was confirmed for the Zambezi, Pungwe and Shire rivers, and provision made for the construction of a railway from Beira to Fort Salisbury.

Thus Britain, and more especially Rhodes, acquired not only Mashonaland and most of Manica, but Barotseland, Nyasaland and the road to the Katanga as well, while Portugal, having lost the better part of Manica, was compensated with an area which, though territorially spacious, was commercially almost worthless. Pioneers in exploration though they could claim to be, the Portuguese lacked the determination to make good their 'archaeological' claims and so to establish a belt of sovereignty across the continent to link Angola with Mozambique. In a world where power counted for more than precedence, they had proved to be no match for the ruthlessness with which Rhodes had set out to grab what he thought to be the richest areas of southern Africa. And as these unhappy truths bore in upon them, the Cortes, with surprising meekness, decided to cut their losses and to approve the new Convention, which was duly ratified on June 11 by the signature of the King of Portugal.

Yet even with all these gains to the credit of his territorial account, Rhodes was not satisfied. Bitterly he criticised Salisbury for giving away Gazaland and his access route to the sea, to 'gain a diplomatic success and get a troublesome problem off his hands.' Loudly he protested at the establishment of a neutral buffer zone in Manica which prevented the Company from carrying their occupation even further to the east. For Rhodes had, of course, hoped all along that the standstill agreement would expire without any agreement being reached, in which case he would have claimed a free hand to seize most of Mozambique and to establish his own trans-African belt from Gazaland to Angola. When the Portuguese had sought to reoccupy Macequece in May, six months after he had been ordered to hand it over, he had blandly protested that it was they who had broken the truce by attacking his forces. Harris had telegraphed on his behalf to the London Directors, saying that they must now press the Government to let the Company take Beira and a strip of territory linking Mashonaland with the sea. Mashonaland could not be developed, he said, 'with 1600 miles of land route. . . . Now is your chance'. Likewise, Rhodes objected violently to Sapte's peace-making efforts in Manica, and complained to his garrison commander that Loch's emissary had not been arrested on arrival and 'put in irons'!

As always where his own ambitions were concerned, Rhodes was unable, or unwilling, to understand the wider needs of British foreign policy. Nor, believing as he did that every man had his price, could he comprehend that, although Portugal's national debt might have soared to £134,000,000, national pride would not allow her either to sell out or be driven out of Africa. Yet, however he might rail at these impoverished 'half-breeds' with their claims to his 'North', there was a point beyond which even he could not force the Imperial Government to go in evicting the Portuguese from their African possessions, for fear of jeopardising Britain's foreign relations and of alienating international support for the British presence in Egypt. That point was reached in the final stages of the negotiations for the 1891 Convention. Although six years later the buffer zone in Manica was abolished in favour of the B.S.A. Company, no other 'improvements' were allowed to them. And after a last-minute attempt by Rhodes to buy Lourenço Marques on behalf of Cape Colony had come to nothing, he was obliged to accept the situation and to turn his attentions inwards upon the vast new empire which he had acquired.

Here there was certainly no shortage of unsolved problems whether to the south or north of the Zambezi. One difficulty concerned the question of land-ownership in Mashonaland. Lobengula's concession to Rhodes gave him the right to dig for gold, but it made no provision whatsoever for disposing of the land. In spite of this, Rhodes had promised every Pioneer 3,000 acres of farm land as well as fifteen gold claims; and the settlers were now asking for their pound of flesh. To complicate matters still further, one of Lobengula's regular visitors, a Mr. Renny-

Taillyour, trading on one of the King's periodical hates against the B.S.A. Company, had procured a concession, which gave to the holder the right for the next hundred years to grant, lease or rent land in Mashona territory. This concession he had subsequently sold to Edouard Lippert, who was a cousin of Rhodes' partner, Beit, and, according to current legend, was the chief agent of German intrigue in the Transvaal and of Boer mischief-making in Matabeleland.

Rhodes knew that, unless he could buy this concession, his entire operation in Mashonaland would be rendered nugatory. But Lippert knew this too and, when Rhodes approached him, he said that he wanted £250,000 for it, failing which he would sell to the highest bidder. Fearing that such a sale might lead to a mass of Boers and 'undesirables' moving into Mashonaland, Loch promptly issued an edict that the concession could not be sold except to the B.S.A. Company as holders of the Rudd concession and hence of the mineral rights of Mashonaland. But Lippert was undismayed. Realising that time was more on his side than on Rhodes', he held to his price and watched with joyful anticipation the continuous flow of land-hungry settlers moving onto the land which he controlled.

A year after the Pioneers had arrived, the number of Europeans in Mashonaland had reached three thousand. And in October 1891, with immigrants streaming in at the rate of over three hundred a month, it was clear that Lippert's tactics were about to pay off. Unable to wait any longer, Rhodes was forced to buy the concession for the equivalent of the asking price, payable in shares in his commercial empire.

But, if he was prepared to pay a high price for a concession that was vital to the fulfilment of his dreams, Rhodes could be niggling in areas of more marginal interest, as was shown by the curious story of his dealings with the African Lakes Company in Nyasaland. Indulging his passion for territorial and commercial acquisition, he had decided, soon after acquiring the Rudd concession, to gain control of the Lakes Company, who held most of Nyasaland under treaties negotiated with the chiefs in the middle eighties. Accordingly, in 1889, he approached their directors with a suggestion for a merger with the B.S.A. Company, which 'combination' would operate under the existing Royal Charter as the British South African and Lakes Company, with head offices in Glasgow to preserve the Scottish character of the original venture. The Lakes Company being at this point near the verge of bankruptcy, the harassed directors could not afford to refuse Rhodes' offer. Indeed, without the backing either of the Imperial Government or of some major enterprise such as the B.S.A. Company, they knew that they would not be able to hold out much longer against the combined pressures of the Arab slavers in the north and of the Portuguese in the Lower Shire valley. And since Salisbury at this point still fought shy of declaring a Protectorate, they had really no alternative but to accept the merger with the B.S.A. Company.

Thus early in 1890 the deal was done and Rhodes rejoiced over the 'absorption' of the Lakes Company which 'brings us up to Tanganyika'. But it was to prove a somewhat abortive and unprofitable venture. For one thing, the Scottish missionaries wanted no part of the B.S.A. Company in their domains, and as Salisbury's actions were to show, their wishes carried great weight in Whitehall and at Westminster. For another, partly from pressures exerted by the missionaries and partly to thwart the Portuguese, Salisbury was prevailed upon in the following year to change his mind and to declare a Protectorate over Nyasaland, with Harry Johnston as chief protector under the august title of Consul-General and Resident Commissioner.

Nevertheless, Rhodes strove to keep a foot in the door by simultaneously appointing Johnston to be his manager for the lands west of Nyasa—later to be known as Northern Rhodesia—where Thomson had obtained concessions for the B.S.A. Company. Although he had not forgiven Salisbury's Consul for his 'desertion' over the 1890 Convention, there was currently nobody else to whom Rhodes could turn. And so he wrote to Johnston, 'My idea of the best settlement over the Zambezi is that, to meet the sentiment of the missions, (a) Nyasaland should be marked out as small as possible and managed by you for the Imperial Government; (b) I think that the balance of the territories over the Zambezi should be placed under the Charter and managed . . . by you also for the Charter and that we should give you £10,000 per annum to do this; (c) any expenditure commercially should be extra and by us and that you should not mix in it in any way, except as having control over our people to see that they do not misbehave themselves.'

Johnston agreed to these terms on condition that he should be allowed to spend the £10,000 subsidy at his own discretion, either in the Protectorate or in the Company's territory. But for such a sum Rhodes tried to secure much too big a return. Among other things, he sought to insist that only the Chartered Company's concessions should be recognised as valid in his new sphere of influence, which would have given him three-fifths of Nyasaland, in addition to all of Northern Rhodesia up to the borders of Tanganyika. But Johnston refused to admit such blatant discriminations in favour of the Company which he held were entitled to no more consideration than any other mining or trading enterprise in the area. He also told Rhodes that he was obliged to spend almost all of his subsidy in the Protectorate—to pay for the police—and that, in the absence of any imperial grant-in-aid, he now needed more money. Rhodes, however, maintained that the Imperial Government should pay the police in the Protectorate and that the Company should not be forced to squander money in shouldering such responsibilities. At the same time, seeing in Johnston's dire need for funds an opportunity to strengthen his hold over Nyasaland, he offered to increase his subsidy to £17,500 a year, on condition that the Company should be allowed to take over all Crown lands and mineral rights in the Protectorate.

Johnston in his penury was obliged to recommend this extortionate proposition to London. But the Foreign Office, who were responsible for the Protectorate, decided that the terms were altogether too one-sided. If Rhodes was to obtain such reversionary rights in Nyasaland, then they must insist that he be committed to continue his subsidy for not less than ten years and that the whole of it should be spent in the Protectorate rather than be divided between Imperial and Company territory at the discretion of a man who was himself a part-time employee of the Company.

On learning of these conditions Rhodes exploded with rage

and indignation. Harris, on his behalf, told the London Directors that the proposal was 'a pure mockery, which gives us nothing and puts us at the mercy of the Government'. Johnston was once again accused of treachery and desertion and of going behind the Company's back to curry favour with his Foreign Office employers by suggesting that they stiffen the terms which he had himself agreed. And protesting that he was not going to spend his money to make Johnston King of the Zambezi valley, Rhodes now refused to pay a penny more than the original £10,000.

But if he hoped to gain his ends by turning the screw on the Protectorate, he was to be disappointed. For, in 1892, Lord Rosebery became Foreign Secretary and, by way of demonstrating his devotion to Liberal Imperialism, readily responded to Johnston's frantic cries for an adequate grant-in-aid. The Foreign Office paid off the Protectorate's deficit and obtained parliamentary sanction for an annual Government subsidy. Rhodes and Johnston had a last acrimonious meeting and parted the worst of friends; and the B.S.A. Company finally withdrew from Nyasaland.

According to Johnston, Rhodes never forgave him for this reverse and, when in 1897 the post of High Commissioner for South Africa became vacant, he attributed his failure to secure the nomination to 'Rhodes' enmity more than any other cause'. But in fact, far from being Johnston's fault, the exclusion of the B.S.A. Company from Nyasaland was largely self-inflicted. In contrast to his willingness to buy out Lippert at almost any price, Rhodes had offered too little and demanded too much in the Nyasa region. No doubt he reckoned that such an addition to his African empire, with its attendant problems of having to deal with Arab slave traders and recalcitrant Scottish missionaries, would in the end prove a dubious commercial asset, however much it might gratify his passion for territorial expansion.

But, if his attitude towards Nyasaland was half-hearted by comparison with his purchase of the Lippert concession, an even stranger contrast was to be found in his behaviour in Barotseland. Here, in April 1890, the B.S.A. Company had acquired from a Kimberley trader named Ware, a concession granted by King

Lewanika of the Barotses permitting him to prospect for gold. At this point, Rhodes still hoped to establish his own 'belt' of paramountcy across Africa from Gazaland to Angola. Two of his agents, Bagley and Fraser, were about to secure concessions as far west as the Cunene river, only two hundred miles from the Atlantic seaport of Benguela. And since Barotseland was an essential link in this chain of claims, he readily paid a high price for Ware's concession—£9,000 in cash and 100,000 Chartered Company shares.

However, Ware's rights gave no preferential position to the holder, and to Rhodes it was essential to secure the same monopoly as he had obtained in Mashonaland. To this end, he decided to send an ex-Bechuanaland Police officer, named Frank Lochner, to negotiate with Lewanika. Lochner had been about to leave for the Katanga to seek concessions for the B.S.A. Company. But, in the prevailing circumstances, Rhodes took the decision—which he was bitterly to regret—that Barotseland was a more urgent priority.

Several weeks later, at the end of May 1890, Lochner reached Lewanika's kraal after a nightmarish journey and suffering so severely from fever that for the last ten days his porters had to carry him lying full-stretch at the bottom of his canoe. He soon learned that he was not a very welcome visitor. Although Lewanika's personal attitude towards Europeans resembled that of Khama—with whom he also shared a deep hatred of the marauding Matabeles—many of his indunas were a lot less friendly and he was by no means secure upon his throne. Known to be pro-Christian and a patron of the Paris Evangelical missionary, Father Coillard, who had established himself and his Scottish wife in Barotseland four years earlier, the King was threatened by a powerful pagan element among the twenty tribes of the Barotse confederation; and he had only recently gained a somewhat inconclusive victory over his opponents in a long drawn-out civil war. Moreover, when Lochner arrived, all the tribe's headmen were, it seemed, away 'at the wars'. He was therefore told, through Coillard, to 'sit quietly and some day we shall talk with you'. And it took nearly a month of waiting before Lochner was able to see Lewanika and persuade him, with Coillard's assistance, to grant the required monopoly rights to the B.S.A. Company in return for an annual payment of £2,000.

But, as had happened with Lobengula over the Rudd concession, no sooner had the deal been made than the King's opponents raised a howl of protest over the alleged sale of the country to the white man. Four months later, in October, Lewanika bowed to these pressures, despite the urgent pleas of his friend, Coillard, not to break faith with this powerful British enterprise. And although Coillard swore that he had faithfully explained during the negotiations with Lochner exactly what the terms entailed, Lewanika now avowed that he had never intended to grant the Company monopoly rights to prospect for gold and had in fact thought that, by his agreement, he was placing himself under the protection of the Queen of England. Recalling the emphasis which Lochner had placed on the Company's royal patronage and connections, he said that he could not understand 'how gold concessions could be mixed up with the name of Queen Victoria or her son-in-law, the Duke of Fife'. He had been, so he informed a rival concession-hunter, 'taken advantage of, owing to my well-known and undisguised admiration of the Queen, who I have always considered to be a champion and protector of black races'. The Queen's name, together with that of the Duke of Fife, had been used to persuade him to sign a document which he now learned gave away a monopoly of his country's mineral and other resources for a paltry £2,000 a year. He objected most vigorously to this deception and, writing to Lochner to return the first instalment of his subsidy, he said, 'I am afraid of your wisdom or deceitfulness. You say you come from the Queen, but you are only a Company. I like the government of the Queen. I consented to the Queen to protect my country and the people. But you look for gold. Oho! Oho! go home. I do not like the Company. Go, leave my country.'

Rhodes, however, was currently too preoccupied with his claims in Manica and Gazaland, not to speak of his duties and responsibilities as Cape Premier, to be greatly concerned about Lewanika's actions. Besides, it was becoming increasingly clear that the Imperial Government would never support his claims up to the Cunene river. Angola was therefore slipping from his grasp and, in consequence, Barotseland had diminished in importance. But if Rhodes could afford to bide his time with the Barotses, the unfortunate Coillard could not. For in the mêlée of in-fighting which was now taking place at Lewanika's kraal, he had become the butt of everyone's recriminations. Fearing for his life, he wrote to Loch asking him to send a British Resident to confirm to Lewanika that he was under the Queen's protection. In reply Loch promised that Johnston would shortly proceed to Barotseland as Her Majesty's Commissioner for Central Africa to explain matters to the King and to undertake the administration of the territory in the Queen's name. Meanwhile Lewanika should rest assured that he was under British protection and that the B.S.A. Company were recognised by the Queen and would fulfil all their engagements to him.

Nevertheless, some seven months later, in April 1892, Johnston had not turned up; and Coillard, now almost desperate and quite unable to calm Lewanika's suspicions, begged Loch to send an emissary without further delay. This time Loch referred to Rhodes, who calmly replied that he hoped that the Company would be 'freer to commence the development of Barotseland', when they had become more established in Mashonaland. Meanwhile Coillard should work on Lewanika 'to look favourably and fairly on this Company and to show a disposition to abide by those concessions, the repudiation of which has caused and must still cause some delay in our work of opening up the country to civilisation'.

It would be hard to imagine an answer less likely to help the luckless Coillard or more likely to enrage the King. And as the months of waiting turned into years, Lewanika's conviction that he had been abandoned by England's Queen, as well as tricked by Rhodes' Company, grew stronger under the influence of those indunas who had from the start opposed his dealings with the white man. Eventually, after three years had elapsed with no sign of Johnston coming to fulfil Loch's promise, Lewanika sent the High Commissioner a stinging rebuke. 'I am uncared for and forlorn', he wrote. 'I have often brought my tears to you, but you do not answer me. To whom else must I cry? Three years ago, you told me that the Great Queen had appointed Mr. Johnston to be the representative of Her Majesty and that I could speak to him all that I have in my heart. Glad with expectation, we waited and strained our eyes watching the road. But he has never come . . . and I doubt now whether he is a real living man . . . . When we see a child restless and crying, we make him all kinds of promises to quiet him. You are too great to do that.'

Loch was certainly 'too great to do that', as indeed he showed by the single-mindedness with which he tackled so many difficult problems during his term as High Commissioner. But alas, Barotseland was the one blot on his otherwise splendid record. For, although Lewanika shortly afterwards reaffirmed his agreement with Lochner and, humbling himself before his own people, dismissed the indunas who had in their 'wickedness' advised repudiation, still no imperial officer was sent to reinforce the King's authority in Barotseland, still no action was taken to force Rhodes to honour his part of the bargain. And it was not until 1897, seven years after Lochner's agreement with Lewanika, that a British Resident was sent up to show the flag and the B.S.A. Company finally moved in to 'commence the development of Barotseland'.

In the light of such callous treatment of Lewanika, it was perhaps only poetic justice that the Chartered Company's efforts to add the Katanga to their empire were blocked by the agents of King Leopold's Congo Free State. This Bantu Kingdom, equal in area to that of Great Britain and lying to the west of Lakes Mwero and Bangweolo on the Tanganyika border, had been created by the single-handed efforts of a native trader's son, called Msiri, an engaging and capable character whose five hundred wives included a Portuguese lady whom he had bought for a load of ivory. Although the area was rich in copper, ivory, iron and salt, few white men had ever penetrated to this remote corner of Africa. Livingstone had passed by Lake Mwero. But by the middle eighties only four Europeans had ever visited Msiri's kraal at Bunkeya; and while the area had been nominally recognised by the Berlin Conference as forming part of the

Congo Free State, Leopold had been too short of money and too busy consolidating his rule against the menace of Tippo Tib's Arab state in the Manyema area of the Middle Congo to be able to make good his claim to the Katanga. The grant of Rhodes' Royal Charter with no limitations on the Company's freedom to extend northwards beyond the Zambezi had, of course, troubled him; but he had taken no active steps to counter this threat. Thus, by the end of the eighties when Rhodes began to formulate his own designs upon this rich and virgin land, virtually the only European influence in the Katanga was a Scottish missionary, Frederick Arnot, a Plymouth Brother following in Livingstone's footsteps who, ever since he stumbled upon Msiri's kraal in 1886, had used all his powers of persuasion to warn the King against ceding his country to Leopold's so-called Free State and so handing over his people to the most brutal of all existing colonial regimes.

Perhaps if Arnot had still been at Bunkeya when Rhodes eventually made his bid for Msiri's favours, he would have been prepared to talk the Chief into signing the necessary treaty. Certainly he had spared no effort in reporting home to arouse the interest of his fellow countrymen in an area which he eulogised as beautiful, rich, healthy and peaceful. And it is very likely that Rhodes would have cast his spell on this guileless evangelist in much the same way as he had succeeded in doing with Moffatt. But it was not to be so. And, when Alfred Sharpe, a Vice-Consul on Johnston's staff, who had been appointed to command one of the B.S.A. Company's two Katanga expeditions, arrived at Msiri's kraal in November 1890, Arnot was back in England. Nothing could have been more unfortunate for Sharpe. For one thing, Msiri firmly believed in a superstition that visitors from the east brought bad luck. For another, Sharpe's bedraggled appearance after a long and difficult march from Nyasaland scarcely accorded in the King's mind with his visitor's claim to represent, however indirectly, the Queen of England. Msiri refused point-blank to sign any treaty ceding his territory to the Company and Sharpe was quickly shown the door.

Rhodes had failed in his bid to grab Katanga while the

Belgians were looking the other way; and Leopold was not going to give him a second chance. Now galvanised into action, he promptly despatched two Belgian expeditions to Bunkeya. Remembering Arnot's warnings, Msiri refused equally to treat with the emissaries of the Congo Free State. Indeed from the behaviour of the second expedition, he became so certain that the Belgians were trying to undermine his authority by inciting his vassal tribes to rebellion that he wrote to Sharpe asking him to return at once. But the message was intercepted and destroyed by a Captain Stairs, a Canadian officer in Leopold's employ, who was leading yet another Belgian expedition to Msiri's capital. Stairs then advanced on Bunkeya where, having ingratiated himself with Msiri by pretending to be a British officer, he hoisted the flag of the Congo Free State. Msiri promptly fled, but was hunted down and killed by Stairs' soldiers before he could reach safety.

Nothing could now prevent the Congo Free State from establishing Leopold's title to the Katanga. Sharpe had returned without even a mining concession for the Chartered Company. And Rhodes' other expedition under the geologist, Joseph Thomson, had been prevented by fever, floods and mutinous porters from ever reaching their destination. So Rhodes lost out to Leopold, whom he ever afterwards called Satan. But for all that, he had not done too badly! By 1892, when the boundaries of these regions had been settled between Britain and the B.S.A. Company and the Governments of Germany, Portugal and the Congo Free State, he had established his claims to all of the territory north of the Zambezi, which is now Zambia, while to the south all of Mashonaland and most of Manica were under Company occupation.

Yet for Rhodes this was still not enough. For one thing, he still itched to fill the vacuum that existed in Matabeleland. For another, when he came to realise that his dreams of a New Rand in Mashonaland and Manica were not to be fulfilled, he was to focus his greedy gaze upon Johannesburg and to direct his conspiratorial mind to contriving ways and means of destroying Kruger's Republic and of forcing the Transvaal into the British, or more specifically the British South Africa Company's, fold.

13 The Matabele War

As was clearly shown by his abortive conspiracy with Frank Johnson at the end of 1889, Rhodes had from the beginning been determined to grab Matabeleland from Lobengula at the first opportunity. His nature was not such as could tolerate this vacuum any longer than was strictly necessary to concoct a presentable pretext for filling it. Besides, other elements had combined to persuade him that the seizure of all Lobengula's Kingdom was essential not only to satisfy the needs of the B.S.A. Company but also to fulfil his patriotic duty. In November 1890, two months after the Pioneer Column had reached their destination, Moffatt had reported from Bulawayo that 'influences and impulses' were working on the Matabeles promoting suspicion and resentment of white settlement in Mashonaland. Wild tales of outrages by some of the Pioneers on native women were circulating among the impis; and it was feared that Lobengula might be driven to succumb to the pressures of the war party in his ranks for fear of losing his throne.

Jameson in Fort Salisbury had dismissed Moffatt's warnings as exaggeratedly alarmist, asserting that the Matabeles would not attack, at least so long as the Company showed no signs of withdrawing. But for all Jameson's self-assurance, the first year or so in Mashonaland was a difficult and dangerous period. Owing to serious floods which prevented the carriage of supplies along Selous' road, there was an acute shortage of food, clothing and tools. Supplies of red and white-eye beads and 'Kaffir blankets' which were bartered to pay for food and native labour had been exhausted. And with much sickness among men and horses, the situation of the Pioneers was highly vulnerable to attack.

Added to these local dangers was the German 'threat' from South-West Africa. Following on Britain's proclamation of the Bechuanaland Protectorate in 1885, the Germans had regarded the territory beyond the Protectorate's northern limit as open to all and, acting accordingly, they had in the following year agreed with the Portuguese to divide these unclaimed areas between them. Hence, when Robinson proclaimed Lobengula's country as a British sphere of influence in 1888, Germany had protested that this constituted an invasion of her rights acquired by agreement with Portugal as the only valid claimant in this area. Then, when they learned that Rhodes was about to receive his Charter, the Germans weighed in again with a demand that Britain should recognise their sovereignty over Ngamiland—the north-western corner of the Bechuanaland Protectorate. This demand was categorically refused on the grounds that the local tribes infinitely preferred British to German rule. In fact, the tribes knew little of the former and nothing whatever of the latter; and the real reason for denying Germany in this area was that to have ceded Ngamiland would have been to allow a wedge of some 50,000 square miles of German Protectorate to be inserted into British South African territory. Even Salisbury felt this to be too high a price to pay for German goodwill elsewhere. And two years later as part of the general settlement of Anglo-German boundaries in Africa, he was able to placate Berlin with the cession of a very much smaller slice of Bechuana territory—to be named after Germany's Foreign Minister the Caprivi Strip—which gave the Germans access to the Zambezi along the southern border of Barotseland.

Rhodes drew little comfort from the fact that Salisbury had prevented Germany from achieving her larger designs in the north of Bechuanaland. Rumours were still reaching him that German expansion was being vigorously pursued in the east and there were reports that a German syndicate had been formed to buy the Delagoa Bay railway concession from

Portugal with the object of controlling, if not of monopolising, all trade with the Transvaal to the detriment of Cape Colony. In South-West Africa, plans were being laid to construct a railway into the interior and to export numbers of emigrants from Germany. To Rhodes, therefore, the Caprivi Strip was a sinister claw of German influence pointing directly at a most sensitive area of British and B.S.A. Company influence—the Zambezi river frontier between the Barotses and the Matabeles. As he saw it, Salisbury, with his infernal inclination to horse-trading in southern Africa, had let the Germans penetrate more than half-way across the continent. Having gained a foothold on the banks of the Zambezi, they might not rest until they had linked up their possessions in Tanganyika and therefore thrown a barrier of German territory right in the path of the British expansion into the north. And all that lay between the Germans and this goal was the vacuum of Matabeleland, proclaimed as a British sphere of influence, but unprotected by any British force and ruled by a King who, while professing eternal trust in the British Crown, had all too often shown a dislike of the B.S.A. Company.

In fact, the German Government had recently concluded on the strength of a report from their Consul in Pretoria, that the B.S.A. Company had effectively prevented any possibility of a German belt from South-West Africa to Tanganyika and that it would be most unwise to attempt such a manoeuvre from an inadequate base which could only end in undesirable complications and a humiliating withdrawal. But Rhodes did not know of this. As early as the middle eighties, he had supported his claims to the north by contending that 'the only thing we have now to work for is that the Germans shall not take Matabeleland.' Thus the prevention of a German advance through the Matabele vacuum was yet another argument for the Company to seize all Lobengula's territory as soon as possible. For, even after the Lippert concession had been bought, neither the Company nor the Imperial Government held any sovereign rights over Lobengula's Kingdom. The Company were merely tenants of the mineral and other rights relating to the use of the land, while sovereignty still rested with the King. And although

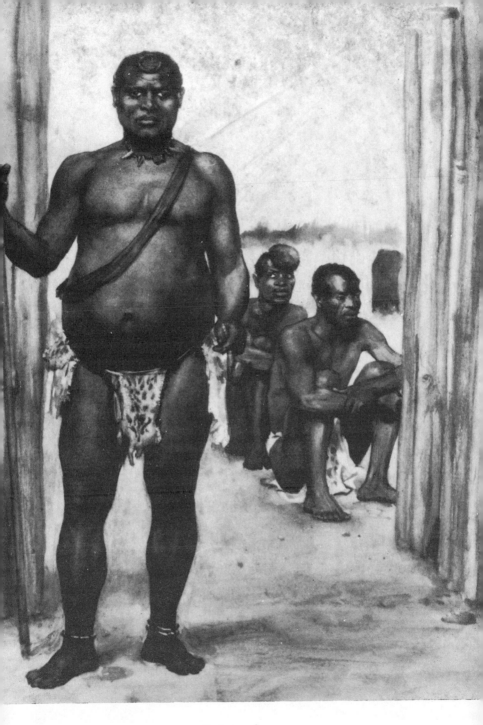

Lobengula

John Smith Moffatt

Lobengula had bound himself in the Moffatt treaty not to cede any part of his Kingdom to a foreign power without Britain's sanction, Rhodes was not prepared to rely on his observing this or any other engagement, if pressed by the Germans to break it.

Nor were the Germans now the only potential threat to the Company's tenure in the Zambezi valley. For in April 1891 it was announced that another Boer trek was about to descend upon Mashonaland. This enterprise owed its initiative to a Transvaal Boer by the name of Adendorff. Adendorff claimed to have obtained in the previous August a concession of land from a petty chief who, it appears, in a moment of *folie de grandeur* contended that he had the right to dispose of any part of Mashonaland. Adendorff's plan was to collect his fellow trekkers on the banks of the Limpopo in the month of May and to cross into Lobengula's country early in June. Once across the frontier a new Boer state—the 'Republic of the North'—was to be proclaimed and a provisional government elected. Announcing his intentions in the Transvaal press, Adendorff invoked celestial authority for the venture, concluding with the words, 'The Lord of Heaven Who governs everything can alone prevent this trek being made, but no man'.

However, he reckoned without Rhodes who, warning Loch that Mashonaland was in imminent danger of being 'jumped by the Transvaal', called for the strongest diplomatic remonstrance in Pretoria. Loch's response was to bombard Kruger with a succession of telegrams reminding him that he had undertaken in the Swaziland Convention to renounce all claims beyond the Limpopo. The Adendorff trek therefore had to be stopped and steps taken to 'prevent an invasion having for its object the establishment of an independent and hostile Government in a country under British influence . . .' By way of reinforcing his démarche, Loch also ordered imperial troops to hasten to Bechuanaland and issued a proclamation warning the would-be trekkers that, while anyone could enter Mashonaland who was willing to observe the rules and regulations of the Chartered Company, any incursion designed to set up a Boer Republic would be resisted as an unfriendly act. Rhodes for his part, persuaded his friend and political ally, Jan Hofmeyr, to support

Loch's ordinance in the name of the Afrikaner Bond and to declare himself strongly opposed to any idea of a Boer Government usurping the Company's rights in Mashonaland. In fact, so staunchly did Hofmeyr and the Bond stand by Rhodes and Loch at this juncture that the High Commissioner felt able to inform Knutsford that 'The Dutch party in the Colony are entirely against the Transvaal Boers in their present action. . . . They speak in stronger terms against Kruger and the Boer of the Transvaal than any Englishman would think of doing'. And after the trek had been stopped, Rhodes wrote to his friend W. T. Stead that his alliance with Hofmeyr had played a decisive part in preventing it.

But, if the Cape Dutch thought it was Kruger who was egging on Adendorff and his trekkers, they were wrong. Kruger, of course, cared little or nothing for the north. What interested him was access to the sea. The Swaziland Convention of 1890 gave him a route to the coast at Kosi Bay. Naturally, he would have liked to have been allowed more territory, and especially Swaziland itself, the better to protect and safeguard the route. But he was the last man to jeopardise the rights which he had gained to the coast for the sake of establishing another Boer Republic in the north. Knowing the Matabeles for what they were, he was quite content to stay on the south side of the Limpopo and to leave the highly tricky business of settlement in Lobengula's domains to Rhodes. But P. J. Joubert, his Commandant-General, was of an altogether different opinion. Having disagreed fundamentally with Kruger's policy at Blignaut's Pont and believing that the north was of greater importance to the Transvaal than Kosi Bay, he had been the prime mover behind Grobler's mission to Bulawayo in 1887; and now he and his son-in-law, A. H. Malan, were actively promoting the Adendorff trek.

This fact was known to Rhodes and Loch from reports which the Company received from a spy in the Transvaal, who was referred to in Jameson's telegrams as 'the subsidised one'. Kruger might, therefore, reply to the High Commissioner that he was well aware of his obligations under the Swaziland Convention and would take steps to prevent the trek; but there was some doubt in Cape Town as to whether he would be able to make his will prevail. For not only did Adendorff enjoy the patronage of Joubert, who commanded considerable support both in the Volksraad and in the country, but there were also the trekkers themselves to be considered. Parties of one to two hundred were already collecting, having sold their houses and farms in the belief that a better future awaited them in Mashonaland. Whatever the Government ordained, they might therefore refuse to turn back on the plea that they had nothing to turn back to.

Indeed, when Kruger duly issued his proclamation forbidding any Transvaal citizen to take part in the trek he had to use all his influence to secure its endorsement by the Volksraad. The opposition, led by Joubert, objected violently to its penal provisions and argued that the B.S.A. Company possessed no sovereign rights in Mashonaland and therefore could not legally prevent anyone from entering the country. But Kruger was now under severe pressure from Loch who was threatening to renege on the pledge given by Hofmeyr during the Swaziland negotiations if the trek should go ahead. Britain, he said, would not be prepared to discuss 'outstanding issues' with Pretoria 'while large bodies of armed men are being openly organised in the Transvaal with a view to invading territory and establishing an independent government . . . within the sphere of British influence'.

To reinforce the High Commissioner's pressures, Jameson paid a visit to Pretoria. And in what he described as 'a very friendly interview: I conciliatory, the President the injured tone re Swaziland', he told Kruger that, 'if he stopped the trek, there was great hope of his wishes being granted in Swaziland'. In fact, Jameson concluded from his talks that the President, whose 'apparent honesty' impressed him greatly, was leaning over backwards to thwart Adendorff's plans. Which judgement was shortly afterwards proved right when Kruger managed to induce a majority of the Volksraad to outlaw the trek, in the hope of obtaining some satisfaction over Swaziland in the promised discussions with the Imperial Government.

With this, most of the trekkers dispersed; Loch telegraphed

his thanks to the President; Adendorff remained in Pretoria; and, on the appointed day, only 112 Boers, led by Malan and a Colonel Ferreira—a veteran of the Bapedi campaign who had been decorated by Wolseley—attempted to cross the Limpopo. They were promptly stopped by a patrol of B.S.A. Company police. Ferreira, who alone refused to go back, was placed under arrest, while his companions returned meekly whence they had come. A brief outcry appeared in the Transvaal press that a group of 'speculators' calling themselves a Chartered Company should arrogate the right to deny the claims of innocent Afrikaners and should insist that anyone entering Mashonaland must undertake to obey the Company's laws. But apart from such newspaper comments and a rather half-hearted protest to the High Commissioner by the trekkers' leaders, what had once been talked of as a possible armed invasion had fizzled out like a damp squib.

Yet the mere fact that a Boer incursion across the Limpopo had been contemplated made Rhodes all the more anxious to occupy Matabeleland with a minimum of delay. True, the Company's forces had been able, without challenge from Lobengula's impis. to take up positions opposite the four drifts on the Limpopo where Adendorff's ox-wagons had been assembled. But the north bank of the river was Matabele, not Mashona, territory. And, although the Company had the right to use the fringes of Matabeleland as a road for their supplies, this sensitive frontier area, which might at any moment be threatened by another Boer trek, was altogether too far for comfort from the Company's bases in Mashonaland and too susceptible to possible Matabele attacks from the rear. To Rhodes, therefore, these dangers had to be eliminated by the decisive destruction of the Matabeles' fighting power and the occupation of their land.

Loch had clearly known for some time that his Premier was thinking on these lines. He had never really trusted this devious and erratic figure and, when the Sprigg Ministry had fallen in 1890, had only sent for Rhodes to form a Government after others had declined to do so. Loch was not so naïve as to have believed Frank Johnson's assertions that the plot to seize Matabeleland was solely his own idea. And warning Knutsford in 1891 that the B.S.A. Company might provoke trouble with Lobengula, he had strongly advised that it would be unwise to entrust to them 'any independent administrative power'. So far the settlers had not impinged on the native population, but it was becoming increasingly obvious that, at the current rate of immigration, the amount of vacant land available for allocation as farms and mineral holdings would soon be exhausted. Clearly implying that Rhodes, as he had hinted to the Pioneers, might then try to grab more territory by force, Loch suggested to the Colonial Office that the administration of Mashonaland, as well as all political negotiations with Lobengula, should be conducted by imperial officers who would be responsible to the High Commissioner and who would be better able than the Company's officials to 'exercise a quite impartial judgement between the white man's wants and the black man's rights'.

Such an arrangement would have taken care of Lobengula's objection to granting to a monopoly company the power to make their own laws, which the King had continued to mutter to Moffatt long after the Pioneers had settled into Mashonaland. But in 1891, to Rhodes' infinite relief, Loch was overruled by Knutsford. Heedless of Lobengula's fears, an Order in Council was issued entrusting jurisdiction to the Company and giving the High Commissioner power to intervene only when the authority of the Company could not be enforced. On top of this, in the following year, Moffatt was withdrawn from Bulawayo to reside permanently at Khama's capital, Palapye. No imperial officer was sent to replace him; and the transaction of all business with Lobengula was left to a Company official, Johann Colenbrander, a colourful Natalian who had served as a trumpeter in the campaign against Cetewayo, had accompanied Lobengula's embassy to Queen Victoria and many years later was to meet his death by drowning, while playing the role of Lord Chelmsford in a film about the Zulu War. Thus, by 1892, with the High Commissioner unrepresented in Matabeleland, the way was left clear for Rhodes, aided by Jameson as his Administrator in Mashonaland, to pursue his plans against Lobengula with little or no imperial interference.

Originally it had been the Company's policy not to interfere with the Mashonas or Makalakas in their territory. Each kraal was left to function under the authority of its own headman. And as a result, these relatively placid natives came to accept employment in the service of the settlers as the natural order of things. As for the Matabeles, it was at first Jameson's belief that they could likewise gradually be absorbed into the Company's economy by turning them into wage-labourers. But before long he came to realise that such a policy would run counter to all the traditions of a warrior tribe and could not therefore work. And, soon after the Order in Council was issued which conferred the administration of Mashonaland on the Company, the attitude of Jameson and his officers on all matters of native policy underwent a radical change. From then on, the Company began to undertake jurisdiction not only over white men, which Lobengula had been obliged to accept as a fait accompli, but over the King's African subjects as well.

In fact, by the beginning of 1892, it was becoming increasingly clear that Jameson was deliberately trailing his coat with Lobengula by, among other things, refusing to admit his right as Paramount Chief to send his impis into Mashona territory. Such action might scarcely accord with the fact that, ever since the Moffatt treaty of 1888, both the Company and the Imperial Government had recognised the Matabele King as 'Ruler of the tribe known as the Amandabele (Matabele) together with the Mashona and Makalaka, tributaries of the same'. It might also run counter to the exchanges with Lisbon over Portuguese claims to Mashonaland, in which the Imperial Government, strongly supported by Rhodes, had insisted that Lobengula was Paramount Chief of Mashonaland as well as Matabeleland, for which reason they could not recognise the claims of any foreign power in what Lobengula had conceded to be a British sphere of influence. But no matter. Rhodes had meanwhile made up his mind to grab Matabeleland and it no longer suited the Company's book to follow any of these interpretations. On the contrary, from 1892 onwards, their efforts were increasingly directed towards provoking Lobengula to fight and so provide them with the pretext to go in and seize Matabeleland by force.

Jameson's tactics were twofold. First, he set out to deny Lobengula his right to levy tribute or otherwise to enforce his paramount authority in Mashonaland. Second, he sought to make the Mashonas subject to the Company's authority and to impose his own arbitration upon the tribes. Kraals were raided and chiefs seized by Company forces intervening in native disputes. In February 1892, a chief was killed and his kraal burned down. Lobengula of course protested at this violation of his preserves. But in the very next month another chief who had assaulted his neighbour found his kraal attacked by a Company patrol led by a particularly vicious young officer called Captain Lendy. With the aid of a seven-pounder and a machine gun, Lendy managed to kill some twenty-one natives, including the chief himself, after which, according to his report, 'deeming the punishment sufficient, I did not burn the huts and left'.

Loch considered this action 'excessive' and, in reporting to his superiors in London, took the opportunity to remind them that their decision to make the Company independent rulers left him powerless to prevent such brutalities. But although the Colonial Secretary was moved to censure Lendy's deed as reckless and unduly harsh, no further action was taken. And while Jameson insisted that the punishment was necessary because the natives were withholding their labour and generally becoming insolent, Knutsford sought refuge in the euphemism that Loch should do nothing 'which could tend to relieve the Company's representatives . . . from a full sense of their primary responsibility for . . . Mashonaland'. Small wonder that, in the following year, the Company were emboldened by this passive attitude in Whitehall to seek approval of a native hut tax as a means of increasing their revenue, in complete disregard of the fact that Lobengula alone had the right to levy tax or tribute from the tribes within his realms.

In fact, nothing came of this request and, for a while, comparative calm reigned over Mashonaland. Lobengula paid a visit to the area without any objection being raised by the Company, although throughout his travels he was constantly shadowed by Jameson's patrols. Even the notorious Lendy, who was appointed as chief shadow, was constrained to report that he had been most cordially received at Lobengula's camp, where the King had insisted that they drink beer from his cup and shake hands after each gulp, and that he had 'never on any occasion detected any threat of animosity' and was 'perfectly confident that Lobengula is most anxious to remain on good terms with us. . . .'

But the peace was short-lived. For in the next few months another serious incident occurred involving a Matabele impi and a Company patrol, again under Lendy's command. This collision which was to lead directly to open warfare between the Company and the Matabeles, originated in the discovery in May 1893 that some five hundred yards of telegraph wire had been cut and removed by tribesmen in the neighbourhood of Fort Victoria. Jameson promptly demanded that the local chief either pay a fine or hand over the culprits for punishment. The chief elected to pay the fine and duly delivered a number of cattle to Fort Victoria. But the cattle belonged by custom, not to him, but to Lobengula. And when the King came to hear of what had happened, he protested vigorously to Colenbrander and to Loch, demanding that his property be returned to him forthwith. His younger warriors wanted to go in and seize the cattle by force, but Lobengula, with commendable restraint, told them that he preferred to settle the matter peaceably. The cattle were promptly given back by Jameson and the matter might have ended there, had it not been that, in the following month, the King decided to send a large impi to 'punish' the miscreant tribesmen.

Whether he did so with the ulterior purpose of reasserting his own authority in Mashonaland or whether he was merely concerned to teach his thieving subjects a lesson, we shall never know. What we do know is that Loch, in replying to the King's protests about the seizure of his cattle, was at pains to impress upon him the seriousness of the crime for which the fine had been levied, and to make it clear that he should put a stop to the all too frequent practice of wire-cutting by natives in the Company's territory. Moreover Lobengula, in answer to Loch's admonishment, said that he realised the seriousness of the offence and would try to prevent any recurrence. He also took

care to notify Jameson through Colenbrander that he was sending the impi to Mashonaland to punish the wrong-doers,
together with certain tribesmen who had stolen Matabele cattle;
and he plainly emphasised that 'the white people should know
that the King has no hostile intention against them'. Besides, as
Colenbrander and therefore presumably Jameson also knew,
Lobengula was momentarily in no position to launch an attack
on the Company, having just despatched six thousand of his best
warriors to wage war against the Barotses who, he alleged, were
responsible for the recent 'disappearance' of one of his sons.
Certainly Loch felt, as he indeed reported to the new Colonial
Secretary, Lord Ripon, that in all the circumstances the
Company's settlers could rest assured that they were in no
danger of attack.

However, on receiving Lobengula's message, Jameson
declined to accept his good faith. Clearly implying that he suspected treachery against the Company's settlers, he replied on
July 10 with a warning that the impi must not be 'allowed to
cross the border agreed between us'. In fact, no frontier had
been 'agreed' between them, the 'border' to which he referred
being merely a line arbitrarily drawn by the Company to mark
the western limit of white settlement. And to a native monarch,
who already felt that the Company were usurping his authority
with his Mashona and Makalaka subjects, this claim to exclude
him altogether from a part of his Kingdom was quite inadmissible. More unfortunately still, some of the younger members of
the impi cut loose when, in defiance of Jameson's injunction,
they advanced to the Victoria area. Numbers of Mashonas were
killed and their kraals pillaged. No white man was molested,
still less injured, but several of the Company's native servants
were murdered. And when the commander of the impi demanded of Jameson that any Mashonas guilty of stealing Matabele
cattle should be handed over for summary trial and punishment, he was naturally met with a categorical refusal. He was
further told that he had 'no right to come over the border', and
the Matabeles were given an hour to depart in peace, after
which time they were warned that force would be used to expel
them.

Much to the disgust of the younger warriors, their commander complied with Jameson's orders. But as the impi wended their way slowly back towards Matabele territory, Lendy, at the head of a squadron of Company troops, caught up with them and, under a barrage of fire, drove them in headlong flight before him, killing thirty-two of their number. Jameson promptly protested to Lobengula about the murders committed by his young warriors, but without mentioning that the Matabeles had been gunned down as they withdrew. To which Lobengula contritely replied 'you are quite right . . . I acknowledge that I was wrong in sending my impi so close to the white people. . . .' But when his warriors returned and told of Lendy's further act of savagery, the King sent for Colenbrander and, inveighing against Jameson, protested that the white men, by their action in firing on a retreating impi, were trying to force him into a quarrel.

Lobengula also wrote to Harris at the Company's Cape Town Office complaining that the authorities at Fort Victoria had refused to surrender the cattle stealers, and had then 'turned their cannon on my people'. With an apt choice of phrase, he concluded by saying 'Tell Captain Lendy he is like some of my own young men; he has no holes in his ears . . . and all he thinks about is a row; you had better caution him carefully or he will cause serious trouble between us'. Lobengula quite genuinely could not understand why his men, having obeyed his orders to leave the white settlers alone and to punish his own subjects for an offence which the Company regarded as heinous and having further complied with Jameson's order to withdraw, should have been fired on as they retired by Company forces. In a message to his old friend and counsellor, Moffatt, he protested that his sole purpose in sending his impi to Mashonaland had been to punish those who had cut the telegraph wire and stolen his cattle. As for Jameson's talk of a border between them, he knew of no such thing and had agreed to no boundary lines whatever.

Fearing further serious repercussions, Loch now decided to intervene with a reminder to Lobengula that the killing and pillaging perpetrated by his impi had dangerously inflamed the white settlers in the Victoria area. Warning the King against allowing his young warriors to get out of hand, he concluded his message with an appeal that, rather than face 'the punishments that befell Cetewayo and his people', Lobengula should 'live in peace with the white men . . . abandon the system of raiding the country, burning villages and taking lives . . . and so enable me, before it is too late, still to continue to sign myself your friend'.

But, although Loch did not yet know it, it was already too late to prevent a war. Immediately after the Victoria incident, Jameson had made up his mind to settle with the Matabeles once and for all by marching on Lobengula's capital at Bulawayo and taking it by storm. Forbes, now promoted to Major following his successes in Manica, was invited to take command of the Company's force which was to undertake the task, advancing in two columns from Salisbury and Victoria. This force was to consist of 700 mounted men, each of whom was promised 6,000 acres of land and twenty gold claims in Matabeleland, plus a share of any loot, as a reward for his service. In addition some 900 armed Mashonas were to accompany the expedition. And to give the venture the flavour of a popular demand for self-protection, resolutions were voted by the settlers in Salisbury and Victoria, at the instigation of the Company's officers, requesting that an end be made of the Matabele threat.

A stiff note was sent to Lobengula on August 16 demanding compensation for the settlers' murdered servants and stolen cattle and couched in tones which Jameson clearly knew would provoke the King to dig in his toes and so provide a pretext for more coercive measures. Meanwhile, from Cape Town, Harris prepared the London Directors for the oncoming storm. There were, he said, only two possible courses of action which the Company could take. One would be to keep 'an armed mounted force of 700 to 800 men on our borders'; the other, to 'break up the Matabele military system once and for all'. Since the first course would cost not less than £120,000 a year 'such a plan is utterly impossible for financial reasons'. More forthrightly, he added that 'if, as all will admit, the extension of English influence into Mashonaland and Matabeleland is greatly to be desired, then it is reasonable to expect that we must be allowed to make it a substantial fact, not a shadow . . . .' His only fear was that Lobengula might have forced the issue upon the Company a year too soon. Nevertheless, he said, 'Mr. Rhodes has determined that, should the Matabele give us an excuse to order an advance upon Bulawayo, he is quite sure the Board will concur in the wisdom of this . . . . Either Lobengula or the Chartered Company must be once and for all supreme.'

It would be hard to find more conclusive evidence that Rhodes was resolved to take the offensive against the Matabeles at the very first opportunity. Although he had wanted to seize Matabeleland from the very outset, he had accepted, once his plot with Johnson was uncovered, the tactical necessity of observing his agreement with Lobengula to leave the Matabeles alone, until such time as the Company had firmly established their roots in the north. But, three years after the Pioneers had arrived in Mashonaland, he and Jameson were feeling strong enough to 'order an advance on Bulawayo' and to ensure that they would be 'once and for all supreme'.

Both Loch and Lobengula now realised this. Loch advised Jameson to be less officious in his language and his treatment of the King and, in particular, to drop his demand for compensation for the Victoria incident, which could only exacerbate a situation which Lobengula was trying a lot harder to calm than were the Company. Lobengula duly refused to pay any compensation and in reply to Jameson's demands shrewdly observed that the Pioneers' recent behaviour suggested that they had come 'not only to dig gold but to rob me and my people of their country as well'. He also recalled his army from Barotseland and told his people to prepare for an imminent attack by the white settlers. And to show his disgust with the Company, he refused to receive any further payments in respect of the Rudd and Lippert concessions, telling Colenbrander he now regarded such stipends as 'blood money'.

Colenbrander was then withdrawn on Rhodes' orders and Bulawayo was left with no channel of communication to Jameson. Yet, since he still retained a touching faith in the 'Great Queen' and in her High Commissioner, Lobengula sought once more to make contact with the imperial authorities.

Towards the end of August emissaries were despatched to put his case to Queen Victoria and to seek Loch's advice in Cape Town. But at this late stage there was nothing that Loch could do to control the situation. From having 'the jumps', as Jameson had earlier described the mood of Fort Victoria, the settlers were now becoming almost hysterical and wild rumours were circulating that Kruger was aiding and abetting Lobengula. With so much fear and uncertainty, the Mashona labourers stayed in their kraals and much of the Company's work came to a standstill. Meanwhile, Jameson stubbornly refused to drop his demand for compensation; and the Company continued to mobilise for the attack with the aid of quantities of arms, ammunition and horses bought from the Bechuanaland Border Police.

Loch, desperately trying to pour oil on the waters, now bluntly told Jameson that war would be 'inadmissible' and demanded that the text of any further messages to Lobengula should be submitted for the approval of the High Commissioner's office before despatch. But Jameson merely retorted that, since relations had been broken with Lobengula, there could be no question of sending any further messages. Rhodes' Viceroy was now completely deaf to all contrary opinions and counsels. Indeed when Colenbrander telegraphed before leaving Bulawayo to say that in his view the King had a case and did not want war, Jameson contemptuously dismissed his envoy's statement as being that of a man who was frightened for his own skin. This, despite the fact that the few English traders still residing at Bulawayo—not to mention Moffatt, Loch and Lobengula's arch-enemy, Khama—also firmly believed that the King did not want to fight and would only do so if forced to act in self-defence. True, when Lobengula sent an impi to reconnoitre near Victoria, Jameson refrained from despatching patrols to engage them, following a further warning from Loch that the Imperial Government would take a most serious view of the Company indulging in 'hostilities that could be avoided'. But he made it clear to the High Commissioner that he could not be expected to maintain such restraint indefinitely and that he was only holding back 'until we are prepared for any eventuality'.

Nevertheless, Loch strove ceaselessly to avert the oncoming tragedy and to soothe tempers in Salisbury and Bulawayo. Jameson was urged to refrain from offensive actions and Lobengula was warned that, while nobody could properly dispute his right to rule the Mashonas and levy taxes from them, Britain could not allow him to punish his subjects by killing and pillaging in areas inhabited by English settlers. If he would only behave as Khama did towards his people, he too would earn the trust and friendship of the white men. But for Loch nothing would go right. For, as he awaited the arrival of the King's indunas in Cape Town, disaster struck again. Due to a misunderstanding, Lobengula's emissaries were arrested as spies by the Bechuanaland Border Police soon after crossing the frontier and, when they tried to escape, were shot dead.

Lobengula, understandably outraged by what he regarded as an act of the basest treachery, thundered that the white men were all liars and cheats. The High Commissioner hastened to express his deepest regrets for this tragic accident and to assure the King that, even at this late hour, he would be glad to explore with him any arrangement to keep the peace. But to no avail. Lobengula, now fully convinced that he was about to be attacked, responded by sending more impis towards Jameson's 'border' and by packing off the Matabele women and children to the safety of the Matopos Hills, south of Bulawayo.

Realising from Jameson's telegrams that he could not indefinitely stop the Company moving against the Matabeles, Loch decided that the only course now open to him was to try to limit so far as possible the extent of the inevitable fighting. He therefore told Jameson towards the end of September that he might send out patrols to ascertain the strength of the impis which the Company claimed were threatening their settlements and, if necessary, require their withdrawal. At the same time, he informed Lobengula of the action he had authorised Jameson to take and appealed to him to keep his impis away from the white people, 'so that there may be peace'. But as luck would have it, the Company's patrols were fired on as they advanced into Matabele territory. Jameson, quickly seeing his opportunity, requested authority to 'go right into the country'. Once again

Loch had to give ground; and on October 2, he sanctioned an advance to drive the Matabeles back from their positions, while stipulating once more that, whatever happened, the Company's troops 'should confine themselves to a defensive policy'.

But it was much too late for any such reservations or requests to either side. The recent brush with the Company patrols, added to the news that Lobengula's indunas had been killed in Bechuanaland, had so inflamed the Matabele impis that the King was finding it almost impossible to restrain them. Jameson, for his part, also made it clear in his reply to Loch's last plea that the Company had no intention of remaining on the defensive. Lobengula, he protested, had been steadily preparing to attack the settlers and, even if his impis were now to withdraw whence they came, failure by the Company to follow them up and destroy their kraals 'would only embolden them to reappear immediately on our border and become more aggressive'. In fact, he concluded, 'a retreat would be infinitely more dangerous than an advance'.

Rhodes, leaving the Government of Cape Colony in the hands of a deputy, now hurried to Salisbury on what was his first visit to the country which he had recently been allowed to call Rhodesia. Reviewing the Company's troops, he proclaimed to the world that they were about to 'eliminate ruthless barbarism in South Africa'. And on October 5, the Salisbury and Victoria columns of the expeditionary force, armed with rifles, machine-guns and a couple of seven-pounder field guns, marched out to claim the new lands which they had been promised in Matabeleland.

At the same time, by prearrangement with the High Commissioner, a force of 400 Bechuanaland Border Police and volunteers under Colonel Goold-Adams, accompanied by 1,800 of Khama's Bamangwato, also crossed the frontier into Matabele territory. Although the effect of this movement was to stab Lobengula in the back by forcing him to fight on two fronts, its purpose was rather to ensure that, when Bulawayo should fall, there would be an imperial presence on the spot to give effect to Loch's orders to the Company's Commanding Officer. Once he knew that he could not prevent Rhodes and Jameson from engaging in a full-scale war against the Matabeles, Loch felt that the sooner the fighting was over the better; and as he thought, Goold-Adams could not only help to accelerate this end, but would also be able, when the Matabeles were beaten, to see to it that the 'Imperial Factor' would not be excluded from the ultimate settlement.

The war was soon over. The Matabele impis were no match for the Company's troops. For one thing, a large number of those who had been recalled from Barotseland had returned suffering from smallpox. For another, just as Rhodes had once forecast, they persisted in their belief that, by putting up the sights of their rifles, their bullets would go further and strike harder. Thus they were worsted in two attacks upon the advancing white men, which cost them more than ten per cent of their total force of five thousand warriors, but which wrung from one of the Company's officers the compliment that 'no civilised troops could have withstood the terrific fire they did for half as long'. Thereafter, the Matabele impis retired and left the way open for Forbes to occupy Bulawayo on November 4, a month after the start of hostilities. Ten days before this, Lobengula had abandoned his capital, after setting fire to all but the houses occupied by the two remaining English residents whom he had protected, together with their property, against any molestation by his people throughout the duration of the fighting. And when the Company's troops entered Bulawayo, they found to their astonishment the two Englishmen waving from the roofs of their houses, completely unscathed among the smoking ruins of Lobengula's capital and surrounded by the broken remnants of the most ferocious Bantu army in southern Africa.

For the B.S.A. Company the capture of Bulawayo was a double victory. Not only had they defeated the Matabeles and could therefore help themselves to the land: but Forbes' men also won the race with Goold-Adams, whose advance from Bechuanaland had been delayed by Matabele attacks and by an outbreak of smallpox among his Bamangwato allies which caused Khama to return home with his entire force. When the fighting began, the Colonial Office, having come to realise their mistake in allowing the B.S.A. Company so free a rein in Mashonaland, had authorised Loch to conduct all peace negotiations with Lobengula and to ensure that the administration of the conquered territory would be under himself as High Commissioner. But Rhodes, seeing what lay behind Goold-Adams' diversionary expedition, had told Jameson to 'be careful when you take Bulawayo to retain management for the Company and (make sure) that Goold-Adams is given clearly to understand that the Company retains management'. When told of the High Commissioner's instructions from Whitehall, he expostulated that this was 'so monstrous, I can't believe it'; and he induced his colleagues in the Cape Government, as well as his London Directors, to demand of the Colonial Office that he, rather than Loch, should be empowered to make the settlement. The Company, having paid for the war, should be allowed to settle the peace, he maintained.

Now with Forbes installed in Bulawayo in advance of Goold-Adams' arrival, Rhodes was in a strong position to resist any imperial intervention. Besides, Lobengula having fled, leaving a defeated and dejected rabble behind him, the question of negotiations no longer arose. So as to avoid any confrontation with Loch until the Company had dug themselves in at Bulawayo, Rhodes promptly despatched Jameson to set up the new administration in Matabeleland and himself stayed in Salisbury through the months of November and December, on the plea that Jameson's absence in Bulawayo made it impossible for him to return to his duties in Cape Town. Jameson, for his part, made haste to establish Company rule in the conquered territory and so to prevent what he called an 'egotistical and vainglorious' High Commissioner from usurping his functions.

Rather than pursue what had largely become a lost cause, Ripon and Loch therefore climbed down and allowed the Company to parcel out the land and mineral rights of Matabeleland to the victorious volunteers. All that Loch was able to gain for the 'Imperial Factor'—and even then Rhodes objected that he was being unnecessarily interfering—was that the Bechuanaland Border Police should stay in Bulawayo to keep order, and a watch on the Company's actions, for the time being. For the rest, he and the Colonial Secretary could only bemoan the fact

273

that Knutsford had two years earlier refused to make the B.S.A. Company subject to proper imperial control.

Meanwhile Jameson, in an attempt to persuade Lobengula to return to Bulawayo, had sent a runner after him with a truly extraordinary message. Totally disregarding Loch's frequently repeated injunctions to avoid any aggressive moves, he claimed that he had taken Matabeleland 'by order of the Queen'! From this he went on to demand that Lobengula should come and see him. He would be guaranteed a safe-conduct for his journey; but, should he refuse, he would be hunted down by the Company's troops. Jameson then signed himself 'your former and I hope your, at present, friend'. The message was duly delivered to the King who replied that he would come. But fearing treachery, he added, in an obvious reference to the indunas who had been killed in Bechuanaland, 'allow me to ask you where are my men which I sent to the Cape?' He also enquired pathetically where he might find a house to live in, since all his houses had been burned.

Whether from fear of treachery or because the indunas who followed him into exile persuaded him not to surrender, Lobengula nevertheless kept on running, 'driven by the wind' and heading north towards the Zambezi, perhaps in the hope of finding yet another country in which to settle. In a prophetic allusion to the way in which the B.S.A. Company were to treat him, he had once told one of the missionaries in Matabeleland, 'England is the chameleon and I am the fly.' So the presumption is that he now feared that he would be killed if he gave himself up. But whatever his motive and wherever his destination, he simply vanished like a ghost never to be seen again.

When the King failed to return, Jameson sent Forbes to try and capture him. And, with the Company's troops hot on his trail, Lobengula made one final desperate attempt to get away. Putting in a bag all the gold sovereigns that he had left over from the Company's annual payments, he instructed an induna to give the money to his pursuers and to ask them to take it and leave him in peace. The money was duly handed to two Company troopers who had become separated from Forbes' column. But, no-one having seen the transaction, the troopers pocketed it themselves, while the column marched on, only to be baulked of their prey by torrential rains which made any further advance impossible. Forbes returned to Bulawayo without his royal captive and minus twenty-two of his column who, on a forward reconnaissance patrol, had stumbled on the rear-guard of the King's impi and had been wiped out. Two months later, in January 1894, Lobengula was reported to have died in the bush from smallpox.

Rhodes celebrated his hour of victory with a speech to his troops at Bulawayo on December 19. Making it clear that the Rhodesian colonists, like their fellows in America in the previous century, would brook no interference from England or from the Cape, he told them to go and select their ground. 'It is your right', he said, 'for you have conquered the country.' And in response to some pointed criticisms made by Henry Labouchere in the House of Commons and by the Aborigines Protection Society, he proclaimed that the settlement of the conquered land should be made by those who conquered it and 'not be left to the negrophilists at Exeter Hall'. Then, with the cheers of his supporters still ringing in his ears, he set off for the Cape to inaugurate an election campaign with a further round of speeches exalting the enterprise of the B.S.A. Company and mocking the cautious timidity of the Imperial Government in terms which Loch described as 'wanting in tact, taste, truthfulness and gratitude' for the solid support which he had received over the past four years from London and Cape Town.

Perhaps the truest judgement of all on this shameless episode came from the London Missionary Society's Reverend Helm, who Jameson admitted was 'the best authority on the Matabele'. From the vantage point of his Inyati mission and after careful cross-examination of several of Jameson's volunteers, Helm pronounced that 'the whole matter of this Matabele war had been so unrighteous that a searching enquiry should be made'. The Matabeles, whose losses in killed and wounded—according to Rhodes' own estimate—exceeded three thousand, had been dragged into a war for the occupation of their country on the basis of false information, exaggeration and rumour. Likewise

Moffatt, from having been one of Rhodes' greatest admirers, was now so disgusted by what had been done that he would have resigned his post in protest, had he not felt that he should stay on at Palapye to protect Khama against similar treatment. Feeling no small responsibility for having introduced the Company to Mashonaland and for having recommended them to Lobengula as men of honour who kept their word, he wrote to Loch, while the fighting was still going on, that he had 'spent several hours of sleepless misery pondering whether it was not my duty to wash my hands of any further complicity in the affair by resigning my appointment'. He had desisted only because he feared that 'when the Chartered Company has worked its will with Lobengula, it will turn and use similar tactics upon Khama'. He did not much like the Matabeles or their King, but the Company were 'pursuing a dishonourable course towards them. . . . Unmitigated falsehoods have been published far and wide by the Chartered Company to colour the excuse for an aggressive policy'.

The Matabele War had proved the truth which had been spoken by none other than Colenbrander, the B.S.A. Company's own ambassador in Bulawayo prior to the outbreak of hostilities, when he said 'the Pioneer at his most highly developed state is a white savage, the most terrible of men'. For, while making every allowance for the fears caused by the Matabele raid on the Mashona kraals near Victoria in the previous July, the premeditated seizure of Matabeleland in cynical disregard of solemn pledges written and spoken to Lobengula could scarcely have been a more savage and terrible act. The Matabeles' treatment of their Mashona and other vassals was undoubtedly barbaric in the extreme. But they had scrupulously refrained from attacking the white settlers. And there was nothing in their conduct which could excuse the 'dishonourable and aggressive' action of the B.S.A. Company in bringing about their destruction.

14 The Encirclement of the Transvaal

As with the Portuguese in Manica, so now in Matabeleland Rhodes had established his 'nine points of the law'. With Lobengula dead and Matabele rule at an end, sovereignty, both in Matabeleland and Mashonaland, was deemed to have reverted to the Crown. And as the Company installed themselves at Bulawayo and parcelled out the land to their own settlers, the Imperial Government recognised the fait accompli and issued an Order in Council confirming them in their new acquisition. Loch still strove vigorously to retain some element of imperial control over their future dealings. Citing the precedent of the East India Company, with its Board of Control appointed by the Government of India, he proposed that the Crown should impose strict limitations on the right of the Company to make war on native tribes and that no member of the Civil Service in Rhodesia should have a pecuniary interest in the Company's commercial undertakings. But Rhodes, determined as ever not to have to conform to any rules or precedents, insisted on the fullest autonomy; and once again he managed to get his own way.

Matabeleland and Mashonaland were now officially joined together to be governed as a single district by the B.S.A. Company. Orders were issued for the general disarmament of the Matabeles. The military kraals, from which Lobengula's impis had in the past derived their training, were broken up and destroyed and their occupants packed off to separate smaller kraals. Also, since it was held that the best way to bring home to the people that the old regime had been swept away was to take and distribute the livestock which were the symbol of the King's authority, huge numbers of Matabele cattle were seized and divided among the Company's agents.

By the end of March 1894, a sullen peace reigned over Rhodes' new territory. All the chief indunas had surrendered and the populace uneasily awaited the outcome of Jameson's avowed intention to redistribute them in special native reserves. But peace was not accompanied by prosperity. The New Rand proved a sad disappointment and the high plateaus of Rhodesia, so healthy and amenable to European settlement, fell a long way short of the Eldorado which Rhodes had so confidently believed they would vouchsafe. Even the agricultural wealth of the country was threatened by periodical plagues of locusts which destroyed the crops and by rinderpest which killed off the cattle. Added to all this, the Company, which had been in debt before the Matabele War, were in even worse straits with the expenses of the campaign to meet. Chartered shares, having almost quadrupled in value in 1890, had now fallen below par. And with the Beira–Salisbury railway still far from complete, the cost of supplying the settlers from the Cape was proving exorbitant.

In the circumstances, Rhodes had been unable even to make a start in the development of the vast territories beyond the Zambezi, which he had reserved for the Chartered Company and which were later to reveal the famous 'Copper Belt' of Northern Rhodesia. Indeed, his progress and plans were even more stultified north of the Zambezi than they were in Mashonaland and Matabeleland. Due to a combination of bad timing on the Company's part and the swift application of force majeure by Leopold, he had lost his chance of adding the Katanga to his dominions; and soon after the Matabele War a further attempt to fulfil his Cape-to-Cairo project was thwarted by the determined opposition of Germany.

Ironically enough, it was King Leopold—Rhodes' Satan—who revived his hopes of realising this dream. Having settled his 'Arab problem' by first recognising Tippo Tib as his Viceroy in the Middle Congo and later, under the banner of an anti-slavery crusade, crushing his successor in a lengthy campaign, Leopold turned his attentions to acquiring access to the Nile and so to linking his Congo empire with the Mediterranean as well as the Atlantic. Ever since the middle eighties when he invited General Gordon to help him secure a foothold on the Upper Nile, Leopold had been casting envious glances in this direction. Following the fall of Khartoum, he had vainly tried to get Emin Pasha, who had served under Gordon as Governor of Equatoria until the Mahdist Revolution, to return to his former governorate and acquire it as an addition to the Congo Free State.

Then, in 1890, he made an agreement with the British Imperial East Africa Company by which the Congo Free State was to cede a strip of territory along the border with Tanganyika to link up the British spheres of influence in Uganda and Northern Rhodesia, in exchange for access to the Nile between Lake Albert and Lado. Nothing came of this deal, because within a few weeks the Anglo-German Agreement cancelled out its provisions. But three years later, to the surprise and concern of the British Government, came the news that a Belgian expedition from the Congo had marched through the southern Sudan and occupied Lado. Rosebery, as Foreign Secretary, was greatly disturbed to learn of this foreign incursion into Britain's sphere of influence on the Upper Nile. But as the ensuing months went by and the threat of France's designs on the Nile valley grew ever more intense, he began to perceive in Leopold's ambitions a means to block a French advance into this area. In March 1894, therefore, on the day after he succeeded Gladstone as Prime Minister, Rosebery offered to lease to 'the sovereign of the Congo' the Sudanese province of Bahr el Ghazal which bordered on the Congo and constituted a buffer between French Equatorial Africa and the upper reaches of the Nile.

A few days later, news reached London that a French expedition was about to march on Fashoda. With alarm bells ringing throughout Downing Street, the Imperial Government promptly proclaimed a Protectorate over Uganda, so as to secure the source of the Nile, and resolved to complete as speedily as possible the arrangements for Leopold to take care of the southern Sudan. Within a few weeks, the necessary treaty was concluded on similar lines to the earlier agreement with the Imperial East Africa Company. Without prejudice to Britain's sphere of influence on the Upper Nile, Leopold was to obtain a lease of the former Egyptian provinces of Bahr el Ghazal and Equatoria, while Britain was to be granted the lease of a corridor along the Congo border with Tanganyika.

For a brief moment it seemed as if Rosebery and Leopold were to grant Rhodes what he had been denied in the Anglo-German agreement four years earlier—a belt of territory linking British South Africa with Egypt. But it was not to be. As with the 1890 negotiations with Berlin, so again with these arrangements, it only required a slight reminder from Germany that, if her wishes were flouted, she could make difficulties for Britain in Egypt, for the Imperial Government to give ground immediately. Thus, when Berlin objected to the British corridor at the back of German territory in Tanganyika, Britain backed down; and when the French added their objections to Leopold blocking their advance to the Nile valley, he abandoned the rest of the treaty.

By the end of 1894, therefore, Rhodes' every project beyond the Zambezi had been frustrated. His Cape-to-Cairo dream had been shattered, the Katanga had been snatched by Leopold and the opening up of Northern Rhodesia could not yet be started, due to a lack of human and financial resources. When, therefore, to his even further disappointment, Matabeleland proved to be no richer in gold than Mashonaland and Manica, he began to turn his attentions back to the Transvaal. 'If only one had Jo'burg', he told a friend, 'one could unite the whole country tomorrow.'

But it was Kruger who 'had Jo'burg'. Moreover, the seemingly limitless wealth of the Rand was not only amassing ever-increasing fortunes for the mining companies and their shareholders, but was also making the South African Republic a serious rival of Cape Colony for the leadership of southern Africa. And for one whose desires for the Cape, at least so long as he remained its Premier, took second place only to his ambitions for his new empire in the north, the prospect of the Transvaal under Boer leadership becoming the commercial and financial centre of South Africa was quite intolerable.

Nor for a man with Rhodes' capacity for deluding himself and others was it very difficult to portray this nightmare as part of a devilish plot by Germany, aided by Portugal and Kruger, to destroy British paramountcy and to create a South African union under Boer supremacy and German protection. As he put it, thanks to his enterprises, the way was now barred to any link-up between the Transvaal and the Germans in South-West Africa and Tanganyika. But the Boers might still be able, with Germany's blessing and the new-found revenues from the Rand, to buy out the Portuguese in Mozambique and so to secure a large area of coast-line on the Indian Ocean. They had, after all, tried to do so when they had been far less rich than they were now.

Besides, the Delagoa Bay railway to Pretoria was nearing completion and in addition the Boers had obtained the thin end of a wedge at Kosi Bay by the terms of the Swaziland Convention. True, Kruger had been forced to climb down and permit the extension of the Cape-Bloemfontein line to Pretoria and Johannesburg more than two years before the completion of the Delagoa Bay railway. But what might have proved a golden opportunity to gain control of this vital artery had, so Rhodes believed, been muffed by the British Treasury's refusal two years earlier to allow an attempt by the Cape to purchase Delagoa Bay, despite the assurances of Lord Rothschild that Lisbon was faced with such dire financial problems that a reasonable offer to buy a lease of the territory would not be refused. With a railway of his own to Kosi Bay plus the Delagoa Bay outlet, Kruger would shortly be largely free of British restraints and pressures. Therefore, if British influence was to remain supreme in southern Africa, the Boers must somehow be shut off from this outlet to the sea. Once this had been accomplished the next step would be for the B.S.A. Company to move in and make Kruger's Republic part of Rhodes' northern empire.

Notwithstanding his problems in the north, Rhodes was, at

this point, at the height of his political power in South Africa. Thanks largely to his 'triumph' over Lobengula, he had won a spectacular victory at the Cape elections early in 1894, and in the Cape Parliament the Opposition now mustered only eighteen members out of a total of seventy-six. No doubt this result was helped by his earlier prudent action in raising the property qualification for voters from £25 to £75 and imposing an educational test to eliminate from the electoral register 'barbarian tribesmen' and down-at-heel half-castes. Thanks to such examples of his native policy, he had had no difficulty in retaining the solid support of the Afrikaner Bond. Jan Hofmeyr, his personal friend and most important political ally, shared Rhodes' desire for union and his policy of Colonial Home Rule in the Cape, and supported his activities in the north in the belief that the Company was a better friend to the Afrikaner than the Crown. Rebuffed by Kruger over the Swaziland negotiations, in 1890, Hofmeyr had been thrown more than ever into Rhodes' arms. And although declining to serve in any Cabinet, he had been persuaded by such devices as a Government programme for the teaching of Dutch as well as English in the Cape's schools that Rhodes stood for the things that the Bond held dear.

Outside the Cape, too, Rhodes' political position was gaining strength. In Natal, a new Government had come into office which, unlike their stand-offish predecessors, had declared themselves in favour of an economic union with the Cape and the Boer Republics. Better still, the Liberal Imperialist, Rosebery, had replaced Gladstone as Britain's Prime Minister. In fact, if anything, Rhodes was perhaps riding too high and his position was too supreme for safety. Following a major scandal involving Government contracts, he had suffered the resignations of three of his ablest colleagues, J. X. Merriman, J. W. Sauer and James Rose-Innes. Always disliking opposition, especially in politics, he was thus becoming increasingly surrounded by yes-men and hangers-on of little character and less honesty. In Parliament there were few to say him nay; in his Cabinet there were none. As for Whitehall, as the issue of the Matabeleland Order in Council had shown, Rhodes had all too little difficulty in seeing to it that the High Commissioner was overruled, whenever he felt that his interests were being challenged.

Due in no small way to this lack of any effective control over his political actions, he was shortly to overreach himself fatally. But for the moment, Rhodes' influence in British South Africa was almost unchallenged. Loch might resent his inability to curb his inexorable Premier, but there was nothing he could do about it. And so, when Rhodes decided to squeeze the Boers in the east and block the outlet to the sea which the Swaziland Convention had given them, the High Commissioner's instructions from London read accordingly.

Following the signature of the 1890 Convention, Loch had made an honest and painstaking effort to do justice to Kruger's legitimate claims in the east. But he was thwarted by a combination of circumstance and suspicion beyond his control. For one thing, the Joint Government of Swaziland failed to work. The Swazis themselves had settled down peaceably enough. Umbandine's young son was presented to his people by his mother, the Queen Regent, seated on the traditional tortoise-shell at the gate of the royal kraal; and with the prohibition of liquor sales to the natives strictly enforced, the people mended their former drunken ways and even abandoned their more barbarous customs. But the Europeans quarrelled incessantly among themselves over concessions and the Boer and British representatives on the Joint Government were more often at loggerheads than in agreement.

By the end of 1890, therefore, Loch was proposing to Knutsford that 'Her Majesty's Government could now retire with honour' from Swaziland and leave the government of the whites there to the Boers alone. Leyds, now State Secretary of the Transvaal and Kruger's right-hand, was pressing hard for the full incorporation of Swaziland in the South African Republic. And the Volksraad, having voted to ratify the 1890 Convention on the understanding that it was a 'transition measure', was chafing at Loch's failure to meet and settle outstanding issues with Kruger as Hofmeyr had promised he would.

But Knutsford prevaricated, afraid of parliamentary and

humanitarian reactions to the idea of Britain 'retiring' from Swaziland; and Loch was obliged to plead such feeble pretexts as the threat posed by the Adendorff Trek as his reason for delaying the promised discussions with the Boers. In vain he pointed out to his superiors that Kruger had loyally kept his word and forbidden the trek. Knutsford insisted that discussions with the Transvaal of controversial issues would not be appropriate at a time 'when the recent agitation is still fresh in the minds of the public'. Loch suggested repeatedly that the talks need not be purely one-sided. The opportunity should be taken, he thought, to raise with Kruger outstanding British grievances such as the disenfranchisement of the Uitlanders in the Transvaal, for it would be only by discussing such matters with him, that he might be persuaded to concede the need for reforms. But it was not until nearly three years after Hofmeyr had given his famous promise that the High Commissioner was able to talk matters over with the Transvaal President; and not unnaturally, throughout this long period of waiting, Kruger saw no good reason to carry out his undertaking to join any customs union with the Cape.

Towards the end of this interval, Ripon succeeded Knutsford as Colonial Secretary. Apart from claiming the rare distinction of having been born at No. 10 Downing Street during the brief premiership of his father, Viscount Goderich, Ripon came from a political background in curious contrast to that of his predecessors at the Colonial Office. Influenced at an early age by the Christian Socialist movement of Charles Kingsley and Thomas Hughes, he had served under Palmerston and Gladstone and for four years had been Governor-General of India. Although he later shocked many of his Liberal friends by his pressures on the Transvaal and by his defence of the B.S.A. Company's action in provoking the Matabele War, initially at least he brought a refreshing element of Radicalism to his conduct of South African affairs. In particular, since he felt morally bound to honour Hofmeyr's promise, he resolved to make a virtue of necessity and allow Kruger's Republic to take over the administration of Swaziland which, in its peculiar geographical situation, all expert opinion agreed would be militarily impossible for Britain to police and protect. He would not go as far as to sanction the incorporation of the country into the Transvaal. But he told Loch that, provided the Swazis were satisfied that their rights would not be impaired, the futile attempt at joint administration should be abandoned in favour of the Boers. Also, without much enthusiasm, he agreed to Loch trying to settle with Kruger such problems as the Uitlanders' franchise and the Transvaal's entry into a customs union.

Armed with this authority, Loch set off to meet Kruger at Colesberg in April 1893 for what both parties agreed should be an exploratory discussion of the many outstanding issues. Kruger opened the talks by asking that the 1890 Convention be revised, so as to permit the Transvaal to annexe Swaziland and the other intervening territories in order to protect his route to the sea. And although Loch felt that this was asking too much, he nevertheless agreed that the Boers should have sole rights of administration in Swaziland and in such tribal lands to the east as were prepared to admit them and their railway. From his own agenda the High Commissioner spoke frankly of the Uitlanders' grievances and appealed to Kruger to reduce the residence qualification for the franchise from the existing fourteen years to two which, he claimed, should allow sufficient time for the Pretoria authorities to sift out any undesirables seeking naturalisation. As for the customs union, Loch suggested it would suffice if the Transvaal agreed to admit free trade in all South African products.

Kruger reacted to all this with moderation and understanding. He admitted the need for reforms, but said that they must be introduced gradually, if he was not to outrage his burghers. His political position was none too strong at this point. He had just been reelected as President by the narrowest of majorities; and his opponent, Joubert, had been making determined efforts to unseat him by charging that the elections had been rigged. Therefore he could only hasten slowly.

All things considered, it was a very friendly and useful meeting, as Loch was at pains to point out in reporting to Ripon. But, in those circles in Whitehall where Rhodes' influence predominated, this encounter aroused grave doubts and suspicions.

Such contacts with Kruger could, it was felt, become positively dangerous, especially if they should lead to a guileless High Commissioner helping the Boers to consolidate their independence. In the face of these unconciliatory counsels, Ripon's attitude rapidly hardened. In reply to Loch's proposal that he should follow up this break-through and offer Kruger a new convention giving him jurisdiction over his outlet to the sea, the Colonial Secretary now seemed firmly resolved to deny the Boers any independent access to the coast. Kruger, he decided, could have Swaziland but the other territories must be kept out of any new agreement.

Disappointed though he was by this halving of his proffered loaf, Loch set out to meet Kruger once again, this time paying the first visit to Pretoria by a British High Commissioner since 1881. From the outset, the omens were against a successful sequel to the Colesberg meeting. At the public reception the platform collapsed while the President and the High Commissioner were exchanging the usual courtesies. And Loch's fears were very soon confirmed that the Imperial Government's renewed determination to encircle the Transvaal would make any further progress on such other issues as the franchise and free trade impossible. For during his stay in Pretoria, the Volksraad, angered by Ripon's restriction of the British offer, authorised the President to accept Loch's terms for Swaziland, but refused to allow 'other subjects or . . . conditions' to be included in the new convention. If nothing was to be said to confirm the right of access to the sea, then nothing would be said about free trade or the franchise.

On this limited basis, therefore, a second Swaziland Convention was drawn up and duly signed in November 1893. The South African Republic was granted the 'rights and powers of jurisdiction, protection and administration over Swaziland without incorporation thereof into the said Republic'. But these rights were made subject to the Swazi people being satisfied that native interests were protected; and when the new convention was duly explained to the Swazis, both the Queen Regent and the young King objected vigorously that they wanted British, not Boer, protection. The Queen was said to have threatened to strangle herself to death with a whip-cord rather than be handed over to the protection of the Transvaal. And since no argument could avail to change their minds, the High Commissioner set off in the spring of 1894 to try to resolve the deadlock with Kruger at a further meeting in Pretoria.

This visit was to prove even more unfortunate than the earlier one, so far as relations between Boers and Uitlanders were concerned. During the interval, the feelings of the British residents had been much aroused by a Government order commandeering a number of them to serve in a Boer commando called out to deal with a native uprising. The British element among the Uitlanders, who then numbered some 35,000 of a total of 40,000, had appealed to the British Agent in Pretoria, Sir Jacobus de Wet, for protection against the enforcement of this order, pointing out the injustice of the law which allowed the authorities to enrol them for compulsory military service after only two years residence but which required fourteen years for them to qualify for the vote. Other nationalities such as the French, German, Portuguese and Belgians were protected from conscription by special treaties and they demanded that similar exemptions be obtained for them by the Imperial Government.

The situation was complicated by the fact that to negotiate such exemptions would require corresponding treatment for Transvaal citizens residing in the Cape: and this had been steadfastly refused by Rhodes' Cabinet. Nevertheless, as de Wet intoned gravely that a crisis was approaching, Loch set off for Pretoria, resolved not to let this obstacle stand in the way of the main negotiations. That he achieved at least this limited result was a tribute to his own palpable honesty and forthrightness in his handling of the ever-suspicious Kruger. For, as from the very moment of his arrival, the behaviour of some of the Uitlanders suggested that they were anything but responsible citizens seeking to exercise their responsibilities by the ballot-box. When Kruger arrived at the railway station to greet his visitor, an angry crowd of Uitlanders assembled, and soon became so hostile that the traditional address of welcome had to be postponed until the official parties could gain the calm and safety of the High Commissioner's hotel. Some of the demonstrators, determined not to be prevented from registering their wrath, leaped onto the box of the presidential carriage as it left the station, brandishing a Union Jack which wrapped itself around the head of the outraged Kruger. Others, to his equal fury, unhitched the horses and dragged the carriage to the hotel, singing 'God Save the Queen' and 'Rule Britannia' along the length of the route. And when the official ceremonies were finally completed, the President's carriage-horses were nowhere to be found and a fresh team had to be sent for to rescue him. To cap everything, the British Uitlanders invited Loch to Johannesburg to receive a petition listing their grievances and requiring the Imperial Government to demand immediate redress from the republican authorities.

In fact, the High Commissioner was no less disturbed by this exhibition of Uitlander temper than was Kruger. From the depths of his very real anxiety that a 'revolution' might happen at any moment, he appealed to the President to exempt the British residents from commando service and to remit the sentences which had been passed on those who had refused to be conscripted. Kruger, acting in what Loch called 'a liberal spirit', saw the danger of the position and conceded the High Commissioner's request. But he begged him not to go to Johannesburg, where his presence could all too easily excite the Uitlanders to fever pitch. Loch, strongly advised by Bower, his Imperial Secretary and a fervent advocate of conciliation, agreed to receive the petition in Pretoria. And when this had been presented, he told the Uitlanders that the President had agreed to exempt them from conscription and to consider their other grievances. But meanwhile they must abide by the laws of the Transvaal and refrain from any violence, which could only make his task of securing reforms more difficult.

As to the question of Swaziland, Loch and the President agreed that, for the moment, all that could be done was to prolong the Joint Anglo-Boer Government until the end of the year to allow time for a more definite settlement to be made. But, while Kruger might believe in Loch's honesty of purpose, he was deeply distrustful of those British politicians and advisers who surrounded him in the Cape and gave him orders from

Sir Henry Loch

King Leopold II

London. Appeals to the British public had not availed to induce in these men a sense of justice towards the Transvaal. Three years earlier he had said in an interview with Flora Shaw of *The Times*, 'You are afraid to give us a seaport. Can our two or three ships upset the balance of the first navy of the world? . . . You think that if I had a port I might give . . . preference to foreigners. It is nonsense. England, if she will but treat me fairly, will have the preference always. . . . I ask nothing better than to work with England as a younger brother might work with his elder, but I will not work with her as a slave.'

But Kruger's appeal had done nothing to soften British attitudes towards him. Whether over Swaziland, where he suspected that British jingoes had prompted the Queen Regent to object to Boer administration, or over the Uitlanders who he believed were being excited to rebellion by Rhodes, he was therefore becoming more and more convinced that Britain was determined to make him her 'slave'. Thus, even as Loch was telling a Swazi deputation that Britain would not undertake the administration of their country and wished the Transvaal to take over, Kruger was drawing up a list of amendments to the 1884 London Convention which would, once and for all, give him the independence which he felt was essential to escape from the machinations of men like Rhodes. And when this was completed, he suggested to the High Commissioner that, having conceded his request to exempt British residents from military service, he deserved this much consideration.

Kruger was, of course, told that he could not expect any reward for a concession which was 'absolute and unconditional'. But Loch, nevertheless, had much sympathy with his appeal; and when he visited London for consultations shortly afterwards, he told Ripon that he thought the President might be seeking 'some golden bridge by which he could retreat from his present untenable position . . . and this he hopes to attain through a revision of the Convention of 1884'. In particular, he suggested that to offer Pretoria such substantial concessions might secure a reform of the franchise. But the only concession Ripon would allow was that the Swazi delegation, which was shortly to descend on London in search of British protection, would be firmly told to make their peace with the Boers. Other problems, such as the Uitlanders' franchise were of little interest to Ripon, who was more concerned to rid himself of the plaintive Swazis. Loch's suggestions for a horse-trade with Kruger were therefore coldly received and he returned to Cape Town in November 1894 sadly empty-handed.

On December 6th, the High Commissioner and Kruger met for the last time, at Charleston on the borders of Natal, to complete the arrangements for Swaziland. Three days later, after Kruger had accepted the necessary safeguards for native rights and autonomy in internal affairs, the third Swaziland Convention was signed. And three months afterwards, at an indaba called by the Queen Regent and the King, the Swazis accepted their fate and the young King was formally recognised as Paramount Chief by General Joubert on behalf of the South African Republic.

Kruger had finally got his own way in Swaziland, because Britain had no interest in a country which was as inaccessible to her troops as it was unattractive to her traders. But the new agreement contained little, if any, satisfaction of his paramount need—an outlet to the sea. On the contrary, it stipulated that no railway might be constructed east of Swazi territory 'save under the provisions of a further contemplated convention'. And within five months of the signature of this new agreement, in the wake of a series of British complaints to Pretoria about alleged illegalities committed by Boers against the tribes to the east of the Swazi border, any hopes that the 'further contemplated convention' would allow a railway to the coast were finally destroyed. In April 1895, Ripon, prompted by renewed fears of an imminent alliance between Germany and the Transvaal, authorised the Governor of Natal to proclaim the annexation of two of the intervening territories. And a few weeks later, on the strength of an assertion by Queen Zambili's successor in Tongaland that 'I am always obeying the British law, because I obey the Queen of England', a further proclamation announced that Tongaland had been annexed by the Crown. Kosi Bay was to be British territory after all and the Boers were to be denied all access to the sea.

Pretoria promptly protested that, 'taking into account previous negotiations and the fact that the territories are not of
the least importance to Her Majesty's Government, this
annexation cannot be regarded . . . otherwise than as directed
against this Republic (and) . . . therefore as an unfriendly act'.
As Leyds put it, 'the acknowledged rights (of the Transvaal) in
the north . . . were exchanged for the promise held out by the
British Government of some advantages in the east; but when
the time for payment came, these in turn were denied to the
Boers'. But such protests were to no avail. The Imperial Government retorted that the Transvaalers, by failing to enter a
customs union, had not fulfilled the condition on which the
earlier Convention had allowed them a railway to the sea. In
fact this was no more than a convenient debating point. For the
truth was that neither Rhodes nor the Colonial Office were any
longer interested in merely drawing the Boers into an economic
union, as had been the intention at the time of the first Swaziland Convention. Rhodes' new aim was to put such pressure
on Kruger as would force him to surrender to British paramountcy or face the alternative of war; and wherever Rhodes
now aimed, the Colonial Office were certain soon to follow.

If proof were needed of this evident change of British policy,
it is to be found in an exchange between Loch and Ripon in
December 1894 shortly after the signature of the third and final
Swaziland Convention. Loch, now more than ever afraid that
serious trouble was brewing between Britain and the Transvaal,
suggested to the Colonial Secretary that he should try once more
to break down the barriers of suspicion which inhibited Kruger's
dealings with Britain. In particular, he wished to hold out the
hope that Britain would be ready to consider certain of the
revisions of the London Convention which Kruger wanted, for
example Article 4 which prohibited the South African Republic
from making treaties with any country or tribe without British
consent. It should not be, he suggested, beyond the wit of man
to find some acceptable modification of this all-important article,
while at the same time insisting that the Transvaal must remain
within the sphere of British influence. Loch also wanted to
disabuse the President of his fear that, if he conceded the

franchise to the Uitlanders after a comparatively short period of residence, the British residents would use their newly won civil rights to further British, as opposed to Transvaal, interests on the grounds that they had not abandoned their old allegiance to Britain. To this end, he proposed to tell the President that, since 1870, English Common Law had held that a British subject, who had been naturalised in another country, was no longer still bound by his former allegiance. But, although such reassurances might have gone very far to remove the President's doubts on this score and might even have turned the scales on the franchise question, Ripon refused to allow Loch to pursue any of these matters with Kruger. Instead, he curtly telegraphed that the Imperial Government were not disposed to agree to any alterations of the London Convention, least of all of Article 4, and that further discussion of this, and other, questions should be dropped altogether.

In fact, so strained had Loch's relations become with his superiors in Whitehall, not to speak of his Premier at the Cape, that at the beginning of 1895 he bowed to the irresistible force of Rhodes' pervasive influence on British policy and resigned his post. But before leaving, he sought to make one final disposition to ensure that, whatever trouble Rhodes might engineer with the Transvaal, at least the 'Imperial Factor' would not be altogether left out of account. This took the form of a plan whereby, in the event of a clash between the British Uitlanders and the republican authorities in the Transvaal, the High Commissioner would first warn the Transvaal Government that Britain could not be indifferent to a state of affairs that might endanger the lives and property of her subjects and, if fighting continued, would then assert his right to intervene and arbitrate a settlement.

As long ago as the previous summer, Loch had felt that Kruger's Government was extremely unstable, with the 'pale and aged' President beset by rival factions. And he clearly suspected that Rhodes and the B.S.A. Company might shortly engage in a conspiracy to topple the Republic and take over the Transvaal by first provoking a Uitlander rebellion and then sending in Company forces to help the rebels. In a remarkably perceptive secret despatch to Ripon he had questioned whether it would be 'altogether consistent with imperial interests' for the British in the Transvaal to take over the Government. For, having suspected that there was something synthetic about the Uitlanders' attitude as it revealed itself on his second visit to Pretoria, and believing that Uitlander opinion was more anti-Boer than pro-British, he doubted that these people, if they gained power, would show themselves to be any more loyal to the Crown than they were to Kruger. 'I should certainly regard with very considerable apprehension,' he concluded, 'if the Transvaal became practically an English, instead of a weak and discredited Dutch, Republic.'

Loch felt that such an eventuality, whether brought about by Rhodes' Chartered Company or by such powerful British 'Randlords' as J. B. Robinson, would give Britain the worst of every world. And for this reason, he believed that the High Commissioner should be empowered to intervene to stop a revolt from getting out of hand. At the same time, if such an intervention were to be effective, military support would be necessary; and at the moment this could only be undertaken at the risk of exposing the Cape to outside attack. On the advice of General Cameron, G.O.C. British troops in South Africa, he therefore coupled with his plan for intervention a request for two additional infantry battalions and a field battery to reinforce the imperial garrison.

In support of this request, Loch contended that there was now a definite possibility that Germany, or France, might try to take advantage of any British digression in South Africa. Recent German naval visits to Delagoa Bay had coincided with 'disquieting' reports suggesting that Germany was developing closer political and economic ties with the Transvaal. Kruger, speaking at a banquet in celebration of the Kaiser's birthday, had recently remarked to his German guests, 'I know I may count on the Germans in future. . . . I feel certain that when the time comes for the Republic to wear larger clothes, you will have done much to bring it about.' There were also persistent reports that Leyds had told Berlin that trouble was brewing with the Uitlanders over the franchise and that, if it came to a rising, only Germany could hold Britain in check. Moreover, it was being suggested that Germany, faced with mounting hostility from the Hereros of South-West Africa and the tribes of southern Tanganyika and with the consequent stagnation of German commercial enterprise in these areas, might soon cast envious glances on the relative peace and prosperity of Cape Colony. The German administration were blaming the resistance of the Hereros on the failure of the Cape Government to prevent arms being smuggled across the frontier, rather than on their own harsh practice of conscripting native labour into chain gangs; and there were fears that they might use this complaint as a pretext for seizing Cape territory.

As for the French, the growing enmity between Britain and France arising from the current struggle for supremacy in the Niger valley might at any moment develop into open warfare. The French were reported to be sending to Madagascar an expeditionary force of some 17,000 to 20,000 men to annexe the island as a French colony and to crush once and for all the Hovas' resistance to the Protectorate which France had held since 1886. England had recognised French sovereignty in Madagascar in 1890, in return for French recognition of Britain's Protectorate in Zanzibar. But, as the situation in West Africa had shown, this agreement had not prevented conflict in other areas between the two countries. Loch therefore argued that, 'Should England be engaged in war with France, a large military force in the near neighbourhood (would be) . . . a source of considerable danger . . . (and) it would be unwise to ignore the probability that every effort will be made by France to seize the Cape.' For if, as was likely in such a war, the Suez Canal were blocked, the Cape would once again be of crucial strategic importance as the only alternative route to the east.

For every reason, therefore, a stronger Cape garrison seemed necessary to the High Commissioner. But although the Foreign Office told the Austrian Ambassador in London—for the information of Berlin—that Britain would go to war to preserve her supremacy south of the Zambezi, Loch received neither the troop reinforcements that he requested nor any authority to intervene in the event of an Uitlander rising in the Transvaal.

Ripon took the view that, so long as Britain had 'hegemony', the Transvaal could be a Republic either under Boer or Uitlander rule for all he cared. And Loch left Cape Town saddened alike by the reluctance of Whitehall to assert the 'Imperial Factor', as by their failure to prevent Rhodes from sabotaging his efforts to arrive at some meeting of minds with the Transvaal Boers.

The fact that, towards the end of the same year, the role of his successor in the Jameson Raid conspiracy was to stand ready to intervene in the expected revolution was later to cause some suggestions that Loch had in fact been as much a conspirator as Rhodes and those imperial officials who were privy to the plot. That this was not true was, however, shown by the fact that Loch's idea of intervention by the High Commissioner was as a means of stopping or, at least, containing a revolt on the Rand, whereas Rhodes' plan was that it should be part of a conspiracy to promote one. But perhaps the clearest evidence to acquit Loch of any charge that he helped to promote the Jameson Raid conspiracy was spoken by Rhodes himself, when he came to London after the abortive Raid had brought resignation and ruin to his premiership. During his visit he dined one night with his former Governor and High Commissioner, now in retirement. Over the port Loch asked him 'Why did you get rid of me?' To put his guest at ease, he added, 'Don't think I'm sorry to be retired. On the contrary, I am very happy. But I should just like to know why you forced me to resign.' Rhodes, caught off guard by Loch's typically straightforward question, could only reply, 'Because you would never have allowed me to do what I did.'

Coming from the man who was to be more responsible than any other single individual for making war with the Boers unavoidable, there could be no finer epitaph on Loch's efforts to restrain Rhodes, to deal justly with Kruger and to keep the peace in South Africa. Merriman had written to Loch shortly before his departure, 'We can ill afford to spare any influence that is above being bought or squared just now.' The next twelve months were to demonstrate the wisdom of that comment.

15 The Jameson Conspiracy

WITH Loch out of the way, Rhodes was able to give full vent to his desire to 'have Jo'burg' and to combine his political power with his financial resources in a ruthless attempt to overthrow Kruger's Republic. Earlier in his career Rhodes had been content to work for South African unity through such economic processes as a customs union, railway agreements between the Colonies and the Republics and free trade in South African products, all of which accorded with his broader ideas of an Empire Federation based on Imperial Tariff Preference. For a brief while he had even seemed ready to let time and patience work to bring the principal opponent of this policy, the Transvaal, into line. But in the past few years his attitude had changed drastically. As Jean van der Poel wrote in her brilliant book on the Jameson Raid, 'Patience gave way to precipitance and for the statesman's policy was substituted the adventurer's plot.' Which transition was due first, to disappointment over the failure of the 'New Rand' in Rhodesia; second, to Kruger's refusal to join an economic union with the Cape; third, to the absence of men of character and wisdom in his political entourage; and finally, to the realisation that, having failed to gain control of the Delagoa Bay railway, he could no longer hope to work his will on the Transvaal by economic pressures.

Certainly no-one could have tried harder than Rhodes to get hold of the Delagoa Bay Railway; and it was not until the middle of 1895 that he eventually had to admit defeat for lack of support in Whitehall and in face of determined Portuguese resistance. In 1893, encouraged to believe that the Portuguese would sell by a dubious Bavarian intermediary called Baron von Merck, he had offered £700,000 to buy Delagoa Bay. But the Portuguese were warned by Germany against accepting an offer which could lead to British intervention in Portuguese East Africa and they therefore insisted that the arbitration case concerning McMurdo's company must first be settled. Then again in 1895, prompted by a statement by the Portuguese Minister of Marine expressing doubts that Portugal would be able much longer to afford the 'burden of glory' of her African colonies, he tried to win the support of Rosebery. But even this usually staunch supporter of his plans bluntly replied that the Government could not help. The German ambassador in London had been at pains to point out that Germany 'could make her power felt elsewhere', i.e. in Egypt, if Britain tried to interfere in Portuguese East Africa. And Rhodes was forced to accept that, so long as Berlin maintained this 'protective' attitude towards the Portuguese and the Boers, he would not be able to block this outlet to the sea. The most that he could get was an undertaking from Lisbon not to cede Delagoa Bay to any other power pending the arbitration settlement.

Unable to strangle the Boers into submission by economic pressures and attributing to them the very desire to dominate all South Africa which inspired his own every action, Rhodes now resolved to overthrow Kruger's Republic by force. Interpreting the rowdy demonstrations during Loch's second visit to Pretoria as evidence of a truly revolutionary spirit among the Uitlanders, he planned to foment a rising on the Rand and to support it with an armed invasion of the Transvaal by a B.S.A. Company force advancing from the Bechuanaland Protectorate. In preparation for this coup he had already taken several important steps. Among other things, he had engineered the return of the complaisant and now ageing Robinson to replace Loch in the office of Cape Governor and High Commissioner. And Robinson had immediately justified his selection by adopting and adapting Loch's plan for imperial intervention in the event of an Uitlander revolution and by persuading Ripon to send the troop reinforcements which had been denied to his predecessor.

Rhodes also took time off to visit England, accompanied by Jameson, to conduct an intensive public relations campaign for a forward policy in South Africa. Playing on the German 'threat', exemplified by the current presence in Berlin of Kruger's State Secretary, Leyds, and by the announcement of a forthcoming German fleet visit to Delagoa Bay to celebrate the formal opening of the rail link with the Transvaal, he drummed up much support for himself as Britain's foremost empire-builder. Though apparently sparing Ripon's Radical conscience, he confided to Rosebery his ideas for an armed raid on the Transvaal in support of a revolution in Johannesburg, to which the Prime Minister reacted by no means unfavourably, insisting only that the Company's forces should not move before the rising was properly under way. Rhodes also charmed Queen Victoria by remarking in the course of an audience that he had just 'added two provinces to Your Majesty's dominions', which prompted the Queen to reply that this was a welcome change from the performance of some of her Ministers, who kept on giving her provinces away. By way of following up this bid for royal support, Jameson addressed the Imperial Institute before an enthusiastic audience, including the Prince of Wales; and in his customary downright manner he proclaimed that the 'handful of Boers', who constituted the only obstacle to a British Federation in South Africa, should be simply swept away.

Rhodes also persuaded the B.S.A. Company's directors to authorise a large increase in the strength of the police force in Rhodesia and the purchase of substantial quantities of arms and ammunition. A senior officer was sent to spy out the land around Johannesburg and Pretoria. And through Rhodes' Consolidated Goldfields Company in Johannesburg, contact was made with Lionel Phillips and Charles Leonard, leaders of the Transvaal National Union—the Uitlanders' pressure group, formed in 1892 to redress their grievances and secure their political rights —with whom Rhodes saw that an opportunity might soon arise to concert an armed attack by Company forces with an Uitlander rising on the Rand.

298

Meanwhile back in the Cape, the credulous Hofmeyr and his Bondsmen, knowing nothing of these conspiratorial moves, continued to give Rhodes their full support. Robinson's reappointment was applauded by the Bond who saw in him an opponent of imperialism and a friend of the man who they still held to be their champion. More perceptive politicians, realising that Rhodes was seeking a completely free hand, deplored Robinson's return as highly inadvisable for the interests of South Africa. And for a brief moment after a change of government in Britain had brought Joseph Chamberlain to the Colonial Office, Robinson—and Rhodes too—feared that these opinions might find an echo in Whitehall and that a further change of High Commissioner might soon follow. An ardent imperialist, the new Colonial Secretary distrusted Rhodes, partly because of his contribution to Parnell's Irish Party at Westminster, but more especially because of his avowed desire to eliminate the 'Imperial Factor' from South African affairs. Also, as Robinson knew from Bower, Chamberlain had worked behind the scenes to get him replaced by Loch in 1889. For his part, Robinson certainly disliked his new overlord intensely, describing him to Bower as 'dangerous as an enemy, untrustworthy as a friend but fatal as a colleague'. Yet, for all this mutual distrust, the anxieties caused by the change of regime at home were soon to be allayed. For while Chamberlain made other changes in the Colonial Service, he decided for the time being to leave Robinson in Cape Town.

Rhodes could therefore breathe easily again. But if he had the High Commissioner that he wanted, he still lacked one essential element in his conspiracy against Kruger's Republic. This was the Bechuanaland Protectorate which, as the nearest point of British territory to Johannesburg, was the best, if not the only, possible launching platform for a rapid strike from outside the Transvaal in support of a revolution on the Rand. For several months past Rhodes had been putting pressure on the Imperial Government to fulfil the undertaking which he claimed had been given by Knutsford at the time of the Charter that the Protectorate would in due course be handed over to the B.S.A. Company. Ripon, Loch and Shippard, the British Resident in

Bechuanaland, were being constantly bombarded by him with demands that the time had come to carry out this undertaking. But Loch, in his advice to the Colonial Office, had held stead-fastly to the view that the Protectorate should be annexed to the Crown Colony of Bechuanaland rather than be entrusted to the Company. Khama dreaded the idea of being ruled by the Company, having seen how they had treated Lobengula. Besides Loch felt that it would be most undesirable for those who governed the Protectorate to have to arbitrate over concessions in which they as a commercial company had a direct interest. This would involve them in awkward political dealings with the Bechuana chiefs and with the Transvaal and Orange Free State, and for such delicate diplomatic transactions the Company's officers, to judge by their performance in Rhodesia, were com-pletely unqualified.

Loch's recommendations had, of course, infuriated Rhodes who angrily accused him of an 'attempt at public robbery' from the Company. The Imperial Government had made, he claimed, 'distinct pledges which placed the ultimate destination of the country with the Charter'. And he insisted that the Company had undertaken the expense of extending the railway from Kimberley to Palapye solely on the understanding that the Protectorate 'should become a portion of the Chartered Terri-tories' which, he claimed, 'a glance at the map will show . . . naturally form one state'.

Loch categorically denied the existence of any such under-standing and reminded Rhodes that, when the Charter had been granted, Knutsford had written to him to put on record that it did not 'supersede or affect the Protectorate of Her Majesty' north of the Molopo river. While not ruling out the possibility that the Company might one day take over the Protectorate, he felt most strongly, as he had told Ripon, that this day was still a long way away. And suspecting as he did, the real reasons why Rhodes was making such an urgent issue of the matter, he ad-vised that the Imperial Government should continue for some time to come to hold the ring in Bechuanaland. Indeed, he went even further and suggested that Rhodes be told not to build the railway extension from Kimberley along the frontier of the Protectorate, since this could lead to trouble between the Transvaal and the B.S.A. Company.

Torn between Rhodes' demands and Loch's advice, Ripon dodged the issue. He did not at all like the idea of handing over responsibility to the Company. Yet he felt that, since Rhodes had undertaken to extend the railway to Palapye, it would not be practical politics, or economics, for the Imperial Government at this stage to refuse him the territory for all time. He therefore sought escape in the Olympian judgement that at the 'proper time' the Government would 'entertain favourably any reasonable proposals' of the Company.

But the proper time never arrived. For within a few months, Khama, prompted by rumours that his country would shortly become part of the Chartered Territories, led his fellow chiefs from the Protectorate to protest vigorously against being handed over to the Company. Khama even expressed anxiety to Loch that the railway which was to traverse his country was to 'belong to the Company and not to the Government'. After what had happened to Lobengula, he would not allow Rhodes to have any part in the administration of his territory. He was perfectly content to be under the Crown, whose officers had always treated him fairly. In fact his only objection was to the hut-tax because it encouraged his people to crowd into fewer huts so as to avoid the tax. And in a disarming plea for its abolition, he told the Colonial Office that, 'Some of us have learnt it is not good to have too many people sleeping in a small place, especially big girls and big boys sleeping in the same hut, although they are the children of one father.' But apart from this, he wished all the existing arrangements under the Protectorate to continue.

Unfortunately for Rhodes' designs, Khama was currently the Imperial Government's favourite South African chieftain. In cooperation with the missionaries he had made determined efforts to suppress the sale of liquor, the curse of the Bantu in the late nineteenth century. Also, within one year of moving his capital from Shoshong to Palapye, he had built a number of schools, in addition to teaching his subjects to plough with modern equipment and to take a pride in their houses and gardens. Thus, when this model pupil of British imperialism raised his voice against Company rule, Whitehall hearkened to his pleas. And when, in June 1895, Chamberlain arrived at the Colonial Office to be confronted by Khama's petition for the continuation of the Protectorate, he had no hesitation in meeting his wishes. All that he would concede in the way of change in that area—which benefited the Imperial Treasury far more than Rhodes' schemes—was that the Crown should hand over British Bechuanaland to be annexed as part of Cape Colony.

Rhodes was seriously discomfited by the Imperial Government's surrender to Khama. Even worse than losing the opportunity of adding another quarter of a million square miles to his empire, the base for his projected invasion of the Transvaal was now threatened. There was, therefore, nothing for it but to bring the new Colonial Secretary into the conspiracy and seek his cooperation. Chamberlain was opposed on principle to Chartered Companies and believed that all colonial advance and development should be conducted by the Imperial Government. Besides, on a more personal level, there was not much love lost between Rhodes and the new Colonial Secretary, who had bluntly told him at the time of the negotiations for the Charter that he did not like his anti-imperialist attitude or his cynical belief that every man had his price. But Rhodes needed the Protectorate for his plans, and only Chamberlain could give it to him.

Early in July 1895, he therefore sent Harris, the Company's Cape Town secretary, to London to put the Colonial Secretary in the picture and to point to the importance of the B.S.A. Company having a police force on the border of Bechuanaland, ready to move into the Transvaal whenever the current unrest among the Uitlanders on the Rand should boil over into a revolution. With this consideration in mind, he was to urge Chamberlain to concede Rhodes' repeated requests that the Protectorate should now revert to the Company. And since a rising of the Uitlanders might happen at any moment, he was to press that the territory be handed over as soon as possible.

At a meeting with Chamberlain and his deputy, Lord Selborne, on August 1, Harris broached the subject on these lines. As he put it in a cable to Rhodes, he informed the Secretary of State 'guardedly reason why we wish to have base at Gaberones and advisable our presence in Protectorate.' According to Chamberlain's later testimony to the Committee of Enquiry into the Jameson Raid, his response to this approach was to protest that he could not discuss the plan for putting Company police on the Transvaal border, and that he did not want to hear confidential information of which he could not make official use. But Harris' cable to Rhodes, not to mention the subsequent cooperation and encouragement which the conspirators received from the Imperial Government, suggests that his reaction was, in fact, far from the outraged innocence which he was later to feign. For Harris concluded his report by saying that Chamberlain was 'heartily in sympathy' with Rhodes' designs. And a few days later, on August 13, a further cable reached Cape Town, telling of the Colonial Secretary's more considered response and saying that, after further discussions, 'Chamberlain will do anything to assist, except hand over administration of Protectorate, provided he does not officially know your plans.' In other words, Rhodes could use the territory as a base, but without prejudice to the Imperial Government's sovereignty in the Protectorate as a whole.

Leaving all moral issues aside, it is an extraordinary reflection on Chamberlain's judgement that he should have so swallowed his distrust of Rhodes as to become a party to the disreputable conspiracy which was to follow and which came close to ruining his political career. No doubt fear of Germany aligning herself with Kruger and making the Transvaal a German Protectorate played a large part in winning him over to Rhodes' scheme. For in the Colonial Office there had for some time been a nightmarish fear that if the Germans took the Boers under their wing, or even the Delagoa Bay Railway, British paramountcy in South Africa would be at an end and Cape Colony, strategically a more vital British interest than Malta or Gibraltar, would then secede from the Crown and make whatever terms might be possible with Pretoria.

Apart from all this, Chamberlain was faced with the indisputable fact that Rhodes, by combining his political power as Cape Premier and ruler of the 'North' with the vast wealth of De Beers and Consolidated Goldfields, had achieved a position which any Imperial Government would have found hard to challenge. Paradoxically for one so resentful of the 'Imperial Factor', Rhodes had become the very embodiment of imperial supremacy in South Africa and the acknowledged champion of Britain in the struggle which he, more than anyone else, had decided must now be waged against Kruger. And it is not to over-simplify the issue to say that, whereas Rhodes decided to beat the Boers in a trial of strength, having failed to make them join an economic union, Chamberlain, realising that he could neither beat nor even check this impulsive and irresistible adventurer, decided to join Rhodes.

Nor, apart from his personal distrust of the man, was it so very repellent for him to do so. For one of the reasons why Chamberlain wanted the Colonial Office above all other departments was that he longed to see Britain break away from the *laissez-aller* policy in respect of the Transvaal, which his predecessors, Tory as well as Liberal, had been content to follow. Ever since the London Convention had been followed by the discovery of gold on the Rand, successive Colonial Secretaries had assumed that the Transvaal would somehow ultimately become absorbed into a British South African federation. To this end they had each in their turn applied varying forms of pressure, such as keeping the Boers from the sea and inserting wedges of British territory on all sides of the Transvaal to stop them linking up with the Germans. Then, when these devices had failed to bring the stubborn Boers to submit, they had for a while tried to lure Kruger into an economic union by offering him access to the Tonga coast at Kosi Bay. But ever since the humiliation of Majuba Hill, it had been settled Government policy that 'every nerve should be strained to prevent such a disgrace as another South African war'. And although, as the years passed, the Transvaal, daily growing richer, began to displace Cape Colony as the economic and political centre of South Africa, the Colonial Secretary of the day had relied on the ever-increasing influx of British immigrants to the Rand to turn the scales and by sheer weight of numbers to bring the Transvaal painlessly into the British Empire.

But these pipe-dreams had failed to materialise. In fact, on returning from his last visit to Pretoria, Loch had reported that the Uitlanders, far from pining for the British Raj, might declare themselves a Republic if they ever achieved political power. Nor was there the smallest sign of Kruger weakening in the face of pressures either from the Uitlanders or from Britain's encirclement policy. In fact, by the middle of 1895, he had completely recovered his poise and seemed to be as deeply entrenched as ever. Although his eyesight was beginning to fail him and he was becoming increasingly deaf, Kruger's recovery from the leadership crisis, which threatened to unseat him following his narrow victory in the 1893 election, had shown that he could still rise to the occasion and become the 'old warhorse', when confronted by a serious challenge. Not only had he ridden out the storm raised by the Opposition's bitter accusations of rigging the ballot, but he had persuaded his election opponent and principal accuser, General Joubert, to resume his place in the Executive Council, thereby ensuring that all Cabinet decisions would be irreversible in the Volksraad. With the aid of his brilliant young Hollander colleague, W. J. Leyds, who in 1888 had become his State Secretary at the age of twenty-nine, Kruger was pursuing a policy of rugged and resolute independence, cleverly playing off the Germans against the British. He was trying to turn his military alliance with the Orange Free State into a formal federation of the two Boer Republics. And following the opening of the Delagoa Bay railway, which had been completed with the aid of a £2,500,000 loan from Rothschilds, he was turning the screw on the Cape railways by raising the tariffs on the Transvaal section of the line from Bloemfontein to Pretoria, so as to reduce the traffic from the Cape in favour of the line from Lourenço Marques.

With the Boers in such a determined frame of mind, reinforced by the continuing flow of British capital and labour to the Transvaal, Chamberlain decided that the time had come to discard the old ways of inertia and to adopt more forceful methods to coerce Kruger's Republic into joining a British South African federation before it was too late and the Boers too strong to be constrained. And whether or not he distrusted Rhodes and suspected that his aim was to add the Transvaal to his own northern empire, there was no other 'agent' available and willing to undertake this dangerous and devious enterprise.

Chamberlain had long been determined to become Colonial Secretary at the earliest opportunity. And like Carnarvon in the seventies, he wished to bring about a federation of South Africa. Ambitious and ruthless, this son of a London shoe-maker had entered politics as a Radical Liberal nearly twenty years earlier, having retired from a highly successful career in the screw-making business of Birmingham at the age of thirty-eight. His Radicalism had caused him to oppose Carnarvon's annexation of the Transvaal in 1877. But five years later, as President of the Board of Trade under Gladstone, he was cheering with the jingos over the bombardment of Alexandria which led to the British occupation of Egypt in 1882. Thereafter his Radical thinking had led him into the paths of Imperialism which, he was convinced, would alone provide for Britain's industrial workers the markets upon which their continued employment depended, while at the same time giving the backward native populations of the world the inestimable benefits of government by the greatest of all the governing races.

From this conversion it was but a short step to resignation, when Gladstone's Government introduced their Home Rule proposals for Ireland which Chamberlain regarded as an attack upon the whole concept of Empire. And having severed his connections with the Liberal Cabinet, he founded a new party in Birmingham, which he called the Liberal Unionists and with which he helped the Tories to defeat his erstwhile leader in the General Election of 1886. Nevertheless he was not to hold any office in the Government over which Salisbury presided for the next six years, during which period of frustrating 'unemployment' he and his famous monocle continued, somewhat paradoxically, to be found on the Opposition benches in the House of Commons, and sometimes even on the Front Bench, alongside the very men whom he had helped to drive out of office. With his middle-class industrialist background, 'Pushful Joe', as some people called him, was out of keeping with the men and manners of a patrician England savouring the last lingering days of its Indian summer. And he had to wait until 1895 before the call came to serve in a Salisbury Cabinet.

But when it came, Chamberlain refused all other offices, including the Treasury, and took over the Colonial Office with a zest that was to blow like an icy wind through the cobwebbed corridors of that 'leisurely and sleepy' institution. He even installed electricity in place of the candles which had cast their pale light upon the labours of his predecessors. Proclaiming that 'we are landlords of a great estate and it is the duty of a landlord to develop his estate', he served immediate notice on the Treasury and the taxpayer that the days of mid-Victorian penny-pinching were over and that, so long as he held office, Britain's colonies would find a ready response to their requests for imperial assistance. At the same time, he made it clear to Britain's rivals overseas that, although that foremost of diplomatic dealers, Lord Salisbury, might still be Prime Minister and Foreign Secretary, there would be no more horse-trading of British colonial interests in Africa or elsewhere. The cause of Empire Federation, later to be followed by Imperial Tariff Preference, had become an article of faith, almost an obsession, for him; and anything and everything that tended to support this cause had his unqualified support.

Chamberlain had for a long time put Africa at the top of his list of colonial priorities. As a member of Gladstone's Cabinet in 1885, he had played a leading part in sending General Warren to deal with the crisis in Bechuanaland. He had been second to none in his determination to secure the road to the north, although he would have infinitely preferred that the north, when secured, had been occupied by imperial agencies rather than by a Chartered Company with far too much autonomy for his liking. Then, when he saw that the Robinson-Rhodes partnership in the late eighties was threatening still further to undermine the authority of the Crown in British South Africa, he had joined with a group of leading public figures who shared his dislike of colonialism in forming the South Africa Committee.

307

With their support he had worked for the recall of Robinson and had pressed for the separation of the office of High Commissioner from that of Cape Governor and hence from the apparently dominating influences of Cape politicians. And now, with the reins of power finally and firmly grasped in his own hands, he hoped to succeed where fifteen years earlier Carnarvon had failed and to establish during his term of office a British Federation of South Africa as a permanent monument to his stewardship of the colonial empire.

Clearly he would have preferred to make the fulfilment of this task a purely imperial enterprise, without having to rely on the colonial element, still less on a Chartered Company, to help him to drive the Boers into a British dominion. But time, and Rhodes, were pressing him too hard to make this feasible. For to do so would require massive imperial expenditure and reinforcements—not just the two extra regiments which Robinson had wrung from his reluctant predecessor. To persuade first the Treasury, then the Cabinet and finally Parliament to sanction all this would take months, maybe years. The German 'threat' might be thought serious in Cape Town and in the Colonial Office, but it was not obvious enough to stampede public opinion at home. Nor were the Uitlanders' grievances yet of sufficient concern to Parliament; and it would have been difficult to persuade the House of Commons that sending a large imperial army to South Africa was the way to counter the Transvaal's threat to outstrip the Cape as the richest country in the area.

Thus when Rhodes came forward with his plan for an armed intervention against Kruger's Republic, Chamberlain, having carefully weighed all these considerations, felt that he had no alternative but to make use of the Chartered Company's services. Besides, such a course offered the great advantage that, if the Company made a mess of things, he could disown them, provided—as he had apparently told Harris—he did not 'officially know' of the plot.

Moreover, Rhodes was very ready to make things easier for him. Quick to take the hint that any help he required would be forthcoming from the Colonial Office, if he would only drop his request for the administration of the Protectorate to be handed over, he now instructed Harris to reduce the requirement to a strip of territory along the frontier of Bechuanaland and the Transvaal, which was to be nominally for the construction of the railway extension to Palapye, but which was in fact to serve as a military base for the concentration of the Company's forces. Rhodes also asked for, and immediately obtained, Colonial Office sanction for a block of twenty square miles of territory at Gaberones where his main encampment was to be placed. And permission was given for B.S.A. Company police to be stationed there, ostensibly to guard the railway workings against depredations by the natives, which task Rhodes had euphemistically suggested the Bechuanaland Police could not be expected to undertake in addition to all their other duties.

No sooner had these military dispositions been agreed between the conspirators than Kruger was to play into his enemies' hands with a foolishly vindictive attempt to squeeze out the Cape Railways from the Transvaal in favour of his own Delagoa Bay line. At the beginning of 1895, following the completion of the Delagoa Bay Railway, the Cape Government, in their efforts to retain the Rand traffic, had reduced the freight rates as far as Viljoen's Drift on the Free State-Transvaal border. However, at Kruger's prompting, the Netherlands Railway Company had promptly retaliated by tripling the rates on the section from Viljoen's Drift to Johannesburg which was under their control. The Cape authorities vigorously protested at this act of gross victimisation. But to no avail; and after attempts to agree on a negotiated settlement had proved futile, they gave orders that their goods should be off-loaded at the border and sent on to Johannesburg by ox-wagon across the Vaal river drifts. Whereupon Kruger promptly announced in September 1895 that, as from October 1 the drifts would be closed to all external traffic.

There was an immediate outcry at the Cape and Rhodes, sensing the opportunity to portray himself as the injured party and hoping for the support of an ultimatum from London, loudly protested in his capacity as the Colony's Premier that this step was 'a breach of the London Convention and should therefore be revoked. Leyds, on Kruger's behalf, insisted that the closure of the drifts had been brought about by 'measures taken by the Cape Government to damage other railways in the Republic'. Nevertheless, he said that the President would be 'ready to discuss a reasonable division of the traffic from different parts to the Transvaal' with the states concerned. To this Rhodes replied that he too was ready to discuss these matters in an inter-state conference, provided that the Transvaal Government meanwhile repaired their breach of the London Convention by cancelling the closure of the drifts. Yet, despite firm pressures by de Wet in Pretoria, Kruger refused to back down; and Rhodes fumed at the failure of the Colonial Office to threaten the President with more than diplomatic displeasure.

Chamberlain however did not want to be rushed into issuing a premature ultimatum. He had already been pushed into one critical and far-reaching decision which had removed him from the driving-seat, but not from the car. He was also anxious to reassure himself about certain problems which would arise when Jameson staged his attack on the Transvaal. For instance, he wanted to know from Robinson what would be the attitude of the Cape Dutch and whether the High Commissioner would be able to ensure that in the event of a revolution on the Rand the revolutionaries would accept the British flag. And it was not until after Robinson had replied with cautious optimism to these enquiries that Chamberlain would agree to step up the pressures on the Transvaal to reopen the Vaal drifts.

Meanwhile Kruger remained adamant. Insisting that the problem of rail tariffs which had given rise to the dispute with the Cape could only be resolved by a conference with all the interested parties, he invited representatives of the Cape, the Orange Free State, Natal and Mozambique to meet him at Pretoria on November 4. In reply to complaints that the closing of the Vaal frontier discriminated against what were with few exceptions British goods, he blandly suggested that he could always put himself on-side with the London Convention by including all colonial goods in the embargo. The nearest he came to making any concession was to suggest that, as a sweetener for the conference, the drifts should be reopened on November 5 for ten days, after which period he reserved the right to close them again, if no settlement should be in sight. But, since both the Cape and the Imperial Government held that under the 1884 Convention Kruger had no such right, this offer was ignored.

At this point, Chamberlain, having overcome his hesitations about issuing an ultimatum, told Robinson that the Imperial Government were ready to make the 'gravest remonstrance' in Pretoria against what was regarded as 'an act of hostility' aimed at Cape Colony. But he warned that, if such a message were sent, it would not thereafter be possible to 'let the matter drop . . . even if an expedition has to be undertaken', and such an expedition could not, as in previous colonial wars, be conducted wholly at the mother country's expense. Therefore he required that, as an essential condition of sending Kruger an ultimatum, the Cape Government should agree to bear half the cost of any expedition, to contribute 'a fair contingent' of troops and to provide 'full and free use' of the Colony's railways and rolling stock.

Rhodes gave the necessary undertaking and the 'remonstrance' was duly despatched to Pretoria. Kruger promptly offered to consult with Robinson before reclosing the drifts on November 15. But, seeing that Chamberlain and Rhodes were not to be bought off by minor concessions and under strong pressure from the Free Staters, who were being hit almost as hard as the Cape by the stoppage of traffic via Bloemfontein, he climbed down and agreed to let the drifts stay open and to leave it to the inter-state conference to find a solution of the problem of railway tariffs.

In his message informing the High Commissioner of this decision, Leyds insisted that responsibility for the whole affair lay with the 'unfriendly acts' of the Cape Government and denied that the closing of the drifts had in any way been an act of hostility on the part of the South African Republic. But, if he hoped thereby to regain some of the sympathy of the Cape Dutch which the Transvaal had lost during the recent crisis, he was to be disappointed. In fact, no action by Kruger's Republic had done more to unite Dutch and English opinion at the Cape in criticism of the Transvaal Boers. Previously the Cape Dutch, together with certain Liberal Englishmen, had had much sympathy for Kruger's desire to forge his own rail link with Lourenço Marques, especially after the British Government had first promised and then robbed him of access to Kosi Bay. But now it was felt that he had gone altogether too far in his railway war against the Colony.

At the time when he had been forced to admit the Cape line to the Rand because the Delagoa Bay Railway was nowhere near completion, Kruger was so determined to cut down traffic from the Cape, and to keep Natal out of a rail and customs union with her sister colony, that he had agreed to admit a line from Durban to Johannesburg to be built jointly by the Natal Government and the Netherlands Railway Company. With the completion of this line more or less simultaneously with the Delagoa Bay Railway, the Cape very soon suffered serious losses. For the Cape ports were some 660 miles from Johannesburg, while the distance from Durban was 480, and from Lourenço Marques only 400 miles, which sizeable differences were to reduce the Cape railways' share in the Rand traffic from 85 per cent to 28 per cent in the space of only three years. And it was enough that the Cape should have to suffer from such accidents of geography without Kruger piling on further artificial discriminations.

Thus, the closure of the Vaal drifts had aroused the deepest indignation among all shades of opinion in the Colony. And with the Cape Dutch in militant mood, any residual qualms which Chamberlain might have felt about Rhodes' conspiracy against the Transvaal were removed. All that the Colonial Secretary now asked of the chief conspirator was that he 'allow a decent interval' to elapse before the 'fireworks'.

16 The Jameson Raid

ONE of the more extraordinary factors in the failure of the Jameson Raid was the complete miscalculation by the conspirators of the Uitlanders' attitude. Normally the shrewdest judge of people and of risks, Rhodes allowed himself to be fatally misled by the grumblings of the British on the Rand into believing that, with the aid of a few rifles and a small invasion force of Company men, they would rise and overthrow Kruger's Republic to gain their political rights.

Nothing could have been further from the truth. In fact, a large proportion of the Uitlanders were far too prosperous to be willing to bestir themselves to attempt a revolution. Certainly they had their grievances; but lack of political rights came nowhere near the top of the list. What annoyed them far more was having to pay taxes on their profits, while such official abuses as the dynamite monopoly granted to Lippert operated against them by raising their working costs. They complained too about railway rates and customs tariffs levied on their imports and about the lack of English education in the schools. The mining companies grumbled that the Transvaal Government were over-lenient in dealing with Bantu miners who absconded from their jobs, and they protested angrily when the Government took from them, and gave to selected burghers, the areas which had been marked out for water storage and residue deposits. But only a small proportion of Uitlanders—some said no more than a few thousand—were sufficiently interested in the vote to agitate for it. Even this small minority were very far from revolutionary material; and the Transvaal National Union which represented them was pledged to seek reforms by constitutional methods, not by violence.

Besides, many Uitlanders were not prepared to give up their nationality to become citizens. Less than half of their number could be considered permanent settlers, the majority being birds of passage anxious to make as much money as possible to spend elsewhere. And for all their grumbles and despite periodical recessions, there was plenty of money to be made on the Rand. Taxation, though it might be levied without representation, compared favourably with other countries. George Albu, a leading 'Randlord', admitted after the Jameson Raid that the mining laws of the Transvaal left with the industry a higher percentage of the profits than those of any other nation. The Uitlanders might pay ninety per cent of all the taxes, but at two shillings in the pound the taxation of the gold seekers on the Rand was minimal by comparison with Rhodesia, where the B.S.A. Company took half of all the profits from mining. Thus, while some of the more irresponsible—and less successful— Uitlanders might have threatened revolution to impress Loch and Rhodes with their earnestness, most of them were by and large doing far too well to risk a collision with the Boer authorities. As Flora Shaw put it in an article for *The Times,* summing up the situation on the Rand, 'Johannesburg at present has no politics. It is too busy with material problems, luxury without order; sensual enjoyment without art, riches without refinement; display without dignity.'

But the fact that the Rand had 'no politics' did not mean that there was little that needed to be remedied in Kruger's Republic. On the contrary, from the filth of Johannesburg's streets which Merriman described as 'ankle-deep in mud' and smelling of the 'pulverised cow-dung that forms Jo-burg's macadam' to the absence of any Treasury control of Government expenditure, which was undertaken at the whim of the President and his Executive Council without either consulting the Volksraad or rendering proper departmental accounts, the Transvaal was still a backward country in all but its new-found wealth. What was more, Kruger and his Volksraad of Boer ranchers and farmers wanted to keep it that way. In the words of Hofmeyr's son, 'It was Kruger who kept alive the inspiration of the past.' But progress, in the shape of the gold discoveries on the Rand, was catching up with the Boers. However much they might try to ignore it out of fear and suspicion of those who had brought it about, the fact remained that in the last ten years the revenue of the Republic had risen from under £200,000 to nearly £4,000,000. And it was the Boers' tragedy that, instead of accommodating themselves to the fact of progress, they sought to resist it until it was too late, in the defiant belief, as Kruger later told the High Commissioner, that they might as well give up the Republic as grant the vote to the 'newcomers' before a long period of residential qualification.

According to a census taken at this period the population of the Rand was a little over 100,000 of whom almost exactly one half were whites, the other half being mostly Bantus with a few thousand Indians and Malays. Of the 50,000 white people nearly 90 per cent were Uitlanders, of whom rather more than two-thirds were British, hailing either direct from England or from Cape Colony, Natal and Australia. The rest were a mixture of Germans, French, Americans and Dutch, together with a small group of Russian Jews. Thus, although in the Transvaal as a whole the Boers totalled some two-thirds of the population, on the Rand they were overwhelmingly outnumbered. And Kruger seriously believed that the only way to keep this large foreign element at bay was to deny them any effective political participation. Not only did he hate Johannesburg and all the material and ungodly values that it stood for; he also could not forget the experience of the early eighties when the first gold-seekers had come up from Natal and threatened to throw out the Boers and hoist the British flag. And he was stubbornly resolved to prevent the Uitlanders on the Rand gaining a position from which they could do what their forebears had threatened.

In 1888, during one of his very rare visits to Johannesburg, the President had been asked by an Uitlanders' deputation to grant to the city the status of a municipality. But, suspecting that an

elected council of 'newcomers' would turn out to be the thin end
of a wedge, he turned down the request. Instead, he suggested
that a Second Chamber of the Volksraad be established for
which any Uitlander would have a right to vote after two years'
residence and which would decide on such matters of interest to
the Rand as the gold mining laws. Two years later the Second
Volksraad was set up.

But this concession was little more than a mockery. For one
thing, all the decisions of the Second Chamber had to be
ratified by the original Volksraad. For another, the residential
qualification for full burgher status, and hence the right to elect
the President and the First Volksraad, was increased from five
years to fourteen and the voting age raised to forty. So far as
political rights were concerned, the Uitlanders had less than
ever. Prior to 1882, the qualification for the vote had been one
year's residence. Then it had been raised to five, as the Uitlander population began to show an increase. Now at fourteen
years, the franchise had been virtually restricted to those who
had been born in the Republic; and those who had come in
with the gold-rush would have to wait until the end of the
century to get full voting rights.

Realising that they had been tricked and that Kruger had
taken away more than he had given them, a group of Uitlanders
began to organise themselves to press for the proper redress of
their grievances. In 1892, the Transvaal National Union was
founded by Charles Leonard, a young Johannesburg lawyer,
and Lionel Phillips, the President of the Chamber of Mines and
a director of Wernher-Beit. And to this new pressure group a
number of Uitlanders were drawn who, although more interested in reducing taxes than in expanding the franchise, had
been aroused by the duplicity of the President's pretended
reform. Another factor which helped indirectly to expand the
membership of the National Union was the discovery in 1893
of new mining techniques, such as the use of cyanide for extract-
ing ore. These developments clearly showed that the industry
could expect a far longer life than had at first been thought
likely. As a result, a number of those engaged in mining realised
that they would probably be spending a lot more of their lives

in the Transvaal than they had originally expected and, although hitherto they had played no part in politics, they too began to lend their support to the National Union.

These developments led even Kruger to seek some means whereby, as he put it, he might 'meet the wishes of the new population for representation without injuring the Republic or prejudicing the interests of the older burghers'. In 1894, therefore, he went once again to Johannesburg to see for himself what reforms could be introduced with safety. But his visit could hardly have been more of a disaster. The Rand was currently undergoing another of its periodical slumps and, with the temporary collapse of the share-market, tempers had become frayed. Certain irresponsible hotheads among the Uitlanders decided to make the President's visit the occasion for a public demonstration; and as an angry crowd surrounded the house where Kruger was staying, the Vierkleur was torn down from its flag-pole and trampled underfoot. Months of patient petitioning by Leonard and Phillips and their followers were now suddenly set at nought. Kruger's quick temper got the better of him and, infuriated by the insult to his flag, he shouted at the Uitlanders' leaders, 'Tell your people I shall never give them anything. I shall never change my policy.'

These words were all that Rhodes needed to prove his case that further pleading with the Pretoria Government was useless. When they were followed shortly afterwards by Kruger's apparent attempt to solicit German support at the Kaiser's birthday banquet, he was able to point out to Phillips that constitutional methods and arguments had produced no result. The time had come, he said, to take direct action to win independence for the Rand before it was taken over by Germany. And although Phillips believed that few people 'cared a fig for the franchise', he personally had become sufficiently disenchanted with the possibilities of achieving anything by legitimate pressures that he required little persuasion to fall in with Rhodes' conclusions.

From then on the conspiracy forged ahead. The financial resources of Consolidated Goldfields and Wernher-Beit were put at the National Union's disposal and rifles and ammunition were

317

smuggled into Johannesburg packed in oil-drums or in the bottom of coal-trucks. Rhodes' brother, Frank, a Colonel in the British Army, was despatched to the Rand to act as director and coordinator of the operation, under the incongruous cover for a serving soldier of 'Manager of the Consolidated Goldfields Company'. The promotion of the revolution was entrusted to a small executive group of the National Union, while Rhodes made haste with his plans for an invasion by Company forces in support of the projected Uitlander rising. When difficulties arose with the local tribe about stationing these forces at Gaberones, Rhodes secured from a friendly Bechuana chief an even better concentration area at Pitsani, only three miles from the Transvaal border. By the authority of the High Commissioner, acting on instructions from Chamberlain, this strip of territory was formally transferred to the Company. Jameson, who had been appointed to lead the invasion, was appointed Resident Commissioner in the area. And at the end of October 1895, some 250 B.S.A. Company police were despatched from Rhodesia to Pitsani.

Meanwhile Rhodes had been busily exploiting the drifts crisis. To Chamberlain he pointed out that the whole episode showed how impossible Kruger was to deal with diplomatically. To his own Cabinet he maintained that, if the Imperial Government and the Cape kept up the pressure, Kruger would climb down and they need have no qualms about guaranteeing to share the cost of a British expedition, as Chamberlain had demanded of them, since the issue would not be pressed that far. He also decided that the High Commissioner must be brought into the plot, since Robinson was going to have to play the arbiter in Johannesburg after Jameson and the revolutionaries between them had overthrown Kruger's Republic.

Rhodes had originally wished to play this role himself, with the support of Hofmeyr and the Afrikaner Bond, his idea being to win over the Boers by claiming to have saved them from British colonial rule, while telling the Uitlanders that he had saved them from the Boers. Had Loch still been at the Cape he would certainly have stuck to this plan, knowing that the High Commissioner would have refused to act as his stalking-horse.

But in the confident belief that he could rely on Robinson not to prejudice the B.S.A. Company's interests, he felt that if it would facilitate cooperation with Chamberlain he should assign the arbitration role to the High Commissioner. No doubt, too, he felt that an imperial officer would be equipped with more authority to ensure that his hated rival from Kimberley days, J. B. Robinson, did not seize power and declare an Uitlander Republic. For, as he himself said, he was 'not going to risk my position to change President Kruger for President J. B. Robinson'.

In the month of October, Rhodes therefore confided his plans to Bower, the Imperial Secretary at the Cape, although carefully omitting to mention that he was arming the would-be revolutionaries. As Bower recorded in a 'death-bed confession', he was told that 'the capitalists [i.e. Rhodes' and Beit's companies plus other British interests on the Rand] had joined the reformers, there would be a rising and he wanted to move Jameson down for "if there is a rising, I will act if you don't" '. After a brief discussion, in which it was agreed that the High Commissioner must be told what was afoot, Bower imparted the scheme to Robinson. But even more than Chamberlain in his first interview with Harris, Robinson did not want to know officially what his Premier was planning. He knew that it would be futile to oppose something to which Rhodes and Chamberlain had set their hands, besides which he was now over seventy years old and a very sick man, suffering from dropsy and a weak heart. But he had never been an enthusiast for forceful measures and had in fact only recently suggested that Kruger be bought off with the offer of a G.C.M.G! Being made a party to Rhodes' schemes, therefore, much as he admired the man, was highly embarrassing to him. Not only did he insist upon the fact of his knowledge being kept completely secret, but when Bower later tried to discuss the matter with him, Robinson refused to talk about what he termed these 'damned conspiracies of Rhodes and Chamberlain'. Also, when Newton, the Resident Commissioner in Bechuanaland, shortly afterwards came to report his anxieties at the bellicose talk which he had heard from Jameson's officers at Pitsani, Robinson refused to see him.

All that he would do was to submit to Chamberlain the draft of a plan, prepared by Bower and Rhodes, for the issue of a proclamation in the event of a rising on the Rand ordering all parties, British and Boer alike, to lay down their arms, after which he as High Commissioner, if possible accompanied by the President of the Orange Free State and Jan Hofmeyr, would hasten to Johannesburg to arbitrate a settlement. Apart from this, Robinson steadfastly refused to discuss the 'damned conspiracy' with anyone and adopted an attitude of strict nonintervention.

Nevertheless Rhodes had got what he wanted—active support from Chamberlain and acquiescence from the High Commissioner. But no sooner had these arrangements been set in motion than he was to receive the first serious warning that all was not as it should be among the Uitlanders. This came towards the end of October in the form of a letter from his brother, Frank, in Johannesburg which said that, with the passing of the previous year's recession and the gold industry booming once again, immigrants were pouring into the Transvaal at the unprecedented rate of 250 a day and that 'so long as people are making money individually in Johannesburg, they will endure a great many political wrongs'. Only another mining slump with serious unemployment would put their backs up enough to risk an explosion.

A more cautious man than Rhodes would no doubt have concluded from such information that the majority of the Uitlanders, far from being ready to take the law into their own hands and fight for a change of flag, wanted at the most to bring about a reformed Boer administration. If they talked of violence, it was only as a bluff which they hoped might influence Kruger to take them and their grievances more seriously; and the only people who were really spoiling for a fight were those irresponsible elements, who had failed to make money and had nothing to lose by starting a rising.

But to Rhodes caution meant delay, and delay, which was always anathema to him, would now be more dangerous than haste. After all, he reckoned, there were nearly 50,000 Uitlanders in the Transvaal, not all of whom could have waxed so fat on the

Sir Hercules Robinson

The Jameson Raid

pickings of the Rand that they would prefer to endure the discriminations of Boer rule to striking a blow for their independence. Moreover, unlike the Boers who were spread about the country in their farms, most of them were concentrated in one area. And however experienced Kruger's men might be in calling their commandos together to fight native wars, with effective preparations by the Company and the Johannesburg Reformers, Jameson and the revolutionaries between them should be able to overwhelm the Boers in a lightning strike and to seize the Rand and Pretoria before the commandos could get started. Had not Jameson, after a visit to Johannesburg to coordinate plans with the National Union, said that 'anyone could take the Transvaal with half a dozen revolvers'? Had he not also proved against the Matabeles, whose impis far outnumbered what the Transvaalers could put in the field, how effectively a mobile force with modern equipment could deal with an enemy vastly superior in numbers? With the revolutionaries striking on the Rand and Jameson stabbing in from the western frontier, the Boers would not know which way to turn and would be hopelessly caught between two fires.

Buoyed up by these euphoric calculations, Rhodes decided to renew his application to the Imperial Government for the transfer of the entire Bechuanaland Protectorate to his Company. Though he had accepted the railway strip as being better than nothing and as a necessary concession to secure Chamberlain's cooperation, he had been furious with the Colonial Secretary for bowing to Khama's pleas and refusing him the rest of the territory. He told Harris that it was 'utterly humiliating to be beaten by these niggers' and protested to the Duke of Fife, as one of his London directors, that so vast an area had been handed over to the Bechuana tribes, 'the laziest rascals in the world'. Now he cabled to Lord Grey asking him to tell Chamberlain that Pitsani and the railway strip gave him too little room to manouevre. And he instructed Harris to follow up with a request to Edward Fairfield, the Colonial Office Under-Secretary in charge of South African affairs, for the immediate transfer to the Company of the whole Protectorate, less an area to be marked out as a Native Reserve. Harris was also to ask that the Bechuanaland Border Police in the concentration area should now be placed under Jameson's command and authorised to take part in the Raid.

Chamberlain was not to be moved on the question of transferring any more territory to the B.S.A. Company: the railway strip would have to suffice for their needs. But he did agree to Jameson taking over the Bechuanaland Police, provided Rhodes assured him that he was working for the British flag. This assurance was only too readily forthcoming. Since he considered himself to be the very embodiment of all that England stood for and to Loch's frequent indignation had claimed, whenever it suited his purpose, to be acting in the name of the Queen herself, Rhodes saw no distinction between the Company and the Union Jack; and he unhesitatingly replied to the Colonial Secretary's cable that, 'I would not risk everything as I am doing, except for the British flag.' (Needless to say, when the Reform Committee informed him that most of the Uitlanders wanted a new government under the Vierkleur and not the Union Jack, Rhodes was equally ready with the assurance that he would not force the British flag upon them.) And so, on November 7, the day when coincidentally Kruger began to climb down about the Vaal drifts, the arrangements were completed for the transfer of the railway strip and the police to Jameson's control and, on November 16, the High Commissioner proclaimed that the B.S.A. Company had taken over virtually the whole frontier between the Protectorate and the Transvaal.

Chamberlain was later to explain his agreement to all this before the Committee of Enquiry by saying that he had been simply trying to help the Company to construct the railway and protect its building operations against native marauders! But in a private message which he sent to Robinson at the time, he told the High Commissioner that he assumed that no 'movement' would take place 'unless success is certain: a fiasco would be disastrous'.

Just how wrong Chamberlain was in his assumption and how right he was in his warning against any premature move was to be shown a few weeks later, when Jameson jumped the gun on the Reformers and advanced to doom and disaster. Indeed it is not unfair to say that the dishonesty of the Jameson Raid was only excelled by the inefficiency with which it was planned and carried out. Whether at Johannesburg or at Pitsani, it was the same story of complacency, indiscretion and inadequate organisation to a degree that resembled more a children's game of cops and robbers than a conspiracy hatched and executed by grown men.

The original plan had been for Harris to smuggle 5,000 rifles and a million rounds of ammunition into Johannesburg, where it was believed there were already some 1,000 rifles privately owned by various Uitlanders. Jameson was to invade with a force of 1,500 men and to bring with him a further supply of 1,500 rifles. These supplies, together with the smuggled arms, would equip a total force of 9,000 men; and they would be further augmented by the seizure of the Pretoria arsenal, which was supposed to contain 10,000 rifles and twelve million rounds of ammunition and which, so the plotters believed, could be easily captured from its few guards in a surprise attack by no more than fifty men. In the event, Harris managed to get no more than 3,000 rifles to Johannesburg and less than half of this consignment was even unpacked by the 'revolutionaries'. Jameson's invaders numbered only five hundred men, because most of the Bechuanaland Police who should have formed the bulk of his force, refused to take part in an action which they considered to conflict with their allegiance to the Crown. The spare horses, forage and rations which Jameson expected never reached him, because the man who was to organise them went on holiday; and since nobody, except the Boers, knew which route the invaders had taken, they could not be sent after them.

As for the preparations in Johannesburg, there could not have been less secrecy or more complacency about them. Uitlanders drilled openly in the streets and every public bar and club hummed with chatter about the arms that were being smuggled in readiness for the rising. Jameson came and went openly between Pitsani, the Cape and Johannesburg; Phillips and Leonard visited Rhodes in Cape Town with no attempt to cover their tracks; and messages were exchanged between the

Cape and the Rand either in the Company's code, the key of which was available at every telegraph office in South Africa, or in *en clair* telegrams, in which the rising was referred to as the 'polo tournament' or the 'flotation', while Jameson was the 'contractor' and the Reformers the 'subscribers', which pseudonyms served more to confuse the plotters than they did to deceive the Transvaal authorities. As for Jameson's base at Pitsani, there was no attempt to keep the forthcoming raid a secret. The cover story was that the force was being readied to deal with a native chief who had objected to the railway passing through his territory, but Jameson's officers and men boasted openly that they would shortly give the Boers as sound a thrashing as they had given the Matabeles.

The date originally set for the 'flotation' turned out to be the day of the Christmas Races and also of the Dutch 'nagmaal' celebrations when large numbers of Transvaal burghers were likely to be visiting Pretoria. And since to the British residents of the Rand racing was more important than revolutions, and even Jameson agreed that it might be better not to attack Pretoria when the place was crowded with Boers, the date was duly postponed. Still more absurd was a story told about Frank Rhodes by Frederic Hamilton, then editor of the Johannesburg *Star*. According to Hamilton, when Jameson visited Johannesburg in November, he called by appointment on Frank Rhodes to discuss plans and to find out how far his fellow conspirators had succeeded in recruiting support for the rising. But on reaching the house, he was met with a message from his 'coordinator', who fancied himself as a great charmer of women, regretting that he could not keep his appointment, as he had to teach a lady-friend how to ride a bicycle!

Yet, in spite of all these set-backs and of the mounting evidence that the Uitlanders were really only playing at rebellion, Jameson plunged ahead with his plans, fortified by the belief that he was destined to be another Clive of India and convinced that, with his Maxim guns, he would 'draw a zone of lead' a mile wide on each side of his column in which 'no Boer will be able to live'. In the third week of November, he arranged with the Reformers in Johannesburg to give him an undated letter in which, speaking as leaders of the British community on the Rand, they asked him to come to the aid of 'thousands of unarmed men, women and children of our race' whose lives were being put in danger by the conflict with the Boer authori- ties. This letter was to be Jameson's invitation to invade the Transvaal. The date was to be filled in directly he received word that the rising had started. And so far as the Reformers were concerned, it was clearly understood that he would not move or publish the letter until they summoned him. But Jameson saw things differently and, as he afterwards claimed, he considered that the letter gave him his 'authority' to march on the Rand whenever he judged the opportunity to be ripe.

By the end of November, however, some of the Uitlanders' doubts and second thoughts were beginning to have their effect on Rhodes who was growing increasingly anxious that all his schemes might only result in the establishment of a Transvaal Republic under J. B. Robinson. Leonard and Phillips had recently visited Cape Town, where they had strongly urged the importance of playing down the British flag and had made it clear that the Uitlanders wanted to rule themselves and had no wish to become a Colony of Britain or of the B.S.A. Company. Having abandoned the idea of appointing himself the arbitrator of a settlement in order to facilitate collusion with Chamberlain, it was therefore more than ever essential to Rhodes that the High Commissioner should be ready to intervene directly the Reformers and Jameson pulled off their coup. But, although Robinson's special train was being kept in constant readiness to convey him at a moment's notice to Johannesburg, Chamberlain had still not given his formal sanction for the High Commissioner to arbitrate between the Reformers and the Transvaal Govern- ment.

One reason for this delay was the Colonial Secretary's current preoccupation with a frontier dispute between Venezuela and British Guiana in which President Cleveland of the United States had intervened with the appointment of a Boundary Commission and an ominous warning to Britain that the United States Government would enforce the Commission's findings 'by every means in its power'. The last thing that Chamberlain wanted was that the Jameson Raid and the row which it would inevitably cause in South Africa should coincide with a serious quarrel, and possibly even hostilities, with America. As he saw it, if Britain should become involved in war with the United States before or during the coming conflict on the Rand, Kruger might feel the more encouraged to hold out against the raiders and their Rand accomplices in the hope of persuading Germany, or some other foreign power, to intervene on his behalf. Yet, as Chamberlain also realised, if the whole scheme were postponed for a year, while the Venezuelan issue was being resolved, it might be altogether impossible to revive it. For word had recently reached Whitehall that the revolutionary spirit on the Rand was wavering as the moment of truth approached. Moreover, if the conspirators were making so little effort to keep their conspiracy secret, delay could only heighten the risk of one of the European powers finding out what was going on. And if this were to happen, it would be impossible for the Imperial Government to give Rhodes the support which had been promised.

It was a tricky set of alternatives. But, on balance and after prolonged meditation, Chamberlain decided that to hasten the Raid would involve fewer risks than to postpone it and that the sooner the operation was mounted, the better would be the chances of Rhodes keeping the Reformers up to the mark. Early in December, therefore, he cabled his approval of Robinson's arbitration plan and, through the Company's London Board, he sent a message telling Rhodes to make haste, since the Venezuelan crisis was moving so fast that, if the Rand rebellion did not come at once, it might have to be postponed for a year or more.

Rhodes received this news with some relief. For, at this point, he was being bombarded by a constant flow of messages from Johannesburg clearly indicating that any enthusiasm for the revolution that might once have existed among the Uitlanders was waning fast. He had just received a telegram from his brother saying that the 'polo tournament' had been put off to the New Year to give time for the Christmas race meeting. Also his own double-talk about the flag was catching up on him, as those Uitlanders to whom he had promised that he was fighting for their independence under the Vierkleur discovered that he had also pledged himself to the Union Jack. A number of Americans promptly refused to join in a rising designed to put them under the rule of their old imperial masters, with whom their country was now once again in dispute over a colonial issue. And Rhodes was told that, whereas it was hoped that even some Boers might support a rising in favour of political reforms, none would lift a finger for the British flag. Added to all this, there was talk that the Transvaal Government were planning to start a counter-rebellion among the mine-workers against the mining companies.

All these adverse developments caused Bower in Cape Town to take so serious a view of the situation that he sought permission to go to London, in order to warn the Colonial Office that, on the Rand, the picture was not as Rhodes had painted it in his sanguine reports to the London Board. In the event, Bower did not go to London, but he did go to Rhodes. So did Newton, after the High Commissioner had refused to hear him out. So too did yet another emissary from Johannesburg, bearing a message which made it clearer than ever that the Uitlanders would not fight for the Union Jack. Bower urged that, in the altered circumstances, the whole operation should be called off and that Jameson be sent back to Salisbury. But Rhodes met all these warnings and objections with the bland assurance that Jameson would 'sit still for years, if necessary', or at least until he received word that the rising had started. He would 'wire him to keep quiet': but he could not send him away, as he had to be ready and available to march on the Rand whenever the revolution took place: otherwise the 'Robinsons, Barnatos and Lipperts would spring an Uitlander republic' on him. Rhodes insisted that he must himself remain in a position to control any rising. Besides, Chamberlain was telling him to hurry things along and he would be disloyal to his 'chief' if he disobeyed these instructions.

In fact, far from telling Jameson to 'keep quiet', Rhodes ignored his brother's message that the 'polo tournament' had been postponed and, spurred by Chamberlain's injunction to make haste, he telegraphed to Pitsani on December 23 that the rising would take place as planned five days later. And it was not until after an Uitlander deputation had hastened to Cape Town to convey the Reformers' definitive decision to 'absolutely condemn further developments at present' and to put off the rising at least until January 4 that Harris instructed Jameson not to move 'until you hear from us again'.

Chamberlain was duly informed of the postponement and on the very next day, December 28, he received an ominous note from Berlin telling him that the German Government would not be prepared to accept any change in the status quo in the Transvaal such as Rhodes might seek to enforce, and that they reserved the right to support Kruger against any such pressures. Several months before this, the German Foreign Office had made very clear to the British Ambassador that they were sternly opposed to any South African federation, political or commercial, embracing Cape Colony, Natal and the Boer Republics. Their latest warning was therefore the plainest evidence that they suspected Rhodes of trying to use the Uitlander agitation to force some kind of British union upon the Transvaal.

Realising that the conspiracy was no longer even an open secret, the Colonial Secretary now decided to cover his own tracks with a message to the High Commissioner, of which an edited version was subsequently published in the Blue Book. Feigning total innocence of any collusion with Rhodes' plans, the message began by saying, 'It has been suggested that an endeavour may be made to force matters at Johannesburg by someone in the service of the [B.S.A.] Company advancing from the Bechuanaland Protectorate'. And it went on to say that, if that someone should in fact advance, Chamberlain would have to take action under the terms of the Company's Charter. Robinson was to remind Rhodes of the relevant clauses of the Charter and to warn him that the Imperial Government would not support him in the alleged conspiracy.

Although infuriated by Chamberlain's change of front, Rhodes decided to temporise. He told Bower to inform the Colonial Office that the revolution had collapsed over the issue of the flag and even managed to convince the Imperial Secretary that he was much relieved. But, instead of personally telegraphing to Jameson to stay put, he instructed Harris to tell him that Goold-Adams would shortly arrive in Mafeking to discuss plans as an emissary of the High Commissioner and that, 'after seeing him, you and we must judge regarding flotation'. Meanwhile, the Reformers had contacted two of Jameson's liaison officers in Johannesburg and sent them hot-foot to Pitsani to tell Jameson, on behalf of the organisers of the revolution, not to move until further notice. But, as Rhodes clearly knew, this was not likely to stop his lieutenant, a gambler alike in public and in private life, who bluntly replied to Harris that, unless he heard definitely to the contrary, he would move 'tomorrow evening', December 29. He had received altogether too many reports that the Boers were arming the mine-workers to rebel against their employers, that Uitlander women and children were fleeing the country in panic and that Boer commandos were being called up to block his route to the Rand. He could, therefore, delay this advance no longer.

Jameson was not only becoming hopelessly confused by all the order, counter-order and disorder emanating from Johannesburg and Cape Town; he was also afraid that any substantial delay would make it impossible to hold his force together, many of whom were becoming decidedly restless. But of still more decisive importance was the fact that by the evening of December 29 he had had no reply to his telegram proclaiming his intention to advance within the next twenty-four hours. Harris having failed to arrange for the Company's Cape Town office to be manned over that fateful weekend, Rhodes did not receive the message until it was too late to do anything about it. Thus, when the liaison officers arrived from Johannesburg, Jameson turned a deaf ear to the Reformers' decision. Asserting that Clive would not have hesitated in such a situation, he told them that he was 'going in'. And late on that same evening, he 'published' his letter of invitation and began his march upon the Transvaal.

Almost simultaneously, Rhodes received the telegram from Pitsani which told him that it was now too late to prevent the raiders from starting their advance. In a state of great agitation and torn between fear for his own future and hope that Jameson might still somehow pull off his coup, he sent for Bower and confided to him the news. Protesting that he was ruined and would have to resign as Cape Premier, he agreed to telegraph to Jameson telling him not to move, though he feared it was already too late to stop him. But the telegram never got through because Jameson's men had cut the wires between Mafeking and the Cape. For the same reason, a telegram from Robinson sent early the following morning telling Newton to stop Jameson failed to reach him. And had the High Commissioner not also instructed de Wet in Pretoria to send a messenger with identical orders to the raiders, there would have been no means whatever of communicating with Jameson, until the Mafeking telegraph could be repaired.

On the following day, after twenty-four hours of anxious reflection, Rhodes decided to try to bluff it out and, as he told his Cabinet colleague, W. P. Schreiner, he refused to give any further orders to Jameson to withdraw. He then cabled his London Directors to say that the raiders had gone into the Transvaal in response to a cry for help from the Uitlanders. 'Johannesburg', he added, 'is united and strong on our side!' And disgusted with what he considered the weakness of the Colonial Secretary—'you cannot expect much of a product of the Birmingham workshop'—he demanded that Chamberlain be told that he would come through all right if the Government supported him and sent no more telegrams repudiating the Company. 'I will win', he concluded, and 'South Africa will belong to England.'

But Chamberlain, more than ever determined to escape from his involvement, responded with a cable to Robinson saying that Rhodes had 'miscalculated the fishing at Johannesburg' and should be told of the serious consequences of 'invading the Transvaal to force a rising'. Robinson duly translated this message to his Premier as a warning that the Company's Charter might have to be revoked as the penalty for their 'filibustering' activities. At the same time, on the insistence of the inevitably outraged Hofmeyr, he issued a proclamation, calling upon Jameson to withdraw and ordering all British residents in the Transvaal to abstain from giving the raiders 'any countenance or assistance'. To strengthen the Imperial Government's alibi still further, de Wet was told to inform Kruger of what he knew of Jameson's movements and to make it clear that the raiders had been ordered to return at once whence they came.

But the Transvaal Boers did not need to be told by the British Agent of Jameson's situation. With so little secrecy surrounding the conspiracy, they had known for many weeks of what was being planned both on the Rand and from outside. When urged by some of his burghers to nip the conspiracy in the bud, Kruger had replied enigmatically that the tortoise must be allowed to stick its head out before he could cut it off. The President had for long suspected that the Uitlanders would shortly be used by Rhodes to overthrow the Republic. His intelligence service had planted spies in the National Union who kept him well informed of what was afoot and, when in November the 'capitalists', including the mine-owners, joined the National Union, he became certain that trouble was not far ahead. Internal security was thereupon strengthened, commandos were quietly warned to be in a state of readiness, and Leyds was despatched abroad to buy arms. As for Jameson's plans, the Boer intelligence service knew exactly the strength of his force and the route he would take as soon as he crossed the frontier; and since the troopers, who were detailed to cut the telegraph line to Pretoria, got drunk and cut a lot of fencing wire instead, Jameson's advance was immediately reported to Kruger's headquarters. Once alerted, the Boers were ready for him. The commandos were called out and the 'tortoise' was kept under constant observation as it slowly poked its head out in the direction of the Rand.

Twenty-four hours after Jameson had started, he was met by a message from General Joubert, the Commandant-General of the Republic, ordering him to withdraw. But Jameson retorted that he had come at the invitation of the Uitlanders on the Rand to assist them in attaining the rights of citizenship in a civilised state. Then, on the next day, December 31, the telegraph having been restored between Mafeking and Cape Town, a messenger from Newton caught up with him and, on the High Commissioner's authority, repeated the order to withdraw immediately. But Robinson's name had no more effect than Joubert's. Jameson rode on towards Johannesburg, convinced that his advance would encourage the faint-hearts on the Rand and so trigger off the revolution, without which his tiny force had no hope whatever of surviving his desperate gamble, except as prisoners of war.

Rhodes, too, was now pinning his hopes on the raiders' premature action forcing the Uitlanders to take up arms. Desperately he tried to delay the issue of the High Commissioner's proclamation, objecting that it made Jameson an outlaw. But Hofmeyr insisted that Robinson should repudiate the raiders and that Rhodes, if he wished to clear himself of complicity, must also denounce Jameson and dismiss him from his post as Administrator in Salisbury. This Rhodes refused to do and, after the High Commissioner had been forced to issue the proclamation, if only to establish the Imperial Government's alibi, he cabled to the London *Times* the text of the Reformers' letter of invitation, which Harris had 'dated' December 28, the day before Jameson began his advance. He also asked his London Directors to persuade Chamberlain to send Robinson immediately to Johannesburg, where he might 'still turn the position to England's advantage'. And in the hope that Jameson and the Reformers might yet turn the position to his advantage, Rhodes contrived to delay his resignation as Cape Premier by persuading Robinson that he already had enough problems to handle without adding a Cabinet crisis to them.

In fact, the initial reactions of the Reformers in Johannesburg to Jameson's recklessness gave scant encouragement to Rhodes' desperate hopes. The leaders of the National Union had been as angry as they were afraid, when they heard on December 30 that the raiders had crossed the frontier on the previous evening, in defiance of their own clearly announced decision to put off the rising until the New Year. In the certain belief that Jameson would stay his hand when he learned of their decision, they had actually decided to make another attempt to negotiate a settlement with Kruger. On December 26, they had published a manifesto listing their grievances and calling for a public meeting to discuss the franchise and, on the very day that the news of the invasion broke, they had sent a deputation to urge Kruger to concede their list of reforms.

Jameson's action in jumping the gun had, therefore, made it appear that their negotiations, far from being conducted in good faith, were part of a conspiracy to disarm the Boers in preparation for the raiders' advance. Besides, there was now a grave risk that the Transvaal authorities would take repressive action against the Uitlanders which they were in no way organised to resist. The 'continental' element, together with such men as Barnato and J. B. Robinson, realised only too well the dangers of such reprisals and refused to have any further dealings with the Reformers. Faced with the censure of their fellows, Leonard and Phillips therefore dissociated themselves from Jameson's action, called on the citizens of Johannesburg to commit no hostile act against the Transvaal Government, and proclaimed their allegiance to the Vierkleur. But apart from deliberately hoisting the Republic's flag upside down, the nearest they came to making any gesture of independence or protest was to set up an emergency directorate entitled the 'Reform Committee', which they announced was intended to preserve law and order on the Rand.

Somewhat to the Reformers' surprise, however, Kruger did not break off negotiations with them. Nor did he even oppose the establishment of the Reform Committee. By the evening of December 31, the Reformers therefore found themselves in apparent control of Johannesburg. Cheered by this success, as by the absence of news from Jameson, which they mistook to mean the raiders were meeting little or no opposition, they recovered their poise sufficiently to resume negotiations with at least the pretence of renewed confidence and determination. 'We come,' said Phillips to the Transvaal delegates who met him in Pretoria, 'with a rifle in one hand and friendship in the other.' Then, after Kruger had agreed to suspend the customs duties on imported foodstuffs and to consider sympathetically the Uitlanders' other grievances, the Reformers began to wonder whether the Boers might not be weakening in face of the double threat posed by Jameson's invasion and by their assumption of power on the Rand. Growing increasingly self-assured as the talks proceeded, they now openly admitted that they had been in league with Jameson and they even proposed that he should be allowed to enter Johannesburg unopposed, on condition that they made sure of his immediate return to British territory. More foolhardy still, they actually gave the Boer negotiators a list of members of the Reform Committee in order to show how representative they were of the citizens of Johannesburg.

In fact, far from weakening, Kruger was very skilfully playing for time. At all costs he was determined not to put himself in the wrong and not to give Britain a pretext to accuse him of breaking the London Convention or of gratuitously causing bloodshed and civil strife. Hence his decision to allow the Reformers to take over control of Johannesburg for the time being. True, he warned Bloemfontein that the situation might lead to war with Britain and obtained from President Steyn an assurance that the Free Staters would, in that event, honour their obligations under their treaty with the Transvaal. But in spite of the temptation to do so, he declined to solicit German, or other foreign, support. For, although he had guessed that, through Chamberlain, the Imperial Government were deeply implicated in the Raid which he termed a 'typically English product of lies, treachery, intrigues and secret instigations against the Government of the Republic', Kruger felt completely confident that the Transvaal, with the support of the Free State, could handle the situation adequately. Besides, once he learned of the High Commissioner's proclamation, he assumed that, with the British Government in full retreat, the National Union would collapse like a pack of cards. And when, in response to the Reform Committee's urgent appeal, Robinson telegraphed to invite himself to Pretoria to help bring about a peaceful settlement, he became more than ever certain that he held the rebels in the palm of his hand.

At their first meeting Kruger had felt it prudent to promise the National Union delegates that he would consider sympathetically such issues as the franchise, railway rates and customs duties. But, now that the High Commissioner had offered to come and settle everything with him, he no longer had to concern himself with the Reformers' demands. He therefore needed no urging to accept Robinson's offer and readily replied to Cape Town that a visit by the High Commissioner would 'assist me to prevent further bloodshed as . . . Doctor Jameson has not given effect to your orders, but has fired on my burghers'. And when the Reform Committee sought to continue negotiations, he now brushed them aside, saying that the Uitlanders must lay down their arms and submit to his authority unconditionally, and refused to discuss, let alone to concede, any of their demands.

Meanwhile, the Boer commandos were waiting to pounce on the slowly advancing raiders. Every attempt by the Transvaal authorities and the High Commissioner's messengers to turn Jameson back had failed. De Wet sent a second emissary to meet him with a copy of Robinson's proclamation. But, ignoring this edict like all the others, Jameson continued his advance; and when another messenger from Pretoria brought orders to withdraw, he had him placed under arrest. But, whether or not he knew it, Jameson's venture was already doomed. After three days and four nights of marching, both horses and riders were in very poor shape; and when they reached Krugersdorp, thirty miles from their objective, the raiders were quickly surrounded. In front were the Boers lying in wait along a strongly defended line of hills, while in their rear were the commandos who had been shadowing their advance from the moment when they crossed the frontier. Jameson's force put up a brief but gallant resistance. But the shells for their field guns soon ran out and, with men and munitions totally exhausted, they surrendered to General Cronje on the morning of January 2, using for a white flag the apron of a Hottentot nursemaid from a nearby farm.

For five more days Rhodes clung to office, using, as Merriman wrote to a friend 'every engine of corruption and intrigue' to keep himself in power. But Hofmeyr determined the issue by insisting that he had no alternative but to resign as Cape Premier. Without the support of Hofmeyr and the Bond, Rhodes had no authority left and could no longer command a majority in the Cape Assembly. On January 7, 1896, therefore, he handed his resignation to the High Commissioner.

So ended the Jameson Raid and with it Rhodes' bid to become master of all South Africa from the Cape to the borders of the Congo and Tanganyika. So ended too an era of five and a half years in which Cape Colony had been ruled, and Britain's name and influence in South Africa all too frequently misused, to satisfy the personal ambitions and to further the financial interests of the man whom Kruger, not without some justification, had called the 'curse of Africa'.

Some time after these events, Jan Hofmeyr's son was to say that, if Rhodes had been prepared to acknowledge his error after the Raid, he might still have been able to recover his authority with the Afrikaner Bond. But it was not to be. Because Rhodes, surrounded by adulating sycophants, so lacked humility that he once told Jameson that his name would be remembered for four thousand years, he could not bring himself to admit that he had been at fault. He could understand well enough the modern use of money as a means to achieve power and of monopoly as a way of holding onto it. But he understood little of men, and still less of the Boers, from whom he was as far removed as is the predatory hawk from the plodding ox. He could never comprehend their slow anger, their long memories, or their Old Testament code of morality. Cynically naming his horses after the men whom he had bought, he thought of the mass of his fellow-beings as so many labour units to be hired and discarded at will and of the Bantu as natives without rights to own or claim land, who were 'bound gradually to come under the control of Europeans'. Like every other dictator, he resented opposition and despised the whole democratic process. And when, in his hour of disgrace, he could not blame everything on Jameson—as he had done with Frank Johnson over his plot to seize Matabeleland—he went about haughtily accusing his critics in the British and Cape Parliaments of 'unctuous rectitude'.

With such insults added to the injuries already dealt to their alliance, Hofmeyr broke completely with his former friend and partner, and never forgave him for his duplicity. In a devastating outburst he told Rhodes, 'We have often disagreed, you and I; but I would no more have thought of distrusting you than a man

and a wife think of distrusting each other in any joint undertaking.' And from then on, Hofmeyr made it his business to press
for a full and proper enquiry into the Raid and for radical
changes to be made in the Charter of the B.S.A. Company whose
activities, he held, had become a grave danger to peace
throughout South Africa.

17 The Whitewashing of Chamberlain

IT would be difficult to exaggerate the evil and divisive effects
of the Jameson Raid in South Africa. In the damage done to
relations between Briton and Boer it far eclipsed any injury
since Slachter's Nek and the repressions of Lord Charles
Somerset. Even the annexation of the Transvaal in the reign of
the egregious Bartle Frere did not match its mischief. For this
act of coercion had at least been comparatively straightforward
in its contrivance. Frere had never made any secret of his
determination to drive the Boers into the British fold. The
reasons officially given for annexation might not have been
adequate grounds for such high-handed action. But there was
nevertheless a body of opinion in the Transvaal which was not
averse to accepting British tutelage at that time; and the whole
performance had been undertaken openly and with little or no
attempt to conceal Britain's real motives.

None of this could be said about the Jameson Raid. On the
contrary, the whole affair had been conducted by treachery and
stealth, a knife-in-the-back conspiracy designed to overthrow
Kruger's Republic on the pretext of fighting for the franchise for
a group of people, most of whom did not want to be Transvaal
citizens anyway. Unlike Frere, Rhodes had long pretended to
be the Afrikaners' best friend and a staunch opponent of interference by the 'Imperial Factor' in the ways of the white
colonist in South Africa. For the past five years his parliamentary
majority had rested on the Bond's complete acceptance of these

338

pretensions. As for Chamberlain, for all his latter-day conversion to imperialism, he had professed his opposition to the annexation of the Transvaal in the seventies and had supported Gladstone's act of retrocession in the 1881 Convention. According to Sir Harry Johnston, only a few years before taking office as Colonial Secretary, he was still claiming to be 'anxious that no injustice be done to the Boers'. Yet now Rhodes was shown to have been scheming and plotting throughout most of his premiership to seize the Transvaal as he had seized Matabeleland, while Chamberlain had emerged as the principal backer of his conspiracy.

Throughout South Africa the Afrikaners now realised how they had been duped by Rhodes' and Chamberlain's previous protestations and, with their awakening, what had been since Slachter's Nek an underlying distrust exploded into an open loathing and disgust for a nation that could produce such perfidious leaders. In the Cape, the unity which had been gradually developing between the two European communities, largely thanks to Hofmeyr's influence, was shattered. The Orange Free State, disregarding its economic ties with the Cape, closed ranks with Kruger's Republic and voted into office as President a Boer nationalist far more uncompromising than Reitz. Burgher opinion in the Transvaal hardened against making any concessions to the Uitlanders. And from the Cape to the Limpopo, Afrikaners and British drew apart into opposing camps, set one against the other by a racial enmity which was to lead inexorably to the carnage and confusion of the Boer War.

Nobody described this calamitous watershed in South Africa's history better than John Merriman. In a memorandum written at the time, he said that the Jameson Raid had 'united all sections of the Dutch-speaking community in determined opposition to what they consider, with some justice, as a treacherous plot aimed at their nationality, and undertaken with the object of stamping out their existence as a separate factor in South Africa'. Nothing could have done more, he said, to effect among that community a revulsion of feeling in favour of the Transvaal Government. Before the Raid, 'there was a very genuine regard among the majority of the Dutch-speaking colonists for C. J.

Rhodes'. While there had always been an undercurrent of suspicion of British policies and politicians, Rhodes' 'personal generosity and undisguised admiration for Boer ways took their fancy. . . . His Native policy which was uniformly harsh and unscrupulous was carefully planned to attract Boer support.' And although all Afrikaners were naturally proud of the growing success and wealth of the Republic beyond the Vaal which had been founded by the sons of the old Dutch settlers, there were many Dutchmen in the Cape, and in the Transvaal as well, who were openly critical of the corruption, immobility and inefficiency of Kruger's Government.

But, as Merriman said, all this had been changed by the Jameson Raid; and the Afrikaners, like the 'dear blind' Hofmeyr, had awakened to the bitter knowledge that, for ten years or more, they had been used to further the aims and plans of a treacherous conspirator, who had the effrontery to demand at the point of the bayonet political reforms for the Uitlanders in the Transvaal, which his own 'autocratic trading company' in Rhodesia denied to 'its own subjects'. As for the Raid's effects on the balance of power and prestige in southern Africa, Merriman concluded that it had 'completely and absolutely rehabilitated President Kruger, who now occupies without dispute the leading position in South Africa. His faults are forgotten in admiration at his success and in the conviction that both in diplomacy and in war he is more than a match for the English. His leaning to German support is condoned . . . . His refusal of political rights and privileges to men who stand convicted of treacherously plotting to destroy the independence of the state, under the specious plea of reform, will certainly meet the approval of his Volksraad. The sense of common danger from similar intrigues . . . will create a solidarity of feeling between the two Republics that for the time makes them the most important European factor in South Africa. . . . There is a renewal throughout South Africa of all the old suspicion and distrust which had been allayed by the gradual withdrawal of the Imperial Government from interference with South African internal affairs, and which may be fanned into active opposition by any well-meant attempt to force reform on the victorious Republic.'

Merriman was, of course, not the only one to see that Kruger was bound to emerge from the recent crisis as the leading figure on the South African scene with the reputation of being 'more than a match for the English'. Chamberlain was also fully aware that Rhodes' conspiracy had boomeranged disastrously. From now onwards, therefore, having decided that South African affairs were far too serious to be left to bungling colonials and Chartered Companies, he took upon himself the direction of a systematic pressure campaign against the Transvaal designed to break Kruger either by a surrender to British paramountcy or by war.

At first behaving as if the Raid had never happened and ignoring the howls of protest from the Transvaal Government and from public demonstrations of the Dutch community in the Cape, Chamberlain instructed the High Commissioner to go to Pretoria and demand redress for the Uitlanders' grievances. When this attempt failed to budge the more than ever stubborn President, he proposed a conference in London to discuss the Uitlander question. Then, after Kruger insisted that the conference agenda should include revision of the 1884 Convention, he abruptly withdrew the invitation and resorted to ever more threatening procedures.

For the time being, however, Chamberlain had to accept a certain measure of restraint. He might itch to retrieve the losses of the Jameson Raid with an immediate ultimatum to reinforce his demands on behalf of the Uitlanders. But the Cabinet had only recently sanctioned General Kitchener's advance into the Sudan which was to secure the entire Nile valley for Britain's sphere of influence in North Africa; and Salisbury maintained that the time had not yet arrived when Britain could risk a second war against the Boers. Besides, under Pushful Joe's aggressive direction, the struggle against France for West Africa, and more especially for supremacy on the Lower Niger, was now approaching its climax. And his colleagues insisted that there must be some limit to the number of fronts on which Britain should be simultaneously engaged. Robinson also minced no words in warning Chamberlain that the Jameson Raid had radically changed the situation in South

Africa and that, if war came, Britain would need at least 30,000 troops at the outset. For Kruger could now count not only on the support of the Free State, but also on the sympathy of the Cape Dutch, who would have no truck with 'any forcible measures undertaken by the Imperial Government to secure the redress of the Uitlanders' grievances'. Even if, in the end, Britain were to win a war fought for these purposes, Robinson maintained that she would find herself having to govern a population 'torn asunder by race hatred and internal dissensions, which would for generations require the maintenance of a large standing garrison'.

Taken all round, the year 1896 marked a frustrating beginning for Chamberlain's forward policy in South Africa. His colleagues were sceptical and Robinson was at this point as unable as he was unwilling to fulfil his wishes. From the outset the High Commissioner's visit to Pretoria was ill-starred. First, Hofmeyr refused to accompany him, although he undertook to urge Kruger by letter to be conciliatory and magnanimous. Then, as Robinson and Bower alighted from their train at Bloemfontein en route to Pretoria, they gave unfortunately contradictory replies to questions from a welcoming delegation of Free Staters as to why the Imperial Government had permitted Jameson's force to assemble on the Transvaal border. Robinson, faithfully echoing the cover story, replied, 'to guard the railway'. But Bower blurted out that they were there 'to watch Johannesburg', which virtual admission of collusion between Jameson and the Reformers by an imperial officer only served to stiffen Kruger's resistance to Chamberlain's demands. Thus, when Robinson rather half-heartedly sought to carry out his instructions, Kruger very quickly cut him short, saying that this was not the time to discuss the Uitlander's grievances. Jameson having surrendered unconditionally, he insisted that what mattered now was to secure the surrender of the arms which Rhodes had smuggled onto the Rand. All other questions were, he insisted, of secondary importance and could only be dealt with when Johannesburg had been disarmed.

In the circumstances, Robinson had no alternative but to apologise for the Raid and to agree to cooperate in preventing further bloodshed. The Reformers were then told that the High Commissioner could not obtain any redress for them at this stage and were advised to comply with the Transvaal Government's demand for their surrender. The only concession which Kruger would grant was that Jameson and his men should be handed over to be dealt with by the British authorities, instead of being put on trial in a republican court, a gesture which provoked angry protests from certain Boer commandants, but which Kruger defended with the wry comment that 'it is not the dog which should be beaten, but the man who set him on to me'. With nothing to be gained by further argument, the Reform Committee therefore accepted Robinson's advice and surrendered unconditionally, whereupon the Transvaal authorities resumed control over Johannesburg. But no sooner had this bloodless victory been achieved than Kruger's police swooped on the Reformers and, helped by the list so conveniently provided by Phillips, arrested every one of their number, including Frank Rhodes, on charges of having committed treason against the South African Republic.

With more than sixty British subjects thus threatened with a possible death sentence, frantic pressures were now imposed on Kruger's Government to bring about their release. Orders for new mining machinery were cancelled by the mining companies and the Transvaal authorities were told that the gold fields would cease to operate if these capital charges were not dropped. Chamberlain, of course, lent his own weighty support to these pressure tactics. Prompted by telegrams from Rhodes suggesting that, despite Jameson's defeat, the Pretoria Government had been badly shaken and Kruger was tottering on his perch, he instructed Robinson to warn the President in the sternest terms against exploiting the Uitlanders and using the Reform Committee as hostages. As soon as possible, the High Commissioner was to return to the charge about the franchise and other Uitlander complaints. Kruger should not 'abuse his victory', and should be pressed to make concessions, even if this involved sending more troops to South Africa to show that Britain was in earnest.

In seeking to apply these pressures, Chamberlain and the other champions of the arrested Uitlander leaders were gambling on the assumption that with a serious outbreak of rinderpest currently killing off the Boers' cattle in thousands, the Transvaal's economy was more than ever dependent on the revenues of the Rand. Both in Britain and amongst the Uitlander community, it was thought that the threat of a stoppage of gold mining would force the Transvaalers to release the Reformers, if not also to make concessions over the franchise. But, as Robinson well knew, such tactics would be self-defeating with a man like Kruger, who was prepared to sacrifice the revenues of the Rand to maintain the independence of the Republic and would therefore be certain to call their bluff. And although, in the light of this advice, Chamberlain agreed to reduce his demands to a request that Kruger should consider the Uitlander's grievances 'at an early date', Robinson still declined to broach the subject. Any attempt to raise these issues at the present moment would, he felt, only make things worse for the Reformers than they were already. All that he would do was to send Kruger a list of the Uitlanders' grievances, but without insisting on their redress.

Chamberlain, however, was not prepared to settle for such weak representations, which he felt put him in the position of admitting defeat. If the High Commissioner would not put pressure on the Transvaal, he would do so himself, and appoint another emissary who could be relied upon to work his will in South Africa. He therefore decided to retire Robinson with a peerage and to send the austere imperialist, Sir Alfred Milner, to take his place. He also summoned Kruger to come to London —or, as he minuted to Salisbury, to 'walk into my parlour'—to discuss the Uitlander question and commissioned the flagship of the Royal Navy's Cape station to convey him to England. But if he really hoped for an acceptance of his invitation, his methods were scarcely likely to bring it about. First, he refused in advance to discuss the very matters which Kruger wished to raise—the limitations imposed on the Republic's sovereignty by the London Convention. Second, he referred to the recent Uitlander agitation as having been 'open and above-board'! And finally, he broke a basic rule of diplomatic etiquette by publishing his communication in the London Gazette on the day after it had been telegraphed and before Kruger had had a chance to consider it, let alone to reply.

Chamberlain was of course not really interested in serious discussions with Kruger. Ultimately he hoped to force him to surrender or fight. But what concerned him even more at this point was the need to protect himself against the exposure of his complicity in the Jameson Raid conspiracy. Hofmeyr had most inconveniently demanded an enquiry and had only with difficulty been dissuaded by Schreiner from further insisting that the Charter be revoked. Added to this, Chamberlain had been somewhat embarrassed by the attitude of the British press which, having at first hailed Jameson as a heroic figure, had veered round completely when they discovered that his venture had ended in fiasco. Calling the Raid a disreputable blunder, some newspapers had actually congratulated the Colonial Secretary for having dissociated the Imperial Government from the whole affair! It was, therefore, essential for Chamberlain to deflect public attention from these dangerous issues by making the fullest possible use of all available red herrings; and for this purpose haranguing Kruger on the injustice of the Transvaal's treatment of the Uitlanders was as good as any other. In fact, Chamberlain even toyed with the idea of forcing a war on the Transvaal as an escape from any public enquiry into the Raid and, to this end, sent a staff officer to look into the military feasibility of an immediate campaign in South Africa.

In the event Chamberlain had no need to go to such grotesque lengths to distract public opinion. For, at this juncture, a diversion as unexpected as it was welcome was to present itself in the form of a telegram from the German Kaiser to Kruger congratulating the Transvaal President on having successfully resisted the recent invasion and asserted his independence. Which initiative the Germans followed up by reinforcing their naval squadron cruising off Delagoa Bay and instructing their Consul-General at Pretoria to ask permission to introduce German marines to protect his consulate in case of a fresh British attack on the Transvaal.

Kruger wisely responded to this request by offering fifty bearded burghers to guard the German consulate. For although he might think the world was flat, he was not so naïve as to let himself be drawn into what Britain would certainly have claimed to be a breach of the London Convention at a time when he was clearly in the right and the British had equally clearly put themselves in the wrong. Besides, as Leyds was not slow to report from his visitations to the European powers, Germany was merely using the Transvaal to twist the lion's tail in an effort to persuade Britain that it would be to her advantage to come closer to the Triple Alliance of Germany, Italy and Austria-Hungary, from which successive British Governments had so persistently fought shy. Leyds had, for instance, failed to secure German finance to help the Transvaal to buy the Delagoa Bay railway as a means of resisting British pressures. And although the Kaiser talked of offering the Boers a German Protectorate, it was becoming increasingly clear that, as the Kaiser's Foreign Minister, Marshal, had told the British Ambassador, Germany's interests were more . European than African and she was not nearly so concerned with supporting the Boers' defiance of Britain as she was with persuading the British Government to seek a closer association with the Central European powers.

But the British press and public were unaware of Marshal's soothing assertions, and the 'Kruger telegram' therefore raised a storm of anti-German protests in Britain which Chamberlain was quick to exploit as proof of the German menace to British interests and influence in South Africa. Even Hofmeyr expressed alarm at what he saw as a recurrence of the threat of a Boer-German alliance. In fact, so vehement was the reaction of the British press and Government that the Kaiser felt it necessary to reassure his 'most beloved Grandmama', Queen Victoria, that he had no intention of getting involved in a row with Britain over the Transvaal. Far from pursuing the idea of offering the Boers German protection, Berlin now proposed no more than a conference of the European powers to consider guarantees for the independence of the Boer Republics. And even this modest proposition was dropped after Kruger declined to take it up for fear that Chamberlain would probably use any conference of the powers to assert British paramountcy.

Meanwhile Kruger had by no means abandoned his efforts to free the Transvaal of the restrictions imposed by the 1884 Convention. Thinking that his Reform Committee hostages put him in a strong bargaining position, he seized on Chamberlain's invitation to London to make his bid for independence. Ignoring the discourteous manner in which the summons was issued, he told the Colonial Secretary that he was ready to go to England, but that the Volksraad would only allow him to do so if the agenda included the questions which the Transvaalers wished to raise with the Imperial Government. First of these was the need to annul the London Convention and substitute a treaty of peace, commerce and friendship concluded as between equals, which would acknowledge the Transvaal's independence, while at the same time safeguarding British interests and ensuring that the Republic would not become a Protectorate of any foreign power. Second, there must be safeguards against a repetition of the Raid, which should include the cancellation of the B.S.A. Company's Charter. Third, the Transvaal must be compensated for the damage resulting from the Raid. And fourth, Swaziland should be fully and finally incorporated into the South African Republic and the Boers granted an independent outlet to the sea.

Chamberlain was naturally unmoved by such demands. Whatever issues might be discussed between them, he told the President that there could be no question of annulling the London Convention and therefore no real independence for the Transvaal. And after further exchanges had failed to persuade Kruger to modify his terms, he bluntly demanded an assurance that the Volksraad should be told that their President would go to England whether they liked it or not. Failing such an assurance, his invitation would be withdrawn.

For Chamberlain it was in all probability something of a blessing in disguise when Kruger, refusing to be bull-dozed by Britain, declined to give the required assurance and allowed the conference to be called off. For the President had listed among his agenda items at least one matter which placed him as Colonial Secretary in a peculiarly embarrassing position. That was the demand that the Charter of what Merriman had called 'that blood-stained sham, the B.S.A. Company' should be revoked, which demand was being supported by the Free Staters and the Cape Dutch and, in the House of Commons, by Opposition M.P.s such as Labouchere. Chamberlain, who anyhow disliked the concept of Chartered Companies usurping the functions of the Colonial Office, knew well enough that the B.S.A. Company's complicity in the Jameson Raid constituted a breach of the spirit and the letter of the Charter and that, properly speaking, his duty was to withdraw the Charter from them. But, apart from the problems which such punitive action would create for the Imperial Government, he was under heavy pressure to let the Charter continue. Indeed his erstwhile partner in the Jameson conspiracy had seen to it that his future career depended on his doing so. For immediately after he resigned as Cape Premier, Rhodes made a dash to London, where he made it abundantly clear to the Colonial Office that, if the Charter were revoked, he would disclose the part which Chamberlain had played in the Raid. On his authority, the Company's London solicitor, Bouchier Hawksley, told Fairfield that, in the event of an enquiry being held, those accused of instigating the Raid could say in their defence that they had been acting on telegrams from the Company's London Board, which could be produced and published and which would show that the Colonial Secretary not only knew about the conspiracy, but actively supported and encouraged it. If, however, the Charter were allowed to run its course, these incriminating documents would be suppressed.

Up to this point Chamberlain had not had a sight of the telegrams in question. In fact, earlier in the year, when the Imperial Government had sent a team of investigators to South Africa to enquire into the Raid, Sprigg, in an effort to cover up for all concerned, had refused to let them peruse the telegrams to and from Jameson, on the grounds that Post Office regulations made it an offence to divulge messages to a third party without the consent of both sender and recipient. Now, however, the Company's London Office were only too happy to oblige the Colonial Secretary by sending him copies of the incriminating cables. And once he had read them, Chamberlain realised all too clearly that, having so palpably dissociated the Imperial Government from Rhodes' plot and condemned the raiders as filibusters, he would face certain ruin, if these messages were now published. Moreover, Kruger would be given the perfect pretext for denouncing the London Convention on the grounds that the Imperial Government had themselves violated it by aiding and abetting an act of aggression against the Transvaal.

For a brief moment Chamberlain thought that he would have to resign. But when Salisbury, whom he had kept largely in ignorance of the conspiracy, told him that he should stay in office and assured him of his support if he did so, he decided to gamble his future on a deal with the chief conspirator. Pocketing his dislike for the man and his commercial enterprises, he told Rhodes that the Charter would be safe, at least pending an enquiry and the forthcoming trial of Jameson and his officers for their part in the Raid. Although the Queen's speech opening Parliament had promised an enquiry, he was doing his best to shelve the whole idea and he hoped to use the Uitlanders' cause as a diversion to this end. All that Rhodes was called upon to do in return, apart from suppressing the incriminating cables, was temporarily to resign, along with Beit, from the Chartered Company's board.

On this basis the required assurance regarding the telegrams was given. From now on Chamberlain adopted the public posture of having known about a possible rising on the Rand, but not about Jameson's decision to invade the Transvaal. And claiming the same for the Company and their directors, he announced to the House of Commons that the Charter was to be continued and, for good measure, paid a handsome tribute to Rhodes as an empire-building patriot.

Rhodes and his subordinates in the Company were not, of course, the only people who could expose Chamberlain. Bower knew of his complicity and of the exchanges which had taken place between the Colonial Office and the High Commissioner prior to the Raid. Besides, Bower had not been exactly discreet when asked after the Raid what Jameson's force was doing at Pitsani. Jameson, too, together with his senior officers, knew that the Imperial Government had colluded with Rhodes at least to the extent of handing over to him the railway strip and the concentration area for the raiders on the Bechuanaland border. And even if Rhodes, to save the Charter, were to silence Jameson, his officers might blurt out the truth at their forth-coming trial from resentment that not only had they been betrayed by the failure of the Uitlanders to stage their revolt, but they were also being made scapegoats for the politicians who were the principal culprits. Besides, there was no telling what precise information the Boers had captured from Jameson's men when they surrendered, or had wheedled out of the Reform Committee members now on trial for their lives. And even if all these trials at home and in the Transvaal passed off without any dire disclosures, there was still an enquiry by the Cape Parlia-ment to be faced, if not by a Select Committee of the House of Commons as well.

To protect the Colonial Secretary against these risks a thorough-going effort was made to conceal all traces of his complicity. Bower was persuaded to accept the role of scapegoat by the argument that, if the High Commissioner's, and hence the Colonial Secretary's, knowledge of the conspiracy were re-vealed, war might well be inevitable. Besides, he was reminded that Robinson's age and health would not stand up to such a revelation. So, out of loyalty to his old and ailing chief and in the wider interests of preserving the dwindling possibilities of peace in South Africa, Bower agreed to admit his own fore-knowledge of Rhodes' plot, but to keep Robinson's complicity secret. As Bower put it in his 'death-bed confession', 'neither Sir Hercules nor Mr. Chamberlain could face an honest en-quiry'. But since he was convinced that in any case an enquiry which revealed the truth would have led to war, he had shielded them both and taken the blame upon himself.

Sir John Willoughby, Jameson's second-in-command, was less inclined to be accommodating. Writing to the War Office from prison while awaiting his trial, he claimed that he and his subordinates had taken part in the Raid 'in the honest and bona-fide belief', based on what Jameson had told them that they were acting 'with the knowledge and assent of the Imperial authorities'. But when the War Office curtly informed him that he had been quite mistaken and that, in any case, he and his fellows had disobeyed the High Commissioner's order to withdraw from Transvaal territory, he agreed not to pursue this line of defence any further.

Perhaps the closest shave of all for the Colonial Secretary was when W. T. Stead, who had guessed the truth, published a book about the Raid under the title *The History of the Mystery*. Although the principal characters were given pseudonyms, each one was easily identifiable to any well-informed reader. And it required the strongest representations from Rhodes himself to persuade Stead to omit from the final text certain passages, which made plain that 'Blastus', his pseudonym for Chamberlain, knew and warmly approved of the Raid and which Rhodes feared would, if published, have condemned the Colonial Secretary and so jeopardised the Company's Charter. Nevertheless, although Stead was successfully nobbled, Garrett, the editor of the *Cape Times*, who had the original proofs in his possession, decided to publish an unexpurgated version in his newspaper. Miraculously, however, this indiscretion attracted scant public notice and, when Stead's book appeared without the incriminating passages, the *Cape Times*' brief exposure of 'Blastus' passed, mercifully for Chamberlain, into limbo.

The trial of the Reformers also passed off without implicating the Colonial Secretary. Death sentences were passed on the ringleaders, only to be commuted within twenty-four hours by Kruger, who anyhow disapproved of capital punishment; and after a brief interval, all those convicted were released on payment of heavy fines, for which the money was provided by Rhodes and Beit. The Transvaal Government thereafter published a Green Book in which they proclaimed, on the strength of documents captured from the saddle-bags of one of Jameson's officers, that the Raid had been a conspiracy to overthrow the Republic, hatched by Rhodes and the B.S.A. Company, together with certain mine-owners on the Rand. The nearest they got to implicating the Imperial Government was by suggesting that Loch's scheme for intervention by the High Commissioner showed that Britain had made contingency plans to exploit a revolution on the Rand. But, since Loch had left Cape Town before the recent change of government in England, this allusion could not harm Chamberlain personally.

As for the Cape Parliament's enquiry in the summer of 1896, Rhodes was censured for conduct unfitting for the Colony's Premier, but was exonerated of having plotted an invasion of the Transvaal; and no criticisms or accusations were levelled at the Colonial Secretary or the High Commissioner. Likewise, the trial of Jameson and his subordinates went without a hitch so far as Chamberlain was concerned. The defendants were found guilty under the Foreign Enlistment Act, but no breath of suspicion fell upon the Colonial Office. Jameson and Willoughby were each sentenced to fifteen months' imprisonment. But after serving only four months of his sentence, Jameson was released from Holloway Prison on the grounds of ill-health to return to South Africa where he lived to become Cape Premier eight years later; and Willoughby later resumed his army career as if nothing out of the ordinary had happened.

By the middle of 1896, therefore, Chamberlain's efforts to cover his tracks had met with considerable success. But, as he knew very well, his enemies in Parliament and in South Africa had seen to it that there were still too many unanswered questions regarding the Raid for him to postpone indefinitely the promised Parliament Enquiry. And it was becoming ever more self-evident that his own reputation and that of the Government would suffer more from shirking the issue than from facing up to it. Besides, the prospect of being confronted by his peers no longer held its earlier terrors. For the interval of time had enabled the Colonial Secretary and the B.S.A. Company's London Board between them to prepare the ground for an investigation. First, there was the guarantee, recently reaffirmed by Rhodes to an emissary of Chamberlain's, that the incriminating telegrams from the Board to Rhodes would not be produced before any enquiry, provided the Charter were not revoked. Also there was Bower's undertaking to exculpate Robinson, and therefore Chamberlain too. To help pack the jury, the Company had been allowed to nominate, as members of the Select Committee which was to conduct the enquiry, two M.P.s who were supporters of Rhodes. But, most important of

Trial of Dr Jameson and his Officers

Joseph Chamberlain

all, Chamberlain knew that the leading Opposition spokesman on the enquiry, Sir William Harcourt, a former Liberal Chancellor of the Exchequer, refused to believe that the Colonial Secretary could have participated in such a treacherous conspiracy and had therefore 'acquitted' him in advance of any investigation. Harcourt was out to convict Rhodes, but he could be relied upon to refrain from asking any questions which might seem to smear Chamberlain or his subordinates with any taint of association with the conspirators. Likewise, those Colonial Office officials who were not directly implicated believed that the reason why Rhodes had agreed with their chief not to produce certain telegrams in evidence was simply to protect the Government from unnecessary and unwarranted suspicion.

Only Lord Grey of the London Board presented a problem, for it was feared that so patently honest a man might, if called as a witness, succumb to cross-examination and admit too much of the truth. But Rhodes took care of this risk by appointing Grey to take Jameson's place as Administrator in Salisbury, where his presence throughout the enquiry was to be described as 'indispensable'. Finally, Chamberlain decided to preside personally over the Select Committee, in which capacity he was able not only to act as judge at what should have been his own trial, but also to lead the Committee to digress as often as possible onto extraneous issues, such as the Uitlanders' complaints, in order to divert attention from the misconduct of Rhodes and his associates. Indeed, when announcing to Parliament the Select Committee's terms of reference, Chamberlain made it quite clear how he intended the enquiry to proceed, by saying that any investigation would be a sham which did not go into 'the grievances which caused the discontent and made the Raid possible'. And to brief himself for these digressions, he ordered the Colonial Office to prepare a long indictment of the Transvaal's treatment of the Uitlanders.

Yet while Chamberlain might have taken every imaginable precaution to ensure that nothing approaching the real truth about himself should emerge from the enquiry, Rhodes was not at all happy to learn that the Select Committee, having investigated the circumstances leading to the Raid, were then supposed to look into the future administration of the Chartered Company. He, therefore, made a last minute attempt to get the enquiry postponed indefinitely. At the same time he had the gall to revert to his demand that the Bechuanaland Protectorate be handed over to the Chartered Company and insisted that their part in the Raid should not prejudice their rights in this territory in the smallest degree.

A few days before the Select Committee were due to assemble, an acrimonious interview took place between him and Chamberlain in which accusations of blackmail rent the air. But it was no good. Rhodes was told that he could not have the Protectorate and that he would have to face the enquiry. Kruger was still insisting that he be brought to trial and that his Charter be withdrawn. And, while the Imperial Government had warned Pretoria that such 'unfriendly and threatening' demands might lead to a war more terrible than anything since the Crimea, they could not refuse to hold any form of inquest into an episode which they had themselves roundly condemned as illegal. Chamberlain had done all that he could by guaranteeing the continuation of the Charter. Rhodes would have to stand his trial.

So, at the start of the next parliamentary session in February 1897, the Select Committee finally met, well and truly rigged to preserve the reputation of the Colonial Secretary and the Charter of the B.S.A. Company. None of the Company's incriminating messages were produced and the enquiry had to rely for documentation on the 1896 Blue Book, with its selection of telegrams and despatches carefully edited to avoid any suggestion of imperial complicity. Bower played his part as the Government's scapegoat, admitting that Rhodes had confided to him the real purpose of Jameson's presence at Pitsani and cutting throughout his testimony a sorry and even contemptible figure, while those far more implicated than he unloaded their guilt upon him, depicting him as a miserable tool in Rhodes' hands, who had betrayed his own chief by failing to warn him of the conspiracy that was afoot.

Robinson, now packing his bags at the Cape to make way for his successor, was said—with some truth—to be too ill to testify in person and the Select Committee had to accept his written answers to certain carefully phrased questions and to forgo any chance of cross-examining him on his statements. Robinson's testimony, such as it was, followed the same line as Chamberlain's own explanations. Admitting that he knew that there might be a revolution on the Rand, he denied any knowledge of Jameson's intention to invade the Transvaal. And when in the absence of the High Commissioner, Rhodes was questioned on this disingenuous statement, he was allowed to parry any awkward thrusts by asserting that he could only answer for his own knowledge and refused to say that anyone except Bower knew of his plans.

As for his own part in the affair, Rhodes knew that, in the light of his exposure at the Reformers' trial and of his censure by the Cape Parliament, it would be futile to try to conceal that he had been the prime mover in the conspiracy. He therefore opened his testimony to the Select Committee by reading a written statement in which he admitted that he had helped with his influence and his money to promote a revolutionary movement in the Transvaal against a Government which had consistently oppressed the Uitlanders and had shown bitter hostility to Cape Colony. He also admitted that he had stationed B.S.A. Company troops in the strip of Bechuanaland territory which had been ceded to the Company and that these troops were to 'act in the Transvaal in certain eventualities'. But he justified all his actions by contending—as Chamberlain had suggested that he should—that he was driven to these desperate measures by the conviction that the Transvaal and Germany were working hand in glove to undermine Britain's paramountcy in South Africa. He even managed to put in yet another plea that, if only to counter these dark designs, his Chartered Company should be allowed to take over the Bechuanaland Protectorate!

In fact, Rhodes accepted responsibility for the whole conspiracy, although he insisted that Jameson had gone into the Transvaal without his authority. But his plea in mitigation—that he was striving to keep Germany out of a crucially important part of Britain's Empire—enabled Chamberlain, himself safely exculpated from complicity, to argue that the conspirators

355

were acting, however wrongly, from patriotic impulses and generally to direct the course of the enquiry so as to make the Boers appear as more culpable than Rhodes and his associates. Apart from Labouchere who constituted a hostile minority of one, the Opposition members of the Select Committee refrained from probing the matter to any appreciable depth. For not only did Harcourt believe the Colonial Secretary to be innocent; he and his party colleagues also knew that Rosebery, before leaving office at the head of the previous Liberal Government, was said to have been given at least some inkling of Rhodes' plans. And since Rhodes would clearly have briefed Chamberlain accordingly, they feared that, if the finger had been pointed at the Colonial Secretary, he would have turned on the Liberals and, out of spite, have smeared them with the 'knowledge' of their former leader.

Only Hawksley and Rutherford Harris gave Chamberlain the slightest qualms. Both of them resented the fact that the Colonial Secretary was to escape any share of the blame which had fallen upon Rhodes. Thus, when Hawksley came to give evidence, he nearly gave the game away by blurting out to the Committee that, according to what Fairfield had told him, Chamberlain had been put in the picture regarding Rhodes' plans. Harris, for his part, referred to having made, as he had telegraphed to Rhodes at the time, a 'guarded allusion' as to the real purpose for which the Company required the cession of the railway strip in Bechuanaland, when he visited the Colonial Secretary in the autumn of 1895. But, although Labouchere did his best to pin down Chamberlain's complicity, without the telegrams there was no proof to substantiate Harris' and Hawksley's indiscretions. Fairfield had died before he could be summoned as a witness and, although the Committee asked the Company's London office to produce the telegrams in question, they failed to press the matter when, inevitably, their request was ignored.

After sitting for five months the Committee's report was published to the world. Nothing could have been more satisfactory for Chamberlain. Bower was censured for 'grave dereliction of duty', as was Newton, the Assistant Commissioner for Bechuanaland, in whose territory Jameson had mustered his raiders. Both men were dismissed from their posts and were, in due course, transferred to insalubrious and unimportant colonies. Robinson was exonerated and the B.S.A. Company's board of directors escaped with a mild reprimand for having failed to keep Rhodes under proper control. Chamberlain's word, supported by that of his Under-Secretary of State, Lord Selborne, was considered to be adequate contradiction of Hawksley's and Harris' suggestions of official complicity. And the Colonial Secretary and his department were cleared of having 'received any information' which could have 'made any of them aware of the plot'. The Company's failure to produce the telegrams for which the Committee asked was explained, in perhaps the most amazing non-sequitur of all, as proving 'that he [Mr. Rhodes] is aware that any statements purporting to implicate the Colonial Office in them were unfounded and the use made of them in support of his action in South Africa was not justified'.

As for the second element of the Select Committee's terms of reference—to enquire into the future administration of the B.S.A. Chartered Company—the matter was not even discussed. Rhodes was, inevitably, condemned for 'grave breaches of duty' as he had already been by the Cape Parliament. But when the House of Commons debated the Committee's report, Chamberlain made amends by paying the warmest tribute to his partner in the conspiracy, whom he described as a great statesman, who had enriched England's history and enlarged her dominions. To the critics, such as Labouchere, he added that there was no question of prosecuting Rhodes or of removing him from the roll of Privy Counsellors. On the contrary, he was to be encouraged to continue his work of expanding the Empire safe in the knowledge that the B.S.A. Company's Charter would not be withdrawn.

Indeed, apart from having to accept the appointment of a Resident Commissioner to represent the Imperial Government in Rhodesia, together with closer imperial control of the police, the Company suffered no loss whatever as a result of the Raid. Company rule continued as before, with the Administrator remaining as the autocratic king-pin of the Government. Even the Transvaal's claim for damages amounting to some £678,000 was to go by default since, when the Boer War broke out in 1899, it was still being disputed by lawyers on the grounds that the Transvaal had in fact profited from the equipment which had been captured from Jameson's force and the fines exacted from the Reformers. Even Rhodes' resignation from the Board was only a temporary affair; and within two years he was to be reinstated to all his pristine powers within the Company.

But if the results of the enquiry smiled on Chamberlain and the Chartered Company, they were a lot less satisfactory to a wide section of the press and public in England and South Africa. Suspicion remained widespread that evidence implicating the Government had been withheld and that the Select Committee had connived at withholding it. The *Westminster Gazette* called the Committee's report 'a hushing up in public'; and in this and other newspapers there were frequent caustic references to the 'Committee of No Enquiry' and, more wittily, to the 'Lying in State at Westminster'. As for South African reactions, while Chamberlain's public acclamation of Rhodes delighted the English community, it aroused the deepest resentment among Afrikaners everywhere. Few, if any, Boers believed that the Imperial Government had not been involved in the Raid and the proceedings of the Select Committee were seen throughout the Afrikaner world as a palpable effort to whitewash and to keep in office the man who had become the Boers' most dangerous and implacable enemy. Kruger, of course, had no doubts on this score, any more than he doubted that Rhodes' Charter would be continued. As he told J. B. Robinson, he knew perfectly well that Rhodes had blackmailed Chamberlain into allowing the B.S.A. Company to keep the Charter by threatening to expose his complicity if it were revoked.

In fact, it may be said that, even more than the Raid itself, it was the manifest attempt to shield Chamberlain from exposure and Rhodes from punishment which convinced Kruger and his Boers, together with Hofmeyr and his Bond, that war was now inevitable between Chamberlain's Britain and the Afrikaner Republics. Even if Chamberlain and his lieutenant, Milner, had seriously intended that the negotiations about the franchise between the Transvaal and British Governments, which were to follow, should bring about a peaceful settlement, the suspicion and hatred aroused, or rearoused, by the Imperial Government's proceedings during and since the Jameson Raid would have made their task well-nigh impossible.

But Chamberlain had no intention of working for peaceful solutions. All that concerned him was the assertion of British paramountcy in South Africa which was to be achieved either by the Boers' surrender or by war. The Uitlanders, whom he called 'a lot of cowardly selfish blatant speculators who would sell their souls to have the power of rigging the market', meant no more to him than a pretext for putting pressure on Kruger. And as he was shortly to demonstrate, any concessions which the Transvaal might offer to satisfy the Uitlanders' grievances only stimulated him to apply further pressures and make greater demands upon the Boers. Even while the Select Committee's enquiry was pending, Chamberlain was publicly proclaiming Britain's paramountcy in South Africa, condemning the internal policies of Kruger's Republic and warning Pretoria in ominous tones that, 'as the paramount power', Britain would intervene if the Boers continued to defy her wishes.

Thus, at the very moment when Rhodes' premiership came to an end in the Cape, an even more dangerous and powerful figure had been brought to the forefront of a massive imperial campaign to unite South Africa by the sword under British supremacy. The process that had begun with Carnarvon was to be reenacted under the ruthless direction of Chamberlain. And henceforth it became a question, not of whether, but of when Boer and British blood would flow to decide this mortal issue.

359

18 Polarisation of the Protagonists

YET another malign product of the Chartered Company's doings at this time was the rebellion of the Matabeles and Mashonas against the rule of the white man in Rhodesia, which broke out in March 1896 and which threatened to annihilate all white settlement between the Limpopo and the Zambezi. Indeed it has been said that it was the Jameson Raid which decided the timing of this upheaval and that the Matabeles deliberately chose to strike at a moment when, in the absence of the major part of the Company's forces, there were only forty police and a regiment of mounted volunteers to keep order in the country. But, whether or not these simple tribesmen had the intelligence resources to make such a calculation, from the Company's point of view they certainly could not have chosen a more awkward time to stage their revolt.

For the past three years since the white man overran their country, the Matabeles had nursed a deep resentment over the Company's treatment of the natives, which they saw as a vindictive exploitation of the victory over Lobengula. As was later to emerge from an official enquiry into the rebellion, the main causes of their disaffection were twofold. The first was the system of exacting taxation by compulsory labour in the mines, which the B.S.A. Company imposed on the Matabeles and which the Chief Native Commissioner in Bulawayo maintained by the use of force and by the employment of especially brutal Zulu policemen. The second complaint arose from the claim made by the Company following the overthrow of Lobengula that all cattle in the country, having been the property of the King, had reverted to them by right of conquest. Coming on top of the occupation of most of the richest loams in Matabeleland as gold claims, this assertion suggested to the natives that the aim of the white settlers was to dispossess them of all their property and evict them altogether from their lands. Some cattle were, it is true, distributed to Matabeles who surrendered after their defeat. But more often they were seized by the Company's agents who regarded themselves as entitled to this profitable source of loot. To make matters worse, these seizures continued even when, as periodically happened, crop failures and the visitations of locusts made milk the only stand-by food for the native population. In due course, orders were issued from Salisbury that cattle should only be seized as punishment for transgressions of the Company's laws. But no sooner had these orders begun to take effect than a violent outbreak of rinderpest swept across the country, killing thousands of beasts and threatening to exterminate the entire cattle population of Rhodesia. Whereupon, to the stunned amazement of the natives, the Company proclaimed that all contaminated cattle must be slaughtered, whether or not they had actually caught the disease.

Little had then been discovered about this plague, although it was supposed to have originated in the Orient and had been known to exist in Egypt from the time of Moses and more recently in Europe. In a few years' time a preventive dip was to be invented which, by removing the ticks which carried the infection, helped to avert further epidemics. But, for the moment, the slaughter policy was probably the only practicable means of stamping out the disease. Nevertheless, it was impossible to explain this to the Matabeles especially when, after all infected animals had been killed, only a few hundred cattle were left alive out of an original total of 100,000. With no Paramount Chief to guide them, the impoverished and resentful natives turned to the religious cult which, after consultation with the 'spirits', asserted that their dead cattle showed how the white men had bewitched their land and that only by exterminating

361

these intruders could happiness and fertility be restored. More-over, the spirits asserted, an impi would soon come and drive the settlers out, together with the pestilence and disease which they had brought with them. And when, in March 1896, rain brought an end to a long period of drought, the Matabeles jumped to the conclusion that this blessed relief presaged the imminent fulfilment of these prophecies and poured forth from their kraals bent on murdering every white man in the land.

At the outset the rebels enjoyed the advantage of surprise and, compared with the paucity of Company police, over-whelming superiority in numbers. Besides, notwithstanding their recent defeat, they were surprisingly well-equipped with weapons. For although many Matabeles had surrendered their arms in obedience to the Company's orders, the policy of wholesale disarmament had proved unenforceable, especially among those impis which had not been engaged in the war and had not, therefore, been rounded up by Company forces. On top of this, three months after the rebellion started, the Mashonas joined in, ordered by the Matabele indunas to rise and support them or face summary punishment for desertion. Within a few days 119 white settlers were massacred within a radius of eighty miles of Salisbury and a situation had been created which the small forces at the Company's disposal were quite inadequate to handle, even with the help of volunteers from Natal and of reinforcements rushed up from Cape Colony. Thus, as the Company desperately strove to recruit a Matabele-land Relief Force from outside Rhodesia, the Imperial Govern-ment were obliged to weigh in with the despatch of a thousand troops under General Carrington and to appoint the High Commissioner to the supreme command of all forces engaged in quelling the rebellion.

To begin with, these imperial reinforcements proved some-what ineffective. Within the first two weeks of their arrival, they lost twenty per cent of their strength and earned the scorn of the Company's officials, who let pass no opportunity of belittling their intervention. But, before long, their superior fire-power told on the rebels who, with no paramount authority to direct their strategy and led by jealously independent indunas, suffered from a lack of coordination. The Matabeles therefore abandoned the field and retired into the Matopos Hills. But, while they had been defeated in battle, they were by no means crushed in spirit. Nobody knew this better than Rhodes who, having gone to Rhodesia to avoid having to testify at Jameson's trial, happened to arrive in Salisbury only a few days after the rebellion broke out. 'They suffer defeat one day', he said of the Matabele impis, 'but the next day they reappear as if nothing had happened'. And he knew too that, however many rebels might be shot down like the rabid dogs that he thought them to be, it would require more than a military defeat to bring the Matabeles to cooperate in peace and harmony with their Company rulers.

Rhodes, therefore, decided to seek out the rebel indunas in their mountain hide-outs and, unarmed and with three white companions and two natives to act as scout and interpreter, he set off into the Matopos to parley with his enemies. Then, for the first time, he heard from the rebel leaders some home truths about the misrule of the Chartered Company, about the insults and oppressions visited upon the population by the Native Commissioners and their Zulu police and tax-collectors and about the way in which the Company's forces had desecrated Msilikali's tomb and, so it was alleged, had even started the killing of women and children.

Wisely enough, Rhodes did not attempt to defend these actions or to argue about who had committed the first or worst atrocities. Instead, he simply told the rebels that in future their complaints would be remedied, provided there was no more fighting. And in October, after a second indaba had been held with some of the younger and more recalcitrant indunas, the rebels accepted that further fighting would gain them nothing that Rhodes had not offered in the way of redress and agreed to come to terms. The Mashona rebels were to maintain a desultory resistance for another twelve months. But the threat to the very existence of white settlement in Rhodesia was now removed and Rhodes, nicknamed by the Matabeles the 'Separator of the Fighting Bulls', returned to a hero's welcome at the Cape, which was to be repeated by his fellow-countrymen when he later arrived in England to face the Select Committee's enquiry.

Indeed, so much was he lionised and lauded for his courageous intervention in the Matabele Rebellion—which undeniably was his finest hour—that Rhodes now became convinced that his political career, far from being ended, was about to start all over again. Hofmeyr and the Afrikaners had, of course, finished with him. So had Merriman, influential among Liberal voters, who was as disgusted by his one-time chief's manoeuvres to salvage his political career as he had been with the duplicity of the Jameson Raid conspiracy. Also, Schreiner who had been one of Rhodes' most devoted admirers, sharing his belief that the white man should keep the black man in his place, had been so disillusioned by the Raid and so embittered by Rhodes' sneering references to the 'unctuous rectitude' of those who condemned it that he seriously considered retiring from public life altogether to return to his career at the Bar. Schreiner now went so far as to describe Rhodes as the greatest enemy of peace in Africa. Yet, for all the enmity of his former colleagues and supporters in the Bond, Rhodes knew that, after the part he had played in stopping the Matabele Rebellion, the English community at the Cape, and in particular the jingos of the South African League, had forgiven him for the Raid—if indeed they had ever really held it against him—and were looking to him for leadership of a kind which no other political figure in South Africa could then provide.

Rhodes was, therefore, still a power to be reckoned with. By his compact with Chamberlain and his handling of the Matabele rebels, he had preserved intact his northern empire. The Company's finances might have suffered severely under the triple impact of the Raid, the rinderpest epidemic and the rebellion. Indeed their shares had fallen from the boom price of £9 during the drifts crisis to just over £3 in 1896. But by the end of the year, two new share issues had been made and, at the start of 1897, they were on their way to recovery. And however much they deserved to lose their Charter on account of the monstrous misrule which had brought about the Matabele Rebellion, let alone because of their involvement in the Jameson

Raid, Rhodes knew that the Colonial Secretary would not dare to lay a finger on the Company for fear of being exposed as his co-conspirator.

The only snag was that this marriage of convenience meant that Rhodes was as dependent on Chamberlain to further his political ambitions as Chamberlain was on him to protect his political reputation. For without Hofmeyr and the Cape Dutch to back him, he had to make his political nest among the imperialists of the South African League and to swallow his prejudice against the 'Imperial Factor' intervening in South African affairs. Whether he liked it or not, he had to accept that the conduct of the campaign against Kruger's Republic was henceforward to be in Chamberlain's hands and no-one else's and that Milner's mission in South Africa would be to make sure that his master's orders were carried out and no longer vitiated by a High Commissioner acting under the influence of Cape colonials. In short, Rhodes was not to be interfered with in his northern dominions, but he was equally not to interfere in Chamberlain's efforts to create a South African federation under imperial rule.

Yet, if playing this new role went against the grain with Rhodes, he certainly showed no signs of it. For such was his ambition to recoup himself politically that, without any apparent hesitation, he now became the foremost champion of Chamberlain's policy of imperial intervention in South Africa. On Rose-Innes' retirement in 1897, he took over as the de facto leader of the amorphous Progressive Party which, with the backing of the South African League, he proceeded to make the spearhead of British imperialism. And in this capacity, he turned to opposing, and even vilifying, his erstwhile political allies of the Afrikaner Bond who, in association with such Moderates as Schreiner and Merriman, were now mobilising to defeat the imperialist challenge at the crucial elections due to take place in the Cape in the following year.

No doubt Whitehall would have preferred at this stage to have had as their champion a politician less compromised than Rhodes. Certainly with him leading the 'loyalist' British party, any chance that might still have remained of winning back the

Cape Dutch was to vanish completely. Chamberlain knew that he could not 'unite the English without giving offence and cause of suspicion to the Dutch'. And while Milner, as he wrote to Selborne, regarded Rhodes as 'the only man big enough' in South Africa to carry out his policy of federation under British rule, he considered him to be 'too self-willed, too violent, too sanguine and in too great a hurry'. He was 'undaunted and unbroken by his former failure, but also untaught by it'; and he was 'much too strong a man to be merely used'.

Nevertheless, just as Rhodes had no option but to seek his political backing from the imperialist elements at the Cape, so Chamberlain and Milner were obliged to settle for Rhodes as their local champion. Sprigg, the eternal stop-gap Premier, who had taken over the Government after the Jameson Raid, was scarcely a valid alternative. Besides, his administration was tottering under the hammer-blows of the newly formed Opposition coalition of Bondsmen and Liberals, styling themselves the South African Party. And every other politician of stature, such as Schreiner—now leader of the Opposition—Merriman and Hofmeyr, was diametrically opposed to Chamberlain's policy in South Africa. They might concede that there was much that required reforming in Kruger's Republic and that the franchise was a farce, the dynamite monopoly a scandal and the corrupt antiquity of the administration a disgrace. They might also be extremely irritated by the prickly manner in which the Boers treated every suggestion for reform as an unwarrantable interference and arrogantly refused to take account of the views of foreigners within or without their borders. Indeed, Merriman had gone so far as to tell the new President of the Orange Free State, Martinus Steyn, that 'the greatest danger to the future' lay in Kruger's unliberal and unenlightened attitude. But he and his Opposition colleagues were under no illusions about Chamberlain's espousal of the Uitlanders' cause, which they saw as a transparent device to assert British paramountcy. Besides, however reactionary the policy of the Transvaal might be, they refused to accept that an issue such as votes for the Uitlanders could conceivably constitute a pretext for war or threats of war; and they insisted on the need for patient negotiations to persuade the Transvaalers to undertake the necessary reforms.

Needless to say, the attitude of the Opposition leaders in the Cape did nothing to cool the ardour of the Colonial Secretary, whose determination to force Kruger to surrender or fight had not flagged since the fiasco of the Jameson Raid. From having once thought of pushing the Boers into war as a diversion to avoid the Select Committee enquiry, Chamberlain, together with his deputy Selborne, had become more than ever convinced that Kruger's Republic had to be forced into the British fold and that no holds should be barred to secure this end.

In the early spring of 1896, the two Ministers set out in a memorandum to the Cabinet their view that, with the centre of political and economic gravity now rapidly passing from Cape Colony to the Transvaal, it was imperative that South Africa be united 'into a Confederacy on the model of the Dominion of Canada and under the British flag'. Otherwise, and if the various states of South Africa were allowed to develop separately, they would in due course 'inevitably amalgamate . . . into a United States', independent of the British connection and under Boer leadership. No longer was it feasible to plan for the future on the assumption of the Cape's supremacy or on the hope that the Transvaal would ultimately be absorbed into a British union by the sheer weight of numbers of British migrants. Such hopes had been denied by the growth of the Rand and the opening of the Delagoa Bay railway. Nor would it stop the drift towards independence, if Kruger could be persuaded to give the Uitlanders the vote. On the contrary, this would probably only change the Transvaal from a Boer to a British Republic. For, as Rhodes had discovered in his negotiations with the Johannesburg Reformers prior to the Raid, the Uitlanders were far from being sold on the idea of imperial rule. For all these reasons, Chamberlain and Selborne concluded that the situation called for action more direct and decisive than anything hitherto contemplated. The Transvaal had to be subjected to every possible pressure and, in particular, made to feel 'irrevocably hemmed in' by the Imperial Government 'securing control' of the Delagoa Bay railway.

The Cabinet were somewhat taken aback by these recommendations, which Chamberlain's more senior colleagues thought altogether too impulsive. The Prime Minister took the view that a war with the Transvaal would have 'pernicious' repercussions in Europe and might even lead to Germany attacking England in order to curry favour with Holland by supporting her kinsmen in South Africa. Chamberlain, nevertheless, continued to try by every available means to put pressure on the Boers and used every wile and argument to persuade the Cabinet to send at least another 10,000 imperial troops to the Cape. The tremors caused by the Raid required a show of British strength, he contended. And when it was argued that such gestures would be more likely to heighten rather than reduce the tension in South Africa, he retorted that the Matabele Rebellion had exposed the inadequacy of imperial reserves: if there were not enough troops even to keep the tribes in order, he could not hope to force Kruger to grant that redress of the Uitlanders' grievances, which public opinion in England was being led to expect. The Transvaal, he maintained, must be shown that Britain's patience was all but exhausted and that a serious situation would arise if Pretoria continued to delay reforms.

But these pleadings were to no avail. The Cabinet preferred to be guided by the advice of Robinson who, as his term of office drew to a close, was at pains to point out that the position had been radically changed by the fiasco of the Raid and that the Transvaalers would not be bluffed or bludgeoned into giving the vote to the Uitlanders. Rather than submit to British dictation in the Republic's internal affairs, Robinson believed that Kruger would risk everything, including war. Thanks to the Raid, he now had the Cape Dutch firmly on his side and against Britain, so that even if the imperial will prevailed in the end the British would find themselves governing a bitterly hostile people who could only be held down by brute force.

In the face of such advice from Cape Town, backed by similar warnings from the Government of Natal, Chamberlain failed to induce his colleagues to sanction his request for troop reinforcements. And although he continued to protest to

Salisbury that the Boers would give way if they 'see that we are in earnest', he was for the moment obliged by the prevailing view of the Cabinet to mark time, and in his public utterances to disclaim any intention of forcing Kruger into a war which would be 'as immoral as it would be unwise'.

However, it was not long before Chamberlain was to find a pretext to resume his pressures against the Transvaal. For, in September 1896, the Pretoria Volksraad played into his hands by passing an Act which gave Kruger's Executive Council power to expel any foreigner from the Transvaal who was considered to be 'a danger to public peace and order'. A few months later the Cape Parliament were to pass, without a murmur of criticism from the Colonial Office, a law empowering the Government to hold anyone in the Transkei in jail for three months without either warrant or trial. But the fact that Kruger had sought the much less despotic power to get rid of undesirable aliens found Chamberlain protesting in vigorous terms that he had breached those clauses of the London Convention which safeguarded the liberty of non-citizens to enter and reside in the Transvaal. And since such action was held to challenge the whole principle of British suzerainty, Robinson was instructed to demand that the Volksraad should promptly revoke this offensive legislation.

Far from making the Transvaal back down, this British remonstrance only seemed to intensify their defiance. For four months later, in January 1897, the Volksraad proceeded to add to the expulsion law an Act providing for the stricter control of immigration into the Republic. This Act, which provided for the registration of all immigrants and required that anyone entering the Transvaal should produce a passport or some proof of his ability to earn a living, was primarily intended to exclude paupers, people with contagious diseases and other undesirables. But, coming so soon after the Aliens Expulsion Act, together with yet another statute designed to curb what Pretoria saw as seditious proceedings in the press and at public meetings, it brought a further outburst from Chamberlain, even though there was some doubt among his legal advisers as to whether in this case the legislation was in breach of the London Convention. Brushing aside all legal niceties with the assertion that the Convention was to be interpreted in whatever way best suited British interests, the Colonial Secretary now publicly accused Kruger of repeatedly breaking his promises to the Uitlanders. He even suggested to Lionel Phillips in Johannesburg that, as an additional means of bringing pressure to bear on the Transvaal, the Rand mineowners should be invited temporarily to close down their mines and so to reduce the revenue of the Republic to almost nothing.

Had such action been practicable, it would undoubtedly have dealt a crippling blow to the Transvaal's economy. For, with rinderpest currently as rife in the Republic as in Rhodesia, the population in the countryside was at this point approaching starvation level and the revenue was more than ever dependent on the production of gold. However, the gold fields were currently also facing a period of comparative stagnation, and it was hardly likely that their owners would be ready to cut off their nose to spite Kruger's face. Thus Phillips, not surprisingly, refused to consider the suggestion for closing the mines; and Kruger responded to Chamberlain's accusations by challenging him to state exactly what promises he had given to the Uitlanders and had since broken.

Foolishly Kruger now went even further. No doubt nettled by the agitation of the local South African League for Britain to intervene on behalf of the Uitlanders, he used his new power to suppress the principal English language newspaper for publishing what he termed abusive articles against himself and his regime. On top of this, he took the equally high-handed decision to dismiss Judge Kotze, the Chief Justice of the Republic, for daring to claim that the judiciary had the right to examine the Volksraad's legislation in order to ensure that it fell within the four corners of the constitution. All of which autocratic proceedings were unhappily to coincide with the enquiry of the Select Committee into the Jameson Raid and therefore to help its chairman to divert attention from the iniquities of the conspirators by castigating the Transvaal Government as an archaic dictatorship bent on suppressing every aspect of liberty and justice.

But even more sinister—in Chamberlain's sight—than Kruger's attacks on the press and the judiciary was the conclusion in March 1897 of a new treaty between the Transvaal and the Orange Free State which, while rehearsing the provisions of the defensive alliance of 1889, proclaimed as its objective the creation of a federal union of the two Republics. True, President Steyn had insisted that the new treaty should provide for consultation between the two Governments, so that he might preserve his own freedom of action pending the establishment of the union. But the fact that the Republics were now openly seeking an Africaner federation was enough to galvanise Chamberlain into frenzied counter-action. For as he saw it, such an arrangement was to be but a first step to a wider union of South Africa under the aegis of Pretoria.

Besides, other sinister reports of Kruger's designs were being relayed to the Colonial Office which stemmed from a Portuguese spy, Baron Matalha, a former Portuguese Consul-General in Pretoria and an employee of Wernher-Beit, who had on his pay-roll a clerk in the State Secretary's office. One such report which was passed to London by the British Agent in Pretoria, Conynghame-Greene, claimed that Leyds had recently gone to Europe to solicit German and French support for the purchase of Delagoa Bay by the Transvaal. And although nothing came of this project, save a plan for a French cable and a Franco-German shipping service to Lourenço Marques, Chamberlain refused to be mollified. On the contrary, his suspicions were, if anything, deepened by further reports that the Transvaal Government had recently bought from Europe large quantities of field guns, rifles and ammunition.

Making the most of these tales of Kruger's anti-British and anti-Uitlander proceedings, Chamberlain lost no time in sending two minatory despatches to Pretoria, the first of which listed various breaches of the London Convention by the Transvaal, while the second demanded the prompt repeal of the Immigration Act. By this time, moreover, he had managed to prevail on his Cabinet colleagues to sanction supporting military movements which gave his demands the force of a virtual ultimatum. A British naval squadron was despatched to

371

Delagoa Bay and, shortly afterwards, it was announced that the imperial garrison in South Africa was to be reinforced. Kruger protested to Conynghame-Greene that Britain was holding a knife to his throat. And for a brief moment the threat of war hung darkly over South Africa. But, since the Transvaal had only just begun to arm on any appreciable scale, his defiance was short-lived. In May, a few days after the announcement that imperial reinforcements were on their way, Kruger backed down. Contenting himself with a counter-proposal that the President of Switzerland should be invited to arbitrate on points of difference between the two countries, he repealed the Immigration Act and allowed the newspapers suppressed under the Press laws to reappear under new names. Two months later, the Aliens Act was modified to provide for an appeals procedure. For good measure, at a banquet in Johannesburg held to celebrate the Diamond Jubilee, the President went out of his way to express his heartfelt admiration for Queen Victoria; and as a sop to the unenfranchised Uitlanders, Johannesburg was granted the status of a municipality with a partially elected council.

The crisis had passed, but at the cost of still further dividing Briton and Boer and of vitiating the few remaining prospects of reform in the Transvaal and of peace in South Africa. In the Cape, Chamberlain's sabre-rattling had badly shaken the Bond and Liberal Members of Parliament who, on Hofmeyr's initiative, asked the Assembly to go on record that war would be disastrous and should be avoided by moderation and conciliation and by the peaceful settlement of differences. To this the Sprigg Government, unable to dispute the letter of the motion, yet infuriated by the spirit of the supporting speeches, responded by performing the political acrobatics of speaking against and voting for it. Whereupon Merriman promptly tabled a motion of no-confidence in the administration. And after a bitter debate and much ferocious lobbying by Rhodes—who wanted to preserve the status quo until he might himself be ready to take over the reins of government once again—Sprigg and his colleagues were saved only by the casting vote of the Speaker.

The polarisation of the Cape parties had begun. But even more serious for peace than the widening of the gulf between the Bond and the imperialists in Cape Colony was the set-back which the war crisis had brought to the prospects of reform in the Transvaal. Before Chamberlain issued his ultimatum to Kruger, a reform party had been gaining ground and, as Major Sapte, now Managing Director of Rhodes' Consolidated Gold-fields Company, confided to an army friend of his, Kruger was beginning to show some sympathy for the Uitlanders. But these auspicious trends had now been brought to an abrupt halt; and any hopes that might have remained of making a settlement with the Transvaal were banished when, in May 1897, Milner arrived at the Cape to carry into effect the simple, brutal design to force Kruger to surrender to British suzerainty or to fight the British Empire.

From now on Chamberlain could rest assured that there would be no conflict of purpose between himself and his appointed delegate in South Africa, no further time-wasting with delicate diplomatic procedures. For Milner was a man who was temperamentally incapable of seeking his ends by patient diplomacy over any sustained period. Even from his under-graduate days at Oxford, he had been described as 'eager to organise rather than to influence'. A tall, cold and aloof creature, 'grave beyond his years', this quarter-German descendant of a Lancashire business family had spent half of his youth in his native Germany and all of it in poverty. From which joyless background he had won a scholarship in Classics at Baliol, Oxford, whence he emerged with the highest graduate distinctions, 'the finest flower of culture' of his generation. On leaving the university, he became a barrister; but, finding too little work to earn him a living wage at the Bar, he tried his hand at journalism, becoming assistant editor of the *Pall Mall Gazette* under W. T. Stead. Two years later, deciding that the Fourth Estate was no longer to his liking, he took up politics. After unsuccessfully contesting an election as a Liberal candidate, he served for five years as private secretary to G. J. Goschen, who succeeded Lord Randolph Churchill as Chancellor of the Exchequer in Salisbury's second Government; and in this capacity he helped in the formation of the breakaway Liberal Unionist Party following the great Liberal split over Irish Home Rule. As a disciple of Ruskin he developed a strong belief in imperialism, which he saw as the best way of simultaneously helping the industrial working class at home and the untutored savage abroad. And in contrast to his frigid and forbidding manner, he became, under the influence of his Oxford contemporary, Arnold Toynbee, an enthusiastic philanthropist and a co-founder of the Toynbee Hall institution in London's East End.

Having established a certain reputation as an administrator and financial expert while serving with Goschen, Milner was chosen to help Sir Evelyn Baring, the British Consul-General in Cairo and the de facto ruler of Egypt, in the herculean task of reorganising the chaotic finances of the Khedive Tewfik; and for this purpose, he was appointed, in 1889, Under Secretary of State in the Egyptian Ministry of Finance. During his time in Egypt, he developed a strong paternalistic sympathy for the poverty-stricken fellahin. But he had no use whatever for any form of Egyptian administration, which he termed 'the most absurd experiment in human government', and he was convinced that, without British rule, Egypt would relapse into the dark ages. When he left Cairo, he wrote in a memoir entitled 'England in Egypt' that 'the difference between Egypt now and Egypt in the latter days of Ismail is as the difference between light and darkness. . . .' And, while the Imperial Government continued to pretend that Britain's ten year-old occupation of the country was still a temporary affair, he made no secret of his own view that, in the interests of both nations, it should become indefinite. For as he saw it, even if the Egyptians learned from the British how to govern themselves, 'command of the army is one of the last things it will be safe to hand over to native management'.

It was while Milner was serving in Egypt that Chamberlain first met him and formed the highest opinion of his intellectual gifts and organising ability. Having read 'England in Egypt', he marked its author down as a man who could be extremely useful to any Colonial Secretary. So, when Chamberlain made up his mind to retire Robinson from South Africa, he decided to offer the post to this coldly efficient imperialist who, although still only forty-three years of age, had meanwhile added a five-year chairmanship of the Board of Inland Revenue to his varied and brilliant career.

For his part, Milner had no hesitation in accepting the offer which met with general applause from the press and from both parties in Parliament, and within a few weeks of his appointment, he was to show that Chamberlain had indeed made the right choice for his purpose. In a public speech before leaving for South Africa, he declaimed that on such issues as Empire Union, 'My mind is not so constructed that I am capable of understanding the arguments of those who question its desirability or its possibility'. Then with a passionate avowal of his imperialist faith, he concluded, 'It is the British race which built the Empire, and it is the undivided British race which can alone uphold it . . . . Deeper, stronger, more primordial than material ties is the bond of common blood, a common language, common history and traditions'. Which stern implicit warning of what to expect from the new High Commissioner for South Africa might have caused the Boers even more concern, had they known that its author passed the time on the voyage to Cape Town reading the works of Machiaevelli!

Nevertheless, for a while after his arrival at the Cape, Milner showed himself in no great hurry to force the pace with the Transvaal. With a purposeful vigour in stark contrast to the lethargy of his elderly predecessor, he toured Cape Colony, Bechuanaland, Rhodesia and Basutoland, and learned to speak the Boers' 'taal' as well as Dutch, so as to be able to dispense with an interpreter when reading the Afrikaner press and addressing his Cape Dutch subjects. Privately, he made it clear that he nursed the darkest suspicions of Kruger as a man bent on creating an Afrikaner federation hostile to Britain. He also left no-one in any doubt that, as he put it, 'we mean to be masters'; and in an early talk with Merriman, he set out his policy with a brutal frankness which caused the latter to comment that the new High Commissioner would 'convert South Africa into Ireland'. But in his public actions and

375

declarations, Milner was content for the time being to feel his way. He even told Chamberlain that, in his view, the Boers might have had some 'excuse . . . for regarding us with suspicion' and that it would be wise to give time for the passions aroused by the Raid to cool and for a reformist movement to develop within the Transvaal which would put pressure on Kruger's regime. When Chamberlain suggested that the Imperial Government should take steps to exploit the depression which descended upon the Rand in the middle of 1897, he advised that it would be better to 'let the Boers stew in their own juice, fight out their internal quarrels and not be able to coin prejudice . . . by pointing to external interference'. Likewise, he declined to intervene on behalf of the down-trodden native mine-workers and labourers in the Transvaal, although the London Convention gave him the right and the duty to do so, because he feared that the Uitlanders might make common cause with the Boers in resisting such interference in the treatment of their employees. He also cautioned the Colonial Secretary against over-use of the term 'suzerainty' in his exchanges with Kruger, in view of the 'curiously maddening effect' which the word had upon the Boers.

Perhaps Milner was applying the lessons of Machiaevelli. But, whatever the reason for his temporary caution, his advice found an echo among the Law Officers of the Crown who were currently none too happy about the legality of the Colonial Secretary's tactics. For, as Loch had pointed out to Ripon after his second visit to Pretoria in 1894, quite apart from the omission of any specific mention of suzerainty in the 1884 Convention, the Imperial Government had as a matter of fact recognised the sovereign status of the Transvaal by negotiating with Kruger for the exemption of British residents from commando service.

But whether it was Milner telling him to go carefully or the lawyers advising him not to go at all, Chamberlain was not to be deterred by anything short of an absolute veto by his Cabinet colleagues. Having only recently forced the Transvaalers to climb down over the Immigration and Aliens Acts, he was now more than ever determined to rub their noses in

British paramountcy. He did not care how 'maddening' Kruger might find the claim to suzerainty and he insisted that, whatever the 1884 treaty might say or not say on the subject, suzerainty stemmed from the Pretoria Convention which had never actually been revoked. As for encouraging a reform party in the Transvaal, it had never been part of his policy to do more than use the issue of the Uitlanders' franchise as a stick with which to beat the Boers. For, as he had made clear to his colleagues, he feared that, if the Uitlanders ever came to a position of real political power, they would probably turn their backs on Britain and convert Kruger's Republic into a Republic of their own.

Therefore ignoring all contrary advice, Chamberlain sent Kruger a despatch on December 1897 in which he reasserted the British claim to paramountcy, contending that the preamble to the Pretoria Convention which conferred suzerainty had not been superseded by the later treaty. He also maintained the right of the Imperial Government unilaterally to interpret the London Convention. And basing himself on Britain's sovereign right to exclude third parties from her sphere of influence in South Africa, he rejected the Transvaal Government's proposal that differences as to the interpretation of the Convention be submitted to arbitration.

The assertion that in any dispute the British Government's view must prevail came as a bombshell to Pretoria. Nothing could have done more to unite all shades of Boer opinion behind Kruger—and at a time, too, when the Transvaalers were about to elect their President for the next five years. Nor was this high-handed declamation unique in this respect. Indeed, at this point, the activities, not only of Chamberlain himself, but of almost every other agency of British influence in South Africa were such as to make virtually certain that Kruger would be re-elected by a decisive vote, and re-elected moreover on a platform of stubborn resistance to any of the reforms demanded by Britain. On the initiative of Dr. Rutherford Harris, the B.S.A. Company showed their lack of contrition for the Jameson Raid by holding a ball in Cape Town to celebrate its anniversary, which tasteless act of defiance alienated still further every

Afrikaner in South Africa. Also the Transvaal branch of the South African League which had taken over the functions of the defunct and discredited National Union, made little secret of the fact that the purpose of their agitation for an Uitlander franchise was not to enable foreigners on the Rand to become responsible and influential citizens, but rather to force the Republic into a South African Union under the Union Jack. Added to this, it was well known that the effective director and coordinator of the League's activities on the Rand was none other than the British Agent at Pretoria, Conynghame-Greene.

Such provocations could only produce one result. In February 1898, having fought his election campaign on the slogan, 'Beware of Rhodes and keep your powder dry', Kruger was returned as President by an overwhelming majority. Hopes of a genuine reformist movement establishing itself in the Transvaal now dwindled faster than ever before. As they were soon to show by such actions as their refusal to end the iniquitous dynamite monopoly in defiance of the recommendations of a recent enquiry into the mining industry, the Pretoria Government were less anxious than ever to change the established order of things.

Milner, certainly, had no doubts that this was what Kruger's re-election portended. For him it showed with crystal clarity that the policy of *laissez aller* had finally failed. As he told Conynghame-Greene in Pretoria, the stubborn old President was even more firmly entrenched than before and all hope that change might come from a growing reformist agitation within the Transvaal had now vanished. Writing to Chamberlain and Selborne, in ominous tones, Milner now avowed that there was 'no ultimate way out of the political troubles of South Africa except reform in the Transvaal or war; and at present the chances of reform in the Transvaal are worse than ever . . . Kruger had returned to power more autocratic and more reactionary than ever'. He then went on to suggest that since Kruger would not himself provoke a fight, British policy should be 'to work up to a crisis' by keeping up the pressure for reforms. At the same time, he prudently warned his Whitehall masters that, in the event of war, they would have to 'rely on

378

British forces alone, more than half the white people in this Colony . . . are at heart fellow-citizens with the Free Staters and Transvaalers'. The Cape Dutch, he asserted, would never support any forceful measures to remove the 'mediaeval race oligarchy' in Pretoria.

The days when Milner felt it advisable to apply only gradual pressures on Pretoria were over. From letting the Boers stew in their own juice, he was now for pushing them into the fire. And convinced that war was the only solution, he henceforth proceeded on the assumption that every man who was not with him was against him. Never exactly tolerant of colonial opinion, still less of the views of moderate politicians in Cape Colony, he now scarcely ever saw such men as Merriman, whom he considered 'a crank', or De Villiers, the Cape Chief Justice, whom he thought a collaborator with the Boers. He accused the Premier of Natal, Sir Henry Binns, of disloyalty for sending Kruger a telegram to congratulate him on his re-election and he bluntly told Hofmeyr that, if he wanted to see peace preserved, he should address himself to Pretoria and stop complaining about British provocation. More belligerently still, having proclaimed his intention to 'separate the sheep from the goats', he issued, in a speech at Graaf-Reinet, an open challenge to every Cape colonist to choose his side in the coming conflict. Commenting on an assertion by some local Bondsmen that their desire for peace did not connote disloyalty on their part towards the Crown, he blustered, 'Well, gentlemen of course you are loyal: it would be monstrous if you were not'. As for their wanting peace, he insisted that they should first prevail on Kruger to concede reform.

Milner's new offensive attitude found its echo in the campaign tactics of Rhodes and the Progressive Party during the Cape elections which took place a few months later. In June 1898, the Sprigg Government was finally toppled from its precarious perch when a motion of no-confidence moved by Schreiner was carried in the Cape Assembly. In the elections which followed, the Progressives concentrated their campaign on the Transvaal issue, supported more or less openly by Milner, who made no secret of his fear that a Bond Government

in Cape Colony would create a 'Triple Alliance' with the two
Boer Republics to the exclusion of British paramountcy in South
Africa. The Bond and their allies were accused from every
Progressive platform of gross disloyalty for daring to question
the wisdom and justice of imperial policy. Schreiner and
Merriman, as leaders of the new South African Party coalition
of Bondsmen and Liberals, were singled out for specially
vicious treatment. Indeed nearly a year before the election
campaign started, Merriman had had to seek a new constituency. For, at the instigation of Rhodes' propagandists, his
Namaqualand electors had declared him persona non grata
on the grounds that he had undermined British supremacy and
disrupted relations between the Dutch and English communities
by supporting the peace motion and other attempts to remove
the Sprigg Government which had 'irritated the great majority
of English Colonists'.

Rhodes went to the extreme of hyperbole in pouring calumny
on his oponents. He attacked the Bond as a 'little gang terror-
ising the country', whose policy was 'anti the North' and whose
aim was to make Kruger's Government paramount in South
Africa. And he used his control over the *Cape Argus-Star* group
of newspapers, together with his influence on Garrett, the
Cape Times' editor, to vilify all who did not agree with his
policies. Merriman was called a fraud and a turncoat for having
espoused the cause of the Reformers and then stabbed their
champion in the back on the grounds that, having earlier
criticised Kruger's seventeenth-century attitude in no uncertain
terms, he had rounded on Rhodes for his part in the Jameson
Raid. Schreiner, too, was pilloried for 'deserting' Rhodes after
the Raid, having previously been prepared to support him in a
war against Kruger over the Vaal drifts. Rose-Innes was termed
a 'Mugwump', because as a former Progressive leader he now
voted with the Bond. And Hofmeyr and the Bond, who for all
the five years of Rhodes' premiership had been the mainstay of
his parliamentary majority, were now portrayed as a traitorous
bunch of pro-Boer agents who, if elected, would take their
orders from Pretoria and hand the Cape on a plate to Kruger.

No expense was spared in the conduct of the Progressives'

campaign and, in what was to be the last General Election in the Cape before his death, Rhodes spent a small fortune on a desperate all-out effort to regain the premiership. He even imported from England an astute election agent well trained in the electioneering stratagems of the Conservative Party. Yet, despite all the expenditure of money and gall and although he and his supporters won a majority of the votes cast, the Progressives failed by the narrow majority of one seat to defeat Schreiner's South African Party. Rhodes made a last minute bid to invalidate the election result by appealing to the Governor that it did not properly reflect electoral opinion and had only proved the need for a redistribution of constituencies. But, much as he personally disliked the outcome, Milner had no option but to overrule this plea. Thus, after a further no-confidence motion had been carried against the Sprigg administration, Schreiner became Cape Premier in October 1898, with Merriman as a member of a heterogeneous Cabinet of Moderates and Bondsmen.

At this juncture Schreiner was infinitely preferable to Rhodes as the Cape's political leader. For one thing, he was an honest and lovable man—'too honest for the age' had been John Molteno's view of him. For another, he wanted to preserve peace in South Africa. But he was a difficult man to work with, often short-tempered and seldom amenable to advice—in short, an unsuitable leader of a diverse coalition, united largely by a common determination to keep Rhodes out of office. Also he laboured from the start of his premiership under the grave handicap of Milner's implacable hostility. For these reasons Schreiner's policies were as ill-fated in their outcome as he and his Government were ill-assorted in age, experience and temperament for their task. And although he was to succeed where all others had failed in persuading Kruger to concede a measure of reform in the interests of avoiding bloodshed, with Milner now resolutely determined on war, the most that he could do towards preserving peace was to postpone the final holocaust by a few months.

19 Milner's 'Helot' Despatch

SCHREINER and his Ministers were not entirely alone in their efforts to avert the catastrophe of a second South African war. Certain of Chamberlain's colleagues, of whom the most influential were Arthur James Balfour, First Lord of the Treasury and Leader of the House of Commons, and Sir Michael Hicks-Beach, now Chancellor of the Exchequer, were also none too happy with Pushful Joe's pressure tactics. Remembering the disasters which had flowed from Carnarvon's forward policies, they had for some time been urging Salisbury to restrain his Colonial Secretary from, as Balfour put it, treating 'the South African sore . . . by the free application of irritants'. And Salisbury, while reluctant to cross swords with the man who had become the most colourful and politically indispensable member of his Government, was not going to allow any digression in South Africa to thwart his purposes in other spheres. In particular, he would brook no threat to his design to establish a British presence throughout the length of the Nile valley, to which end General Kitchener was currently embarked on the desperate race with France's Colonel Marchand which was to lead the two men to Fashoda and their countries to the brink of war. Thus, at the very moment when Milner came to the conclusion that the bullet offered the only hope of dragooning the intractable Boers, his chief found himself once more obliged by the nervousness of his colleagues and the edicts of his Prime Minister to put a little water in his South African wine.

382

Apart from this, Chamberlain himself had preoccupations other than his quarrel with the Transvaal, which involved him in a number of different areas of colonial, foreign and even domestic policy. Salisbury might want a free hand to establish a British monopoly on the Nile, but the Colonial Secretary was no less determined to keep the French at bay on the Niger, where the struggle for mastery had reached its most crucial stage. Likewise, he was determined to stand firm in the Far East, where the encroachments of the European powers, especially Russia, were threatening to undermine Britain's position and influence. On a still broader plane, Chamberlain was busily promoting his concept of Empire Union. A conference of Colonial Premiers, coinciding with the Queen's Jubilee, had recently rejected as premature his scheme for an Imperial Federation with a political Council of Empire and an integrated system of defence and free trade between Britain and her dominions. But there was still a chance of their agreeing to make a start in this direction with a system of preferential tariffs within the Empire, and he was busily canvassing this modified project with the Colonial Governments. On the home front, Chamberlain had to steer that brain-child of his Radical thinking, the Workmen's Compensation Act, through a sceptical House of Commons. And in the sphere of foreign affairs, believing—like Rhodes—that the Anglo-Saxon powers and Germany should keep the peace of the world between them and that Britain could no longer find security in her traditional policy of 'splendid isolation', he was engaged in certain personal diplomatic initiatives designed to bring about an alliance with Germany and the United States.

Distracted by such wider problems and pressed by the Cabinet to moderate his tone towards the Transvaal, Chamberlain therefore sent instructions to the Cape to conduct a holding operation in South Africa for the time being. 'We must keep our wickets and not force the pace', he wrote a few days after reports of Milner's Graaf-Reinet speech reached London. Conynghame-Greene was instructed to damp down the ardour of the South African League. And when the now militant High Commissioner wanted to intervene after Kruger had replaced Kotze as Chief Justice with the judge who sentenced the Reform Committee's leaders to death—which Milner claimed would remove the Uitlanders' last safeguard against despotism—he was ordered to stay his hand. Only 'a most flagrant offence', he was now told, would justify the Imperial Government departing from a policy of peace: public opinion would not support a clash merely to reinstate a judge who was not even a British subject.

Milner showed considerable irritation at this change of emphasis in Whitehall. Like Rhodes three years earlier, when he was not worrying whether the Uitlanders would remain loyal to the Empire, once they got the vote, he was inclined greatly to exaggerate the militancy of their attitude. He bitterly resented being told that Parliament—for which institution he anyhow had very little use—would not accept that the reactionary repressions of the Pretoria Government constituted a casus belli. As he said to Conynghame-Greene, he would never rest until he had shown the Colonial Office that non-intervention would only weaken Britain's influence and strengthen Kruger's throughout South Africa. And while, in acknowledging Chamberlain's order not to force the pace with the Boers, he said that he hoped by combining 'caution and bluff to worry on without discredit until we are in a better position to "round" upon them', he equally made it clear that he did not for one moment believe that 'an attitude of forbearance' on Britain's part would long be possible.

In fact, Milner need not have been so concerned about his new instructions. Far from abandoning his campaign against Kruger, Chamberlain was merely following the axiom, *reculer pour mieux sauter*. Like Milner himself during his own early months in South Africa, he was advancing cautiously because he needed a breathing-space to enable him to attend to other pressing problems. Directly a solution had been found, or was in sight, for these problems, he intended to bludgeon his colleagues into resuming the strongest pressure on the Boers. Indeed, when the scramble for West Africa was concluded a few months later by the Niger Convention of June 1898, Chamberlain immediately turned his attentions back to the Transvaal

Sir Alfred Milner

Dr W. J. Leyds

and set about isolating the Boers in preparation for the final onslaught.

His plan for so doing was typical of the man. By a lucky coincidence, the Imperial Government was to learn at this point that the Portuguese required a considerable sum of money to pay the compensation which the Berne Arbitration was likely to award to the expropriated shareholders of McMurdo's former railway company. Seeing in this situation a fresh opportunity to gain control over the Delagoa Bay line, Chamberlain therefore persuaded the Foreign Office to offer Portugal a loan, on condition that Britain be granted in return a share in the management of the railway and harbour and, in case of war, complete control of both for the duration of the hostilities. But, soon after the negotiations started, the Germans got wind of his proposals and, intervening in Lisbon and London, staked their claim to be consulted and, even compensated, should any change take place in the status of Portuguese East Africa. Lisbon was threatened with international control of Portugal's finances on the Egyptian model; and London was told that Germany would not hesitate to join with France in making serious difficulties for Britain in Egypt, if Delagoa Bay passed under British control without the Germans obtaining satisfaction elsewhere. Moreover, the 'satisfaction' which Berlin demanded included the transfer of Walvis Bay to German South-West Africa, of Blantyre to Tanganyika and of the 'Volta Triangle' on the Gold Coast to Togoland, plus the reversion of two-thirds of Portugal's African colonies and Portuguese Timor in the East Indies.

These demands, accompanied by such dire threats to both sides, brought the talks between Britain and Portugal to an abrupt end. The Portuguese, seeing all too clearly the dangers of dealing with the two powers who wanted to squeeze them into relinquishing their African possessions, promptly turned to France for help in propping up their shaky finances. As for Britain's reactions, it was equally plain that Germany could all too easily jeopardise Salisbury's plans in the Nile valley by simply voting in the Committee of Control against the expenditure of Egyptian funds to finance Kitchener's advance in the

Sudan. London was therefore no more able than Lisbon to persevere with the negotiations in defiance of German displeasure.

Still Chamberlain was not to be denied in his efforts to impose a British barrier between the Boers and the sea at Delagoa Bay and, with the acquiescence of Salisbury and to Milner's great delight, he now turned to negotiating to this end an arrangement with Berlin. A deal was suggested by which Britain and Germany were to cooperate in getting Portugal to mortgage her colonies and, when she could no longer meet her creditors, to divide Portuguese East Africa so that Delagoa Bay and its railway would be handed over to Britain. After two months of haggling with the Wilhelmstrasse, a treaty on these lines was concluded in August. Even Balfour, who signed on Britain's behalf, could not forbear to cheer this achievement for securing, as he saw it, 'the absolute exclusion of every other power including Germany from . . . our sphere of influence'. For, whatever might become of the Portuguese, at least the Germans had conceded Britain's contingent rights to take over Delagoa Bay and, in doing so, had, in effect, abandoned 'all concern in Transvaal matters'. And by the way of confirming this happy conclusion, the German Ambassador now informed the Foreign Office that his Government had warned Kruger not to expect any help from Germany if he became involved in war with Britain, which news Chamberlain was to comment made 'very nice reading'.

But, apart from implicitly removing a German menace which had always been more convenient than real to the advocates of a forward British policy in South Africa, the new treaty was soon to become a dead letter. Portugal declined to fall into the trap set for her by Britain and Germany. Despite the efforts of the two powers to see to it that she should only borrow money from them, she succeeded within two months in raising the necessary loans in Paris, where the French Government, smarting bitterly under the recent humiliation of having to withdraw Marchand from Fashoda, were only too delighted to seize an opportunity to spoil Britain's designs elsewhere.

For the last time, a British attempt to get control of Delagoa

Bay had been foiled. And as the year 1898 drew to its close, it became apparent that Britain was no nearer to asserting her supremacy over the Boers by political and diplomatic pressures. Germany had abandoned the Transvaal to its fate, but Portugal would not let Britain into Mozambique. Rhodesia had proved to be no conceivable rival to the Rand. And the Uitlanders had utterly failed to topple Kruger or even to weaken his hold over the country. The Orange Free State had abandoned any pretence of neutrality and had joined the Transvaal in a military alliance. And in the Cape, a Bond-supported Ministry ruled over a population of which more than half had been driven by Rhodes and Chamberlain into bitter opposition to Britain's policy.

For all these reasons, Milner was undoubtedly correct when he said that only by war could Kruger be brought to his knees. Moreover, as he saw it, the time to strike was clearly fast approaching. Germany had no longer to be reckoned with as an antagonist; and in those other areas of Africa which had recently caused anxiety to Salisbury and Chamberlain, British interests were no longer at risk. West Africa had been partitioned in such a way as to confirm almost all of Britain's claims in the rich Niger valley, while satisfying the prestige-conscious French with a vast acreage of what Salisbury 'delighted in calling 'rather light soil'! And on the Nile, Fashoda had given Britain an even more important and conclusive victory by destroying for ever the French dream of a 'Niger-to-Nile' belt of French territory stretching across Africa from the Atlantic to the Red Sea. In short, the ground had been cleared for imperialism to take the offensive in South Africa. Nobody understood this better than Milner. But, because he also feared that, if left to themselves, the Cabinet would let this opportunity pass until a further crisis in some other part of the world should once again divert their attention away from South Africa, he now decided to return home to convey his views to Chamberlain in person.

It was for him a propitious move. For, although he was soon to find, as he feared, that the no-war policy still held sway among the older members of the Cabinet, he drew no small reassurance from the palpable evidence of Chamberlain's growing ascendancy over his colleagues and of his increasing popularity with a public growing ever more spellbound by the evangelical fervour with which this most forceful of politicians preached and practised his own special brand of Radical Imperialism. More important still, Milner discovered that he and his chief were at one as to strategy and tactics, and that between them there was complete agreement that Kruger should now be pushed to the extreme limit to concede reforms to the Uitlanders and to acknowledge British paramountcy by threat of war and, if that failed, by war itself. Thus, when Milner returned to the Cape in February 1899, it was with a feeling of confidence that, as he wrote to Selborne, 'If I can advance matters by my own actions, as I still hope I may be able to do, I believe that I shall have support when the time comes.'

In fact, matters had already been well 'advanced' during the High Commissioner's absence in London by an incident involving a British working-man named Tom Edgar who, in the month of December, was shot dead by a Transvaal policeman when resisting arrest for brawling in the streets of Johannesburg. The South African League lost no time in seizing on this affray to mount a furious campaign against the Republican authorities. Protest meetings were held both in the Cape and in the Transvaal and, on the Rand, signatures were collected for a petition seeking the protection of the Imperial Government for the Uitlander community. In reply, far from seeking to calm things down, the Transvaal Government elected to pour petrol on the flames by arresting the organisers of the petition and by inciting gangs of rowdies to break up the League's meetings. Worse still, certain Dutch language journals demanded that all demonstrators should be shot out of hand.

By so doing, the Transvaalers only helped the imperialists' cause. In vain Schreiner protested to the Colonial Office that the League were trying to 'foment and excite ill-will between the two principal European races' and argued that patience was needed to bring Kruger to accept reform. Equally unavailing were the efforts of General Butler, the British forces commander acting as High Commissioner in Milner's absence, to defuse the situation by pigeon-holing the Uitlander petition on the 'technical' grounds that, having been made public before it was presented, it could not be officially recognised. The League merely trebled the number of its demonstrations and bayed all the louder for Britain to assert her authority to protect her subjects against their 'oppressors'. For the jingoes knew well that, however much Schreiner or Butler might try to damp down the fires of racial enmity which they had kindled, Milner was on the side of the League. And it was Milner's influence which would carry weight where it mattered most. Because Butler, a self-educated Irish Catholic with nationalist leanings, who was more at home writing adventure stories for boys than governing irascible British colonists, had opposed the policy of working up to a crisis, Milner made no secret of his disdain for what he called 'this worn-out Lieutenant-General'. On returning to the Cape, he seized on his deputy's handling of the League's petition to demand his recall. And when this was refused by Whitehall, he made life so intolerable for this conciliatory spirit that Butler was driven to resign a few months later. Milner would also have dearly liked to dismiss Schreiner who, as he later told Chamberlain, he feared would try to 'hamper' him in the event of war by refusing the use of the Colony's troops. But for this he had to wait a little longer to work his will and Schreiner managed to hold onto office until, some eight months after hostilities began, he was driven to resign, paradoxically over the Imperial Government's decision to disenfranchise those Cape Dutch who sided with their brothers in the Republics in the war against Britain.

Meanwhile Chamberlain required little prompting from the Cape to realise how easily the passions aroused by the Edgar incident could be exploited. Seizing his opportunity, he immediately took steps to associate the Imperial Government with Uitlander sentiment and, more particularly, with the capitalists of the Rand. In February 1899 he fired at the Transvaal Government a vigorous protest against the iniquities of the dynamite monopoly which had for some time constituted the mining industry's principal grievance. For as Chamberlain well knew, by picking on this legitimate complaint

389

of abuse as being 'inconsistent' with the terms of the London Convention, not only would he align himself with the most powerful element of the Uitlander community, the mine-owners; he would also draw his Cabinet colleagues a stage further down the slippery slope of intervention in the internal affairs of Kruger's Republic.

Needless to say, this significant move met with an immediate and resolute rebuff in Pretoria. For as Kruger saw it, by attacking the dynamite monopoly, Chamberlain and the mine-owners were asking the Transvaal Government to surrender control over the means whereby the Republic manufactured its armaments. And to Kruger, there was no area of the Transvaal's affairs more sensitive than this. Kruger contended that 'at the time of the Raid, the Republic was practically defenceless. The burghers had none but Martini-Henry rifles and many did not possess a rifle at all. There was not sufficient ammunition to wage war for a fortnight'. Yet by the law of the land every burgher was bound to be armed. Hence the determined efforts by Leyds following the Jameson Raid to purchase arms from Europe. Hence too Pretoria's vehement reaction when Chamberlain decided to join in the mine-owners' campaign to break up the dynamite monopoly.

All the same, Kruger was reluctant to kick the ball out, of play by merely rejecting Britain's demands for the cancellation of the dynamite concession. He knew that a purely negative response was exactly what Chamberlain and Milner wanted to enable them to step up the pressures on the Transvaal. The acting British Agent had only recently warned Jan Smuts, the new State Attorney, that Britain was getting tired of Pretoria's efforts to play an independent role and had decided to show that 'England was master in South Africa'. Besides, the Republic was currently in need of a loan; and with the European powers growing cooler with each succeeding month, according to Leyds' reports from abroad, the Rand 'capitalists' offered the most likely alternative source for borrowing money. Kruger, therefore, devised the idea of making a deal directly with the capitalists which would sweeten relations with his putative creditors, while at the same time keeping the Imperial Government out of the negotiations. With this end in view, Lippert was deputed to offer a number of concessions to the mining companies which, without touching the dynamite monopoly, went some way to meet their grievances and those of the Uitlander community as a whole. These concessions included the appointment of a financial adviser to the Government, whom Leyds was to recruit from Europe and whose task it would be to examine the system of taxation, to reorganise the Republic's finances and to ensure that proper control was kept of government expenditure. Also included was an offer to seek Volksraad sanction to reduce the franchise qualification for the Uitlanders to five years.

As an opening bid, this was a great advance on anything that the Transvaal Government had previously shown willing to concede. Had the matter been left to the capitalists to decide on their own, a settlement might well have emerged from these negotiations which would have satisfied at least the bulk of the Uitlander population. But, if only because they had been asked as part of the deal tacitly to accept the continuation of the dynamite monopoly against which the Imperial Government had weighed in on their behalf, the capitalists felt obliged to consult Whitehall and Cape Town. Needless to say, in both places they were warned most severely against accepting Lippert's terms, even as a basis for further negotiations. Milner voiced the gravest suspicion of the franchise offer which, he claimed, was far too vague and indefinite to be of any real value and Chamberlain advised that the capitalists should beware of being drawn into a fool's bargain. This, he contended, would only put them at odds with their fellow Uitlanders, who would not cease their agitation until a full and proper political settlement had been conceded to them.

Nevertheless the capitalists persisted in thinking that the Transvaal's new offer showed that Kruger's policy might be softening slightly under the more conciliatory influences of Smuts and Reitz. Reitz, who had recently succeeded Leyds— now appointed as Pretoria's roving ambassador in Europe—as State Secretary, had mellowed considerably since the day, ten years before, when as President of the Free State he had reversed

Brand's policy of standing in with the Cape. Smuts, too, had yet to become one of the firebrands who were to inspire the Boers to challenge the might of the British Empire for nearly three years of conflict. In fact this brilliant prodigy of Cambridge University had until very recently been a fervent admirer of Rhodes and an enthusiastic believer in Briton and Boer combining to create a new Afrikaner nation in which neither would seek to dominate and both would work for the enrichment of South Africa. Following the Jameson Raid, he had become so disillusioned with his hero that he had left his native Cape Colony to take office in the Transvaal as Kruger's State Attorney at the age of twenty-eight. But he had not yet abandoned hope of a reconciliation between the two European races in South Africa. Like Reitz, he recognised that there was much that needed reforming in the Transvaal and among the Uitlander community these two men were known to be working on Kruger to move with the times.

For these reasons the capitalists were inclined to pursue their talks with Lippert and to ignore the jaundiced advice of the Colonial Secretary and his High Commissioner. But any hopes that further discussions might lead to a settlement were soon to be disappointed. For one thing, Chamberlain chose this moment to inject into his reply to a Parliamentary debate on colonial affairs a repetition of his old accusation that Kruger had persistently gone back on all his promises to the Uitlanders, which was inevitably taken in Pretoria to mean that Britain wanted to kill the negotiations. For another, one of the capitalist representatives, Sir Percy Fitzpatrick—later to find more fame as an author than as a Randlord—decided that the time had come to break up the talks. And, after a dispute had arisen with the Transvaal delegates over the interpretation of certain statements made in the discussions, he took it upon himself to publish the secret correspondence exchanged between the two sides. Then to heap still more fuel on the fires of conflict, the policeman who had shot Edgar was not only acquitted of manslaughter by a Transvaal jury, but was warmly commended by the judge for the manner in which he had done his duty.

This was hardly the time for such foolishly provocative

gestures by either side. Immediately the South African League plunged into the fray. A further Uitlander petition was organised, with more than 21,000 signatures, protesting against the deprivation of political rights, the lack of English educational facilities, the unnecessarily high taxation and the hostility of the police. The Transvaal Government responded with a counter-petition signed by 23,000 Uitlanders who declared that they were satisfied with the administration of the country. And as feeling again ran high, the capitalist negotiations collapsed in acrimony and disarray.

With the Imperial Government committed by the 'dynamite despatch' to direct intervention in the internal affairs of the Transvaal, Milner now stepped in to assume command of all the forces both on the Rand and elsewhere in South Africa that were to be mobilised against Kruger's Republic. Writing to Conynghame-Greene in Pretoria, he said that the Uitlanders were proving useful adjuncts in the struggle for British supremacy, but that they must be kept up to the mark. As pawns on his chess-board they had been 'admirably played so far', but for the game to be won required continued 'persistence . . . (and) pegging away' on their part. He acknowledged that the Uitlanders would not be prepared to risk an 'open policy of unrest' unless they felt assured that the British Government would intervene on their behalf. Admittedly Whitehall had so far been 'slow to move', but he hoped that this would soon be changed. Certainly he would spare no effort to speed things up.

Chamberlain was, of course, every bit as eager as his High Commissioner to force the issue with the Transvaal. But, although Egypt and West Africa no longer presented any grave problems, pressures within the Cabinet and Parliament were still obliging him to hasten slowly. Milner might demand that the latest Uitlander petition be used as a pretext to force Kruger to accept British 'mediation between the Transvaal Government and its discontented subjects'. But Milner had also expressed the view that Kruger would rather go to war than submit to Britain's demands. Besides, Parliament and the public knew little about the Uitlanders and Chamberlain was loath to send an ultimatum to Pretoria, until he could be certain that his Cabinet colleagues were ready to go to war to enforce it. At the same time, he felt that he could not ignore the petitioners because of the damage which British influence in South Africa would suffer if the Uitlanders, feeling abandoned by Britain, should declare for a Republic of their own outside the imperial fold. For should this happen, he feared that the Cape and Natal might well follow suit.

Faced with this dilemma, Chamberlain decided that the time had come to arouse public opinion in Britain to demand a confrontation with Kruger's Republic. His reply to the Uitlanders' petition was carefully worded to avoid any suggestion of an ultimatum, while at the same time making it clear to the Transvaal Government that Britain could not 'permanently ignore the exceptional and arbitrary treatment of her countrymen'. But, having thus put himself on record as a rational and moderate statesman seeking to uphold the rights of British subjects in an alien land, he proceeded to invite Milner to paint, for the same record and for early publication, a picture in the most lurid tones of the plight of the British Uitlanders under Boer repression. 'Mr. Chamberlain', Selborne cabled to Cape Town at the end of April, 'wishes you to send fully your views expressed as frankly as you consider it to be possible or advisable.'

Milner needed not to be told what purpose lay behind this request. He had all too often been told by Chamberlain that, much as he would like to step up pressure on the Boers, the British public were not yet ready to face the possible consequences. Realising what was now expected of him, in the words of Chamberlain's biographer, he therefore 'let himself go'. All his journalistic training was brought into play in the concoction of his response. In much the same vein as Hitler was to use forty years afterwards to justify his claims on the Sudetenland of Czechoslovakia, Milner contrasted what he termed the 'perfect equality for Dutch and British in the British Colonies' of South Africa with the 'permanent subjection of British to Dutch in one of the Republics'. Britain's influence, he claimed, was being steadily undermined by the 'spectacle of thousands of British subjects kept permanently in the position of helots'. Citing two Transvaal newspapers—which the British Agent's office in Pretoria had only recently told him were only 'little known and less read'—he suggested that an organised press campaign of 'malignant lies' was being pursued against the British Government. And he added that, 'A certain section of the press, not in the Transvaal only, preaches openly and constantly the doctrine of a Republic embracing all South Africa and supports it by menacing references to the armaments of the Transvaal, its alliance with the Orange Free State and the active sympathy which, in case of war, it would receive from a section of Her Majesty's subjects' in Cape Colony. In such a situation, he concluded, 'it is idle to talk of peace and unity. . . . The case for intervention is overwhelming.'

Milner's 'helot' despatch, as it came to be called, reached Chamberlain's office on May 5, where it was immediately welcomed as exactly fitting the requirements of the case to be made against the Transvaal. But within a few days of delivering himself of the Olympian judgement that the case for intervention was no longer arguable, Milner was obliged to apply the brake to his own war-chariot and to agree, albeit purely as a tactical device, that one more effort be made to 'get into negotiations' with Kruger's Republic. For, even as the 'helot' despatch was on its way to London, Schreiner decided to make a last-minute effort to preserve the peace by appealing to Kruger to grant a more liberal franchise and to meet the British High Commissioner to discuss outstanding issues.

Milner was, of course, greatly put out to learn of the Cape Premier's initiative. But short of exposing himself as an outright war-monger, there was nothing that he could do to prevent it. Accordingly de Villiers set off for Pretoria as Schreiner's emissary and, after several meetings with Smuts and Reitz, persuaded Kruger's Ministers to recommend to their President that a conference with the High Commissioner should be held, on condition that the British demands were presented from the outset in full and final form, so that Milner would not be able to raise a fresh claim as soon as the previous one had been conceded. It was also agreed that, if Kruger

395

could be persuaded to attend such a conference, the venue should be neither Pretoria nor Cape Town, but rather the more 'neutral' ground of Bloemfontein. Hofmeyr then followed up Schreiner's initiative with a request to President Steyn to act as host and chairman of the proposed meeting, coupled with a sombre warning to Kruger not to pass up this opportunity to preserve peace in South Africa, which might well be the last that would come his way. For Schreiner's political position in the Cape was, he claimed, hanging by the merest thread, and he might at any moment be forced out of office, in which case Rhodes would probably take his place.

Thus, just as Milner had decided that all that now remained to be done was to prepare British public opinion for 'intervention' in the Transvaal, both he and Chamberlain found themselves faced with the unpalatable alternatives of agreeing to a conference with Kruger or of outraging those elements of public opinion at home and in the Cape which their tactics required should be humoured up to the last minute. The furthest that Milner could go in seeking to thwart Schreiner's peace move was to suggest that Pretoria should be the venue rather than Bloemfontein, where the presence of Steyn would, he thought, be an awkward additional hindrance. But even this attempt had to be abandoned, when Steyn forestalled him by issuing an invitation to the two protagonists to meet with him at Bloemfontein, which was promptly accepted by Kruger.

With no option but to agree to the proposed encounter, Chamberlain was obliged to postpone for the time being his campaign to arouse public opinion. Publication of the 'helot' despatch was put off: even the delivery of his judicious reply to the Uitlanders' petition was deferred. Milner might fume that the idea of a conference at this stage was 'a very clever move of mollifying the British press ... and relaxing for the moment, unfortunately, as I think, the screw upon the enemy. . . . A good stroke which spoils, or at least delays, a great stroke on our part.' Chamberlain too might 'regret the proposal as placing us in some difficulty', if only because an important section of public opinion expected the Government to make every effort to avoid a breach with the Transvaal. But, as both men well knew, however determined they were to wreck any negotiations with what Milner now habitually termed 'the enemy', they had at least to go through the motions of a conference with Kruger, if only to prepare the ground for the 'great stroke' with which they planned to smite him at the earliest contrivable opportunity.

20 Breakdown at Bloemfontein

IF on the British side there had been at this point a real desire for a peaceful settlement, now was the time to grasp the opportunity. But as the telegrams between Cape Town and the Colonial Office showed all too clearly, it was not settlement but stage-setting which interested the Imperial Government. Nor were Chamberlain and Milner the only malignant influences at work in this direction. Natal's Governor, Sir Walter Hely-Hutchinson, weighed in with the assertion that a widespread and deep-rooted conspiracy existed among all the Dutch in South Africa, which was dedicated to the destruction of British supremacy. Needless to say, Rhodes too, although stripped of Government office, continued to exercise powerful pressure from Cape Town. Indeed, according to Merriman, Milner was 'to a great extent under the domination of Rhodes'.

This may well have been a somewhat exaggerated description of the relations between the High Commissioner and the leader of the Opposition in the Cape Parliament. Yet, in spite of Milner's aversion to Rhodes' peculiarly commercial attitude to politics, the fact remained that the aims of the two men were certainly complementary. As Merriman succinctly put it, 'a peaceful Transvaal would mean Rhodes effaced, and he knows it.' Besides, Rhodes was still striving to realise his dream of a Cape-to-Cairo railway and telegraph and, to this end, had visited Germany two months earlier to solicit the Kaiser's agreement to transit rights through Tanganyika.

Quite apart from the resentment which he felt over Kruger's recent triumph at his expense, he was convinced that his plans required that Britain should assert her supremacy over the Boer Republics, rather than negotiate a settlement with them. In short, therefore, as the Radical M.P., Philip Stanhope, contended soon after the Boer War began, Chamberlain, Milner and Rhodes had between them decided that 'war, and war only could be the termination of this crisis and . . . worked with that conviction for the last twelve or fourteen months'.

Certainly, Chamberlain's 'instructions' to Milner for handling the Bloemfontein conference showed quite clearly that he regarded the meeting with Kruger purely as an exercise in setting the stage for war and that he had no intention of coming to terms with the Transvaal. In the first place, although he knew full well that Milner's intention was to force a war, he gave his High Commissioner a virtually free hand. His only specific suggestion was that the thorniest question of all, the franchise, should be raised at the very outset. And he then went on to say that, if no agreement were reached on this issue, there would be no point in continuing the negotiations. 'You should lay all the stress on the question of the franchise in the first instance', he cabled. '. . . If fair terms on the franchise are refused by the President, it appears hardly worth while to bring forward other matters, such as aliens, coloured people, education, dynamite, etc., at the Conference, and the whole situation must be reconsidered'. In fact, Chamberlain's only concession to diplomacy was to propose that, if immediate reform of the franchise were to be refused, Kruger might be asked to grant Home Rule for Johannesburg. And while he suggested that it might be politic to comply with Schreiner's wish to attend the conference, he did not argue the toss when Milner refused to do so on the grounds that he would only be hampered by the presence of what he regarded as an agent of the Cape Dutch.

Thus the Bloemfontein Conference, which opened on May 31 and ended five days later, was doomed even before it started. With the best will in the world it would have been no easy task for two such opposites as Kruger and Milner to reach an understanding at this, their first and last encounter. If Rhodes and

399

Kruger had little in common, save a love of the South African veldt, the contrast was even greater between the slow, ponderous manner of the stubborn and suspicious old Boer, who epitomised the pastoral oligarchy over which he presided, and the cold, quick and razor-sharp intellect of the 'finest flower' of Oxford, representing all the modern might of Britain and her Empire. But apart from the difference in age, temperament and intellectual capacity, the two protagonists were separated by a gulf of mutual mistrust. Milner had convinced himself that Kruger would never concede reform. Kruger knew that Milner was working for a breach and had no intention whatever of allowing diplomacy to function. And when, on top of all this, Milner insisted on publishing a verbatim account of the discussions, any chance that they might try to understand one another across the table, instead of merely speaking for the public record, vanished immediately.

As instructed by Chamberlain, Milner opened the Conference with a demand for a reduction in the residence qualification for the franchise to five years, to be applied retrospectively, together with an increase of seven seats in the parliamentary representation of the Rand. Kruger immediately asked what concession he might expect in return, explaining that the Volksraad could not be persuaded to grant such far-reaching reforms without some quid pro quo. They would, for instance, want to see Swaziland formally incorporated into the South African Republic: they would also expect reparation for the Jameson Raid and some agreement on the machinery of arbitration for the settlement of any future disputes between the Transvaal and Britain. But Milner curtly dismissed any idea of what he called a 'Kaffir bargain'. The Uitlanders' claims for the franchise were valid and just, he maintained, and they must be conceded on their own merits and not as part of a package deal involving irrelevant issues.

To this Kruger retorted that what Milner was proposing for the franchise was no less than another form of annexation. If his demands were conceded, the Uitlanders would soon get a majority of the seats in the Volksraad and would then be able to take over the Republic. Nevertheless, on the third day of the conference, he put forward a counter-proposal in the shape of what Milner termed 'a complete Reform Bill'. Those Uitlanders who had settled in the Transvaal before 1890 would, he suggested, after two more years be entitled to vote for the Volksraad, although not for the election of the President or Commandant-General; those who had come later and had been resident for two years would get the vote after a further five; and for the future, the qualification would be seven years residence. Added to this, Kruger offered to drop the existing requirement that aliens should renounce their former citizenship on becoming naturalised and he suggested that there should be five new seats in the Volksraad to ensure adequate representation for Johannesburg and the Rand.

In return for these reforms, Kruger expressed the hope that an agreement could be reached at least on a system of arbitration which would include a neutral umpire. For, as he saw the problem, if he were to concede such an increase in the political power of the Uitlanders, there should be a counter-balancing dilution of the powers of the Imperial Government to interfere in the affairs of the Transvaal. Chamberlain and Milner had made it all too clear that they still regarded the 'suzerainty' provisions of the Pretoria Convention as valid and in no way superseded by the later London Convention. And without some third party representation on whatever tribunal might be set up to arbitrate on differences between Britain and the Transvaal, Kruger felt that to give political power to the Uitlanders would be to surrender the Republic's destiny to the whim of Whitehall.

Even Milner was forced to admit that the President's franchise offer was a considerable advance on anything which had previously come out of Pretoria. With one stroke of his pen, Kruger had halved the residential qualification for the vote. Contrary to a life-long belief that political power should be exercised solely by those who owned a stake in the soil, he had conceded that a foreign community, whose property consisted of such disposable assets as mining shares rather than land, should obtain a foot in the door to what could all too soon become a dominating position in the Parliament of his beloved

Republic. But, instead of taking this offer at least as a basis for further negotiation, Milner coldly rejected any idea of arbitration with a foreign referee and continued to press his own demand for a five year franchise qualification. Then, when this was refused, he switched to Chamberlain's alternative of Home Rule for the Rand.

Coming from such a source, Kruger could not refrain from regarding this proposition as a piece of astonishing effrontery, reflecting that 'it was the very question of Home Rule in Ireland which caused Chamberlain to withdraw from Gladstone's party and barter his Radicalism for his present Jingoism'. But apart from the irony of the situation, he saw something deeply sinister in Milner's absolute refusal to negotiate on any point, or even to discuss other issues on his agenda, unless his demands for the franchise were conceded in full. This could only mean that the Imperial Government's aim was to 'cause the negotiations to fail'. And as the conference staggered towards its inevitable collapse, Kruger, almost in tears, was constrained to utter the despairing but discerning cry, 'It is our country you want'.

At this point, Chamberlain, having heard from Bloemfontein that the negotiations were 'likely to fail', cabled to Milner suggesting that he should 'not break off hastily' and reminding him that it was 'of the utmost importance to put the President of the South African Republic clearly in the wrong'. He also suggested as a possible basis for discussion that, if Kruger would concede a five-year franchise, he should in return be offered a formal guarantee of Transvaal independence, plus an arbitration body which would consist of the Judicial Committee of the Privy Council, with the additional participation of leading Afrikaners such as de Villiers.

Whether or not such an offer would have served to keep the conference alive—and it is hardly likely that it would—the issue was never put to the test. For on the day before Chamberlain's telegram reached Bloemfontein, Milner decided to break off the negotiations. On June 5, having cabled to London regretting that his 'studiously conciliatory' attitude had failed to secure agreement, he proclaimed to Kruger and Steyn, 'This conference is absolutely at an end, and there is no obligation on either side arising out of it'.

Nine days later, in a long letter to his chief summing up the results of the Bloemfontein encounter, Milner admitted that he had been wrong to break up the conference quite so quickly. But he explained that, having established 'a clearish issue', he had felt it inadvisable to allow the discussions to drag on and the issue to become blurred. With a candour extraordinary even for this blunt-spoken pro-consul, he contended that 'if we went on and on, as the other party seemed inclined to do, we might get a little more and a little more, each new concession being made to appear very big, and finally feel unable after so many concessions to break off. . . .' Equally astonishingly, he went on to say—in a vein reminiscent of Rhodes before the Jameson Raid—that British South Africa was united as never before under his leadership, that the Cape Dutch were wavering in their attitude towards their Transvaal brothers, that Schreiner was pressing Kruger to go to the limit in conceding reform, and that, if it should come to war, the Orange Free State would be lukewarm in its support for the South African Republic.

Armed with this euphoric report from his representative on the spot and with the 'evidence'—published as a Blue Book—of Kruger's intractability at Bloemfontein in face of Milner's 'studiously conciliatory' attitude, Chamberlain now sought and obtained the Cabinet's approval in principle for an ultimatum to Pretoria demanding the repeal of all legislation passed since 1884 restricting the rights of aliens in the Transvaal. But before this demand could be sent on its way, Kruger made the shrewd move of asking the Volksraad to approve a Bill giving effect to his own Bloemfontein proposals for a seven-year franchise.

Thus, towards the end of June, the Transvaal President could fairly claim to have taken unilaterally a major step towards enfranchising the Uitlanders and without insisting on prior agreement about arbitration, Swaziland or any other contentious issue. Certainly the Cape Government made it clear enough that they regarded the Bill 'as adequate, satisfactory and such as should secure a peaceful settlement'. Yet, in total disregard of Kruger's gesture, Chamberlain now elected to publish Milner's 'helot' despatch with all its vilification of the Transvaal Boers as tyrants and oppressors and its open demand for British aggression, euphemistically termed 'intervention'. And Milner, as the self-styled leader and rallier of 'loyal South Africa', prompted the South African League to stage a new series of demonstrations on the Rand and elsewhere, protesting against the Transvaal's treatment of the Uitlanders and denouncing all who did not echo their war-cries as 'disloyal'.

If after Bloemfontein there had been—as the High Commissioner claimed—any 'wavering' among the Cape Dutch, there was certainly none now. Immediately a wave of indignation swept through the Afrikaner community. But neither Chamberlain nor Milner were taken aback by this. On the contrary, they were far too excited by the effect which publication of the 'helot' despatch had had upon opinion in Britain to care about Cape Dutch reactions. Milner received word from the editor of *The Times* that public opinion had 'veered round in favour of you and your policy' and Chamberlain hastened to inform him that, if war should now come, 'the Government could rely upon the vast majority of its own supporters and a minority of the opposition'. Then with a candour matching that of Milner's own most blatant utterances, the Colonial Secretary went on to say, 'I believe that, to some extent, we have been able to show that the question at issue is greater than any particular grievance or special act of oppression and that, if we have to go further, it will not be for the franchise, or Edgar or dynamite, but for the maintenance of our position in South Africa. . . .' The only snag seemed to be that, according to newspaper reports, Kruger was making further concessions, for 'if these are really substantial, it will be practically impossible for us to find a casus belli in minor differences'.

No longer was there the smallest pretence that the 'question at issue' was the political emancipation of the Uitlanders. It was British supremacy over South Africa which was at stake. Nothing else mattered. Kruger might offer a concession here, a reform there. But his very existence as the symbol of Boer independence and as the leader of the richest and most influential state in South Africa was intolerable, because it effectively made nonsense of Britain's claim to paramountcy over the Boer Republics. Kruger must therefore be pushed beyond the limit; and to contrive a casus belli acceptable to British opinion, the terms would have to be raised whenever he made any concession until he was faced with the alternative of abject surrender or total war.

Milner required no encouragement to raise his terms. In fact, he had already decided to answer Kruger's latest concession with a demand that the Transvaal Government should in future submit any franchise legislation to him as the Imperial Government's representative before presenting it to the Volksraad. To put this proposition to Pretoria he selected as his intermediary an Orange Free State politician and a close associate of President Steyn, named Abram Fischer. But, as it turned out, Fischer was not the kind of man to play stooge to the British High Commissioner. Besides, he was under no illusions that Milner's aim was to force the Boers to accept British paramountcy. Far from being prepared to help in provoking a casus belli for Britain, he conceived as the purpose of his mission to Pretoria to secure reform and peace.

With this aim steadfastly in view, Fischer traipsed between Cape Town, Pretoria and Bloemfontein, consulting in turn Hofmeyr, Smuts and Steyn and ceaselessly urging Kruger and his Volksraad to press ahead with the seven-year franchise regardless of the provocations of London and Cape Town. In all this, he was constantly hampered by the interventions of Milner and Conynghame-Greene, who feared that the atmosphere of détente which Fischer was helping to create was 'demoralising' the Uitlanders and that, as had happened on the eve of the Jameson Raid, their resistance would rapidly evaporate if they were offered substantial reforms. Milner tried to prevent the passage of Kruger's franchise proposals through the Volksraad by insisting that the Imperial Government must be allowed time to consider them before they became law. To rush ahead with such complicated legislation would, he contended, only increase the risk of misunderstandings arising in the future between Britain and the Transvaal as to the interpretation of the law. Besides, he contended that it was in any case Britain's right as the paramount power to scrutinise legislation which affected her subjects abroad. Chamberlain also did his best to sabotage Fischer's peace efforts by ominously intoning in a speech to the Liberal Unionists of Birmingham, 'We have tried waiting . . . we can wait no more . . . we have reached a turning point'.

Nevertheless Fischer was able to win his point with Pretoria, thanks in no small way to some plain-spoken advice from Hofmeyr, who warned Kruger that in a war with Britain the Republic would be isolated and alone and that he and his Bondsmen would be powerless to give them any effective support. On July 19, therefore, the Volksraad placed Kruger's Reform Bill on the statute book. The residential qualification for the franchise was reduced from fourteen years to seven, Uitlanders were to be allowed to keep their citizenship after naturalisation and four new parliamentary constituencies were to be created for the Rand.

Milner now realised how seriously the Fischer mission had boomeranged on Chamberlain and himself. But, for the moment, he seemed quite unable to decide how to deal with Kruger's move which, by reforming the franchise without insisting on neutral arbitration, had met the objection which he had voiced at Bloemfontein. Having thus lost the initiative, he was left lamenting in his diary that British opinion was very likely 'going to be befooled' into inaction by these reforms. Chamberlain seemed equally nonplussed. Having been at pains to assure Salisbury and his colleagues that he was seeking reform by peaceful methods, he too was hard put to find a pretext to reject this Boer olive-branch.

Indeed, in an impulsive moment, he even told *The Times'* parliamentary correspondent that 'assuming the most recent telegrams from Pretoria to be true . . . the crisis in the relations between Great Britain and the Transvaal may be regarded as ended'. And to Milner he cabled that, although his Bloemfontein terms had not been met in full, it would not be possible to fight over a difference of two years between what he had demanded and Kruger had conceded. However, he added that he intended shortly to propose another conference, this time in Cape Town, which would probe the details of the new Volksraad statute in order to ensure that it in fact provided all that it pretended. He would also insist on settling the question of arbitration 'without any foreign element', together with other outstanding issues. Then, in a somewhat tortuous statement to the House of Commons, he sought to temper the optimism with which he had spoken to *The Times*. 'It would be easy', he now said, 'by subsequent legislation to alter the whole character of the concessions now made. But Her Majesty's Government feel assured that the President, having accepted the principle for which they have contended, will be prepared to reconsider any detail of his schemes which can be shown to be a possible hindrance to the full accomplishment of the object in view.'

Meanwhile Milner, fearing that Chamberlain's comment to *The Times* indicated that he was about to renege under pressure from colleagues acting 'from simple ignorance of the situation', had been frantically cabling to warn his chief against taking Kruger's reforms at their face value. The new law, he said, 'leaves it practically in the hands of the Government of the South African Republic to enfranchise or not enfranchise the Uitlanders as it chooses.' For this reason he proposed that, rather than engage in a further confrontation with Kruger, he should be authorised to demand the establishment of a Joint Enquiry consisting of British and Transvaal commissioners whose task it would be to examine the new franchise law and to determine how far it met the need for reform.

In fact, according to Chamberlain's biographer, Milner had no real cause for alarm. For the Colonial Secretary had no intention of taking the new reforms on trust and we are told that, 'it had never entered Chamberlain's head that anything but a bilateral settlement could be a guarantee'. Certainly, he was only too ready to agree with Milner's suggestion of a Joint Enquiry, if only as a means of keeping the Imperial Government's foot in the door and asserting British suzerainty. On July 27, he therefore put this demand to Pretoria in a despatch which gave little credit to the Volksraad's efforts to meet the Uitlanders' case and which reeked of suspicion that the Transvaalers were acting in bad faith. Rehearsing all the old accusations that the South African Republic had broken the

Conventions and had subjected the Uitlanders to a 'position of political inferiority', Chamberlain went on to suggest that under the new law the Transvaal Government might still 'take away with one hand what had been given with the other'. Therefore, he claimed, a Joint Enquiry into the operation of the franchise reforms was essential.

Having sent this high-handed demand on its way, the Colonial Secretary felt that the time had come to arouse jingo sentiment in support of his real aims in South Africa. On the very next day, in a speech to the House of Commons, he made it clear that the 'humiliating inferiority' of British subjects in the Transvaal called in question the far more important issue of British paramountcy. The difference between Britain and Kruger was not, he said, a mere quibble about a seven-or a five-year franchise; and Pretoria had to understand that, 'the great mass of the people of this country are prepared to support us, if the necessity should arise, in any measures we may think necessary to take to secure justice to the British subjects in the Transvaal'. In the House of Lords, Salisbury too spoke with unaccustomed belligerence, saying that the English in the Transvaal had been reduced 'to the condition almost of a conquered, certainly of a subjugated, race'.

The purport of all this menacing language was not lost on the leaders of Afrikaner opinion in the Cape. Hofmeyr, Schreiner and de Villiers knew all too well that Chamberlain and Milner, embarrassed by Kruger's gesture, were trying by every means to provoke him into withdrawing it and so to 'put him in the wrong'. Accordingly, they used all their influence to urge the President to accept the British demand for a Joint Enquiry and not to spoil the chance of a settlement for a mere matter of form. De Villiers even suggested that the Joint Enquiry should be treated as an 'olive-branch'.

It was obviously no easy task to persuade Kruger to play his hand in this way. His immediate reaction, endorsed by his Executive Council, had been to draft a reply to London flatly rejecting the Joint Enquiry as prejudicial to the independence of the Republic. In answer to de Villiers' promptings, he maintained that all Britain's talk about the franchise was 'but a pretence' and that Chamberlain's real aim was to rob the Boers of their freedom. Britain, he said, did not want 'any franchise under a Republic' and her latest demand, like every other, was intended as an attack in the Transvaal's autonomy and as another assertion of British suzerainty over the Boers.

In this view he was upheld by his most influential friends and advisers in the two Republics. Steyn, for instance, agreed fully that to accept the Joint Enquiry would be 'equivalent to the destruction of our independence'. Smuts too advised rejection. Although opposed to risking a head-on collision with Britain, he firmly believed that Chamberlain was bluffing and that, in the final analysis, he would be overruled by the 'obstinate caution' of Salisbury, Balfour and others among his Cabinet colleagues.

Nevertheless, when it came to the point, Kruger not only hearkened to the advice of the Cape Dutch leaders; he exceeded their every expectation. Replying to Chamberlain's demand for a Joint Enquiry, he expressed the hope that this latest British proposal was not intended to encroach upon the autonomy of the Republic which had been guaranteed by the London Convention. With studied politeness he went on to say that, if the Imperial Government wished to seek clarification of the new franchise reforms, the Transvaal Government would be happy to answer any question they cared to put. Then, on the following day, August 13, Smuts called on Conynghame-Greene to put forward a counter-proposal on behalf of the South African Republic which was not short of amazing. If Britain would drop her insistence on suzerainty and her demand for a Joint Enquiry, Smuts said his Government would concede a five-year franchise to become law within a fortnight and to be applied retrospectively. In addition, there would be eight new seats for the Rand which would increase its representation to a total of ten out of a Volksraad of twenty-six and which would never be reduced; the new burghers would have equal rights in the election of the President and Commandant-General; arbitration machinery would be established with no foreign element; and the details of the franchise proposals would be discussed with the British Agent prior to becoming law.

It was all and more than Milner had demanded at Bloemfontein. Without prejudice to the independence of his own country, Kruger was now conceding all that had been asked of him on the franchise, on arbitration and on consultation with Britain and he was offering more seats for the Rand than Milner had in fact requested. Even Chamberlain was forced to admit that the Boers had made 'an immense concession' which was 'a considerable advance' on Britain's own proposals. In fact, so total was this sudden act of compliance with the Imperial Government's demands that one wonders whether Kruger was not indulging in a piece of gamesmanship designed to put him in the right, in the certain knowledge that, whatever he conceded short of outright capitulation to British suzerainty, Chamberlain and Milner would find some way to rebuff him and that he would therefore never be called upon to fulfil so far-reaching an undertaking to the Uitlanders.

But whether this was his purpose or whether Kruger was at this point so anxious to get Chamberlain off his back that he was genuinely prepared to go to such lengths to gain a respite from British pressures, Milner reacted predictably in reporting the new proposals to London with the utmost scepticism. Dismissing this 'immense concession' as merely showing 'a superficial conformity to my Bloemfontein suggestions', he concentrated on the fact that the Boers were insisting that suzerainty and the Joint Enquiry be dropped. This, he insisted, could only mean that they were determined to deny 'our claim to have a voice in their affairs as the Paramount Power in South Africa'. Britain was 'not fighting for a five-year franchise retrospective, but a principle'. What mattered was not what Kruger had now conceded to the Uitlanders, but the fact that he was resisting British paramountcy. And in the High Commissioner's judgement, such resistance called for an ultimatum to be issued from London and supported by troop movements to the borders of the two Republics.

Milner also advocated a demand for the immediate disarmament of the Transvaal. For the past month he had become obsessed by reports that the Boer Republics were arming themselves and he had written to Chamberlain in the middle of July to say that there was a serious danger of the Cape and Natal being 'overshadowed by the South African Republic as a military power'. Since the collapse of the Bloemfontein Conference, Kruger and Steyn had indeed greatly stepped up their imports of arms from Germany. To Milner's disgust, the Schreiner Government were also permitting ammunition to the tune of a million Mauser cartridges a month, together with other armaments, to pass through the Cape ports en route for the Transvaal and Orange Free State. Likewise the Portuguese, still smarting from the humiliations inflicted on them by Rhodes in the early nineties, were readily allowing arms to be landed in Mozambique for onward transmission to the Pretoria arsenal and were turning a deaf ear to British remonstrances in Lisbon.

As a result of this rearmament effort, Milner estimated that the Republics could put 50,000 men into the field, not to mention the 40,000 Cape Dutch, who he now realised were no longer 'wavering' in their attitudes towards the Transvaal and would, in fact, constitute a serious menace in the event of war. Against this, apart from the colonial militia and territorial units, there were only some 9,000 British troops in South Africa. And the fact that the Cabinet had recently rejected the advice of Lord Wolseley, the Commander-in-Chief, that this number should be doubled, made it all the more imperative that the Boers should be required to disarm. He had tried to point out to Steyn the dangers of an arms race and to persuade him to intercede with Pretoria to stop it. But the Free State President had merely retorted that the recent British troop movements near the Republic's borders, which Milner had ordered, showed how necessary it was for the Boers to take every precaution to defend themselves. Besides, the law of the Free State and of the Transvaal required that every burgher should be armed.

Milner's considered advice was therefore that, whatever Kruger had now offered, the Imperial Government should continue to insist on the Joint Enquiry and should, in addition, demand the disarmament of the Transvaal. But this was too much even for Chamberlain. Although he commented that 'I dread above all the whittling away of differences until we have no casus belli left', he nevertheless felt that it would be unwise to 'snub the Boers at this stage'. Besides, Salisbury had minuted on Milner's recommendations that it looked as if he was 'spoiling for a fight'. And faced with an offer from the Boers which his own Colonial Secretary had admitted conceded more than anyone had asked of them, the Prime Minister decided that more than enough had been done for the Uitlanders. The 'subjugated' English of his recent outburst in the Lords now became, according to a letter from him to Lord Lansdowne at the War Office, 'people whom we despise' living in 'territory which will bring no profit and no power to England', but in whose name England had been committed to 'act upon a moral field prepared for us by Milner and his Jingo supporters'.

Instructions were therefore sent to Cape Town to seek official confirmation of the new proposals from the Transvaal Government so that they might be further examined in London. And Milner was told, pending such examination, to 'avoid any language which would lead the South African Republic to think that we are determined to pick a quarrel'. Conynghame-Greene duly passed on the request; and a week after his momentous meeting with Smuts, he was handed a memorandum setting out the new concessions in writing. The only difference between this version and what Smuts had offered by word of mouth was that the written proposals spelled out the fact that the new concessions were expressly conditional on Britain renouncing suzerainty and ceasing to interfere in the internal affairs of the Transvaal. Also, Smuts now informed the British Agent that there could be no improvement on these proposals and that Britain would have to accept or reject 'the terms stated as they stand'. But apart from this attempt to clarify matters beyond any possibility of misunderstanding, nothing had been either added to or subtracted from the proposal made verbally a week earlier. Provided the British would leave him alone, Kruger was still ready to concede all and more than had been asked on behalf of the Uitlanders.

Nevertheless Milner immediately seized on the Transvaal memorandum to claim that, by spelling out the conditions, Pretoria had vitiated the original Smuts offer and that what Pretoria was now asking constituted a moral ultimatum. Chamberlain promptly took up the cry, proclaiming with the voice of doom that this 'was the darkest date in the history of South Africa' and that Kruger 'had presented terms to which the British Government could not yield'. Then, on August 26, in a speech to a constituency garden party at his country home, he thundered that 'Mr. Kruger procrastinates in his replies. He dribbles out reforms like water from a squeezed sponge and he either accompanies his offers with conditions which he knows to be impossible, or he refuses to allow us to make a satisfactory investigation of the nature and the character of these reforms . . . . The issues of peace and war are in the hands of President Kruger . . . . Will he speak the necessary words? The sands are running down in the glass. . . .'

Not a word was said to acknowledge how Kruger had in fact offered better terms than had been demanded of him at Bloemfontein and was prepared to discuss the provisions of the new five-year franchise law with the Imperial Government's representative at Pretoria. The 'immense concession' of the previous fortnight was now ignored. All that counted with Chamberlain, as with Milner, was that Kruger had refused to allow a Joint Enquiry to become a precedent for British intervention in the Transvaal's internal affairs. And for this he was to be threatened with the wrath of Britain and the Empire.

Two days later, on August 28, the Colonial Secretary cabled his answer to Kruger's offer. It was an effective rejection of both of the required conditions. The Imperial Government hoped that 'the fulfilment of the promises made' would 'render unnecessary any further intervention', but they refused to give any undertaking in this respect. As to suzerainty, they rejected the Transvaal's claim to be a sovereign state and insisted that the suzerainty granted to Britain under the Pretoria Convention had never lapsed and was still valid. The only concession which Chamberlain was prepared to make was to drop the Joint Enquiry in favour of Kruger's proposal that the new reforms should be discussed with the British Agent before becoming the law. Apart from this, it was made plain that Britain expected the Transvaal to grant all that Smuts had offered unconditionally. Conynghame-Greene was also told that, when communicating this reply to the Transvaal Government, he should add a 'personal' warning that, if Kruger insisted on his conditions, the Imperial Government would in all probability issue an ultimatum and support it with the despatch of further troop reinforcements to South Africa.

Having despatched this menacing retort, Chamberlain set about persuading his Prime Minister that behind the apparent reasonableness of Kruger's promises lurked a sinister Afrikaner conspiracy designed to eliminate British paramountcy and to establish a union of South Africa under Boer leadership. As always reluctant to interfere with departmental Ministers—and particularly with the Colonial Secretary—except when their activities impinged on his foreign policy, Salisbury soon capitulated to the force of these arguments. On September 2, Chamberlain therefore gleefully informed Milner that he had arranged for an early Cabinet meeting to decide the terms of an ultimatum. He admitted that 'the technical casus belli is a very weak one' and that the existence of Schreiner's 'Afrikaner Government at the Cape' would raise awkward constitutional problems. But he drew comfort from the progress which he had made in indoctrinating public opinion. As a result, he said, 'the majority of the people have recognised that there is a greater issue than the franchise or the grievances of the Uitlanders at stake and that our supremacy in South Africa and our existence as a great Power in the world are involved . . . . Three months ago we could not—that is, we should not have been allowed to—go to war on this issue. Now we shall be sufficiently supported.'

Almost as an afterthought, however, Chamberlain concluded by saying that, due to the existing paucity of British forces in South Africa, the argument over Kruger's franchise proposals should be exhausted and a clear refusal obtained from Pretoria 'before we ask for more'. For 'if and when we ask for more, it means war'; and it was essential that, when war came, there should be sufficient imperial troops to hold the position while 'a full fighting force' was on its way to South Africa.

Thanks to the earlier hesitations of his colleagues, the military preparedness necessary to carry Chamberlain's policies into full fruition had in no way matched the political truculence of his dealings with the Transvaal Government. Repeatedly the Cabinet had agreed to his making exorbitant demands upon the Boers, but had declined to back him with adequate reinforcements. Consequently, the Boer commandos from the two Republics, although far from constituting the aggressive menace which Milner attributed to them, currently outnumbered the British Army in South Africa by nearly four to one and when the war began a month later, the Republican forces were still almost double the strength of their opponents. Indeed, such was the state of British military unreadiness that, after nine months of fighting, Milner's Military Secretary had to tell Schreiner that, at the forthcoming ceremony for the opening of the Cape Parliament, the traditional artillery salute would have to be dispensed with, since there were no guns available due to the exigencies of the war!

Thus, even as Chamberlain was able to rejoice that public opinion was now prepared to support a war to assert British supremacy in South Africa, he realised that he must still play for time. Before the final show-down could take place with Kruger's Republic, reinforcements must be sent to the Cape and Natal, lest the Boer commandos might overrun the British garrisons before help could reach them from outside.

21 War

ON the same day that Chamberlain had told Milner that the Cabinet were about to decide on the terms of an ultimatum to Pretoria, Kruger despatched his reply to the British demand that his offer of a five-year franchise should be unconditional. Taking Chamberlain's last despatch to mean that the Imperial Government had rejected his proposals, he announced that the five-year franchise was no longer on offer and reverted to his earlier proposal endorsed by the Volksraad for a seven-year qualification, plus four new seats for the Rand. At the same time, in an effort to keep negotiations going, he implied that, subject to further clarification, he might now be prepared to accept the Joint Enquiry.

This was a sad and serious mistake. Having conducted his case with consummate skill since the breakdown of the Bloemfontein Conference, Kruger had now played directly into Milner's hands. By revoking the five-year franchise and halving the offer of additional seats for the Rand, he gave Chamberlain and Milner a pretext to claim that he had not been negotiating in good faith. And by suggesting that he might now accept the Joint Enquiry, he raised hopes of an eventual surrender on his part to British paramountcy. To Chamberlain's way of thinking, Kruger had at last put himself 'in the wrong', while simultaneously suggesting that he might be weakening on the crucial issue of suzerainty.

Yet even now Milner was none too happy. Fearful lest the

416

General Joubert

Boer Commandos

Transvaalers should still force a compromise on a British Cabinet whose only resolute member, as he saw it, was Chamberlain, and more than ever resolved that the South African Republic should 'disappear from the map', he warned his chief that, even if they should 'climb down' at the last minute, 'the Pretoria gang' would end by 'cheating us' of the victory without which British paramountcy could not survive. But the Colonial Secretary needed no such prompting. Determined to lose no time in exploiting the advantage which Kruger's reply had given him, he told the Cabinet, 'What is now at stake is the position of Great Britain in South Africa . . . . Everyone, natives included, sees that issue has now been joined and that it depends upon the action of the British Government now whether the supremacy, which we have claimed so long and so seldom exerted, is to be finally established and recognised, or for ever abandoned'. The Government, he concluded, should now 'formulate its demands in a form to which a categorical yes or no may fairly be demanded'. War was now not only possible but inevitable and to prepare for it and guard against another Majuba humiliation, he insisted that 'the troops in South Africa should be largely reinforced'. A terrible responsibility would rest upon the Government, he concluded, 'if owing to want of proper preparation, reverses should be suffered by the British forces, or British Colonies should be invaded and British troops have to fall back'.

Not all the caution of Salisbury and Balfour could now stay Pushful Joe's hand. On September 8, the Cabinet were talked into agreeing to raise the number of regular British troops in South Africa to a total of 22,000 by reinforcing the garrison of Natal, the most vulnerable of the territories concerned, with units of the British Army in India. On the same day, the terms of Chamberlain's 'final offer' to the Transvaal were approved. This 'penultimatum', as it came to be called, began by repudiating the Republic's claim to be a sovereign international state and went on to reject as totally unacceptable Kruger's reversion to a seven-year franchise. Five years was the maximum which the Imperial Government could accept. In addition, the Rand should have a quarter of all the seats in the Volksraad and Uitlanders should be entitled to vote on equal terms for the election of the President and Commandant-General. Moreover, so as to ensure that all of these concessions were in fact secured, the Transvaal Government had to accept without equivocation a Joint Enquiry. But, if their answer to these demands were to be negative or inconclusive, the Imperial Government reserved the right to reconsider the situation de novo and to formulate their own proposals for a settlement.

Thus were the Boers told to surrender, without condition, compromise or compensation, to the requirements of British suzerainty. Chamberlain utterly refused to entertain the idea of substituting a seven-year franchise with a Joint Enquiry for a five-year franchise without one. He had manoeuvred his adversary into a corner by pocketing every concession he had offered, rejecting every condition he made, and then 'asking for more'. Well might Kruger fume before the Volksraad that, when the British had asked for his trousers, he had given them and, when they asked for his coat, he had given that too, but now they were asking for his life and he could give them no more. And while Pretoria's reply, which was handed to the British Agent on September 16, accepted the Joint Enquiry unequivocally, it made it equally clear that the subject of the enquiry was to be a seven- and not a five-year franchise.

At the same time, well knowing that the troop reinforcements announced from Whitehall a week earlier were intended to enforce Chamberlain's final settlement, the Transvaal Government began to prepare for war. In the last two weeks Smuts had come to realise that Britain was not bluffing after all and that a collision was now inevitable, if the Boers were not to become what he called 'wood-cutters and water-carriers for the hated race'. With the delivery of Chamberlain's 'penultimatum', he had suggested to Kruger that the Boers should seize the initiative by striking the first blow while the British reinforcements were still on their way from India. His plan was for the Republican forces to invade Natal and, with a lightning thrust, to capture Durban. In this way, they would gain the double advantage of securing their own supply route from the sea, while at the same time denying this landfall to their enemies and obliging them to disembark their forces at Cape ports several hundreds of miles further away from the scene of the fighting.

In the event General Joubert was to reject this daring scheme and, instead of seizing Durban after the initial surprise of the Boer attack had opened the way to the sea, wasted precious time in trying to reduce the beleagured British garrison at Ladysmith, which fatal blunder was to allow time for the British army to stem the Boer advance. But Smuts' general thesis that the Transvaal should seize the initiative was accepted by Kruger and the first steps were now taken towards general mobilisation of the Boer commandos.

In vain Schreiner and Hofmeyr appealed to both sides to avoid war. Kruger knew that it was too late. He had been told to expect an ultimatum which would force him to fight. And even though Schreiner steadfastly refused to be a party to Milner's policy of provocation and stoutly maintained his Government's neutrality, he had lost all influence in Pretoria. Kruger had responded to his earlier pleas to meet provocation with conciliation. But now he was cornered and would have to surrender or fight; and not even his most trusted friend could ask him to surrender.

Schreiner was equally powerless to restrain the High Commissioner. Never exactly the soul of tact and somewhat over-inclined to be cocksure of his own opinions, he had from the start been at loggerheads with Milner who, for his part, had made little secret of his disappointment that Rhodes and the imperialists had been defeated in the last elections by Schreiner's South African Party. More recently, the Cape Government's refusal to be manoeuvred or pressured into stopping the transit of arms to the Republics via Cape ports had deepened the gulf of bitterness and suspicion between the two men. In all the circumstances, it was hardly likely that Milner would respond other than negatively when Schreiner, on September 21, sent him on behalf of the Cape Government an official minute entreating that Britain should pause before plunging into war. 'Ministers', he said, 'unanimously beg Her Majesty's Government . . . to weigh well their earnest conviction that the situation is now one in which great efforts should be made by the exercise of a spirit of magnanimous compromise to avoid the calamity which seriously threatens not only the Republics, but the British possessions in South Africa. The issue of war could only be a victory for the Imperial arms. That matter is not open to doubt. But the evil consequences (affecting alike the European and native populations) of the perhaps prolonged struggle would be far-reaching and abiding for generations. . . . They are deeply persuaded that a large measure of consideration shown by Her Majesty's Government at this present juncture is the main, they fear the only, hope of avoiding such a calamity. . . .'

As a statement, or understatement, of the responsibility devolving on the Imperial Government for the critical impasse which had been reached, this declaration was as masterly as was its forecast of what would follow if the 'calamity' was not avoided. But Milner, totally ignoring its implications, replied that the 'spirit of magnanimous compromise' for which Schreiner was asking appeared to him to 'have been already exhibited by the Imperial Government in a remarkable degree' during the protracted exchanges with the Transvaal. Chamberlain, replying on his own behalf, similarly refused to accept any responsibility for the fact that South Africa was now poised on the brink of war. It was, he declared 'still open to the South African Republic' to secure a peaceful and satisfactory settlement. Her Majesty's Government appreciated the anxiety of Cape Ministers, but they had already shown all possible consideration in their dealings with Pretoria.

The Cape Government had made their last unavailing effort to prevent catastrophe. And Merriman could now only lament how unpleasant it was 'as an Englishman to see one's country playing the part of a bully'. Chamberlain's and Milner's actions, he said, had 'in a few months implanted in the breasts of a people so dogged and so resolute (as the Boers) an unextinguishable hatred of our country. A wilderness of gold mines will not repay us for that criminal blunder'. As a last desperate gesture fifty-eight out of a hundred and eleven members of the Cape Parliament petitioned Her Britannic Majesty praying for a peaceful settlement. But it was already too late for such entreaties to have any effect. For on September 22, the day after Schreiner penned his last desperate appeal to the Imperial Government, Milner received his anxiously awaited orders to break off negotiations with the Transvaal forthwith and to stand by for the promised British ultimatum.

With this final breach the Transvaal Government accelerated their plans to seize the military initiative. Commandos were assembled in small ward units where numbers, horses and supplies were checked before they were assembled into district commandos and moved to their appointed places on the Republic's frontiers. The womenfolk took over the running of the farms and virtually every male Boer between the ages of thirteen and eighty enrolled in the country's service. Together with the contributions of the Orange Free State, a total of 40,000 burghers were to answer the call to arms, supported by the Transvaal's mounted police force and a small, well-armed corps of artillery from each Republic.

As an essential corollary of his plan to get in the first blow, Kruger decided to anticipate the British ultimatum with one of his own. But when he consulted his Free State allies about the terms and timing of the Boer demands, he found that Steyn was none too happy about his intended tactics. In the first place, Steyn knew that the Free State, not having had occasion to call out its burghers since the days of the Basuto Wars, would take much longer to mobilise than the Transvaal. And since this would probably reduce the military advantage of a pre-emptive Boer offensive to a matter of a few days at most, it might be wiser to make a virtue of necessity and await the British ultimatum, which would make Britain the aggressor in the eyes of the world. In spite of Leyds' recent lack of success in drumming up European support, Steyn felt that the possibility of foreign intervention on behalf of the Boers should not be completely excluded. And unless the actual advantages of taking the initiative were a lot better than marginal, it would be advisable not to do anything which might put the Republics in the wrong and alienate European opinion.

Faced with these arguments, Kruger was obliged to postpone his proposed initiative, at least for a few days. Apart from the fact that his own mobilisation scheme had run into difficulties over problems of supplies, he felt that he could not altogether ignore his ally's views. Steyn had recently been under considerable pressure from Milner who was trying all he could to detach the Free Staters from the Transvaal. If war should come, the High Commissioner had told him, the Imperial Government would expect Bloemfontein to observe strict neutrality. But Steyn, firmly refusing to be browbeaten, had tartly replied that any breach of relations with Britain would not be the fault of the Boers. And even while his consultations with Kruger were proceeding, the Bloemfontein Volksraad had passed a resolution declaring that, although they saw no reason why peace should not be preserved, they would nevertheless honour their obligations to their Transvaal allies in the event of war. Therefore it was, as Kruger saw it, merely a matter of a few days before the two Republics would be in a position to act in concert. And as it turned out, within a week of their discussions ending, Steyn, urged on by Kruger to hesitate no longer, informed Milner that mobilisation of the Free Staters had begun in response to the continued concentrations of British troops along the Republic's frontiers.

Meanwhile, having told the Transvaal to expect a British ultimatum, Chamberlain had talked his colleagues into agreeing to the terms of his final settlement. These were to include the repeal of all Transvaal legislation since 1881 which prejudiced the Uitlander's political rights, together with guarantees for the independence of the judiciary, 'Home Rule' for the Rand, arbitration with no foreign element, 'surrender' of the right to import arms through Portuguese East Africa, and disarmament of the Republics. In return for this total capitulation by Kruger, Britain was to offer the Transvaal the status and the guarantees of a British Protectorate. As Chamberlain told Milner, the Imperial Government had decided to exact 'a complete surrender on the part of the Boers either by agreement or by war, else they would forfeit all rights to intervene in the Transvaal's affairs'.

All that now remained was to settle the precise timing of the ultimatum; and on this point Salisbury and Milner found themselves for once in full agreement. Having, albeit reluctantly, accepted that war was now 'the most probable alternative', the Prime Minister insisted that Chamberlain should 'do nothing to precipitate an attack until our reinforcements arrive'. Milner too accepted the need to delay further provocations until adequate forces were available to shoulder the consequences. There was, of course, a danger that the Boers might anyhow decide to attack before the reinforcements reached Durban. But this, he felt, was a risk that had to be taken and was no reason for Britain to invite a military reverse before she was ready.

Thus, with Kruger staying his hand while the Free Staters girded their loins, and with Chamberlain holding back his ultimatum until British reinforcements arrived, all South Africa held its breath and waited for the first shot to be fired in the war which had now become a certainty. September passed, October came and still neither side made any move. Conyng-hame-Greene informed Smuts that 'the only chance for the South African Republic was an immediate surrender to the Bloemfontein minimum'. Steyn had another exchange with Milner in which he suggested that, if Britain wanted a settlement, she should stop threatening the Republics and withdraw her troops. And Milner replied regretting that Steyn should require, as a condition of further negotiations, that Britain must surrender her right to deploy her troops on her own soil after Kruger had converted the Transvaal into an armed camp. But, apart from these exchanges and an ironical suggestion by Reitz to Conynghame-Greene that the Imperial Government should hurry up and issue their ultimatum, no communication passed between Pretoria and London for all of that tense first week of October. Poised on the edge of catastrophe, both parties seemed unable to speak, yet afraid to shoot at each other. As in a motion picture when the reel is stopped, the characters in the drama were frozen into immobility.

Then, on October 7, came the announcement that Britain was mobilising the army reservists and that an Army Corps would very shortly leave for South Africa. On the very next day the first of the British reinforcements from India disembarked at Durban; and with their arrival the reel was restarted, the actors

423

suddenly came back to life and motion. Chamberlain and Milner now busily made ready to deliver their ultimatum to Pretoria within the next forty-eight hours. But the Boers moved faster still. Kruger immediately contacted Steyn and obtained his agreement to deliver the Transvaal's ultimatum without waiting so much as another day. For although the delay over the past week or more had cost him much of his advantage, all was not yet lost. By no means all the British reinforcements had yet arrived; the burghers of the two Republics still outnumbered their adversaries; and Kruger considered it as essential as ever to seize the initiative and march on Natal while the British were still collecting themselves. The only reason, he said, why Britain had not already forced a war on the Boers was that she had not been ready 'to overwhelm the Republics from every side'. But this could be changed within a few months, possibly even weeks.

These arguments, reinforced by the news of British troop landings, finally convinced Steyn that to delay further would lead the Boers into a trap of their own making. And on October 9, with his full approval, the Transvaal's ultimatum was presented to the Imperial Government. The Note began by insisting that the Boers had scrupulously observed the terms of the London Convention, while Britain had persistently violated her obligations by interfering in the Transvaal's internal affairs and by threatening the Republic with troop concentrations on its borders. It went on to say that, since the Imperial Government had not yet vouchsafed the 'final solution' foreshadowed in the message with which they broke off negotiations, the South African Republic must ask for certain assurances to be given within the next forty-eight hours. These assurances were to include first that the British Government agreed that all outstanding issues should be settled by arbitration or other peaceful methods; second, that all British troops on the borders of the Republic should be instantly withdrawn; third, that Britain would remove within a reasonable time all reinforcements which had arrived in South Africa since June 1; and fourth, that those British troops still on the high seas would not be landed at any South African port. The ultimatum concluded by saying that, if by 5 p.m. on October 11 no satisfactory answer had been received to these demands, the South African Republic would consider itself to be at war with Great Britain.

The mouse had roared at the lion. Chamberlain, exclaiming 'They have done it!' as he read the Boers' demands, could not believe what his biographer called his 'almost unbelievable good fortune'. Thanks to Kruger's ultimatum, he would be able to answer his critics on the Opposition benches and win the support of the Liberal Imperialists by representing the Boers as claiming the right 'to sweep imperial influence' out of South Africa and summoning the Queen 'to reduce her exiguous garrisons to a derisory footing . . . and to accept in effect the domination of the Transvaal Republic over an extensive portion of her Empire'. Lansdowne, from the War Office, echoed his colleague's elation. 'Accept my felicitations', he wrote, 'I don't think Kruger could have played our cards better than he has. . . . My soldiers are in ecstasies'. In a few hours Chamberlain cabled to Milner instructing him to tell the Transvaal Government that their demands were 'such as Her Majesty's Government deem it impossible to discuss'. And on October 11, Conynghame-Green, having relayed this message to Kruger, asked for his passports.

Milner made a somewhat half-hearted last-minute attempt to detach the Free State from its alliance, enquiring whether, in the light of the Volksraad's recent reassertion of their obligations to the Transvaal, Steyn would support his ally 'whatever may happen'. Bloemfontein's answer was an unqualified yes. The Free State Government had endorsed the terms of the ultimatum and, come what might, they would honour their obligations. On a similar note of defiance Kruger told the *New York Herald*, 'The Republics are determined that, if they must belong to England, a price will have to be paid which will stagger humanity'. And on October 12, the Boers opened their account with Britain by striking simultaneously at Mafeking, Kimberley and Ladysmith. The second, and most terrible, South African War had begun.

In all modern history there can scarcely have been a more

unnecessary or more futile struggle than that which now engulfed South Africa and was to drag on for the next two and a half years. As they had shown at the time of the Jameson Raid, the Uitlanders, for whose deprivations the British public were being lashed into a frenzy of chauvinistic indignation, did not want to fight their rulers. They were much too busy making money out of the Rand and cared little or nothing for British supremacy in South Africa. Far from helping them, the war crisis caused a severe economic depression and serious unemployment and turned several thousands of prosperous Uitlander families into penurious refugees. Nor did British business require that the Union Jack should fly over Pretoria. The City of London was perfectly happy to invest vast sums of money in the South African Republic regardless of whether Kruger accepted or rejected British paramountcy. The Rand paid handsome dividends; and that was what mattered to the investors. Likewise British traders cared little whether or not their exports to the Republic passed through British territory and were carried on British railways. They were far more concerned to send them by the cheapest route which would make their prices competitive with their rivals. And although the Cape railways had undoubtedly lost a great deal of traffic to the relatively much shorter and more convenient line from Delagoa Bay, this was scarcely a reason for going to war, save perhaps for the more rabid elements of the South African League. True, the loss of rail traffic was only one of many symptoms of the comparative decline in the Cape's former supremacy and of the rising influence of the Transvaal. But this did not mean that a majority even of the English colonists, let alone the Cape Dutch, thought that this decline could or should be arrested by shooting down their competitors with rifles and machine-guns.

The war that was forced on the Boers was the deformed and evil brain-child of three men—Chamberlain, Milner and Rhodes—who were driven by a combination of ambition and fear to compound the notorious errors and injuries done by Carnarvon and Frere some twenty years before. Their ambition had been to create a South African Union under British rule which, together with Canada and Australia, would be a source of strength and unity to the British Empire and, as such, would promote and enhance the concept of Imperial Federation, so dear to Chamberlain's heart. To this end, the frontiers of British South Africa had to be extended to embrace the two Boer Republics which had for so long impudently refused to be painted red on the map and in which an Eldorado had been discovered incomparably greater than that of all the British territories combined.

Their fear had been that, thanks to its new-found wealth, under the 'malignant' rule of President Kruger, the rapidly growing stature of the Transvaal would shortly eclipse the standing of the British Colonies to a point where British influence would no longer count in any part of South Africa and where the English, not only on the Rand but also in the Cape, Natal and the Chartered Company's territories in the north, would decide to sever their ties with the British family of nations and make common cause with the Boers in a republican union with its capital in Pretoria. Since the Voortrekkers had moved away from the Cape in the 1830s and in between attempts to impose upon them the policy of confederation, successive British Governments had only been prepared to tolerate the existence of another white man's government in South Africa and to accept the Boer Republics, as long as the Boers remained weak, isolated and impoverished. But with the rise of the Rand all this had changed. And as Selborne had put it, it was now feared that 'in a generation the South African Republic will by its wealth and population dominate South Africa. South African politics must revolve around the Transvaal which will be the only possible market for the agricultural produce or the manufactures of Cape Colony and Natal.'

Consumed with their ambitions and obsessed by their fears, Chamberlain, Milner and Rhodes had pulled out every stop in their campaign to arouse their fellow-countrymen. By ceaseless appeals to the jingo spirit, by parading on every suitable occasion the bogey of German, French and Portuguese intrigues and ambitions, and by constantly attributing to Kruger the very desire to dominate South Africa which inspired their own policies, they contrived to overawe a sceptical Cabinet and to convert an apathetic public into a chauvinist mob baying for blood and British supremacy. The Liberal Opposition—apart from Rosebery's disciples—remained a notable exception, refusing to be stampeded by such rhetoric and protesting, in the words of their leader, Henry Campbell-Bannerman, that the deprivations of the Uitlanders, however wrong, could never justify 'the senseless appeal to arms' and that to go to war to help British subjects get the vote 'a little sooner' was absurd. But a large part of the press, including *The Times*, the newly established *Daily Mail*, the *Westminster Gazette* and the *Daily News*, plus of course the *Cape Times* and *Argus*, had been stimulated by the publication of Milner's 'helot' despatch to join the chorus of hatred for Kruger's Republic and were demanding extreme measures to gain the Uitlanders their electoral rights. Queen Victoria too, having not forgiven Gladstone for giving away the Transvaal, made no secret of her support for Chamberlain's treatment of the Boers whom she considered a 'horrid people, cruel and overbearing'. To her the war, although regrettable, was a necessary struggle to avoid the intolerable humiliation of seeing the influence of the Transvaal progressively increasing at Britain's expense. In fact, so powerful and pervasive were the fears which Chamberlain and Milner between them had managed to conjure up of South Africa defecting from the Empire that even such a normally severe critic of Pushful Joe's methods as Hicks-Beach was in the end constrained to agree that Britain could not afford to risk the loss of her supremacy for fear of losing the Cape, 'perhaps the most important strategic position in the world and one of the main links of our great Empire'.

Blinded by the dread and distrust of Kruger and his associates which had thus been instilled into them, the British Government and people could not foresee that Chamberlain's pressures and the war which they produced were bound in the end to bring about the very result which they were so desperately anxious to prevent. Ignoring the lessons of the American War of Independence and disregarding Kruger's awesome warning of the price which the Boers would exact for being forced to belong to England, they plunged into war to restore imperial supremacy by demolishing the Republics. Borne forward on the high tide of jingoism, they could not see that their objective was no longer attainable. For the magic moment during the governorship of Sir George Grey, when the Boers might have been brought painlessly into the British fold, had long since passed and could not now be recalled. And as Ronald Robinson and John Gallacher concluded in their masterly work *Africa and the Victorians*, the restoration of imperial supremacy in South Africa was to prove impossible because it 'cut against the grain of . . . historical experience. The empire went to war in 1899 for a concept that was finished, for a cause that was lost, for a grand illusion.'

After two and a half years of attrition, the futile war came to an end. In 1902 the Boer Republics' endurance was finally exhausted by sheer weight of numbers and, through the peace of Vereeniging, Milner realised his ambition to see the South African Republic 'disappear from the map'. Kruger was a political refugee in Europe and the Union Jack fluttered over the Government buildings in Pretoria and Bloemfontein. But, even with Kruger out of the way and the Boers conceding unconditional surrender, neither Milner nor all the might and majesty of the Imperial Government could achieve what they had set out to accomplish. They could annexe the Transvaal but they could not wipe out its ascendancy in South Africa. They could arraign Cape Dutchmen on treason charges for showing sympathy to the enemy during the war, but they could not turn Boer burghers into loyal British subjects by coercion.

Besides, Britain's reputation in the world suffered grievously from the war. Her armies, which had ultimately to be increased to 400,000 men, including a quarter of a million regular troops, were sadly humiliated as the Boer commandos first pinned them back on every front and then kept them at bay in the long drawn out phase of guerilla warfare which followed the fall of Bloemfontein and Pretoria. More than that, as Merriman had rightly prophesied when the war started, world opinion soon forgot about Kruger's misgovernment and remembered only that Britain had forced a war on 'two petty Republics who happened to have the richest goldfields in the world'. Thus the jingo spirit was to wilt before the deadly fire of Boer mausers at Colesberg, Colenso and Spion Kop. As the war and the casualty lists lengthened, the hysteria of 1899 turned to frustration; and when the end finally came, the Imperial Government, now under Balfour's leadership, were more concerned to repolish their tarnished reputation than to exploit their all too empty victory.

The scramble for South Africa had produced its inevitable result. After a hundred years British territory had increased tenfold in area from 125,000 to 1,148,000 square miles. But the purpose for which it had been prosecuted was soon to be lost. Britain might have won the war, but Afrikanerdom was to win the peace. The South African nation which was to emerge from the crucible of British imperialism was to be British in name, but Afrikaner in reality. The Transvaal was confirmed in its supremacy as the focal point of South African industry and commerce. And as the Imperial Government soon relinquished the absolute suzerainty for which Britain had contended for so long, the English communities gradually opted out of the political scene, content as they had always been to conduct their businesses under Boer rule. Afrikaner systems and policies, notably in native affairs, were substituted for British: republicanism and Afrikaner nationalism, Milner's twin nightmares, grew apace. A hundred years of effort to implant an exclusive British dominion in South Africa only proved that the roots of Dutch tradition were everywhere too deep to dislodge; and in the shadow of van Riebeeck's oaks, the 'grand illusion' was finally to wither and die.

Bibliography

UNPUBLISHED SOURCES

British South Africa Company Archives, Salisbury

1 *Division of the Administrator*

Documents concerning:
Boundaries
Land
Mining
Native Affairs

In Letters:
L. S. Jameson
Jameson Raid
London Board
Manica
Mashonaland
Matabeleland
Native Unrest
Portuguese Territory
1896 Rebellion
Renny Tailyour Concession

Bibliography

> Out Letters:
> > Cape Town Office
> > Cape Town Office Private
> > Confidential
> > High Commissioner
> > Matabeleland Administration

2 *London Office*

> Board of Directors Minutes
> Executive Committee Minutes

> In Letters:
> > Bulawayo
> > Cape Town (Kimberley) Office
> > Salisbury
> > Miscellaneous

> Out Letters:
> > Administration
> > Special Report on Causes of Matabele **Rebellion**

> Agreements, Concessions and Legal Documents

3 *Cape Town (Kimberley) Office*

> In Letters:
> > Administrator, Mashonaland
> > Agreements, General
> > Barotseland
> > Boer Trek to Mashonaland
> > Gazaland
> > High Commissioner
> > Jameson Raid
> > London Office
> > Manica
> > Matabeleland
> > Matabele War
> > Native Unrest
> > Nyasaland

Railways, Beira and Bechuanaland
Matabele Rebellion

Out Letters:
Administrator, Mashonaland
Directors, London Board
High Commissioner
L. S. Jameson
Nyasaland
Dr. Rutherford Harris

4 *Personal Papers*

Lord Baden-Powell, Reports
Sir John Graham Bower, Letters and Papers
Sir Drummond Chaplin, Letters
Francois Coillard, Letters
Johannes Colenbrander, Letters and Diaries
James Dawson, Diaries and Notebooks
Thomas Dhlamini, Letters
German Consul, Pretoria, Reports
M. D. Graham, Reminiscences
Earl Grey, Letters
Sir F. Hamilton, Letters
Sir H. Heyman, Letters
H. M. Hole, Collected Papers
Sir L. S. Jameson, Letters
Sir W. A. Jarvis, Letters
Sir Frank Johnson, Letters and Papers
Sir Harry Johnston, Letters
Bishop Knight-Bruce, Diaries
T. S. Leask, Letters
Lobengula, Concessions
Lord Loch, Diaries
London Missionary Society, Letters
E. A. Maund, Letters
Major T. Maxwell, Letters
Captain R. D. E. MacMahon, Reminiscences

Sir Lewis Michell, Letters
Sir William Milton, Letters
J. S. Moffatt, Letters, Telegrams and Reports
G. L. Parker, Letters
Rev. D. R. Pelly, Letters
Col. E. G. Pennefather, Letters
Gen. Sir J. Ponsonby, Letters
Rt. Hon. C. J. Rhodes, Letters
C. D. Rudd, Letters and Journals
H. L. Sapte, Letters and Reports
F. C. Selous, Letters
Col. J. A. Spreckley, Letters
H. M. Stanley, Letters
Lt.-Col. Stevenson-Hamilton, Diaries and Notes
Rev. T. M. Thomas, Journal
W. F. Usher, Letters
H. H. Williams, Letters
Sir John Willoughby, Reports
Benjamin Wilson, Letters and Journals
W. J. Wood, Letters

Cape Colony Archives, Cape Town

Government House 1806–1885
Prime Minister 1872–1902

Minutes:
Governor to P.M. 1879–1902, Vols. 1–84
P.M. to Governor 1882–1902, Vols. 286–294, 305–306
P.M. to Executive Council, 1873–1902, Vols. 312–339
Prime Minister's Correspondence, 1875–1903, Vols. 259–264
Correspondence re Closing of Vaal Drifts, 1895, Vol. 247
Despatches from Imperial Military Authorities, 1887–1904, Vols. 95–96
Despatches from Agent-General, London, 1884–1902, Vols. 97–104

Despatches from Orange Free State, 1889–1899
Despatches from South African Republic, 1889–1899

Executive Council, 1867–1902
  Minutes 1867–1902, Vols. 8–19
  Ministerial Minutes to Executive Council, 1873–1902,
  Vols. 29–154

Defence Department 1877–1902
Native Affairs Department 1872–1902
Bechuanaland Crown Colony 1883–1895
Griqualand West Government 1870–1880
British Kaffraria 1827–1866.

South African Library, Cape Town

Personal Papers of:
  Sir John Graham Bower
  Jan Hofmeyr
  J. X. Merriman
  Sir John Molteno
  W. P. Schreiner

French West African Archives, Dakar

Gouvernement Général de l'Afrique Occidentale Française
Série F.—Affaires Etrangères, 1809–1921.

Relations with:
  Gambia 1820–1898
  Gold Coast 1848–1898
  Great Britain 1809–1898
  Liberia 1892–1898
  Nigeria 1889–1898
  Portuguese Guinea 1820–1898
  Sierra Leone 1818–1898
  General 1876–1898

The Personal Papers of Sir Henry Loch, 1890–1895 privately
printed and edited by James Headlam.

PUBLISHED WORKS

AMERY, L. S., *German Colonial Claims*, (Chambers, London, 1929)

AXELSON, E. A.: *The Portuguese in South-East Africa 1600–1700*, (Witwatersrand University Press, Johannesburg, 1960)

——: *Portugal and the Scramble for Africa 1875–91*, (Witwatersrand University Press, Johannesburg, 1967)

BAXTER, T.: *Rhodesian Epic*, (Government Archives, Salisbury, 1967)

BINNS, C. T.: *The Last Zulu King*, (Longmans, London, 1963)

BLAKE, ROBERT: *Disraeli*, (St. Martin's Press, New York, 1966)

CARTWRIGHT, A. P.: *The Corner House*, (Purnell & Sons (Pty.) Ltd., Cape Town, 1965)

CECIL, Lady Gwendolen: *Life of Robert, Marquis of Salisbury* (3 vols) (Hodder & Stoughton, London, 1931)

CLOETE, STEWART: *African Portraits*, (Collins, London, 1946)

COLVIN, IAN: *Jameson* (2 vols), (Arnold, London, 1922)

CROMER, LORD: *Modern Egypt*, (Macmillan, London, 1908)

CROWDER, MICHAEL: *Senegal*, (Oxford University Press, 1962)

DAVENPORT, T. R. H.: *Afrikaner Bond*, (Oxford University Press, 1966)

DECHARME, PIERRE: *Compagnies et Sociétés Coloniales Allemandes*, (Masson, Paris, 1903)

DESCHAMPS, HUBERT and CHAUVET, PAUL: *Gallieni Pacificateur*, (Presses Universitaires de France, Paris, 1949)

——: *Le Sénégal et la Gambie*, (Presses Universitaires de France, Paris, 1964)

EDWARDS, J. E.: *The 1820 Settlers in South Africa*, (Longmans, London, 1930)

ENSOR, R. C. K.: *England 1870–1914*, (Oxford University Press, 1936)

FLINT, J. E.: *Sir George Goldie*, (Oxford University Press, 1960)

FULLER, T. E.: *Rt. Hon. Cecil John Rhodes*, (Longmans, London, 1910)

GANN, L. H.: *History of Southern Rhodesia*, (Humanities Press, New York, 1969)

GARSON, N.: *The Swaziland Question and a Road to the Sea*, (Archives Year Book, Cape Town, 1957)

GARVIN, J. L.: *Life of Joseph Chamberlain* (3 vols), (Macmillan, London, 1932–4)

GOODFELLOW, C. F.: *Great Britain and South African Confederation 1870–1881*, (Oxford University Press, 1966)

HAILEY, LORD: *African Survey*, (Oxford University Press, 1957)

HALPERIN, V.: *Lord Milner and the Empire, Evolution of British Imperialism*, (Odhams, London, 1952)

HANCOCK, SIR KEITH: *Smuts, The Sanguine Years*, (Cambridge University Press, 1962)

——: *Smuts, Selected Papers* (2 vols), (Cambridge University Press, 1966)

HANOTAUX, GABRIEL and others: *L'Empire Colonial Français*, (Libraire Plon, Paris, 1929)

HARDY, GEORGES: *Histoire de la Colonisation Française*, (Libraire Larose, Paris, 1931)

HARGREAVES, J. D.: *Prelude to the Partition of West Africa*, (St. Martin's Press, New York, 1963)

HEADLAM, CECIL, edited by: *Milner Papers 1897–1905*, (Cassell, London, 1931)

HOFMEYR, J. H. and REITZ, F. W.: *Life of J. H. Hofmeyr*, (de Villiers, Cape Town, 1913)

——: *South Africa*, (Ernest Benn, London, 1931)

HOLE, H. MARSHALL: *The Making of Rhodesia*, (Macmillan, London, 1926)

——: *The Jameson Raid*, Allan, London, 1930)

HOSKINS, H. L.: *European Imperialism in Africa*, (Henry Holt, New York, 1930)

INNES, J. ROSE-: *Autobiography*, (Oxford University Press, 1949)

JACKSON, M. V.: *European Powers and South-East Africa*, (Longmans, London, 1942)

JOHNSON, FRANK: *Great Days*, (Bell, London, 1940)

JOHNSTON, Sir H. H.: *British Central Africa*, (Methuen, London, 1898)

JOHNSTON, Sir H. H.: *History of the Colonisation of Africa*, (Cambridge University Press, 1913)

——: *The Story of My Life*, (Chatto & Windus, London, 1923)

KENNEDY, A. L.: *Salisbury, Portrait of a Statesman*, (John Murray, London, 1953)

KRUGER, P. J.: *Memoirs of Paul Kruger*, (Fisher & Unwin, London, 1902)

LANGER, W. L.: *The Diplomacy of Imperialism 1890–1902* (2 vols), (Knopf, New York, 1951)

LEONARD, A. G.: *How We Made Rhodesia*, (Kegan & Paul, London, 1896)

LEWIN, EVANS: *The Germans and Africa*, (Cassell, London, 1915)

LEYDS, W. J.: *First Annexation of the Transvaal*, (Fisher & Unwin, London, 1906)

——: *Transvaal Surrounded* (2 vols), (Fisher & Unwin, London, 1919)

LIEBRECHTS, MAJOR C.: *Congo 1883–1889*, (J. Lebegue, Brussels, 1909)

LIVINGSTONE, DAVID: *Missionary Travels & Researches in South Africa*, (John Murray, London, 1857)

LOCKHART, J. G. and WODEHOUSE, C. M.: *Cecil Rhodes*, (Hodder & Stoughton, London, 1963)

LONGFORD, ELIZABETH: *Victoria R.I.*, (Weidenfeld & Nicolson, London, 1964)

MAGNUS, PHILIP: *Gladstone*, (E. P. Dutton, New York, 1964)

MARAIS, J. S.: *Fall of Kruger's Republic*, (Oxford University Press, 1961)

MARQUAND, LEO: *People and Policies of South Africa*, (Oxford University Press, 1962)

MAUGHAM, R. C.: *Portuguese East Africa*, (John Murray, London, 1906)

McCORD, J. J.: *South African Struggle*, (J. H. de Bussy, Pretoria, 1952)

Correspondence of James Xavier Merriman (3 vols), (van Riebeeck Society, Cape Town, 1960)

MICHELL, L. L.: *Life of Rt. Hon. Cecil J. Rhodes* (2 vols), (Arnold, London, 1910)

MILLIN, S. G.: *Rhodes*, (Chatto & Windus, London, 1937)

438

MILNER, ALFRED: *Egyland in Egypt* (7th Edition), (Arnold, London, 1899)

MOCKFORD, JULIAN: *Khama, King of the Bamangwato*, (Jonathan Cape, London, 1931)

MOFFATT, R. V.: *John Smith Moffatt*, (John Murray, London, 1921)

MOLTENO, P. A.: *Life and Times of Sir J. C. Molteno* (2 vols), (Smith, London, 1900)

MOREL, E. D.: *King Leopold's Rule in Africa*, (Heinemann, London, 1904)

MORLEY, JOHN: *Life of William Ewart Gladstone* (2 vols), (Macmillan, London, 1903)

PERHAM, MARGERY: *Lugard, The Years of Adventure 1858–1898*, (Collins, London, 1956)

——: *Colonial Reckoning*, (Collins, London, 1962)

POPE-HENNESSY, JAMES: *Sins of the Fathers*, (Alfred A. Knopf, New York, 1968)

RAPHAEL, L. A. C.: *The Cape-to-Cairo Dream*, (Columbia University Press, New York, 1936)

REITZ, DENYS: *Commando*, (Faber & Faber, London, 1929)

ROBERTS, S. H.: *History of French Colonial Policy 1870–1925*, (P. S. King, London, 1929)

ROBINSON, R. and GALLACHER, J.: *Africa and the Victorians*, (Macmillan, London, 1965)

SCHREINER, OLIVE: *Trooper Peter Halket of Mashonaland*, (Unwin, London, 1897)

Schreiner, Letters of Olive, (Unwin, London, 1924)

SLADE, RUTH: *King Leopold's Congo*, (Oxford University Press, 1962)

SMUTS, J. C.: *Jan Christian Smuts*, (Cassell, London, 1952)

STANLEY, H. M.: *The Congo and the Founding of the Free State*, (Sampson, Low, Marston, Searle & Rivington, 1885)

STEAD, W. T.: *The History of the Mystery*, (Review of Reviews, London, 1896)

——, *Last Will and Testament of Cecil J. Rhodes*, (Review of Reviews, London, 1902)

STENT, VERE: *Personal Incidents in the Life of C. J. Rhodes*, (Maskew & Miller, Cape Town, 1925)

439

STERN, JACQUES: *Les Colonies Françaises*, (Brentano's, New York, 1943)

THEAL, G. M.: *South Africa*, (Fisher & Unwin, London, 1894)
——: *Portuguese in South Africa*, (Fisher & Unwin, London, 1896)
——: *History of South Africa 1795–1895* (5 vols), (Swan Sonnerschein, London, 1908–1910)

VAN DER POEL, JEAN: *Railway & Customs Policies in South Africa, 1885–1910*, (Longmans, London, 1933)
——: *Jameson Raid*, (Oxford University Press, 1951)

VERBEKEN, AUGUSTE: *Msiri*, (Louis Guypers, Brussels, 1956)

'VINDEX': *Cecil Rhodes. His Political Life and Speeches*, (Bell, London, 1900)

VULLIAMY, C. E.: *Outlanders—Study of Imperial Expansion in South Africa 1877–1902*, (Jonathan Cape, London, 1938)

WACK, H. W.: *Story of the Congo Free State*, (Putnams, London, 1905)

WALKER, E. A.: *The Great Trek*, (A. & C. Black, London, 1934)
——: *Cambridge History of the British Empire*, Vol. VIII (South Africa, Rhodesia and the Protectorates), (Cambridge University Press, 1936)
——: *W. P. Schreiner*, (Oxford University Press, 1937)
——: *History of Southern Africa*, (Longmans, London, 1957)

WARHURST, P. R.: *Anglo-Portuguese Relations in South Central Africa*, 1890-1900, (Humanities Press, New York, 1962)

WILLIAMS, BASIL: *Cecil Rhodes*, (Constable, London, 1921)

WOLF, L.: *Life of the First Marquis of Ripon* (2 vols), (John Murray, London, 1921)

Index